The World of the Roosevelts

Published in cooperation with the Franklin and Eleanor Roosevelt Institute
Hyde Park, New York

General Editors:
Arthur M. Schlesinger, Jr., William vanden Heuvel, and Douglas Brinkley

FDR AND HIS CONTEMPORARIES
FOREIGN PERCEPTIONS OF AN AMERICAN PRESIDENT
Edited by Cornelis A. van Minnen and John F. Sears

NATO: THE FOUNDING OF THE ATLANTIC ALLIANCE AND THE INTEGRATION OF EUROPE
Edited by Francis H. Heller and John R. Gillingham

AMERICA UNBOUND
WORLD WAR II AND THE MAKING OF A SUPERPOWER
Edited by Warren F. Kimball

THE ORIGINS OF U.S. NUCLEAR STRATEGY, 1945–1953
Samuel R. Williamson, Jr. and Steven L. Rearden

AMERICAN DIPLOMATS IN THE NETHERLANDS, 1815–50
Cornelis A. van Minnen

EISENHOWER, KENNEDY, AND THE UNITED STATES OF EUROPE
Pascaline Winand

ALLIES AT WAR
THE SOVIET, AMERICAN, AND BRITISH EXPERIENCE, 1939–1945
Edited by David Reynolds, Warren F. Kimball, and A. O. Chubarian

THE ATLANTIC CHARTER
Edited by Douglas Brinkley and David R. Facey-Crowther

PEARL HARBOR REVISITED
Edited by Robert W. Love, Jr.

FDR AND THE HOLOCAUST
Edited by Verne W. Newton

THE UNITED STATES AND THE INTEGRATION OF EUROPE
LEGACIES OF THE POSTWAR ERA
Edited by Francis H. Heller and John R. Gillingham

ADENAUER AND KENNEDY
A STUDY IN GERMAN-AMERICAN RELATIONS
Frank A. Mayer

THEODORE ROOSEVELT AND THE BRITISH EMPIRE
A STUDY IN PRESIDENTIAL STATECRAFT
William N. Tilchin

TARIFFS, TRADE AND EUROPEAN INTEGRATION, 1947–1957
FROM STUDY GROUP TO COMMON MARKET
Wendy Asbeek Brusse

SUMNER WELLES
FDR's GLOBAL STRATEGIST
A Biography by Benjamin Welles

THE NEW DEAL AND PUBLIC POLICY
Edited by Byron W. Daynes, William D. Pederson, and Michael P. Riccards

WORLD WAR II IN EUROPE
Edited by Charles F. Brower

FDR AND THE U.S. NAVY
Edward J. Marolda

THE SECOND QUEBEC CONFERENCE REVISITED
Edited by David B. Woolner

THEODORE ROOSEVELT, THE U.S. NAVY, AND THE SPANISH-AMERICAN WAR
Edited by Edward J. Marolda

FDR, THE VATICAN, AND THE ROMAN
CATHOLIC CHURCH IN AMERICA,
1933–1945
Edited by David B. Woolner and Richard
G. Kurial

FDR AND THE ENVIRONMENT
Edited by Henry L. Henderson and David
B. Woolner

VAN LOON: POPULAR HISTORIAN,
JOURNALIST, AND FDR CONFIDANT
Cornelis A. van Minnen

FRANKLIN ROOSEVELT'S FOREIGN
POLICY AND THE WELLES MISSION
J. Simon Rofe

FDR'S WARTIME LEADERSHIP
Edited by David B. Woolner, Warren F. Kimball,
and David Reynolds

ROOSEVELT AND FRANCO DURING
THE SECOND WORLD WAR
FROM THE SPANISH CIVIL WAR TO PEARL
HARBOR
Joan Maria Thomàs

ROOSEVELT AND FRANCO DURING THE SECOND WORLD WAR

FROM THE SPANISH CIVIL WAR TO PEARL HARBOR

JOAN MARIA THOMÀS

palgrave
macmillan

ROOSEVELT AND FRANCO DURING THE SECOND WORLD WAR
Copyright © Joan Maria Thomàs, 2008.

All rights reserved.

First published in 2008 by
PALGRAVE MACMILLAN®
in the United States—a division of St. Martin's Press LLC,
175 Fifth Avenue, New York, NY 10010.

Where this book is distributed in the UK, Europe and the rest of the world, this is by Palgrave Macmillan, a division of Macmillan Publishers Limited, registered in England, company number 785998, of Houndmills, Basingstoke, Hampshire RG21 6XS.

Palgrave Macmillan is the global academic imprint of the above companies and has companies and representatives throughout the world.

Palgrave® and Macmillan® are registered trademarks in the United States, the United Kingdom, Europe and other countries.

ISBN-13: 978–0–230–60450–6
ISBN-10: 0–230–60450–1

Library of Congress Cataloging-in-Publication Data

Thomàs, Joan Maria.
   Roosevelt and Franco during the Second World War : from the Spanish Civil War to Pearl Harbor / Joan Maria Thomàs.
     p. cm.—(The world of the Roosevelts)
   Includes bibliographical references and index.
   ISBN 0–230–60450–1
     1. United States—Foreign relations—Spain. 2. Spain—Foreign relations—United States. 3. United States—Foreign relations—1933–1945. 4. Spain—Foreign relations—1931–1939. 5. Spain—Foreign relations—1939–1945. 6. Spain—History—Civil War, 1936 1939 Diplomatic history. 7. World War, 1939–1945—Diplomatic history. 8. Roosevelt, Franklin D. (Franklin Delano), 1882–1945. 9. Franco, Francisco, 1892–1975. I. Title.

E183.8.S7T48 2008
327.7304609′044—dc22   2008025844

A catalogue record of the book is available from the British Library.

Design by Newgen Imaging Systems (P) Ltd., Chennai, India.

First edition: December 2008

10 9 8 7 6 5 4 3 2 1

Printed in the United States of America.

Contents

Acknowledgments   vii

Part I   Background: From the Spanish Civil War to the Second World War

1. Roosevelt and Franco during the Spanish Civil War (18 July 1936–1 April 1939)   3

2. Between Two Wars: From the Spanish Civil War to the Second World War (1 April–1 September 1939)   25

Part II   The United States and Spain from the Second World War to Operation Torch

3. The First Stage of Alexander W. Weddell's Embassy (May 1939–August 1940)   47

4. The Second Stage of Alexander W. Weddell's Embassy (August 1940–March 1942)   103

Conclusion   215

Notes   219

Sources and Bibliography   255

Index   265

Acknowledgments

You are holding a book that is the outcome of a study on the relations between the United States of America and Franco's Spain during the Civil War and the two years of United States' neutrality in the Second World War. The study largely focuses on the diplomatic relations between the two countries and the internal problems that were raised within the Roosevelt administration by the fact that Spain had become a dictatorship that was on good terms with the Axis—a real "red hot potato," as one of the protagonists was to remark at the time.

The main threads running through my research are the attitudes and decisions of President Roosevelt toward the Franco regime; the reconstruction of the policy implemented by his administration on Spanish affairs (the leading players, and the relations between the State Department and the Madrid Embassy); and the relations between the United States and Great Britain in their dealings with Franco. My study takes into account the complexity of the Franco regime, which Spanish historians and Hispanists have been trying to understand for the past thirty years.

Although recently, several valuable studies have been made within Spanish political historiography of the relations between the United States and the Franco regime, and vice versa, they tend to deal with periods after the Second World War: the agreements of 1953 and the years up to 1995.[1] U.S. historiography, on the other hand, dealt with the issues that I have studied in the 1960s and 1970s. Of particular note are those of historians such as Charles R. Halstead, James W. Cortada, and the former economic adviser of the State Department Herbert Feis. Some studies, particularly the doctoral thesis by Bert Allan Watson, were never published. However, at the beginning of the 1980s, interest in the subject started to flag and has yet to revive.

I began my research, and therefore the book, with a six-month stay as Visiting Associate Fellow in the Department of History of the University of Wisconsin in Madison in the second half of 2002. This was made possible by the good will of Stanley G. Payne, the Jaume Vicens Vives-Hilldale Professor of the Department, and the award of a mobility grant for university teaching staff from the Spanish Ministry of Education, Culture and Sports on 18 April 2002 (call published in the BOE [Spanish State Gazette] on 29 October 2001).

I made the basic research in the United States in two stages. The first was during the stay just mentioned, when I worked in the National Archives and Record Administration (NARA-II) in College Park (Maryland); in the Franklin D. Roosevelt

Presidential Library in Hyde Park (New York); and in several libraries, among which are the Memorial Library of the University of Wisconsin and the library of the Wisconsin Historical Society. The second stage was in 2006 when I spent the month of January at the Virginia Historical Society researching the personal archive of one of the leading characters in the book: the ambassador Alexander Wilbourne Weddell. This second period in the United States was made possible by the award of two grants: one from the VHS itself—the Virginia Historical Society's 2006 Mellon Research Fellowship—and the other—Acces 2005—from my university, the Rovira i Virgili in Tarragona. In Spain I continued my investigations in the archives of the Presidency of the Government, at the Ministry of Foreign Affairs and in the General Archive of the Administration in Alcalá de Henares. The drafting stage of the process was funded by the Central Library of the University of Otago in Dunedin (New Zealand).

Throughout my research I have incurred debts of gratitude with many people. First of all, I would like to thank Stanley G. Payne for his constant encouragement, support, and trust. I will have great difficulty in repaying all that I owe him on both a personal and professional level. James W. Cortada—Jim—the pioneer author of a study on the relations between the United States and the Franco regime during the Second World War and a veritable historiographic corpus on Spain, has honored me with his friendship and his knowledge. Jeremy Suri gave me invaluable advice on the NARA-II. Norman J.W. Goda, the historian who has done most to get to the bottom of the Nazi policy on Spain and northeastern Africa, provided me with contacts in the National Archives that proved to be crucial. All of the above and Wayne H. Bowen, one of the leading "new Hispanists" in the United States, read the manuscript and made interesting comments. Paul Preston guided me through the British sources and his own studies have always been particularly revealing to me. Enrique Moradiellos, the leading Spanish expert on the history of Anglo-Spanish relations during the Republic, the Civil War, and the beginning of the Franco dictatorship, was a source of knowledge and a sound guide. I am grateful for his comments on the book. I am also grateful to Florentino Rodao for lending me documents on Ambassador Carlton J.H. Hayes.

Also of great help were the archivists Greg Bradsher (from NARA-II), Robert Clark (from the Franklin D. Roosevelt Presidential Library in Hyde Park, that beautiful town on the banks of the Hudson), and Nelson D. Lankford (director of the Virginia Historical Society in Richmond). I would like to thank Dr. Lankford for his advice on my research on Weddell and for the receipt of a grant from the VHS. Of the Spanish archivists, I would like to mention Ignacio Ruíz Alcaín, from the Archive of the Presidency of the Government and Pilar Casado, from the Archive of the Ministry of Foreign Affairs. I am grateful to both of them for their guidance and patience.

Finally I would like to thank Casimiro Molins Ribot, Joaquín Maria Molins Gil, and the lecturer and personal friend Joaquim Molins López-Rodó for all their help. It has also been a pleasure to work with my translator, John Bates, and my editor in New York, Christopher Chappell.

On a more personal note, the book is dedicated to my dear children Joan Maria and Àngela.

PART I

BACKGROUND: FROM THE SPANISH CIVIL WAR TO THE SECOND WORLD WAR

CHAPTER 1

ROOSEVELT AND FRANCO DURING THE SPANISH CIVIL WAR (18 JULY 1936–1 APRIL 1939)

THIS IS THE STORY OF A STANDOFF BETWEEN TWO HEADS OF STATE: President Franklin Delano Roosevelt (1932–1945) and General Francisco Franco Bahamonde (1936–1975), *caudillo* (leader) and generalissimo of the so-called Spanish New State. It is also the story of the relations between a president who liked neither Franco nor any other dictator, and a general who not only despised and hated democracies but also regarded them as being responsible for all of the ills afflicting Spain. As shall be seen in the pages below, however, Franco had a vital need for the democracies he so reviled, since they provided the essential supplies that enabled his regime to survive. Roosevelt and Franco were never to meet but were very aware of each other. At that time, in both the United States and in Spain, there was much talk of "the other": the Franco regime was the subject of many news items and articles of opinion; and the United States was systematically reviled by the state-controlled Spanish press.

The story that we shall reconstruct is much more than the story of two statesmen. It is the story of the relations between two states, between two administrations, and it focuses on the policies of the United States of America toward the Franco regime.

It is sometimes quite difficult to identify and understand Roosevelt's criteria and personal opinions about the policies implemented by his administration. This difficulty increases if we attempt to discover his specific criteria and opinions concerning foreign policy. This is not only because the president felt disinclined to write down his points of view; there are also deeper reasons. It should not be forgotten that FDR did not feel very secure with topics of international politics and that when he became president he was neither a declared isolationist nor an internationalist.[1] Rather, Roosevelt seemed to play "diplomatic chess by seeking fresh counsel with every new move."[2] It is hardly surprising, then, that ambivalence was to be the dominant feature of his policy.[3] At the same time, by having in his government and family environment such people as the Secretary of State Cordell Hull, the Under Secretary of State Sumner Welles, the Secretary of the Treasury Henry Morgenthau, the Secretary of the Interior Harold L. Ickes and his wife Eleanor, among others, he was ensured of very different (not to say contradictory) points of view when decisions had to be taken. And, as has been pointed out by many studies on the president—which seem to be well founded—if Cordell Hull was Roosevelt's book of rules, Morgenthau, as Mrs. Roosevelt often said, was her husband's conscience.[4]

If there is one event that exemplifies this, that event is the Spanish Civil War, which raged between 18 July 1936 and 1 April 1939. The Roosevelt administration's official attitude to the war was adopted by the president and the secretary of state at the very beginning and remained unchanged throughout. Franklin Delano Roosevelt's personal opinion, however, depended on such factors as the advice he was given, the pressure he was subject to, the fluctuations in North American public opinion or the evolution of the international situation. Roosevelt made no policy changes, although he attempted to do so on several occasions and—much more surprisingly—even encouraged several undercover military operations in support of the Second Spanish Republic. Had these attempts prospered, he would have violated his own policy. But the fact is that, when the Spanish Civil War ended, the president was deeply unhappy about General Franco's victory. Secretary Hull, on the other hand, was satisfied with the policy implemented by the United States during the conflict. And he was to remain satisfied until his death.

President Roosevelt's Belated Involvement in the Spanish Civil War in 1938

There is a common consensus among historians that until 1937 and 1938 President Roosevelt showed little interest in international issues, and focused largely on domestic policies.[5] It has also been stated that at that time Roosevelt gradually took the responsibility for Europe and left Asia and the Pacific in the hands of the Secretary of State Cordell Hull.[6] In any case, for European issues and diplomatic issues in general, it was Sumner Welles who became his right-hand man. This strange situation—a president who worked more closely with his under secretary than with his secretary—was one of the reasons for the tension between Hull and Welles and was to end in the dismissal of the latter at the request of the former in 1943 after several clashes and the use of some rather questionable methods.[7] In the final analysis, this situation came about because the president, who had been paralyzed from the waist down since 1921 when he was 35 years old, needed people he could trust to act as his eyes and ears.[8] Sumner Welles was one of these people. Harry Hopkins was the other.

It is generally considered that the turning point in the attitude and policies of FDR took place in the period immediately after the Munich Conference of 29 September 1938, which was when he became fully aware that Adolf Hitler's policies of annexation would inevitably lead to a new war in Europe.[9] His attitude to the war in Spain is also believed to have changed at this time. I believe, however, that these dates are not entirely accurate: the president's attitude to the war in Spain changed several months before, probably between February and March 1938.

FDR had never been attracted by the Spanish.[10] At the outbreak of the Spanish Civil War his main preoccupation, and that of the State Department, had been to prevent the conflict from spreading throughout Europe. That is why the United States decided to join the French and the British in their policies of nonintervention. But another factor that had an influence on the president's decision was the loathing that the Catholic hierarchies in the United States and much of Catholic world felt for the Spanish Republicans or Loyalists—those who defended the Republic against the military and the civilians who had come out against it (Rebels)—and their revolutionary and bloody excesses during the first few months of the struggle. However, little by little, the president became more concerned with the aid that Nazi Germany and Fascist Italy were providing the military rebels. And by February 1937 it seems that he had become more sympathetic to the Loyalists.[11] Or, to be more accurate, he had taken a greater dislike to the Republic's military opponents and, particularly, to their Nazi and Fascist friends.[12] FDR, then, was against those who had rebelled and against the Fascist powers—Hitler's Germany and Mussolini's Italy—who supported them. All this aside, the president's attitude to the Spanish Republic was always slightly less favorable than that of two members of his cabinet—the Secretaries of the Treasury and the Interior Henry Morgenthau and Harold Ickes, respectively—his wife Eleanor and his friend, the ambassador to the Spanish Republic Claude G. Bowers. But the undisputed fact is that, above and beyond any likes or dislikes, the policies applied by the Roosevelt administration—and in general the policy of nonintervention—always indirectly benefited Franco.

Nevertheless, in 1938 FDR began to make political, legislative, and even secret and illegal plans to help the Spanish Republic in an attempt to prevent what at that time seemed to be the more than probable victory of Franco and his allies, the Fascist powers, in the south of Europe. All these plans, however, were to no avail. The policy of his own administration did not change and the undercover operations in support of the Loyalists (at least the most ambitious of them) were never carried out. On the contrary, Franco came out on top and the number of Fascist countries (or Fascistized countries, as was the case of Spain)[13] in Europe increased by one. None of this satisfied the president who was well aware by now of the threat to European peace posed by the Nazi and Italian Fascist powers and their Asian ally Japan, with whom they had signed the Anti-Comintern Pact in November 1936.

The attitudes that President Roosevelt adopted toward the Spanish Civil War and the action that he took may not have been fundamental to his increasing commitment to defending freedom and democracy against the Fascist threat to world peace, but they were certainly important. Particularly after 1938, this commitment encouraged him to lend support to the democratic powers. He provided material aid during the first two years of the Second World War because, although the United States was formally neutral, it was in fact a nonbelligerent country that supported the democratic nations at war, first with Germany (as from 1 September 1939) and then with the Germany-Italy axis (as from 10 June 1940). And after France's surrender, also in June, it supported a solitary United Kingdom in its struggle against Hitler and Mussolini. This was the same commitment that, since 1937, had led the United States to support China after yet another Japanese attack.

When it broke out on 17, 18, and 19 July 1936, neither the people nor the president of the United States paid much attention to the Spanish Civil War.[14] But interest gradually grew, not only because of the dynamics of the war and its horrors—people were slaughtered, the civil population was bombed, and land and factories were expropriated in a revolutionary frenzy—but also because of the symbolic nature that various sectors attached to it. One part of public opinion in the United States tended to think of the war as a confrontation between Nationalism and communism while another part regarded it as the first act of a world struggle between Democracy and fascism. At the same time, the possibility of lifting the embargo on the sale of arms that the Roosevelt administration had imposed on both the sides involved in the conflict became a controversial issue between the pro-Loyalist and pro-Franco sectors of the U.S. population. This same controversy also raged within the administration and government of the United States.

In fact, shortly after the war broke out, the pro-Loyalists in the United States denounced that the embargo on the sale of arms imposed by the democratic powers on Franco and his Republican adversaries clearly benefited the former. That is to say, although Franco was openly being supplied with arms, equipment, and troops by Nazi Germany and Fascist Italy—thus blatantly infringing the resolutions of the international Committee of Non-Intervention set up two months after the outbreak of the war—the Republic could not obtain arms from North America, Britain, or France and was obliged to buy them from such countries as Mexico and, after September 1936 and on a much larger scale, the Soviet Union.[15] What is more, they were obliged to pay a fortune for the arms they did manage to acquire[16] but they never arrived in the same quantities or as regularly as the arms supplied by the Fascist powers.

Nevertheless, in February–March 1938 Roosevelt changed his attitude toward the Spanish Civil War. And from that point on he became increasingly concerned until the conflict ended at the end of March 1939. His concern was not only due to the evolution of the conflict itself, in which the Republican forces experienced increasingly greater difficulties after the defeat in Teruel at the beginning of 1938 and made increasingly anguished pleas for aid. It was also due to the massive military support that Germany and Italy were providing Franco, and the further steps that Hitler had taken in the spring of 1938 in his offensive to modify the map of Europe. This was one more manifestation of the escalation of European and world demands that the Fascist powers had been making since 1935. For example, Hitler had repeatedly demanded that the Treaty of Versailles be revised, Italy had invaded Abyssinia in 1935, both Italy and Germany were intervening in Spain, Austria had been annexed in March 1938, and Germany had demanded to annex the Sudetenland (Czechoslovakia) in May 1938. In February and March 1938, Roosevelt responded to the desperate requests of the ambassador of the Spanish Republic in Washington, Fernando de los Ríos.[17] The ambassador was a prestigious socialist who had been minister of foreign affairs for some months in 1933, after being the minister of justice of the Second Republic between 1931 and 1933, and he was a friend of the Secretary of the Treasury Henry Morgenthau[18] and Eleanor Roosevelt.[19] He made his first appeals for aid to the Under Secretary of state Sumner Welles on 23 February and again personally to the president at the beginning of

March 1938. Roosevelt agreed to secretly provide the Republic with arms via France.[20] He set to work at once and his brother-in-law Gracie Hall Roosevelt—Eleanor's brother, former aviator and fervent pro-Loyalist—was to play a leading role in the operations, which had the support of the president's wife. As a result, in March and April 1938, thirty consignments of strategic material were sent to the Spanish Republic via France.[21] However, despite the fact that FDR had ordered the head of the Office for Arms and Munitions Control, Joseph Green,[22] not to investigate the false applications for export licenses and that Eleanor had written to Ambassador Bullit in Paris asking him to help her brother (although she did not explain exactly why he might be in need of help), the most important operation—the sale of 150 new and secondhand North American airplanes—was to end in failure.[23] And it did so because the pressure brought to bear by the British premier Neville Chamberlain on the French president Edouard Daladier, for reasons totally unconnected with the operations just described, led to France's border with Spain being closed on 13 June 1938.[24] It also seems that the State Department as such had no previous knowledge of the operation but, when it did find out, it undoubtedly played a part in the failure Harold Ickes said that "not having been told of the President's interest, the State Department promptly clamped down so that this plan of getting arms into Spain failed."[25] If the Republican forces had been in possession of the North American planes in July 1938 when they engaged in the Battle of the Ebro, the most important offensive in the three years of warfare, they may have had a better chance against Franco's superior troops and arms. The defeat in this battle in the month of November meant that Republican Spain's die had been cast.

After the Munich Conference on 29 September 1938, which had so fleetingly seemed to bring hope of a lasting peace to Europe, President Roosevelt took another important step in his defense of democracy from the Fascist threat in Europe, of which his interest in a Republican victory in Spain was a part. It was at this time that FDR was most committed to finding ways of preventing a Franco victory, which he believed would reinforce the Fascist powers. At the end of October, then, when the Battle of the Ebro seemed to have brought the war to a conclusion, he took up the Franco-British idea of an armistice and entrusted the assistant Secretary of State Adolf Berle with presenting a request to the Vatican. He also considered the possibility that Cordell Hull[26] should propose a call to armistice in Spain at the Lima Conference of December 1938. This proposal, however, was not approved because of disagreements between the Latin American countries.[27]

But in the very fall of 1938 that he launched these initiatives and after the failure of the secret operation in support of the Republican forces of the previous June, Roosevelt contemplated lifting the embargo on the sale of arms to Spain. One way of lifting the embargo was to take the issue to Congress when it met in January 1939. Another way was for him to use his presidential powers. This possibility was based on his belief that the discretionary powers (which he had used in the case of Spain) granted to him by the Neutrality Act of 1 May 1937 not only allowed him to impose an embargo on arms to countries engaged in a civil war but also to lift an embargo, merely by withdrawing his request. The embargo imposed on Spain a few months before was mandatory, the result of the Spanish Embargo Act, a joint resolution of Congress that had been ratified by Roosevelt on 8 January 1937.[28]

This law had been passed specifically to ban the sale of arms to the adversaries in the Spanish Civil War.

When he formulated this plan, the president was probably influenced by a letter he had been sent by the Secretary of the Interior Harold L. Ickes after a lawyers' conference in Washington. It contained two appendices: a "Petition of Members of the American Bar to the President of the United States with Accompanying Memorandum on the Embargo against Spain" and a request from the "Lawyers's Committee on American Relations with Spain" to be received at the White House. In his letter of 23 November 1938,[29] Ickes convincingly set forth some of the arguments that had been presented at the conference. He referred to the need to lift the embargo in view of the "very significant change that has occurred since May 1, 1937, the day when the embargo proclamation now in force was promulgated. At that time there was an operation that seemed at least to be an honest effort to stop arms shipments to both sides in the Spanish War through the mechanism of a four-power naval and border patrol of Spain which, as you know, was abandoned soon after our embargo went into effect." Because the situation that had led to the embargo being imposed had changed, Ickes believed that the president had the authority to lift it. He echoed the opinions of some of those who had attended the meeting, who were also influential Catholics: among others, Frank P. Walsh, Louis F. McCabe, and Dean Francis Shea. All their opinions were liable to affect a president who was concerned by what he perceived to be a Fascist threat not only in Europe but, by extension, throughout the Western Hemisphere. According to Ickes "they [the lawyers mentioned] all take the view that however the situation may have appeared at the beginning of the Spanish War, the question now is whether Hitler, by gaining mastery of Spain, will be able ultimately to dominate Latin America (...) they feel quite naturally that this possibility constitutes a terrific threat to the Catholics of Spain and Latin America." And he added that "our arms embargo against the Spanish Republic inevitably creates a doubt in Latin American governmental circles as to whether a liberal government threatened by Fascist-aided insurrection can assume that it will be accorded the right to purchase military equipment in this country for the suppression of such insurrection." The Italian and German emissaries to the Lima Conference were to play on these doubts and use the cases of Spain and Czechoslovakia to show that the friendship of a democracy was of little value and that only the friendship of totalitarian states could bring material advantages. He concluded:

> If, at this time, we should reopen to the Spanish Republic facilities for purchasing arms, would we not go a long way toward counteracting this type of propaganda? And is not this moment when our action in according such rights to the Spanish Republic, regardless of his material effect, would have a tremendous moral effect not only in Latin America but in Europe as well?

In this last respect, it should be pointed out that President Roosevelt's strategy to confront the Fascist threat to Latin America was to reinforce the Good Neighbor policy, which was based on respecting the independence of the Latin American countries and moderating the interventionism of previous decades. This had become apparent on 18 March 1938 when the Mexican president, Lázaro Cárdenas, had expropriated the assets of the North American oil companies. In response, Roosevelt had opted to come to an agreement with the Mexican government. He took no notice of the Secretary of State Cordell Hull who had proposed in no uncertain terms that they should break off relations and who complained bitterly of having to "deal with these communists down there [Mexico]."[30]

After receiving Ickes' letter, FDR was determined to use his presidential powers to lift the embargo on the sale of arms to the Spanish Republic. He sent the letter to Sumner Welles and asked for his advice on how best he could change the application of the Neutrality Act of 1 May 1937 to Spain, and lift the embargo on the sale of arms to Spain. Welles' response, however, came as a complete shock. He said:

> The assumption underlying the arguments in the petition enclosed with the letter addressed to you by the Secretary of Interior, viz., that the Joint Resolution of January 8 [in fact it was 6 January but it was signed by FDR two days later] was repealed by the passage of the Neutrality Act of May 1, is entirely without foundation. On this point, the legal officers of the Department are unanimous.

And also "Even if you were to revoke your proclamation of May 1, 1937, the original prohibition upon the export of arms, ammunition and implements of war to Spain laid down by the Congress on January 8, 1937, would still remain in force." Therefore, it was up to Congress to decide whether or not to lift the embargo.[31] This was the point of view of the State Department and its lawyers, and it was a point of view shared by both Welles and Hull.[32] Three days after receiving this negative advice, the president, far from discouraged and unwavering in his endeavor, explained the legal dilemma posed by a possible lifting of the embargo and his personal stance on the issue to the attorney general in the following terms:

> The State Department lawyers and the Secretary of State believe that if I were to revoke my proclamation of May First [1937] the original prohibition of January 8th [1937] would still remain in force. The other side claims that the resolution of May 1st cancelled out the resolution of January 8th—and I think there is some merit to this contention. What do you think?[33]

The response of the Attorney General, Homer S. Cummings, was by no means definitive. Indeed, some members of his staff believed that the president's decision to use his presidential powers so that the law of 1 May would no longer apply to Spain could have legal grounds. However, they also believed that the arguments against this possibility were very solid and that any official declaration by the president stating that the Spanish Civil War had ended would raise considerable controversy because it was so clearly false.

Faced with these legal difficulties and determined to lift the embargo and help the Spanish Republic, the president considered the possibility of having Congress change the general Neutrality Act. He was prompted to do so not only by the Spanish conflict but also by his conviction that the United States had to prepare for the Nazi threat. This threat was compounded by the horror of what Hitler's followers had done after 30,000 people had been arrested and synagogues, shops, and homes had been destroyed on the previous 5 November, the so-called Night of Broken Glass.[34] On 15 December 1938, he tried to get Senator Key Pittman, chairman of the Senate Committee on Foreign Relations, to take the initiative for this legislative reform. However, Pittman's doubts about acting without consulting the other committee members and the launch on 23 December 1938 of what seemed to be Franco's definitive offensive on the territory that still remained in Republican hands prompted Roosevelt to take the initiative himself. And in his State of the Union Address of 4 January 1939 he spoke of the growing danger of war, of the need for countries to provide themselves with arms for defense and the dangers to democracies of indifference to international lawlessness anywhere. He added:

> At the very least, we can and should avoid any action, or any lack of action, which will encourage, assist or build up an aggressor. We have learned that when we deliberately try to legislate neutrality, our neutrality laws may operate unevenly and unfairly—may actually give aid to an aggressor and deny it to the victim. The instinct of self-preservation should warn us that we ought not to let that happen anymore.[35]

However, his attempt to take this particular path was to be thwarted almost immediately. Although Senator Key Pittman had agreed to start hearings on the various new Neutrality bills presented to the Senate, he warned the president that if he were to support any of them, he would be encouraging a united front against him. Here the leadership of the senator, a seriously ill alcoholic, failed.[36] What FDR was trying to do was remove arms embargoes from the new law but maintain the cash-and-carry system, and the prohibition on loans, transport, and trips.[37] What is more, the reality of the war in Spain was getting increasingly desperate for the Republicans as in January 1939 Franco continued his march on Catalonia, which was to reactivate the public controversy on the embargo between the pro-Loyalist and pro-Rebel sectors of the North American population. The debate immediately became public and was to play a decisive role in short-circuiting FDR's plans. The pro-Loyalists buried the Senate under an avalanche of letters, petitions containing millions of signatures and telegrams in favor of lifting the embargo and promptly providing the Spanish Republic with aid, but Franco's supporters responded in exactly the same way and also sent millions of signatures demanding precisely the opposite. These conflicting pressures led the Senate Committee on Foreign Relations to suspend any decisions that had to be taken on the new Neutrality Act and the Spanish embargo,[38] effectively blocking, at least temporarily, the second path that Roosevelt had wanted to use in an attempt to provide a desperate Republic with aid. At this point he decided to take no further action and he stopped pressuring the committee.

The reason he took this decision was that the legislative elections of November 1938 had weakened President Roosevelt's position in Congress and reinforced the coalition of conservative Republicans and Democrats that opposed him. More specifically, the elections had ended with the victory of the Democrats over the Republicans in the House by 261 to 164 and with the reinforcement of the most conservative sector of representatives of the Democratic Party itself, who were extremely reluctant to accept the New Deal and against what they considered to be the "dictatorial tendencies" of the President.[39] FDR was afraid of jeopardizing the revision of the Neutrality Act. In fact, he was aware of the extreme difficulty of getting North American arms to Spain in time to save a Republic that was in its death throes. He even decided not to respond to those who publicly requested an executive revocation of the embargo. As he bitterly explained in a cabinet meeting on 27 January 1939, the day after Barcelona had fallen into Franco's hands:

> [It] had been a grave mistake... The policy we should have adopted was to forbid the transportation of munitions of war in American bottoms. This could have been done and Loyalist Spain would still have been able to come to us for what she needed to fight for her life against Franco—to fight for her life and for the lives of some of the rest of us as well, as events will very likely prove.[40]

FDR, THE UNITED STATES, AND THE OUTBREAK OF THE SPANISH CIVIL WAR

What had happened? Why had the United States of America not adopted a policy at the beginning of the Spanish Civil War that would have allowed the Spanish Republic to purchase North-American arms and defend itself against the military coup? And what were the factors, both inside and outside the United States and its administration, that had determined the embargo policy that was to prove to be so harmful to the Republic's survival? In our attempt to find an explanation, we must understand that, for much of the Spanish Civil War, President Roosevelt's sympathies for the Loyalists were compatible with the policy designed within his administration by the State Department not to sell arms to either side. This confirms the appraisal made several years later by the president's wife, Eleanor Roosevelt, about some of her husband's political beliefs: "Franklin frequently refrained from supporting causes in which he believed because of political realities."[41]

However, as we have just seen, FDR gradually began to take a more committed, firmer stand against the Fascist threat of Germany and Italy to European and world peace. And, as the fortunes of the Spanish Civil War turned against the Loyalists, he seriously questioned the advisability of the embargo and, in particular, the harm that it was causing the Spanish Republic in its struggle against the rebels. When he decided to act in support of the Loyalists, however, he either could not or he no longer had sufficient will to do so. But it was always clear to him which part of his administration had designed the policy and where the (continuous) efforts to maintain it came from: the State Department. When the war was coming to an end and Franco's victory was assured, Roosevelt replied to a journalist who asked him about "the wisdom of retaining the embargo" with a curt "you will have to ask the State Department about that." Likewise, in a cabinet meeting, he admitted for the first time that the embargo had been a mistake because it "controverted old American principles and invalidated established international law."[42]

The Roosevelt administration's first reaction to the outbreak of the Spanish Civil War had been to refrain from taking any action on behalf of either of the two sides. Not all the Western democracies had acted likewise. France, for example, had been favorably disposed toward the Spanish Republic, although only for a short period of time. The original decision taken by the socialist prime minister of the French Popular Front government, Léon Blum, to sell arms to the Spanish Republic, which was governed by a so-called Popular Front coalition, had immediately met with opposition from sectors of his own government, the right wing, Catholic opinion, and influential sectors of both the civil and military administration. And his hopes were finally dashed when, on top of all the domestic opposition, Stanley Baldwin expressed the reluctance of the British Conservative government to lend any sort of help to a Republic that on 26 July 1936 had been nicknamed "the Russians!";[43] that is to say, alleged followers of Soviet dictates. The British standpoint on this issue had been communicated to Blum during a visit he made to London on 24 July.

Any attempt to explain the reluctance of the British Conservative cabinet to support a formerly friendly democratic state such as the Spanish Republic must take into account that since the monarchy had fallen and the new regime had been established on 14 April 1931, the British Conservatives had considered it to be dangerously left wing. This was largely because of the nationalist economic policy that the young Republic implemented during the first two years of center-left governments (1931–1933), which was relaxed somewhat during the center-right governments (1933–1936), and which was taken up once again when a new version of the center-left—the Popular Front—came to power in February 1936.[44] In fact, the threat that this policy represented to the economic interests of the United Kingdom was politically exaggerated by the British conservatives: in London it was generally thought that the Spanish Republic was some sort of Kerensky regime that, as had happened in Russia, was destined to be the prelude to the rise to power of Bolshevism. These fears took even firmer hold after the Popular Front's victory in the elections of February 1936 and the disturbances that took place in Spain in the spring and first weeks of the summer of the same year. Therefore, the military coup of 17–19 July 1936 was perceived by the British cabinet as a necessary response to the prevailing disorder and to the problems that British interests were experiencing, symbolized by the labor conflicts at the Río Tinto mines.[45] And, after the military uprising had failed and revolutionary activity had broken out in the Republican-controlled territory, the British cabinet believed that their fears of Bolshevism were being confirmed even though the disturbances were more anarchist and radical socialist in nature than Communist. We should not, then, be surprised that the sympathies of most of the British cabinet lay with Franco's rebels throughout the Spanish Civil War. That is to say, they supported those who, in their eyes, appeared to be the guarantors of law, order, and private property[46] and resisted the Communist threat. The destruction of Spanish democracy that might be the consequence of Franco's victory was regarded as being rather awkward but the lesser of two evils in comparison with the disaster that a red victory would have signified for British interests.

British policy toward the Spanish Civil War, however, must also be inscribed within the general policy of appeasement that the United Kingdom was applying to Germany on the continent and Italy in the Mediterranean. At the outbreak of the Spanish Civil War, Great Britain had had several objectives: namely, the conflict should remain within Spanish borders, the country should remain territorially intact, and Spain should not be hostile to the United Kingdom in the future, or at least remain neutral in the event of a new war. By the end of hostilities on 1 April 1939, the last and most important of these objectives was by no means ensured.[47] On the contrary, at the end of the previous March Spain had joined the Anti-Comintern Pact and also secretly signed a treaty of friendship with Germany similar to the one with Italy signed in November 1936. And on 1 March 1939, Spain entered into another treaty of friendship with Portugal, one of the objectives of which was to close the door on a possible British attack through the neighboring country.[48]

In response to the surprising refusal of the French and British governments to provide supplies and arms (surprising, that is, from the point of view of international law, and particularly so in the case of the French Popular Front), the government of the Spanish Republic approached the United States in search of war supplies. As was soon to be discovered, this approach would be fruitless.

Ever since the Second Republic had been established in Spain, the State Department had shared Britain's fears that the country was on the brink of bolshevization. During the Civil War, the department was horrified by the thought of a Loyalist victory and its most probable direct consequences: the expansion of Communism throughout Europe and a new continental war that could arise out of the internationalization of the Spanish Civil War.[49] Of more immediate concern were the North American interests in Spain, represented by such companies as International Telephone & Telegraph (ITT) and the great automobile manufacturers, which had set up their manufacturing or assembly plants in the country and which were now being seized by the Loyalists. For all these reasons, and also because they believed that the Republic would soon be asking the United States to purchase arms, the secretary of state, Hull, and his closest collaborator, the Under Secretary William Phillips—who was to sent to Italy the following fall and replaced by Welles—decided to prevent the United States from selling by campaigning for a "moral embargo." It could only be "moral" because the sale of arms to a country torn by civil war was, at that time, perfectly legal in the United States according to the legislation in force (the Neutrality Act of 31 August 1935).[50] This law, which had been hastily passed in response to Italy's invasion of Abyssinia and the resulting fear that it would lead to another world war, had made it illegal for U.S. citizens to sell arms once the president had officially announced the existence of the war in question. This was a radical departure from the traditional policy that had been followed up to that time. In February 1936, it was also made illegal to grant loans to the belligerents, and in May 1937 sailing on belligerent vessels and, especially, transporting arms for belligerents on U.S. vessels were added to the list of prohibitions.[51] However, the Act did not cover civil wars.

The positioning of the State Department on the Spanish Civil War did not reflect unanimous internal agreement but Hull and Phillips convinced the president of the wisdom of total abstention from the war in Spain by means of the moral embargo mentioned above and which Roosevelt announced on 11 August 1936.[52] So the first and fundamental decisions concerning the Spanish Civil War emanated to a much greater extent from the State Department than from a president who was at that time throwing himself heart and soul into preparing the elections that were to be held in November 1936.[53]

For their part, the British had also received requests from the Republic to purchase arms and they, too, had managed to find a way of justifying their (diplomatically speaking) hardly justifiable refusal: they supported the proposal by French President Léon Blum to enter into an international agreement not to intervene in the Spanish conflict.[54] In fact, Blum's initiative concealed his desire to provide the Spanish Republic, which he was unable to help directly, with indirect aid. That is to say, it was politically impossible for him to send arms, so he was attempting to prevent any other country from helping either side. In this way, given their material and economic superiority, and their more numerous human reserves, he hoped that the war would end in a victory for the Republicans. Although his ultimate hopes were not to be realized, Blum's proposal was successful and on 9 September 1936 the International Committee for the Application of the Agreement regarding Non-Intervention in Spain was set up in London.[55] Despite its international nature, this committee did not depend on the League of Nations, which was still traumatized by the conflict in Abyssinia and which had contemplated intervening in the Spanish conflict when it began. However, it had finally decided that it was an internal issue, shelved it and applauded the creation of the committee. In particular, the Non-Intervention Agreement prevented all twenty-six signatory countries from interfering[56] by prohibiting them from exporting or reexporting arms to either of the Spanish belligerents. Its main aim was to stop the Spanish War from spreading to the rest of the continent. With their signature, the British managed to confine the Civil War to Spain and "also make politically credible what had been their unilateral political tactic: a neutrality that was malicious to the Republic and, therefore, benevolent to the military uprising."[57]

The policy designed by the State Department, which pursued the same objectives as the United Kingdom, was shaped in a somewhat different manner. The United States did not formally join the committee mentioned above but applauded and supported it. And the State Department's successful attempt to encourage President Roosevelt to announce a moral embargo on the sale of arms to Spain was along the same lines. However, it was to be seen in the following months that the policy they had decided to adopt was difficult to implement: because the embargo was merely "moral" and neither legal nor mandatory, any U.S. trader who wished to sell arms to the warring sides in Spain had every right to do so by virtue of the Neutrality Act of 1935, which was still in force. And this is precisely what happened on 29 December 1936, when the State Department had to authorize an export license requested by a North American trader for a consignment of arms for the Spanish Republic. Aware of the weakness of the policy, the State Department reacted to this situation and, within twenty-four hours of granting the authorization, Secretary Hull sent acting Secretary of State R. Walton Moore to see the president and ask him to approve a new Neutrality Act designed specifically for Spain and explicitly prohibiting the sale of arms to the belligerents there. Once Roosevelt's support had been obtained, this law was to be passed almost immediately, on 8 January 1937. It was officially known as the Spanish Embargo Act.[58] Four months later, on 1 May 1937, another Neutrality Act was passed, this time of a more general nature, which granted the president discretionary powers in the case of civil wars. He was to use these powers on the very day that the Act was signed. He specifically declared that Spain was in a state of civil war and also that "under such conditions (…) the export of implements of war would threaten and endanger the peace of the

United States."⁵⁹ The law prohibited the sale of arms, munitions, and materials to the two sides, the shipment of other products—which the president had the power to choose—in vessels under the U.S. flag and the granting of loans by U.S. citizens so that these items could be purchased.⁶⁰ Among the products that were not prohibited from being sold but were subject to the above conditions FDR included oil and its derivatives. Although the discretionary powers he had been granted by the new Act were quite considerable—he had the authority to put all the nonarmament trade with the warring factions on a cash-and-carry basis if he felt that this was necessary for the peace and security of the United States—he had wished for more.⁶¹ But the domestic situation, and in particular the New Deal, dissuaded him from confronting Congress in order to extend them.⁶²

In our attempts to explain Franklin Delano Roosevelt's attitude to Spain, we must bear in mind that in 1936–1937 his main concern was not to prevent a Fascist victory: he was more concerned with falling in line with the Anglo-French policy of nonintervention. The aim of this policy was to prevent the war from spreading throughout Europe but, from the perspective of the interests of the British Conservative government and the North American State Department, it also reflected strong anti-Communist feeling and the desire to protect both their countries' economic interests in Spain. The issue of anti-Communism is paradoxical since the refusal of the democratic powers to sell arms forced the Spanish Republic into the arms of the Soviet Union that, since September 1936, had become its main arms supplier. Given that Stalin and the Communist International had been following an anti-Fascist policy since 1935, this did not mean that the USSR was intending to take advantage of its privileged position to sovietize Spain. Nevertheless, this cut little ice with the State Department and the Foreign Office, who immediately interpreted the Soviet aid and intervention as yet further proof of bolshevization.

General Franco was elected generalissimo and head of the state government (a title that was soon to be changed to head of state) on 1 October 1936 and he clearly stated that the U.S. Spanish Embargo Act was extremely favorable to the rebels and extraordinarily harmful to the Republic in their fight to the death. At that time, he said, "President Roosevelt behaved in the manner of a true gentleman. His neutrality legislation, stopping export of war materials to either side—the quick manner in which it was passed and carried into effect—is a gesture we Nationalists shall never forget."⁶³ Two years later when the Civil War ended, however, Franco did forget and in fact displayed considerable hostility toward the president.⁶⁴ And to Roosevelt's surprise, Franco's Spain showed the United States very little gratitude.

Of course, the moral embargo and the lack of commitment to the Spanish conflict had been useful to the Roosevelt administration since the president had been victorious in the November elections of 1936—his first reelection after four years of controversy over the New Deal. The following January he had no qualms about establishing the mandatory embargo that prohibited the sale of arms, perfectly legal from the point of view of International Law, to a state—the Spanish Republic—that the United States recognized diplomatically. As Hull pointed out, this policy satisfied both the isolationists and the internationalists in the country. He said: "For once, our position seemed acceptable to both the apparently irreconcilable isolationists and internationalists. Isolationists approved because we were keeping aloof from the conflict. Internationalists approved because we were cooperating with Britain and France."[65] The secretary said not one word about defending the interests of North American corporations in Spain or the anti-Communism that was rife within the State Department. The Under Secretary Sumner Welles made this clear several years later: "Loyalist links to the Communists had created suspicion and hostility at the State Department."[66] And another high-ranking Department official admitted "high echelon officials were strongly pro-Franco."[67]

Another factor to take into account when explaining the United States' embargo policy was the attitude of the North American people. In 1936, public opinion was largely in favor of avoiding any sort of alignment that would mean getting involved in a European war.

However, the Roosevelt administration's policy toward the Spanish Civil War was to encounter new problems very soon, even before the new Neutrality Act was passed in May 1937. Various events disrupted the position that had been adopted and prompted President Roosevelt to consider extending the Spanish embargo to include the Fascist states that were providing Franco with aid for there was increasing evidence that Germany and Italy were participating in the conflict. In March 1937, a large contingent of the regular Italian army was captured after their defeat at the Battle of Guadalajara, and in the following April the German bombardment of Guernica was reported in the media. Voices started to be heard in favor of extending the embargo to Nazi Germany and Fascist Italy. At the same time, petitions requesting this same action from pro-Loyalist sectors and personalities rained down on the president's desk. One of these was from the U.S. ambassador to the Spanish Republic and personal friend of the president, Claude Gernade Bowers (1878, Westfield, Indiana), who insisted that in its conception the war in Spain was in fact a struggle between Democracy and Fascism, not between Nationalism and Communism. On 24 June 1937 he wrote to him to complain that "We know damn well that Italy and Germany are at war with Spain—but we sell them arms and ammunition."[68] However, when Roosevelt responded to these petitions and tried to apply the effects of the Neutrality Act to the Fascist powers, he came up against the State Department. He was informed by experts from the department that extending the embargo in this way would merely strengthen the relation between Germany and Italy, precisely at the moment that North American and British diplomacy was trying to force them apart. In this issue, Secretary Hull, former Under Secretary Phillips from Italy[69] and Robert W. Bingham, the ambassador in London, played a leading role. For its part, and just as it had done since the outbreak of the Civil War, the Foreign Office believed[70] that extending the embargo could lead to the war spreading throughout Europe. It also seems to be clear that the British believed that a Franco victory would not endanger British interests in Spain: on the contrary it would be very positive for them. After some initial hesitation, the president accepted the opinions of the State Department and the Foreign Office and decided against extending the embargo to the Fascist powers.

The international situation, however, was getting increasingly complicated. In July 1937, Japan attacked China once again, this time from the west, a continuation of the occupation of Manchuria in 1931–1932. This led to the outbreak of an undeclared war in which U.S. interests were directly affected. Shangai suffered a succession of intense bombings—which preceded the fall of the city in the following month of November and the Japanese atrocities in Nanking in December—similar to those that the Germans inflicted on the Spanish town of Guernica in the previous month of April. In order not to harm Chiang-Kai-Shek's China, FDR did not apply an arms embargo in this conflict. He opted for an intermediate solution, which he subsequently regretted not having used in the case of the Spanish Civil War: that is to say, "government-owned ships would not be allowed to transport munitions to China or Japan, that other ships flying the American flag would conduct such trade at their own risk, and that the question of applying the Neutrality Act would remain open."[71] His concern for the Chinese conflict and the increasingly strained situation in Europe prompted Roosevelt to make his famous Quarantine speech in Chicago on 5 October 1937. In this speech he announced the need to put the hostile nations into quarantine but this concept was never subsequently defined or specified in any detail. Shortly afterward, at the Brussels Conference in November, FDR proposed that boycotts or blockades should be imposed on Japan, or naval units sent to the Pacific. He became even more convinced of the need for such action after the U.S.S. Panay incident in December 1937, when the North American gunboat was attacked by Japanese planes in the China Sea. However, he was dissuaded from taking any action by the force of the pacifist sentiment in the United States and their compliance with the basic British policy of appeasement. In fact, it was this same compliance with the policy of appeasement that just a few months later—March 1938—would lead him to accept the Austrian Anschluss. And in another turn of the screw, and despite the fact that by then his personal aversion to events was considerable, he then agreed to an official and public display of U.S. sympathy for Britain's diplomatic acceptance of the Italian conquest of Abyssinia. Neither did he come out against the Foreign Affairs Committee and in favor of those members of Congress and senators who in March 1938 had pointed out the lack of effectiveness of the Neutrality Act in the cases of Spain and China and introduced bills to allow discriminatory embargoes against the aggressors.[72] The president's official attitude was being dictated by a variety of factors: seven months of recession and four million more unemployed in the United States, the desire to follow British policy, pressures from within the Democrat party itself and, as we shall see below, desire to avoid a confrontation with the U.S. Catholic hierarchy.

However, unofficially, we know that ever since February–March of 1938 President Roosevelt was supporting secret, and politically risky, operations involving members of his close family to sell war material to the Spanish Republic. And all this was happening at a time that the lifting the Spanish embargo had once again become an issue of public debate in the United States, just as it had been the year before as a result of the possible extension of the embargo to include the Fascist powers that were supporting Franco. Whether it was interpreted as being a struggle between Fascism and Democracy or between Nationalism and Catholicism, the Spanish Civil War was raising greater interest than the Italy-Abyssinia or China-Japan conflicts.[73] Of course, this interest is only relative because until as late as May 1939 North-American public opinion was dominated by domestic concerns. In fact, the string of victories earned by Franco's army in the first months of 1938 increased the prevailing conviction of United States pro-Loyalists that the embargo was damaging to the Republicans, and that Fascism was making new and dangerous inroads into Europe and was even threatening South America.[74] Consequently, the pressure on the president to lift the embargo grew more intense. Franco's offensive in March-April 1938 had been very important in this respect because it had split Republican Spain in two and isolated Catalonia from the rest of the Republican area.

Proof of this greater pressure were the petitions that Roosevelt received from Henry L. Stimson, a Republican, former secretary of state with President Hoover and secretary of war with Taft;[75] from leading scientists and academics, including Albert Einstein; from liberal and left-wing political parties, organizations and committees; and from notables of the Methodist Church and well-known rabbis. Likewise, the Democrat representative for California Byron Scott presented legislative initiatives in the House in April 1938. The fervent isolationist senator Nye did the same in the Senate in the following month of May. In particular, Nye sought to lift the embargo and allow arms to be sold exclusively to the Loyalists. To back up his proposal he invoked the Havana Convention of 1928, "the declared purpose of which was [and here he quoted] 'to prohibit the traffic of arms and war materials, except when it is destined to a government, so long as the belligerency of the rebels has not been recognized, in which case the rules of neutrality shall be applied.'" This would have been a revocation "only insofar as it applied to the Spanish government, since the ban of shipments to the Insurgents would not have been affected" and as long as U. S. vessels did not take part in the shipments.[76] However, as on the previous occasion, the pressure in favor of lifting the embargo was considerable, but so was the pressure in the opposite sense. The main defenders of the embargo were Secretary Cordell Hull and other high-ranking officials from the State Department such as Pierrepont Moffat—Chief of the Western European Division—and James Clement Dunn, the secretary's main advisor on European affairs,[77] who Eleanor Roosevelt referred to as an "ardent Francoist" and to whom Ambassador Claude Bowers attributed the authorship of the State Department's and United States' policy on Spain.[78]

This powerful group was prepared to go to any lengths to prevent the embargo from being lifted. For example, at the beginning of May 1938 Secretary Hull himself leaked the news of the possible lifting of the embargo to the press, which, as he had intended, provoked the irate reaction of the pro-Franco Catholic sectors[79] and the subsequent avalanche of telegrams and letters against the initiative. Influential figures from the Catholic Church such as Dougherty from Philadelphia and Mundelein from Chicago played a leading role in the campaign.[80] Prominent Democrats from the large cities in the East feared—as the president did himself—that a group of voters who could be crucial in the next presidential elections in 1940 would be alienated and they pressurized the president accordingly. In this respect, although in the United States as a whole Franco's supporters were mainly Democrats, the pro-Loyalists were divided between Democrats and Republicans. The recently appointed ambassador to London, Joseph Kennedy,[81] a Catholic and ardent supporter of the policy of appeasement practiced by Neville Chamberlain, the British prime minister since May 1937, also expressed his disagreement with the lifting of the embargo. His opposition to the administration's support of Nye's proposal was based on the familiar argument that the war might spread throughout Europe.[82]

Finally, in the month of May 1938, the external and internal offensive against the modification won through and it was decided to stick to the policy that had been followed until then, as Cordell Hull informed Senator Key Pittman. Indignant, Harold Ickes complained to the president that not supporting the Spanish Republic was "a black page in American history." Roosevelt replied with an explicit "to raise the embargo would mean the loss of every Catholic vote next fall and that the Democratic Members of Congress were jittery about it and didn't want it done."[83] However, despite this offical stance and all the negative consequences that it had for the Spanish Republic, Roosevelt was secretly encouraging operations to supply North American arms to the Loyalists. That the most important of these operations—a consignment of 150 airplanes—was to fail should not conceal the fact that the president was clearly in favor of the Republic. And above all, he wanted to do all he could to halt Franco's German and Italian allies. Paradoxically, all this was occurring at a time when three quarters of the U.S. population were in favor of the Loyalists.

Also in May, the international situation in Europe deteriorated further because of the pressure that Hitler was to bring to bear on neighboring Czechoslovakia. The Sudeten conflict was provoked by Hiltler's demands on the German-speaking people living in this country and the territory—Sudetenland—they occupied. In the ensuing months and until the Munich Conference in September, Roosevelt believed that the democratic countries should stand up to the Führer's threats although he also agreed with Chamberlain's option of negotiation. He was finally to accept the results of the Munich Conference although, as we have seen, he held no great hopes that the agreement would prevent the outbreak of a new war. It was in this context that in October 1938 he considered the Franco-British idea of an armistice, reformulated at the Lima Conference in December 1938,[84] and in November, the possibility of lifting the Spanish embargo (either by way of Congress or his discretionary powers). Subsequently, until January 1939, he was to try to modify the general Neutrality Act. All these initiatives would have helped the Spanish Republic's cause and they all failed.

ROOSEVELT AND THE END OF THE SPANISH CIVIL WAR

Events took a turn for the worse from the Republic's point of view after 23 December 1938 when, taking advantage of his recent victory at the Battle of the Ebro, Franco launched a general offensive on Catalonia. The lack of resistance he met there—the direct result of the long and bloody defeat just inflicted on the Republican army—meant that the whole of Catalonia was conquered in little more than a month. This conquest culminated with the Nationalists reaching the French border at the beginning of February 1939. In between, on 26 January, the capital of Catalonia and of Republican Spain, Barcelona, also fell and the government was forced to flee to France. On this very day, 26 January, and after he had received another plea from the Spanish government through Ambassador De los Ríos[85] to lift the embargo,[86] FDR was to make his last attempt to help a Republic that was still in possession of a large portion of territory in the center and east of the Iberian peninsula. As there were legal impediments to lifting the embargo, Roosevelt considered the possibility of urging the warring factions in Spain to reach an agreement.[87] However, he had to forsake this idea as there was no real possibility that Franco would accept. Finally, then, the president had to accept the inevitability of the end of the Spanish Republic.

Unlike the president himself, the State Department was anxious for the United States to diplomatically recognize Franco's Spain. On 4–5 February, Pierrepont Moffat presented his arguments to Cordell Hull, the main one of which was the need for "protecting our vast investment in Franco territory."[88] The United Kingdom and France hurried to do the same. Ambassador Bowers and the department also had differing opinions on the issue of the diplomatic recognition of Franco's New Spain. All this was to affect the president's decision-making process.

Thus, on 16 February 1939, in a personal letter to Roosevelt, the ambassador forcefully argued against prompt recognition. These arguments[89] had a profound effect on FDR, who was fully convinced by now that the policy implemented by his administration during the Civil War had been mistaken. And he was even more convinced of the need to halt the advance of the Fascist powers in Europe. In his letter, Bowers stated many arguments in favor of his standpoint: the Loyalists were still in control of a sizable amount of Spanish territory (the center and southeast of the peninsula was in their hands, including the main cities of Madrid and Valencia); they still had between 400,000 and 500,000 men at arms; and they were faced by the whole of the Italian army and thousands of German soldiers. Diplomatically recognizing Franco's Spain, he argued, would be "the bestowal of a blessing on aggression." What is more, he added, the Franco press "has carried out a vicious and abusive campaign against the U.S., its President, yourself and American institutions and ideals." This campaign had been inspired by Germany and Italy, and was related to the efforts they had made to distance Latin America from the United States, as had been seen during the Lima Conference the previous December. And Franco's government was "encouraging and sponsoring the organization of South and Central Americans in Spain into a Fascist society having for its purpose, as the press proclaims, the aggressive urging of Fascist and Nazi doctrines and plans on South and Central America." Although these last statements do not seem to be too plausible, Bowers believed them to be true and, as we know, the president himself was sensitive to them. He must also have given careful thought to the ambassador's premonitory insistence that "Franco has refused to forego reprisals and I predict that the wholesale killing of liberals, democrats, republicans will shock mankind when the facts behind the Spanish military censorship emerge." For Bowers, the only way that Spain could be granted diplomatic recognition in the future was, in the first place, to wait for the war to end and then for Franco to make a formal request. He specifically—and rightly—stated that "I have talked with many outstanding men from Franco's side and I gather from these that they are hoping for loans and financial assistance generally from the United States. We certainly do not need Spain as much as Spain needs us, and they, not we, should be the suppliants in the matter of recognition."[90]

The State Department, however, continued to insist on prompt diplomatic recognition of Franco's Spain even before the war had formally ended in order to gain favor with the victors. Hull actually sent a telegram to the president—who was on board the USS Houston—suggesting that he rang Bowers in Washington "to guarantee total freedom of action" on the recognition issue. In an extremely torturous fashion, Hull demanded the following:[91]

> We had been officially advised that the British government has decided to recognize the Regime of General Franco as the "de jure" government of Spain and will do so not later than tomorrow.[92]
> We understand that the French government may be expected to accord similar recognition within the next few days. The Netherlands Foreign Minister has just informed our Minister at The Hague that the Netherlands government has decided to recognize Franco and will probably make public announcement thereof tomorrow. Since the First of this year Ireland, Switzerland, Peru and Uruguay have extended "de jure" recognition to Franco. Prior to that time the government of twelve other countries had so recognized the Franco Regime. In these circumstances in order to insure our having complete freedom of action to meet any contingencies in our relations with Spain you may wish me to send telegraphic instructions to Ambassador Bowers to proceed to Washington for consultation. I shall be glad to have any instructions you may wish to give me on this matter.

The president agreed that Bowers should be contacted, although he pointed out that he would rather appoint him to a different ambassadorial post. On the more important issue, he said—surely to the secretary's desperation—that, although diplomatic recognition would eventually be granted, there was no immediate hurry and that, meanwhile, Franco should be surreptitiously informed that the United States expected the losers to be treated magnanimously. It is worth reproducing his exact words:[93]

> I have no objection to sending for Bowers, but as soon as it is known it will of course be obvious that he will not return to Spain as Ambassador and when we recognize Franco. It seems to me therefore that you should consider possibility of sending Bowers to another post at the same time you announce his recall from Spain.
> In this connection I think there need be no haste in recognition of Franco government. Without having any official statement made should not mind if it leaked out that we expect to recognize Franco but are watching first to see whether he treats the Loyalists with the Christian magnanimity that ought to be shown by the victors in a long and destructive civil war. To persecute the losers will take from Franco the good will of most people in the Western Hemisphere and this thought can, I think, be unofficially conveyed to him and to the public.

Relieved by the president's attitude, Hull told him of the steps he was taking on this issue and, arguing that the preparation of a new destination for Bowers would involve some considerable delay, requested permission to call him to Washington immediately. In the words of the secretary,[94]

> In accordance with the policy you have outlined we are sending the following telegram to Bullitt [the U.S. ambassador in France]:
> Please see Quiñones de León [the representative of the Franco government in Paris] at earliest possible opportunity and speaking purely informally tell him that

in view of changed conditions in Spain this government is naturally giving careful consideration to the problem of recognition of the Insurgents as the 'de jure' government of Spain; you should point out that public opinion in this country has followed developments in the Spanish conflict with interest and that both this government and public opinion would be gratified at receiving indications from the Franco authorities that there would be no policy of reprisal against their opponents in the civil strife. As a second point this government would desire to receive assurances that the Insurgent authorities are ready to protect American nationals and their property in Spain and otherwise to fulfill the obligations and responsibilities incumbent upon a sovereign state under international law and treaties.

The difficulty of delaying orders to Bowers to return to this country for consultation until we are able to announce his appointment to a new post is the time element involved a new post, obtaining agreement, etc. May I suggest for your approval ordering him home and announcing at the proper moment that he is coming for the purpose of consulting with you and me on developments in Spain as well as on the question of a new diplomatic assignment which you desire to tender him.

The president accepted and Bowers was called to Washington on 1 March. Once there, he said to Roosevelt in the Oval Office "We made a mistake. You have been right all along."[95] The ambassador remained in the United States while the president held the diplomatic recognition of Franco's Spain on standby for the rest of March.[96] Subsequently, in May, Bowers returned to St. Jean de Luz, but when he requested permission to travel to the embassy in Madrid to collect his things, it was denied by Under Secretary Welles,[97] who was very probably afraid of irritating Franco's authorities. While he was in St. Jean de Luz, the Ambassador to France Bullitt gave him two options for diplomatic posts: the embassy in Canada or Chile.[98] Claude G. Bowers accepted the latter and in the following years he was to follow Spanish affairs from Santiago, intervening in some cases directly for the president.

As we have said, Roosevelt had decided to delay the diplomatic recognition of the Franco regime, despite being pressurized by some Congressmen[99] and the large corporations with interests in Spain.[100] Meanwhile, in Republican Spain a new war had broken out, this time confronting the socialists and anarchists with Communists, which made any reversion in the result of the war even more unlikely. To evaluate Roosevelt's attitude, we must bear in mind that Great Britain and France had both recognized the regime on the previous 27 February.[101] The recognition by these two democratic powers had been granted after Franco had formally assured them that he would be merciful to the Republicans. These assurances were not respected in the slightest. Under Secretary Welles also told Bowers in Washington[102] that Franco had given the same guarantees to the United States of America, which does not seem to have been true. What is more, the under secretary denied Ambassador De los Ríos' request to evacuate Republican refugees to French ports with the argument that "we had felt it necessary to adhere to a rigid policy of not permitting our warships to be used as a place of refuge by other than American nationals and the nationals of some of the other American republics."[103] Finally, when Madrid fell into Franco's hands on 28 March 1939, the State Department was a bundle of nerves. The next day Hull, Welles, Moffat, Dunn, and other high-ranking officials met and decided that the United States could delay no longer and should grant recognition immediately, in two or three days at most. According to Moffat, this was "partly because our business interests demand it [and] partly because we and Soviet Russia alone have not recognized the inevitable—an embarrasing partnership." Two days later, in a second meeting, Hull managed to convince a reluctant Roosevelt to establish relations as from 1 April 1939,[104] the very day that the Franco regime was to proclaim a national festival: Victory Day. It was on this day that the president revoked the "state of civil war" in Spain that he had announced on 1 May 1937 and declared null and void Congress's joint resolution of 8 January of the same year, which had imposed the embargo.[105] The delay in diplomatic recognition had been a small presidential victory over the State Department.

The divergences over the war in Spain in the upper echelons of the Roosevelt administration were not an isolated phenomenon. They also existed in the heart of the Conservative cabinet and throughout the British government in general. Behind the British controversy was the policy of appeasement that the Conservative cabinet had been implementing to cope with the aggressive attitudes of the Fascist powers in the international arena. However, since January 1937, Foreign Secretary Anthony Eden—who was very close to the anti-appeasement stance of the influential Conservative minister Winston Churchill—had declared his opposition to this policy. He believed that the rapprochement between Franco's Spain and the Axis powers, the steps taken toward fascistization, and Spain's irredentism toward French North Africa were potentially dangerous for Britain's strategic interests.[106] His view on these matters meant that he was constantly, and fruitlessly, clashing with the Chancellor of the Exchequer Neville Chamberlain. The following fall, by which time Chamberlain was prime minister (he had been elected in May), Eden and the Under Secretary of the Foreign Office Robert Vansittart reiterated their disagreement not only with the prevailing viewpoint of the cabinet of the Italo-German aid to Franco but also more generally with the policy to appease Hitler and Mussolini. They also warned of the threat to peace that this policy entailed.[107] Subsequently, in February 1938 and on the eve of the Nazi *Anschluss* of Austria, Eden resigned as foreign secretary, and was replaced by Lord Halifax, who was in tune with Chamberlain. Vansittart was also replaced.[108] Among those ministers who were in favor of a really applied policy—which was based not only on the defense of British interests in the Mediterranean but also on a profound anti-Communism—was Sir Samuel Hoare, the future ambassador to Spain (from June 1940).

But even the British policy of appeasement had its limits. And these limits were reached when Germany invaded Bohemia and Moravia on 15 March 1939 and destroyed Czechoslovakia as a sovereign state.[109] Two days after the occupation, Prime Minister Chamberlain announced that he was not prepared to sacrifice the freedom of the United Kingdom in the interests of European peace. And less than two weeks later he committed his country to defending Poland, a country that Germany had already threatened and presented its territorial demands.

CHAPTER 2

BETWEEN TWO WARS: FROM THE SPANISH CIVIL WAR TO THE SECOND WORLD WAR (1 APRIL– 1 SEPTEMBER 1939)

IN THE MIDDLE OF TURBULENCE IN EUROPE, in April 1939, diplomatic relations were initiated between the United States of America and the Franco regime. Symbolically speaking, however, the Spanish Civil War was not over in either the United States or the rest of the world. North American public opinion was still divided[1] and, more importantly, so was the administration. Differences between its members had first come to the fore in 1936 and progressively widened in the three following years. Now, in the spring of 1939, these differences arose once again, but this time over how the United States should behave toward Franco and *his* Spain. And, as had occurred during the war, the policy that was finally adopted was determined to a much greater extent by the State Department than by President Roosevelt himself or those closest to him who were committed anti-Francoists. As was brilliantly portrayed by Jay Allen—the anti-Francoist journalist who had interviewed the Spanish Fascist leader José Antonio Primo de Rivera in Alicante prison in October 1936, one month before he was shot by the Republicans—in a letter to Mrs. Roosevelt on 10 July, the U.S. policy toward Spain had two quite different aspects:

> It is all very ironical and not a little frightening. We propose such fine ideas. We said we were going to embargo agressors. What we did, in the case of Spain, was to embargo the agressee and maintain that embargo as part of the Non-Intervention set-up long after the true character of Non-Intervention was—or should have been—apparent to everyone. We propose to subsidize exports to South America to help to counteract the politicocommercial penetration by the totalitarian states. And now the Export-Import Bank undertakes to subsidize exports to Franco through whom in South America the Germans and the Italians are doing their most effective penetration (one has only to

look at the recent riots in Mexico City where Franco Spaniards did the dirty work, on inspiration from the German, Italian and Japanese consulates).

It is frightening to see the good ideas go into reverse so soon. And please let me presume so far to say, as a foreign correspondent who can look at his government as he looks at others, with a certain degree of detachment, that there is a curious Jenkyll and Hyde quality to our administration in foreign policy at this moment. As Dr. Jenkyll we propose some very fine and workable ideals; As Mr. Hyde, that other half (?) of us—I would not attempt to name individuals in the Department [of State] or elsewhere because in naming some I would be neglecting others—proceeds to undo all that Jenkyll has done. And permit me to say that I think that Hyde is ahead.[2]

A few days before, Allen had gone with the former president of the Government of the Spanish Republic Dr. Juan Negrín to visit the first lady at her home in Hyde Park, the town in the state of New York where the president was from and where they lived. Eleanor, however, also had another house of her own, Val-Kill, where she spent much of her time, because of the special relationship she had with her husband. Since 1918 they had drifted apart because Eleanor had found out that Franklin was having a relationship with one of his secretaries, Lucy Mercer. And although Franklin put an end to the affair, they were to be definitively estranged. In the following years, Eleanor fashioned her own political career and by 1932, when Franklin was elected president, she had deservedly become a leading figure in the social movements. During her husband's presidency, she played a major role in the New Deal and fought for the rights of women and young people, and against racism.[3] And, in consequence, as we have pointed out, she had been an active supporter of the Republican cause in the Spanish Civil War. On the same day that he met with Mrs. Roosevelt, Negrín had had dinner in the home of Secretary Morgenthau,[4] a neighbor of the Roosevelts in the Hudson Valley.[5] On both occasions, he had spoken out against the granting of a loan to buy cotton that Franco's government had requested from the Export-Import Bank two months previously, and which was generating considerable controversy and tension within Roosevelt's cabinet. He also offered to act as intermediary to improve North American relations with the president of Mexico Cárdenas (which had deteriorated partly due to the clandestine activities of Germany and Italy there).[6] But Allen was right: it was Hull and the State Department that were still calling the shots.

Everything seems to suggest that, after the president had deliberately delayed the diplomatic recognition of the Franco regime and from the moment that the Spanish Civil War ended, the issue of Spain had ceased to be one of his main concerns. The main conclusion that he had drawn from the defeat of the Loyalists in the Spanish conflict was that the embargo—in fact all the embargoes affected by the Neutrality Act that was then in force—benefited the aggressors and were against the interests of the victims. So, during the summer of 1939, he persisted in his attempts to have the law changed.

In 1939, and before the World War II broke out on 1 September, Roosevelt was mainly concerned with two international scenarios: China, which was being subject to the full might of Japanese belligerence and, even more importantly, democratic Europe, which was under the threat of Germany. However, although Roosevelt was to have some success in the first scenario, he was unable to become effectively involved in the Old Continent. At this time, as a result of the war that had broken out in July 1937, Japan was in control of much of North-West China. This war, and in particular the brutal Japanese conquests of Shangai and Nanking, had increased sympathies in the United States for a country that was being regarded as a martyr. What is more, thanks to the efforts of the missionaries, it was also thought to be open to the West, especially as far as religion was concerned, and Chiang-Kai-Shek, whose wife had been educated in America, was considered to be a "modern" leader. All this was in stark contrast to the image portrayed by Japan: more aggressive by the day, interested only in itself and tending to dictatorship.[7] Public opinion in the United States identified more with the situation in China than with the European conflicts, and was even more prepared to go to war with Japan than with a European country. Nevertheless, the U.S. policy toward China and Japan was being directed by the State Department, and particularly by Cordell Hull. The main feature of his policy was to avoid clashing with Japan, although this did not mean that he approved of its activities and conquests;[8] it was a policy that irritated Morgenthau, Ickes, and the anti-Fascists in the cabinet. And, of course, President Roosevelt.

In July 1939, Roosevelt responded firmly to yet another example of British appeasement, this time with Japan. The British and the Japanese had been involved in an incident over the United Kingdom's use of the port of Tiensin, south east of Peking, and out of which nationalist guerillas were operating. The British had refused to hand over four of these guerillas to the Japanese military, but after a land blockade by the Japanese, they had agreed to sign the Craigie-Arita agreement in Tokyo on 24 July by which the British ambassador Sir Robert Craigie recognized in the presence of the Japanese foreign minister Arita Hachiro the "special situation of Japan in China" and the right of his army to maintain law and order in the territory that it had already occupied.[9] That is to say, he accepted the Japanese incursions into China. Roosevelt, who had just been witness to Congress rejecting his Neutrality Act, reacted by announcing to Japan on 26 July that he was giving the mandatory six months' notice of his intention to withdraw from the trade agreement that had been in force between the two countries since 1911. He carried this threat into effect in January 1940.[10] This response, which Morgenthau had been contemplating for some time, was designed to warn and pressurize the Japanese leaders, and it was implemented by means of a bill that was presented by the Republican Senator Arthur A. Vandenberg (also opposed to strict neutrality in European affairs).

In August, in a clear display of foresight, he attempted to convince the Soviet Union, who was negotiating at the same time with France, Great Britain, and Germany and doubting about which way to turn for a possible alliance, that signing an agreement with Hitler would only delay the certain Nazi attack on the USSR until after France had been defeated in the imminent European war. Stalin took no notice and on 23 August he signed the German-Soviet Non-Aggression Pact that left both Hitler and himself free to attack Poland. Three days previously he had decided to end the conversations about the border between Manchukuo and his country by launching a surprise attack that overcame the Japanese troops. The combination of the attack and the pact with the Germans—who thus seemed to distance themselves from Japan despite having signed the Anti-Comintern Pact in 1936—led the

Japanese to make peace with Stalin. And from this point on, until the defeat of France in June 1940, they were to make no further moves in Asia. Chiang-Kai-Shek, on the other hand, turned his back on the USSR and did his utmost to curry favor with the United States.[11]

Roosevelt's anti-appeasement attitude showed itself once again in the final days of that fateful month of August 1939 when he refused to follow the advice of the ambassador in London, Joseph Patrick Kennedy, who was as much an appeaser as Chamberlain and in the face of the German threats urged the president to bring pressure to bear so that Warsaw[12] would make concessions to Germany and thus avoid war. Weeks later, when the European war had already broken out, his indignation at *Joe* Kennedy's request was to prompt him to exclaim, "He's just a pain in the neck for me."[13]

Thus, as the president himself and U.S. diplomacy had been predicting, the German attack on Poland, and with it the war in Europe, began on 1 September 1939. The president's attitude to the conflict was consistent with the policies he had been following for more than a year: he announced that the United States would remain neutral and, at the same time, he redoubled his efforts to change the law that codified this neutrality, all in an attempt to be able to help Great Britain and France. For Roosevelt also, Hitler was the enemy to be defeated. And when he finally achieved what he had set out to do, after he had personally intervened in a joint session of the House of Representatives and the Senate and convinced representatives and senators, the new revised law of 4 November did away with the embargo on selling arms to belligerent states and permitted all sorts of sales on a cash-and-carry basis, although only by private companies not the U.S. government.[14] What was maintained, however, was the ban on granting loans to the belligerents and the transport of goods for countries at war in U.S. vessels. Likewise, U.S. citizens were prohibited from traveling on ships belonging to nations at war. That is to say, warring nations could go and fetch all sorts of supplies—including war material—from the United States simply by paying for them in cash. The law clearly favored the United Kingdom who had an enormous merchant and armed navy, and considerable financial reserves.[15] The law granted discretionary powers to define "combat zones" in which the ban on transporting goods and people was to apply. FDR focused on the North Atlantic. And in September and October 1939, at the Panama Conference, the United States persuaded the other American countries to accept a common neutrality policy toward the war and an exclusion zone of 300 miles into the Atlantic Ocean that would be patrolled by U.S. navy vessels.

THE BEGINNING OF RELATIONS BETWEEN THE UNITED STATES AND FRANCO'S SPAIN AFTER THE END OF THE CIVIL WAR: H. FREEMAN MATTHEWS, CHARGÉ D'AFFAIRES (APRIL–MAY 1939)

In fact, after the end of the Civil War, the only policy implemented by both the State Department and the Madrid Embassy was to take care of North American interests and restore the economic relations between the two countries (until then they had dealt with both of the warring factions). They also did what they could to help any of their citizens who were in Franco's concentration camps for having voluntarily fought on the side of the Republicans. These issues led them to their first clashes with the authorities of Franco's New State who, under the aegis of the Caudillo, enjoyed considerable autonomy and rarely felt the need to coordinate. This only served to increase the confusion of the North American diplomats. At the head of the new Spanish authorities was Ramón Serrano Suñer, minister of the interior since the end of January 1938 and Franco's right-hand man in the cabinet. At the end of the war, the U.S. diplomats were to find an atmosphere that was, to say the least, somewhat unfavorable. H. Freeman Matthews had been the first secretary at the embassy in France and was appointed to the same position in Spain on 3 April 1939, two days after diplomatic relations had been established with the Franco regime. He acquired firsthand experience of this unfavorable atmosphere very soon.[16] On the same day, the secretary of state asked the Spanish foreign minister to accept Matthews as *Chargé d'Affaires ad interim:* that is to say, until the new ambassador, Weddell, was to arrive. The minister, Conde de Jordana, agreed. Matthews arrived on 12 April[17] and, on the 25 of the same month, after an interview with the Under Secretary of the Ministry of Foreign Affairs Domingo de las Bárcenas in Burgos,[18] which was still the capital of Spain because the government yet to move to Madrid, he wrote to Hull that

> It is (...) quite obvious (...) that resentment is still strong over the attitude of public opinion in the United States with respect to the Nationalists and our "delay" in extending recognition (for instance, when I entered his office Bárcenas said with a smile when I told him I was enjoying Spain "You see we are not the terrible people you thought us in the United States. Frankly, you have never understood our cause, et cetera").

What is more, the self-satisfied tone of the under secretary's words expressed a widespread feeling among the authorities and particularly among the military:

> It would be difficult to exaggerate, however, the existing feeling of self-assurance in Nationalist Spain today specially in military circles. With that feeling goes the extremely bitter thought that Spain's "rebirth" was accomplished to say the least without the aid of the United States and the cost thereof in Spain lives greatly increased by the Brigades of which our unfortunate prisoners were members.

The *Chargé's* words must have only made matters worse in Washington since Hull and other high-ranking officials from the State Department had feared that the delay in diplomatic recognition would lead to such attitudes.

Of course the Francoist perception that had been transmitted to Matthews of the role played by the United States of America in the Spanish Civil War was considerably biased. There had not been a single standpoint but two conflicting ones among the U.S. population, companies, and—more opaquely—within the Roosevelt administration. Hull and the State Department had always supported Franco and the military rebels of 1936 because they believed that they defended property and free trade from the Russian hordes, so they were first taken aback and then exasperated and outraged by the treatment they received at the hands of the victors of the Spanish Civil War, who were soon to prove to be ultranationalist in both economic and political issues. For Hull and his subordinates, all great advocates of free trade, it was as if the unpleasant experience of having economic dealings with the Spain of the Second Republic, which had been marked at various points by economically nationalist and protectionist policies, had come back to haunt them but on a much greater scale. In fact these policies were magnified to the extreme. From the very beginning the Franco regime set about limiting foreign-owned property and put into practice an economic policy that aimed to achieve autarky.[19] That is to say, Hull and the State Department were now obliged to deal with Spanish authorities who were filled with pride and unlimited feelings of superiority for having been victorious in a war that, paradoxically, they had won largely as a result of foreign aid, some of which had been provided by North American companies.

In particular, they should have been grateful for the support of such companies as the Texas Oil Company (Texaco), the *nacionales*' main supplier of gasoline and petrolem products, which had proved to be so crucial. Since 1935, Texaco had been the main supplier[20] of the Spanish monopoly CAMPSA (Compañía Arrendataria del Monopolio de Petróleos SA), a consortium of private investors—mainly banks—with a state participation created in 1927 and which was the sole distributor in the petroleum market in peninsular Spain and in the Balearic Islands. Texaco had run some quite considerable risks to get round the Embargo and Neutrality Acts of January and May 1937 in order to supply Franco with gasoline and petroleum. They transported it in U.S. vessels that were supposedly heading for the port of Amberes, when in fact they were heading for ports in the National Zone. And they even provided loans so that these operations could be carried out. For this, its president and driving force behind the aid to Franco, Captain Thorkild Rieber, was fined by the administration, personally reprimanded by President Roosevelt, and ran the risk of being taken to court.[21] Subsequently, the countries managed to find their own ships or ships sailing under other flags to provide them with gasoline and petroleum, but they still enjoyed loans from Texaco. To understand this situation, we must bear in mind that Rieber was an ardent anti-Communist and a friend of Goering, who, one month after the outbreak of the war, had spoken to Franco in Burgos, and offered his help. This help included information about Loyalist purchases of gasoline.[22] Of course, there was also a business side to the whole affair and Texaco made a considerable amount of money from the *nacionales*, selling them a million tons of petroleum products for a value of 20 million dollars. Franco had only managed to keep hold of a small part of the CAMPSA fleet but he possessed the only petroleum refinery in the country, in Tenerife (Canary Islands). This was the property of the second Spanish petroleum company, CEPSA (Compañía Española de Petróleos SA), which operated in the islands and in the Protectorate (that is to say, outside the area of the CAMPSA monopoly) and which had shares in oil fields in Venezuela. It was the problem of the lack of tankers that Texaco solved. Franco did not forget the company's vital support and when Rieber was forced to resign in August 1940, after a press campaign against him (which highlighted his proximity to the German embassy in Washington), CAMPSA made him their chief buyer in the United States.[23]

But Texaco had not been alone. Standard Oil of New Jersey (subsequently known as Esso or Exxon), Socony Vacuum-Standard Oil of New York (subsequently known as Mobil) and Atlantic Refining, and the British company Shell had been selling petroleum products to the *nacionales*.²⁴ And it was not only oil companies that were involved: General Motors, Ford, and other companies sold enormous quantities of their products to the *nacionales* (although they also sold to the Loyalists). Of course the Republicans had also bought from the oil companies, but most of their gasoline came from the Soviets. In general, the U.S. companies felt more disposed toward Franco and gave him better terms, because they believed him to be a better bet than a Republic that was undergoing revolutionary events that were affecting foreign interests.²⁵ Once the war had ended, none of this, none of the help that the Franco rebels had received from the United States, could even be mentioned in their presence.

The issues that Matthews was to concentrate on in his short term in office were the same as the ones that were to occupy the first U.S. ambassador in Franco's Spain, Alexander W. Weddell, during the first of the almost three years he held the post. This says a great deal about the difficulties in the relations between the two countries from the very beginning. The issues in question were, among others, humanitarian aid, Franco's request for a loan to purchase wool from the United States, the United States' demand for the release of the prisoners from the Lincoln Brigade, and Spain's refusal to grant an entry permit into Spain for the U.S. colonel (so called—he was really a lieutenant colonel) Sosthenes Behn, founder and leading shareholder of the ITT of New York, and also leading shareholder of the Compañía Telefónica Nacional de España (CTNE).

The Beginning of Two Disputes: The Refusal to Allow Colonel Sosthenes Behn, President of ITT, to Enter Spain, and to Release the Remaining Prisoners of the Lincoln Brigade

La Telefónica, or CTNE, had been founded in April 1924 as a public corporation. One month later, and as a direct result of this company being founded, the government—known as the Directorio—of the dictatorship of General Primo de Rivera (1923–1930) appointed a commission to decide which company would be entrusted with reorganizing the telephone service in the country, which up until that point had been divided into many different companies, all with many different problems. The CTNE was competing against the Sociedad de Teléfonos Ericsson and the New Antwerp Telephone and Electric Works, but did not win: all the projects were rejected. But on the following 25 August, a Royal Decree by Alfonso XIII awarded the company the contract for reorganizing the service. It was clear that the Directorio was giving the company preferential treatment. What is more, ITT had bought shares in CTNE when the company's capital had been increased from 1 million pesetas when it was founded to 115 million pesetas in the following month of July. Of this amount, 114,400,000 pesetas belonged to ITT while the remaining 600,000 pesetas were divided equally between the Banco Urquijo and the Hispano Americano, as stated in the contract signed by CTNE itself and the U.S. company.²⁶ The contract between the state and the CTNE was signed for a period of twenty years and, if after this time the company were to be confiscated, it would receive compensation, paid in gold, for the amount it considered it to be worth. The company was not required to pay direct taxes and enjoyed considerable expropriation rights of land and property. What is more, it gradually bought out the existing telephone franchises. It was to pay a tax of 10 percent of its net profits to the state, which was much lower than the tax the previous franchises had had to pay. This meant that the public Treasury was to make considerably less money.[27]

Two conclusions can be drawn from these two contracts: first, that CTNE was being given preferential treatment by decree; and second, that although it was formally a Spanish company—as the Directorio had required—it did in fact belong to ITT and was therefore a U.S. company. Likewise, although its president was the marquis of Urquijo, the effective owner and real director was Colonel Behn. At the beginning of the Second Republic in 1931, Manuel Azaña's Republican-Socialist government had questioned ITT's dominant position and, at the end of 1931, the minister of communications Diego Martínez Barrio presented a bill denouncing the illegality of the contract that was in force. ITT had gone to Washington in search of help, and the administration had agreed to put pressure on the Spanish government. No further interest was taken in the matter until a year later, in 1932, Azaña presented it once again to the Spanish parliament. Nevertheless, as had happened on the previous occasion, pressure from ITT and the public condemnation of the U.S. government of how foreign investments were being treated in the country forced the president of the cabinet to change his mind and take the issue to a parliamentary committee for debate. ITT had people in Parliament who were prepared to defend its interests (e.g., Alejandro Lerroux, the leader of the Radical Party, and the former minister Miguel Maura). In the end, the issue was shelved when Lerroux himself was elected president of the government after the victory of the center-right and the right wing in the November elections of 1933.[28]

The refusal to allow Behn into Spain was the result of the hostility and suspicion created not only by his behavior during the Spanish Civil War but also by that of all the other Americans connected with the company in what was known as the Red (Loyalist) Zone. In fact, the strategy adopted by ITT during the war had been to keep the American directors of CTNE in the Republican Zone while the marquis of Urquijo and the representative of the Banco Hispano Americano were in the National Zone. But during the three years that the war lasted, the two parts that the company had been split into were taken over. The part of the company in the Republican Zone was militarized by decree on 29 October 1936, and the part in the National zone was taken over and Demetrio Mestre Fernández was put in charge. In the months before the Civil War, Mestre had been in charge of a CTNE plant in the Canary Islands, where he had met General Franco, the military commander of the Islands, who undoubtedly promoted him.

The suspicions of Franco and his supporters were made official on 4 August 1939 when the *Auditoría de Guerra de Ocupación* (literally, the War of Occupation Audit, the body entrusted with imposing military law during wartime) initiated a lawsuit against four U.S. directors and one British one, with President Sosthenes Behn and Vice President Fred Caldwell at the top of the list.[29] This was just the first of the obstacles that Franco was to put in the path of ITT at the beginning of the company's new relation with the Regime. Franco's aim was to keep control of the company while the issue of whether the monopoly should or should not be continued was debated internally and secretly. Behn had requested permission from the Minister of Foreign Affairs General Conde de Jordana to enter Spain and take charge of La Telefónica in 1938, even before the Civil War had officially ended. But by then he had begun to fear that if Germany were to enter the communications business in Spain, ITT would be displaced from its privileged position.

Permission for him to enter Spain, however, was not granted until the end of July 1939. Matthews, an experienced diplomat, immediately understood the reasons for the refusal and, realizing the political implications of the affair, he explained these to an incredulous Behn: among the leaders of the regime there was considerable resentment against him, and he was accused not only of having traveled twice to *red* Barcelona but also of not having provided the *nacionales* with aid during the war. Matthews pointed to the minister of the interior, Serrano Suñer, and the military legal advisor of the Generalissimo's Headquarters, Martínez Fuset, as the instigators of this attitude.[30] However, more importantly, and what neither Matthews nor Behn realized was that it was Franco himself who felt particularly offended by the president of the CTNE. Matthews also believed that the contract of 1924 and the ITT monopoly was something that the New Spain, in the grip of an explosion of nationalistic feeling and interventionist policies, wished to reconsider in an attempt to "free" the country from "the foreign monopoly which controls their vital communication system." When the *nacionales* had entered Madrid, they had forced the U.S. directors and technicians to leave the CTNE premises, telling them that the company was being taken over and that it would remain so as long as the country was in a state of war. On top of all this, according to Matthews, Mestre was maneuvering in an attempt to keep his post and all the staff of the company that had been in the Red Zone were subject to the procedure of cleansing (a general procedure that had been systematically applied to all civil servants, professionals, and companies and that investigated the behavior of individuals during the war). Nevertheless, in the words of the Chargé and as Colonel Behn was soon to recognize, the main issue was that "the real motives behind the Goverment's attitude at present arises first from an intention to restrict the rights or privileges hitherto enjoyed by the Company (refraining from even toying with the idea of Government acquisition of the telephone system) and secondly from definite animosity against the Company for its "failure to help in the war."

The second objective, the release of U.S. prisoners who had fought for the Lincoln Brigade, one of the International Brigades, was not fully achieved until one year after the embassy had made its first demands—that is to say, until February 1940. The prisoners in question were a group of 11[31] who had not been included in a previous man-for-man exchange with 71 Italian prisoners in Republican hands,[32] as well as an undetermined number (Ambassador Weddell later found out that there were eight of them) who had to undergo criminal proceedings because they had been accused of various criminal activities. In this case it was not Matthews but the previous ambassador, Bowers, who sensed the turn things were going to take as soon as the war had finished. In a letter to Hull on 20 April 1939 he wrote that

> It would seem of course entirely logical now the war is over that the Spanish Government would be glad to release all foreign prisoners of war (not tried or convicted on other counts) immediately. Such is apparently far from the case, however,

and I sense a desire on the part of the authorities to take their own good time on this and other questions. This applies particularly to those whom they feel declined to help them—at the very least—in their hour of need [that is to say, La Telefónica].[33]

Although the U.S. diplomatic authorities took an interest in the situation and provided the prisoners with aid, the Roosevelt administration did not cover the costs of repatriating the men who they considered had gone to fight in Spain illegally.[34] It was the association Friends of the Abraham Lincoln Brigade[35] who took charge of the repatriation, despite the fact that they were in some financial difficulties[36] because of the extent of the support they were providing to former brigadists.

To solve all these disputes, once Matthews had been replaced by the new ambassador Alexander Wilbourne Weddell in May 1939, the Roosevelt administration had to resort to what was soon to prove to be its main weapon: the granting, or not, of loans for buying raw materials. So despite the revulsion it made him feel, the great advocate of free trade secretary Hull was to take advantage of Spain's request to acquire cotton in an attempt to set in motion an almost paralyzed Catalan textile industry. It was in this way that the United States was to achieve its objectives several months later and having been made to fight all the way.

ALEXANDER W. WEDDELL, U.S. AMBASSADOR AGAINST FRANCO'S SPAIN

Alexander Wilbourne Weddell was appointed ambassador to Spain on 13 April 1939. After leaving the United States on 17 May and spending some time in Paris when he got to Europe, he finally arrived in St. Jean de Luz where he took charge of the embassy, which was still based in the French Midi. It was to return to Spanish territory shortly afterward, to San Sebastián in the Basque Country, and it was not to be established in the embassy building in Madrid until the fall of 1939, following behind the Office of the Head of State and the government ministries that had been located in various cities in the National Zone during the war. The capital had only been partly reconstructed after the devastation caused as a result of being part of the front line of combat. Thus it was that the Madrid Embassy was not to return to the magnificent palace of the dukes of Montellano, its former headquarters, until the end of October.[37]

The palace, which was rented from the duke, was an impressive building with a garden in the center of the city. Among the artistic treasures it contained were several paintings by Goya. Apparently, the Caudillo himself had considered it for his own residence before he finally opted for the El Pardo Palace in the outskirts. Weddell and his wife, who had a vast fortune and refined tastes, would have been very much at home in the building. In fact, in Richmond they lived in Virginia House, an English medieval mansion that had originally been called Warwick Priory. They had purchased it to prevent it from being demolished and transported it stone by stone from Warwickshire to the capital of Virginia.[38] In Madrid, thanks to the Weddells, the embassy was to become an important center for social relations over the next three years. Among their circle of friends were members of Madrid's aristocracy[39] and, in general, the high society not only of the city but of the whole country, which as we shall see was to have an influence on the ambassador's opinions on some Spanish issues.

While searching for a substitute for Bowers, both the State Department and the president had been very aware that "since Bowers was so definitely anti-Fascist in his views, it was necessary to replace him with an Ambassador who would work more in harmony with the group in power."[40] Nevertheless, after Weddell had been appointed, Roosevelt wanted to make his opinion of the Franco regime quite clear. He did so during a meeting that took place in the White House on 10 May, before Weddell's departure for Spain. In response to Weddell's request to give Franco a personal message from the president, Roosevelt authorized him to mention "the historic friendship between the United States and the Spanish people" and the desire that this friendship would be reinforced. But he immediately pointed out that he was referring only to "the Spanish people." And he added, "You know how I feel; we Americans don't like dictators (...) You may tell him that I feel confident that under his leadership Spain will make great strides forward under a representative form of government."[41] Weddell noted down the phrase and read it back to the president for confirmation. The president then asked him to inform him fully if he should learn of any groups that were seeking to establish a legislative power in Spain, which is yet another clear indication of his anti-Franco views and that he was giving the new ambassador quite a demanding program. He immediately added, however, that "such elements would probably be new ones as he supposed the old crowd were either in exile or in hiding."

Roosevelt was to discuss two more issues: one had to do with Spanish domestic concerns while the other—much more important—concerned safeguarding the security of the United States. On the first of these points, he spoke of the wealth and influence of the Catholic Church in Spain. He said that "some years ago Cardinal Hayes of New York, conscious of an irritation or hostility which arose when the church acquired properties outside of New York, for example, along the Hudson river, for orphanages, etc., prescribed it as a rule in his archdiocese that in the future all such properties exclusive of buildings actually occupied would pay taxes especially for monastic orders." Something similar "had taken place near Chicago, in a town called Mundelein, called after the Cardinal of that name, where taxes were being paid on all Church properties except buildings." Weddell replied that he would mention it to Cardinal Gomá, primate of Spain, when he arrived in the country. On the second issue, he expressed his concern for the security of the Atlantic. He said, "Remember Alex, if there should be any question of ceding the Canary Islands to Germany or any other power it would create a most serious situation."

Although they were somewhat disordered, the president's remarks showed not only that he was essentially anti-Franco but also that his main concern was the security of the United States. He must also have been aware that Weddell was not another Bowers, who had been pro-Loyalist and anti-Franco. In fact, the new ambassador did not seem to feel too much sympathy for the defeated Republic or for its political leaders. In a letter that he was to write later, deploring the anti-Franco feeling prevailing in the United States, he complained that "unfortunately Americans translated the title of 'República de España' as Spanish Republic with all the implications of the latter word as known in England and the United States."[42]

Likewise, the speech that he gave in the presence of Generalissimo Franco when he presented his credentials on 15 June in Burgos, the city where the Spanish head of state was still residing at the time, did not have the slightest democratic overtones. Consider the following extract:[43]

> The President of the United States has charged me to avail myself of this opportunity to convey to Your Excellency the assurances of his high esteem and fervent good wishes for your personal felicity and for the welfare of the Spanish people, as well as his desire that happy relations between the two countries may flourish, and that there may be constant growth in those spiritual and material interests which they have in common. (...)
>
> Today I enter a new-born Spain, one which has undergone a baptism of fire and of blood, and whose sufferings have provoked the poignant sympathy of men and women in my own country as throughout the civilized world. (...) The recollection of these vital things moves and inspires me as I enter on my mission, in which it will be my sincere endeavor fairly and fully to communicate and interpret to my Government the aims and ideals and aspirations of this new Spain and its Government. (...) Equally it will be my effort to translate to Your Excellency and to your Government the sentiments of friendship which animate the Government and people of the United States. (...)
>
> In these undertakings I nourish the hope that I may receive the generous and comprehending assistance of Your Excellency and of those whom you have chosen to collaborate with you in your lofty endeavor.

The last paragraph was to prove to be frankly ironic in the light of the difficulties that Alexander W. Weddell was soon to encounter as the U.S. ambassador in Spain.

Weddell was sixty-three years old when he arrived in Madrid. Born in 1876 in Richmond (Virginia), he was the son of an Anglican minister who died when he was still very young. So, from an early age, he had to work to help support his family. One of the jobs he held was that of clerk in the Copyright Office of the Library of Congress in Washington. At the same time he was studying at the George Washington University, where he graduated in English Literature in 1908 when he was thirty-two years old. In the same year, and in a chance encounter, he met the North American ambassador to Denmark, who contracted him as his private secretary and then as a clerk in the embassy in Copenhagen. It was here that Weddell became interested in following a diplomatic career and started preparing for the examinations that would allow him to opt for the position of consul. He passed and held posts in various places. First, between 1910 and 1914, he was posted to the African island of Zanzibar (a British colony) and Catania (Sicily, Italy) and he used these years to complete his higher education by enrolling on course at the universities of Catania and Lausanne (Switzerland). He was soon made consul general and between 1914 and 1919 he was posted to Athens and Beirut and subsequently, between 1920 and 1928, to Calcutta (India) and Mexico. He spoke French, Italian, and Spanish, and in 1928 he retired from the diplomatic career for unknown reasons.[44] In 1923 he had married Virginia Chase Steedman, from Saint Louis (Missouri), a widow and the only heiress to the family fortune of one of the city's important industrialists. After the marriage she was to share this fortune with Weddell who in his home town was now ironically known as Wed-Well.

Weddell shared with his wife a fondness for art and literature and became so involved in sponsoring the arts in Virginia that the results of his work are still evident today. This involvement in the associations and the cultural life of his hometown meant that in these years he was to hold posts in museums, educational institutions, and cultural societies[45] and his patronage was to earn him various honorary degrees from the College of William and Mary, the Hampden-Sydney College and the University of Richmond. He wrote just one book, *Introduction to Argentina*, which was published in 1939.[46] For her part, Virginia devoted much of her energy to various welfare and charity organizations. In her youth she had experienced many ups and downs in the family fortune and her personal experiences had made her very sensitive to social and charity issues. She was to continue this work in Spain.

Weddell decided to return to active service and in June 1933, after the presidential elections of 1932, Roosevelt appointed him ambassador to Argentina, largely because of the considerable contributions he had made to the Democrat Party. Although he was a member of the diplomatic service,[47] he was appointed for political reasons, something with which he never felt comfortable. A good example of how he felt about this was the satisfaction he displayed in 1940 when the department informed him that since ambassadors were government employees he was entitled to receive a state pension. The words he wrote at that time are highly indicative of the corporate insecurity in which he had moved up to that time: "The Department has just informed me that I am eligible for retirement. My satisfaction in this is that I should be considered a career officer. It always stuck in my craw that people should look on me as a political apointee, which perhaps I am, but I never liked it."[48] This recognition was soon to be made permanent. In December 1940, after his reelection as president, Roosevelt asked all the ambassadors to present their resignations and then refused to accept Weddell's—just as he probably refused to accept several others—saying that he was "eminently satisfied" with his work. And subsequently, in April 1941, when Weddell was about to turn sixty-five and retire, the president sent him a telegram informing him that he was about to issue an executive order postponing his retirement.[49]

But the fact that he was an appointee between 1933 and 1940 was never frowned upon within the State Department. Quite the opposite. And he was also treated quite differently from his predecessor in Spain, Bowers, who had been scorned for this reason and also for his pro-Republican sympathies. The Department employees, however, considered "Alex" as "one of us." It was not for nothing that he had good connections in the department, where he had worked for a year in 1923. This became clear from the steps that he took to form the staff that he wanted to take with him to Madrid. His first choice was the influential James Clement Dunn, adviser for Political Relations. However, although he was unable to acquire the services of his friends Alexander Kirk and Pierrepont Moffat for the post of counselor (the former was sent to Germany because he spoke good German and the latter already held the post of head of the Division of European Affairs), he was successful in recruiting Robert M. Scotten from the embassy in Brazil, who he also knew and who also spoke Spanish.[50]

So, in April 1939, and after a great deal of personal effort (according to him, this was the only time he ever took steps to secure an appointment[51]), Weddell was given the post of ambassador in Madrid. The fact that he spoke Spanish[52] played a role in the decision to appoint him, although under the Roosevelt administration a knowledge of the language of the country was not always taken into account when diplomatic assignations were made.[53] But another decisive contribution to the decision was the fact that he had never expressed any opinions about, or any sympathies toward, either of the sides in the recently finished Spanish Civil War, quite unlike his predecessor and pro-Loyalist Bowers, the memory of whom the State Department was trying to obliterate in Franco's New Spain.[54]

Weddell's appointment raised some protest in the U.S. press. "Newsweek" responded to the praise that the "New York Times" had heaped on Roosevelt for having appointed him by publishing a bitter biographical sketch of the new ambassador. He was portrayed as a former Library of Congress clerk who had managed to enter the diplomatic service for having married a rich widow. And it was made quite clear that he would be no match for the other Western ambassadors in Spain such as the French ambassador Mariscal Pétain or the British ambassador Sir Maurice Peterson.[55] None of these criticisms were to have any consequences.

The Franco Regime's Hostility toward the United States of America

In the disputes that the Roosevelt administration had to cope with at the end of the Spanish Civil War, the Spanish New State made its attitude quite clear. This attitude persisted throughout the period that we are studying and its main features were extreme national pride; little sympathy, not to say outright hostility, toward the U.S. administration, which was regarded as having supported the defeated side in the Civil War; extreme economic and political nationalism; and extreme eagerness for repression. Weddell had to struggle against all of this from the moment he arrived in Spain in May 1939. Neither he nor the State Department found it easy to deal with and understand the Francoist idiosyncrasy. In March of that year, Franco's regime had signed agreements of friendship with Germany and Portugal to add to the already existing agreement with Italy, which had been signed in the fall of 1936. Also in March, Spain had joined the Anti-Comintern Pact. And there was more. On 8 May 1939, Franco's New Spain withdrew from the League of Nations just twenty-four hours after Germany and Italy had signed their so-called Pact of Steel military alliance. In this way, the regime took one more step toward the Fascist powers at the same time as it was paying tribute in both Spain and Italy to the German and Italian soldiers who had fought for the National army. And very shortly afterward, on 5 June, Franco made a speech to the National Council of the sole political party, the Spanish Traditionalist Phalanx of the Assemblies of the National-Syndicalist Offensive (hereinafter, the Falange), in which he made reference to the (alleged) "secret offensives" of the "false democracies" to lay economic siege to the country and prevent its national and imperial revival.

In the months immediately after the end of the Civil War, then, Franco's pro-Axis leanings and, above all, the New State's hostility toward democracies were to be displayed in all their virulence. The roots of this hostility lay in the conviction that the recent victory was the beginning of a new era in the history of Spain, and that the leading players in this new era were the Francoists. The new Spain had broken away from the liberal-democratic political model on 18 July 1936, had just won the war and believed that the time had come to do away with the country's economic dependence on the more advanced democratic nations like the United Kingdom, France, and the United States of America. The time had come for Spain to present itself to the world as a really great power, as the power it had used to be until, according to Franco's version, these three countries and several others weakened its spirit with the ideological pollution of rationalism and liberalism, colonized it economically, and amputated some of its territory by appropriating such possessions as Gibraltar, Cuba, the Philippines, and Puerto Rico.

All this was accompanied by a policy designed to encourage the idea of the Hispanic world, which was particularly directed at Spanish America and the Philippines. Since the beginning of the twentieth century, Spanish Hispano-Americanism had had both liberal and authoritarian features but it had been this latter aspect that had been given the most political encouragement during the dictatorship of General Primo de Rivera. And now, the Francoists were to use their extreme authoritarian and imperialist nationalism to reformulate the idea. Not only did they criticize the lack of effectiveness of previous policies, they also aspired to Spain's leading a community of Hispanic nations that would be capable of facing up to the influence of the United States. And although the results were to be nonexistent and, as we shall see, the consequences extremely negative for Spain, they also aimed to counter the Pan-Americanism, secularism, and democratism of the United States with the Pan-Hispanism, Catholicism, and authoritarianism of the Franco regime.[56] Of these three factors, the first—Pan-Americanism—was little more than an invention of the United States and the second and the third—secularism and democracy—were present in many of the Hispano-American countries. The Francoist idea of the Hispanic world (*Hispanidad*) was to go through two stages in these years: the first was Catholic-inspired by the minister of foreign affairs in 1939 colonel Juan Beigbeder; the second, more fascistized and aggressive, was also initiated under the same minister after the defeat of France in June 1940 but it reached its maximum expression when Franco's brother-in-law and chief political adviser at the time, Ramón Serrano Suñer, took up office.[57]

But it was not all future plans. The Francoists believed that Spain was already being reborn, just as Germany and Italy were. And this rebirth could not be based exclusively on the architecture of a single-party regime that was loosely inspired by the Fascist model, and which was antiliberal, antidemocratic, and eager to remove its enemies once and for all, whether they were democrats or leftists. Franco, advised by Serrano, had begun to shape the regime after the Decree of Unification of 19 April 1937 by which the single party, FET y de las JONS, had been created and he had taken other political and institutional steps throughout the war. No, it could not be based just on this. What was also required, as the Caudillo pointed out in his speech of 5 June 1939, was an autarkical, interventionist economic policy similar to the policies of Spain's Fascist's friends. The time had come for the famous "produce, produce, produce!"[58] in an attempt to industrialize the country and make it economically independent and find alternatives to as many importations as possible. This policy went against the interests of those countries that had traditionally supplied Spain and that had a great deal of property and considerable investments in the country: that is to say, Franco's *bêtes-noires*, the countries that were responsible for all of Spain's economic ills, the United Kingdom, the United States, and France.

This desire for autarky, which was to be the hallmark of Franco's economic policy for more than a decade, was accompanied by an increase in the economic intervention and price and salary control that had been initiated in the National Zone during the Civil War. But the main aim behind the autarky was to take part in a future war that would provide the definitive solution to Spain's old irredentist disputes—such as Gibraltar—and more recent ones such as the "just and necessary" extension of its African colonial territories at the expense of France. This participation in a new war was regarded as a medium-term objective and the fact that it was to break out so soon—on 1 September 1939, just five months after the end of the Civil War—took Franco and the other leaders of the regime by surprise. From as early as the end of October 1939,[59] they began to make preparations not only to go to war but also to provide aid to Germany. They were also to do exactly the same when Italy entered the war in June 1940. Of course, all this took place in the utmost secrecy because officially Spain had declared its neutrality on 4 September 1939, although in the early years this neutrality was to be totally favorable to the Axis. One example is the fact that on 30 November Franco authorized, at the request of Germany, a secret operation to provide supplies to the Nazi U-boats.[60]

THE ECONOMIC WEAKNESS OF SPAIN IN 1939: THE ACHILLES' HEEL OF THE FRANCO REGIME

The objectives of an autarkic regime and a new war could not be attained quickly in a country that was weakened and partially destroyed by the war, and economically dependent on foreign powers, particularly bearing mind that Franco's Spain was taking its first steps in the middle of a continental, Mediterranean, and Atlantic environment that was about to embark on a war of a world scale. And although Franco's aim was to take active part, he could not do so immediately. Paradoxically, he pinned all his hopes of a future military conflict, autarky and economic independence on his providing aid to Germany and Italy. At least in the short term, then, he aimed to replace his dependence on the democracies by a new dependence on the Axis powers. Hopes and desires were one thing; reality quite another.

And Spain's current reality was absolute dependence on the United States and the United Kingdom for the supply of a wide range of raw materials and products essential to economic survival. Eighty percent of Spain's requirements of oil products (and particularly gasoline, given the relatively small capacity of the only Spanish refinery in Tenerife) came from the wells that the USA[61] and the United Kingdom owned in Colombia and Venezuela. The main raw material of the Spanish textile industry, cotton, was also imported from the United States and the British colonies in India and Egypt.[62] Likewise, the United States also provided Spain with scrap metal, essential in the manufacture of steel. Another issue was wheat, the base of the Spanish diet and a crop in which Spain had been self-sufficient before the Civil War.

However, after the whole of the Spanish territory had been occupied by Franco's forces in 1939 with the fall of the Loyalist cities of Madrid, Barcelona, and Valencia, Spain had had to resort to importation once again. The decrease in cultivated surface area and, above all, the lack of fertilizers, working animals and machinery had led to a wheat deficit, which was in turn to lead to paroxysm, shortages, and famine in 1940, as we shall see. Wheat, however, unlike oil, cotton, and scrap metal were obtainable from other markets and Spain was to import from both the United States and Argentina.[63]

The crude reality of Spain's economic dependence prompted the Caudillo to revise his childish objective of a short-term improvement in the trade deficit. All the above factors formed a framework of foreign economic relations in which Spain was obliged to deal not only with the hated United Kingdom and the United States, but also with its allies Germany and Italy. And as the World War progressed, Spain's dependence on the United States and the United Kingdom would increase for supplies such as oil products and for the British certificates (navicerts) that were required if vessels were to be allowed to cross blockades.

This dependence conflicted with the political sympathies of the regime and with the official propaganda, controlled up to 1941 by the minister for governance and president of the Political Committee of the Falange, Ramón Serrano Suñer. And the United States was to prove to be more sensitive than the United Kingdom to the violence of the attacks made by Franco's press and radio on their respective democracies. The American reaction was much more hostile than the British one, because the British feared that, if Spain were to intervene or to allow German troops to pass through their territory, the Germans might take Gibraltar or occupy the coast of North Africa, thus cutting the supply lines from the Suez and the East. For this reason, the British were quick to define a specific Spanish policy, which aimed to maintain Spanish neutrality and which was put into practice several months before the outbreak of the war. In fact, this policy was constructed on the basis of a disappointment. Just like Matthews and the regime's relations with the United States, the British had also come up against a hostile New Spain. Prime Minister Chamberlain had had high hopes and in February 1939 he wrote the following in his diary: "I believe that we will be able to establish excellent relations with Franco, who seems to be well disposed towards us."[64]

In its attempts to deal with the proud, ultranationalist, and hostile New Spain, the United Kingdom, which was slowly but surely heading toward armed conflict, was obliged to use a twofold Spanish strategy.[65] Even before the outbreak of the World War, the strategy was to maintain Spanish neutrality. On the one hand, a representative from the Ministry of Trade was sent (and given a very frosty welcome[66]) to try to restore full economic relations and Franco was repeatedly assured that Britain would respect his regime, thus scotching the rumors that suggested that Britain would support attempts to restore the monarchy.[67] And on the other, the United Kingdom was aware that Spanish neutrality would be benevolent toward Germany so, at the request of the military high command, began to reinforce the lines of defense in Gibraltar, extend its airport and reinforce it with new equipment and more weapons. The possibility of a naval blockade was also studied in the event that Spain were to decide to intervene in the war against Great Britain and France.

The British, then, had a Spanish policy during the five months between wars. The United States of America, on the other hand, did not have a similar policy in this period or in the immediate subsequent period. Despite the efforts of their new ambassador, they did nothing more than defend their economic interests and their property in the country. In fact, the U.S. policy toward Spain between the end of the Spanish Civil War on 1 April 1939 and shortly before Pearl Harbor on 7 December 1941 (that is to say, more than two years) was simply to go along with the United Kingdom in its struggle against the Axis. But even though they had embarked on the same journey, the Americans were to lag behind the British, following them idly, wearily, and bad-temperedly. And, of course, the leaders of the Franco regime were not oblivious to this situation.

THE UNITED STATES AND SPAIN FROM THE BEGINNING OF THE SECOND WORLD WAR TO 8 NOVEMBER 1942 (OPERATION TORCH)

> The American policy was throughout stamped by emotion, confused thinking, indecision and lack of coordination. It reduced Ambassador Weddell to despair and still strikes the historian as one of the least impressive chapters in the history of American foreign relations
> Willian L. Langer and S. Everett Gleason, *The Undeclared War, 1940–1941* (New York: Harper & Brothers, 1953) 766

During the period that we shall study below—the more than two years of U.S. neutrality at the beginning of the Second World War—the differences that had existed within the Roosevelt administration with respect to Spain during the Spanish Civil War tended to persist although there were some considerable changes. Roosevelt's family environment and some of the members of his cabinet—his wife Eleanor, his brother-in-law Hall, Secretary Morgenthau and Secretary Ickes, and, after June 1940 the new Secretaries of War and the Navy Henry Stimson and Colonel Frank Knox—maintained their pro-Loyalist and anti-Franco attitude and was to come to the fore at certain crucial moments in the relations between the two countries. The attitude that the State Department had entertained toward the *nacionales* during the Civil War, however, often tended to turn sour and become reluctant annoyance with Franco's Spain, whose propaganda expressed extreme hostility to all democracies and in particular to the United States, its president, and its influence in the Western Hemisphere (through the policy of *Hispanidad*). Neither was this hostility limited to propaganda: Spain was to make things very difficult for the United States in many sensitive issues concerning the relations between the two countries.

Within the department there were now differences regarding how to deal with Spain between Secretary Hull, who felt increasingly alienated from a New State that was against free trade, and Under Secretary Sumner Welles, who was more in favor. Welles was on excellent terms with the Spanish ambassador in Washington Juan Francisco de Cárdenas y Rodríguez de Rivas, who was a personal friend,[68] and he was also more receptive to the opinions of Ambassador Weddell. And above all, he was not hostile to Franco's Spain, as Morgenthau and the other anti-Franco members of the cabinet were. The result of all this was a policy that was, in fact, no policy at all, in spite of the unflagging efforts of Weddell and the Madrid Embassy to convince the United States to adopt a decisive policy in support of Franco (who they mistakenly believed was successfully resisting German pressure to enter the war). The policy that was applied was marked by the disputes over Telefónica and the Lincoln prisoners in 1939 and much of 1940. And when they were finally resolved and it seemed possible for the United States to consider a new framework for their relations, other more serious disputes arose, such as the confrontation between Weddell, Serrano Suñer, and Franco. These clashes were sparked off by personal disagreements and Franco's policy of Spanish nationalism, and they were also used by the Franco regime in its relations with the Axis. Meanwhile, the country that really affected policy toward Spain was the United Kingdom, because if Spain was to remain neutral, or at least not join the belligerent Axis powers, the United States had to keep sending supplies.

Nevertheless, the situation started to change shortly before the attack on Pearl Harbor in December 1941, when the United States began to design a specific Spanish policy, encouraged not only by the desire to keep Spain out of the war to help the United Kingdom but also for their own strategic and commercial interests. Their policy was to be similar to that of the British but tougher and more demanding. So it was not until the months of October and November 1941 that the United States finally started to have a fully fledged Spanish Policy. However, the person responsible for implementing it was no longer Weddell, disillusioned by his years of struggle and controversy with Serrano Suñer and Franco, but a new ambassador, Carlton J.H. Hayes.

Part II

The United States and Spain from the Second World War to Operation Torch

Chapter 3

The First Stage of Alexander W. Weddell's Embassy (May 1939–August 1940)

Alexander Wilbourne Weddell's time as head of the Madrid Embassy can be divided into the several periods. The first of these ran from his arrival in Spain in May 1939, just four months before the outbreak of the Second World War, to August 1940, when he managed to resolve the main issue that he had had to deal with: the return of the Compañía Telefónica Nacional de España to its U.S. owners, the ITT. The other major issue, the release of the Lincoln Brigade prisoners who were still in the hands of Franco's forces, had been solved six months earlier, in February of the same year.

During this period, the issues at the center of the U.S. international policy were the outbreak of the Second World War and the decision to remain neutral. Despite this decision, the United States soon started providing aid first to the Franco-British Allies and then to Great Britain who in June 1940 had been left to continue the struggle alone after Germany had surprisingly and devastatingly occupied Belgium, Holland, Luxembourg, Denmark, and Norway, and then gone on to defeat France. Since the beginning of the war on 1 September 1939, and largely because of President Roosevelt's own policy, the intentions of the United States had been somewhat contradictory: on the one hand, they did not wish to take part in the war but, on the other, they were prepared to provide France and the United Kingdom with aid. Fundamental to this policy was the fact that the president had changed the Neutrality Act so that private individuals could sell arms and all sorts of materials to the adversaries on a cash-and-carry basis. However, as was to be expected, putting this regulation into practice was not free of problems. Although President, Secretary Morgenthau and other anti-Fascist members of the cabinet supported and encouraged French and British purchases of U.S. war material, the volume of the orders was not to the liking of the military high command or the war Secretary Woodring, a fervent isolationist. At the beginning of 1940, when the French and British orders of planes and engines from the United States increased significantly, they believed that the sales could endanger the supply needs of the U.S. armed forces, and in March, Secretary Woodring refused to sell some of the planes' fittings arguing that they were secret. Such was his opposition that one month later Roosevelt forced him to accept the sales or resign.[1]

The president stood firm in his resolve to support the Allies and not to take direct part in the war. In his speech on the state of the nation on 3 January 1940 he clearly stated that there was "a vast difference between keeping out of war and pretending that war is none of our business. We do not have to go to war with other nations, but at least we can strive with other nations to encourage the kind of peace that will lighten the troubles of the world, and by so doing help our own nation as well."[2] Deep down, however, he was pessimistic about the situation of the French and British forces. Until March he seriously considered the possibility that the European conflict would end in an early armistice. There was so little activity on the fronts and the seas that this period became known as the "phony war" or "drôle de guerre," and Chamberlain actually entertained the possibility that the Nazi regime would collapse and that he would be able to come to an agreement with a new German government.[3] With no great hopes of success, Roosevelt began to take steps to reach a peace agreement before the Germans could launch their expected spring offensive against France. He asked a high-ranking executive from General Motors with good connections in Berlin to sound out the possibilities of a negotiated peace; he asked forty-six neutral countries for an exchange of views on the postwar scenario and the possibilities of maintaining peace on the basis of international economic stability and arms control; and he sent the Under Secretary and his right-hand man in the State Department Sumner Welles to Paris, London, Berlin, and Rome to secretly explore the possibilities of a negotiated peace (although no proposal was made that could implicate the United States) and perhaps even persuade Mussolini not to involve Italy in the war.[4] The real reasons behind the trip were not explained to the general public for fear that Germany would only be encouraged and that the numerous U.S. isolationists, always reluctant to intervene excessively in Europe, would grow suspicious. It was presented as a mere fact-finding mission for the president (which, of course, it also was). The result was only to be expected. On his return at the end of March 1940, the under secretary concluded that there was not "the slightest chance of any successful negotiation at this time for a durable peace." Meanwhile, the Allies had taken the decisions to place a joint order with the United States for 4,600 planes and to mine Norwegian territorial waters to prevent Scandinavian raw materials from being transported to Germany.[5]

Welles' impression was to be confirmed almost immediately by the triumphant German invasions of Denmark and Norway on 9 April 1940, and then again by the invasions of Belgium and Holland on the following 10 May. On 16 May, in the middle of the frenzy of advances and occupations and when the Germans were already on French soil, Roosevelt asked Congress for extra funds for the army and announced a program to build 50,000 planes a year, some of which would be sold to the Allies. They were to be the United States' first line of defense. These decisions were partly a response to further desperate requests for arms from the British and the French. Britain's new prime minister, the Conservative Winston Churchill, who had succeeded Neville Chamberlain on his resignation after the defeat of Norway on 10 May, put an end to his predecessor's policy of buying products such as tobacco or fruit from the United States (which had infuriated Hull) and he set about spending on a large scale.[6] Some of the purchases he hoped to make included planes, old destroyers from the First World War for escorting convoys, anti-aircraft guns and munitions. To accompany his "blood, toil, tears, and sweat" speech program he also asked the United States to abandon the policy of neutrality and become nonbelligerent, to keep Japan at bay in the Pacific (because they feared that they would enter the war and pose a direct threat to the British empire in Asia), to send a naval force to Ireland in an attempt to dissuade Germany from invading with parachute troops, and to sell strategic materials to the United Kingdom.[7] The president ignored all the requests for a change in the neutral status of the United States but was receptive to many of the others. He promised to provide planes, send a naval squadron to Ireland, and establish a naval presence in Hawaii as a deterrent.

However, making plans to manufacture planes, vessels, and war supplies, and getting Congress to approve the necessary funds was one thing; having sufficient quantities available for immediate shipment was quite another. There was, then, a considerable difference between what had been ordered and what was available. At the height of the Franco-British War crisis in May, the United States laid its hands on anything it could (mainly rifles, machine guns, and cannons from the First World War that were still used for training purposes), prepared the shipments and completed the transactions using private intermediaries to get round the Neutrality Act.[8] To complicate matters further, the Department of War was reluctant to release the supplies and it took Roosevelt and Morgenthau three weeks to get them to do so.[9] Subsequently, in July, General Marshall and Admiral Stark, the leaders of the army and the navy respectively, brought pressure to bear on the Senate to introduce a provision into the Neutrality Act by which all sales of United States' arms had to receive their authorization[10] because they were extremely concerned about the lack of armaments. It is clear, then, that the United States made a real effort to assist the European Allies.

Toward the end of May, Roosevelt ignored the anguished pleas of the French President Paul Reynaud begging the United States of America to join the war. Even so, France's dramatic situation had a considerable impact on public opinion in the United States, because it was becoming increasingly clear that the country was not prepared for the eventuality of having to defend itself against an external aggression. In this context, Congress approved extra funds for the armed forces at the same time as voices started to be heard in favor of a joint candidacy between the Democrats and the Republicans in the November presidential elections.[11] Roosevelt turned a deaf ear. However, during a speech at the University of Virginia in Charlottesville on 10 June 1940, he attacked the isolationists and reaffirmed his resolve to assist France and the United Kingdom. On the same day, Fascist Italy decided to enter the war, not wanting to miss out on the spoils in France, which was on the verge of defeat. Roosevelt qualified this action as a "stab in the back"[12] During the following week, Reynaud and Churchill continued to send messages asking the United States to intervene. But on 17 June 1940, Reynaud handed over the presidency of the Cabinet to Marshal Philippe Pétain, who officially asked Germany for an armistice.

The defeat of France was to be as fundamental to Roosevelt's attitude as Munich had been and the German invasion of the Soviet Union one year later. It reaffirmed his resolve to continue supporting the anti-Nazi and anti-Fascist cause, now by supporting a solitary Great Britain. Hitler's movements in Europe in 1938 had led him to change his mind about the whole continent in general and the Spanish Civil War in particular, and the fall of France convinced him that the path taken at that time had been the correct one. Despite the strong current of opinion in the country in favor of limited rearmament and the defense of the American continent, and against the wishes of the Department of War, he opted to continue providing the United Kingdom with aid.[13]

His decision was influenced by his sympathies for the Allied cause and the need to gain time for the United States to rearm. At this point, 19 June 1940, he finally replaced Woodring and Edison (the secretary of war and the secretary of the navy, respectively, and two of the most fervent isolationists in his cabinet) for Henry Stimson and Colonel Frank Knox, both Republicans and supporters of the anti-Nazi cause. The former had been the secretary of war with Taft and the secretary of state with Hoover[14] and he was determined to send supplies in convoys escorted by the U.S. Navy, even if this meant a new modification to the Neutrality Act. The latter aimed to raise an army of half a million men, create the most powerful air force in the world, and send the most modern fighter planes to the British. With these appointments, Roosevelt was attempting to reinforce the consensus with the Republican Party on a basis of anti-Nazi commitment and implication with the British cause.

On the American continent, the fall of France increased Roosevelt's fears that the Axis would instigate coups in the Latin American Republics. Several ambassadors, including Claude Bowers in Chile, fuelled these fears and rumors, and although they were largely unfounded Franco was not unaware of them and exploited them to the full. For example, because the defeat of France had given fresh impetus to Spanish imperial aspirations, Foreign Minister Beigbeder adopted a new, more aggressive and Fascistized version of the policy of Hispanidad after June 1940. Hispanidad was to peak and subsequently fall into decadence during the period in which Serrano held the post of foreign minister after October 1940. As a policy, it was a complete failure and had negative consequences for the regime because it aroused the suspicions and the hostility of the United States.

The reality of the situation, however, was that Latin American exports were increasingly being sent to European countries that were in the hands of the Axis powers. This gave Hitler unforeseen influence, which he was to use to try to establish friendly regimes on the American continent and undermine the hegemony of the United States. Even so, this was a far cry from Roosevelt's fear that Germany or Italy would occupy the French and Dutch colonies in Latin America and establish a foothold in the Western Hemisphere. Equally unrealistic was his fear that Hitler was aiming to take control of the French fleet (which he could not do because, among other reasons, part of it had been destroyed by the British) and the French North African bases stretching from Algeria to Senegal, and use them to attack Brazil and other South American countries. Although we now know that Hitler was planning a new war against the United States[15] after the first one was over, it does not seem in the least likely that he had considered occupying the American, French, and Dutch colonies in the summer of 1940.

But Roosevelt did not know this. At the Conference of Panama he had obtained an agreement on general neutrality and a 300-mile exclusion zone. And at the Conference of Havana, which had been convened at the request of the United States at the end of July 1940, he managed to persuade the Latin American Republics to protest against any direct or indirect attempt to transfer the sovereignty of the European colonies in the continent and it was agreed that, if any such attempts were to be made, they were to be put under inter-American guardianship until they could be returned to their mother countries or prepared for independence.[16] But to Roosevelt's surprise, he found that during and after the conference both Getulio Vargas' Brazil and Ramón del Castillo's Argentina were reluctant to follow the United States' leadership and were in fact making advances toward Germany. Brazil was trying to take advantage of its reluctance to follow the United States to get on the right side of Berlin and Argentina was suggesting some form of future economic support.[17]

The Asian scenario had also been thrown into confusion by the defeat of France and it was now Japan's turn to mobilize. During the previous winter, the war in China had made no significant advances despite the enormous quantities of weapons, the 850,000 soldiers deployed, and the trade agreement with the United States that had been abrogated in January 1940 (which did not put a stop to trade but it did remove its legal protection). Encouraged by the German victory in France, the Japanese decided to try and make the definitive strike in China and demanded that the Allies cease supplying their enemies with provisions. In July the British agreed to close the so-called Burma Road for three months, largely in an attempt to avoid entering into a new conflict with Asia, but before they did so they asked the United States to stop exporting to Japan and to send their fleet to Singapore as a show of strength and support. The Japanese put pressure on Holland to continue supplying oil, rubber, and tin from their colonies in the East Indies,[18] and France to close the border between Indochina and China.

Britain's agreement was regarded by Washington as a sign of weakness and the anti-appeasers among the secretaries in the cabinet—Morgenthau, Stimson, and Knox—reacted with outraged indignation. However, on 18 July 1940 they met with the British Ambassador Lord Lothian, who drew their attention to U.S. sales of aviation gasoline to Japan and suggested that they order an embargo. Morgenthau decided to make the proposal to the president, in application of the National Defense Act, which had been passed on 2 July 1940. The objective of this act was to facilitate national rearmament and enable the president to ban the export of particular materials and products, including oil. Hull had agreed to it on the condition that it should not be applied to Japan.[19] The embargo proposal was also directed against Spain because Morgenthau, Ickes, Stimson, and Knox suspected that part of their oil supply was being siphoned off for the Axis powers. In the end, the embargo was restricted to aviation gasoline and high-quality scrap iron, but it was to have little effect on either Spain or Japan, at least as far as this type of gasoline was concerned. As it happened, the U.S. planes used 100 octane fuel and restrictions were placed on sales of all fuels with octane ratings of 87 and above. The Japanese planes, however, used fuel with octane ratings of 86, which Japan was able to continue purchasing.[20] Roosevelt took more notice of the State Department than the Treasury because he was convinced that the priority of the United States at that time was not Asia and the Pacific, but Europe and the Atlantic (at least until Germany had been defeated).[21] An annoyed Secretary of the Treasury Henry Morgenthau, who was in favor of quite a different policy, wrote in his diary that the president had spoken to him in the same way as S. Welles.[22]

Before moving on to analyze Spain in depth, we should mention that the combination of the defeat of France and the new Japanese advances in China prompted Roosevelt to decide to run for reelection, breaking with the "no third term" tradition established by George Washington. This decision was a sudden one because just one month earlier he had accepted an offer from Collier's magazine to become a columnist and he had speeded up the transfer of his documentation to the new presidential library in Hyde Park. But he dropped the idea of retiring and decided to carry on and run for reelection with Henry A. Wallace from Iowa in an attempt to remain at the helm of the United States on an increasingly gloomy world stage.[23]

In Spain, the embargo coincided with a series of restrictions on the supply of oil. At the request of the French and the British and on the initiative of Morgenthau himself, these restrictions were applied from June to the end of August 1940, when the British finished negotiating a trade agreement with the Spanish. They led to severe supply problems and made a decisive contribution to solving the most important of the two disputes between Spain and the United States: that is to say, the dispute over the restoration of the Compañía Telefónica Nacional de España to its managers and owners of the ITT, which had become the focal point in the relations between the two countries alongside the issue of the release of the Lincoln Brigade prisoners. Let us start from the beginning and take a look at the situation in greater detail.

Alexander W. Weddell, the State Department, and Their Perceptions of the Franco Regime: The (Alleged) Franco-Serrano Dichotomy and the (Alleged) "Two Forces" in Franco's Government

Ambassador Weddell was a man interested in Hispanic culture in general and openly professed his sympathy for the Spanish.[24] After he had been in the post for two years he said that he had come to Spain "with an open mind."[25] This may be so but, whether he had or not, he was immediately impressed by the figure of Franco and the extreme complexity of the Spanish political situation. In the letters and reports that he wrote in his first days in Spain, he described the Generalissimo as a "first-rate soldier" with the "peculiar gift" of "great personal charm." And he fully agreed with information provided by the military that praised his "lofty personal life" and described him as "a saint of the sword (...) using the words applied to the Argentine hero, Saint Martin."[26] He was to keep this high opinion of the figure of the Caudillo for some considerable time and he was only to revise it somewhat in the last year of his term of office. During the two years of the Second World War that he was in Madrid, he also believed that Franco was a man who would strive to keep Spain neutral, and constantly resist the pressure brought to bear by Germany and Italy.

Weddell's high opinion of the Generalissimo was in stark contrast with his low opinion of Ramón Serrano Suñer, who he privately referred to as his "particular headache." One of the main reasons for this opinion, which was shared not only by the Madrid Embassy but also the State Department and Great Britain, was that of all the regime's leaders Serrano was the most vociferous supporter of the Axis powers and the one who was most in favor of Spain's entering the world war. One of the constant features of the analyses that Weddell, the Roosevelt administration and the United Kingdom made of the leaders of the regime was the dichotomy of a prudent, neutral Franco and a pro-Nazi, interventionist Serrano. Serrano himself was particularly interested in fostering this impression because he had great political aspirations and wanted to appear to the Axis—and the Italian leaders in particular—as if he were their best Spanish friend and partner. It was also useful in Spain's relations with the United States and Great Britain. The Allies' perception of the two leaders was to last until Serrano disappeared from the political scene in September 1942, although it was qualified somewhat when Franco gave a speech on 17 July 1941 in which he was extremely hostile to the United States and the United Kingdom. The perceived difference between the two leaders, however, remained unchanged and this came in extremely useful for the Spanish. After his brother-in-law's speech, Serrano said to the German ambassador in Madrid Von Stohrer that "so far the English government in particular has thought that only he, the minister of foreign affairs, was in favor of going to war, whereas the 'wise and prudent' Caudillo did not wish to put Spain's neutrality at risk on any account. This illusion has been totally broken."[27]

However, this was not the only alleged dichotomy to affect the United States and Great Britain in their dealings with the Franco regime. They also believed that within Franco's government there were two forces: one totalitarian, Falangist and pro-Axis, in the form of the single party (the Falange) and its maximum representative Serrano Suñer; and the other an alleged group of monarchists and men "from the center" with leanings toward Western democracies,[28] which in the period we are studying is highly debatable. The fact that there were different sensitivities within Franco's government does not necessarily mean that those who were not strictly speaking Falangists were liberals or democrats. It should be pointed out that all the members of the cabinet and those in the upper echelons of the regime, as well as much of the power base, shared a profoundly antiliberal and antidemocratic ideology; they felt a certain sympathy for Germany and Italy, and varying degrees of hostility toward the democracies as a result of their convictions and of the attitude of France, Great Britain, and the United States during the Civil War. It is certainly true that at times some ministers approached Great Britain and the United States in search of economic aid (e.g., Beigbeder and Alarcón de la Lastra in 1940) because they were aware of the extremely serious situation within Spain and they were not quite so insensitive to it as Franco, Serrano, and many others. But under no circumstances can this sensitivity to the plight of Spain be mistaken for democratic sympathies.

Quite another thing were Beigbeder's maneuvers shortly before and just after he was relieved of his duties, the opposition of an important group of generals to participating in the war, after months of campaigning to do so (they were in fact unaware that they were being bribed by the British), and minister Carceller's double dealing with the Axis powers and the Allies, as we shall see below. In fact, in the autumn of 1941, even Serrano Suñer himself was to approach the Allies in search of essential economic aid after the months of problems that he and Weddell had created with their clash in April of the same year.

When he first arrived in Madrid, Weddell went to some considerable trouble to counteract the antidemocratic and anti–United States feeling among the authorities and the press, which was controlled and directed by Serrano Suñer in his capacity as the minister of governance. In the first place, he showed "nothing but cordiality, both officially and socially."[29] He took this attitude to the extreme with Franco himself, and after an interview with him in the month of July 1939, he said that he had told Franco that "confidence was a thing of slow growth but that with the passage of time he would come to realize that I was a sincere friend of the Spanish people." With this statement, he was merely following the instructions that he had been given by the president but he could not conceal his real admiration for the Caudillo. For his part, Franco, who was pleased because both Weddell and the State Department had played a fundamental role in the United States agreeing to grant Spain a loan, responded with a smile and said "we are already convinced of that,"[30] which, in turn, pleased the ambassador. Weddell always tended to believe that Franco had little to do with the difficulties he encountered in his dealings with the regime. Also, the fact that both Weddell and his wife were involved in providing and financing humanitarian aid to orphans and disabled servicemen through their collaboration with the Falangist Auxilio Social (Social Welfare) organization and the Cuerpo de Mutilados del Ejército (the Army's Group of Disabled Servicemen), did much toward reaching his objective.

It should also be mentioned that Spain confused Weddell at first: he had great difficulty in understanding the political situation. This confusion can be seen in some of the private letters that he sent to his friends back in the United States. In one of them he wrote the following: "The thousands in prison, strange to say, want a King, hoping for clemency. The Traditionalists of the Pyrenees equally wish the monarchy restored. The Church is disinclined to give this Government what it conceded to Their Catholic Majesties and this is provoking irritation; in the north, in Cataluña [Catalonia], and perhaps elsewhere, the tide of Separatism runs strong; the single political party is fighting a difficult battle in trying to regiment Spaniards, who through their very individualism are more easily inclined to Anarchy, and who naturally and consistently resist Communism or Fascism or Nazism. I am a bit bewildered."[31] His belief that the several hundreds of thousands of people[32] who were in prisons and concentration camps for having fought on the side of the Loyalists and/or for being Republicans and/or Leftists wished for a benevolent king was certainly highly dubious in general terms, although this does not necessarily mean that some may not have dreamt of it. What is more, the Traditionalists or Carlists—who have no particular connection with the area of the Pyrenees—were profoundly divided between those who had agreed to join the Falange and the so-called *intransigentes* (the intransigents), who wished for nothing more than the reestablishment of their particular branch of the monarchy. In fact, the Carlists were not the leading group of monarchists in the country; this privilege belonged to the *Alfonsinos,* the supporters of the deposed Alfonso XIII. In both Catalonia and the Basque Country, which had been granted a statute of autonomy during the Republican period and the Civil War, the repression of their regional characteristics was so brutal that they could be considered to have been subjugated. The attempt of the regime's single party to create "regiment Spaniards" speaks for itself.

However, Weddell believed that the Spanish problem did not lie in the physical scars left by the recent Civil War but in the spiritual ones. He said that "if Spaniard could forgive Spaniard, the rest would be easy." The problem with this was that, as he would soon find out, Franco was not prepared to forgive his enemies. Quite the contrary. This was not a fundamental characteristic of the Spaniards (he also said "it was not in a Spaniard's nature to forget so easily") but rather the desire of the victorious Francoists to make sure that correct punishment was meted out. As far as he was concerned, the most promising aspect was that "at least in the top ranks, especially in the case of Franco, the leaders are men of personally lofty character, if marked with the inescapable defects of their own race. And Franco has set a high social ideal in the rehabilitation of Spain."[33]

Weddell's view of the United States' attitude during the Spanish Civil War tied in nicely with his high opinion of Franco. In a conversation with the Conde de Romanones, the former president of the Spanish cabinet during the reign of Alfonso XIII, he described his country's actions in glowing terms and stated that Franco had been helped by "the unwavering attitude of our Government in the matter of the embargo against shipments of munitions to Spain; (…) since the Republican Government then had all the money, this attitude had been a very positive help to the Franco forces, and that our Administration's position had been maintained despite terrific pressure from many directions for its abatement."[34] And although he wrote to Secretary Cordell Hull in December 1939 that "I am allowing widening my contacts here with the special desire to learn the viewpoint of the more liberal elements,"[35] it seems clear that Weddell, quite unlike Bowers and acting against the instructions he had personally been given by Roosevelt just before he left for Spain, came into contact with the reality of the regime in 1939 more through his acquaintances in the wealthy, monarchic, and Francoist sectors than through the liberal elements.

It seems that Franco's rhetoric on social reform and the search to find a solution to the enormous economic inequalities among the Spanish convinced the North American ambassador of his commitment to social issues. In one of his letters, after mentioning the complex Spanish political situation, he wrote:

> the task of this Government as I see it is for a group of victorious generals and an equally if not more powerful group of civilians, the latter charged with totalitarian sympathies, to create a civil government. Hostilities between the two groups are marked, and no one can see what the result will be. What I am trying to say is that the situation is like a kaleidoscope and with any movement the pattern changes rapidly.

And he added:

> But the toughness of fibre of these people and a certain inherent vitality makes me hopeful that with time they will work out their problems in satisfactory fashion. But

the task is a vast one. Centuries-old privileges to be uprooted, sectional differences to be overcome, prejudices and envies having their base in the very heart of the people to be softened.[36]

Proof that Weddell had encountered a political scene in Spain that was far more complex than he had expected was provided at the beginning of December 1939. He showed that he was aware of the main factional divergences within Franco's universe when he wrote that "the rivalry between elements in the Army and the Falange seems to have been accentuated in recent weeks, while (...) the active hostility of the Requetés (or Traditionalists) toward the Falange, which is cordially reciprocated, has been manifest in actual conflict." In a previous communication, he had made reference to the conflicts between the Church and the Falange on the issues of education and youth associations.[37] The Spanish Church and the Vatican, he wrote, were struggling against Franco's desire—which was to become a reality in 1941[38]—to have privileges that had once belonged to the King of Spain, such as the presentation of bishops. It should not be forgotten that the Church had just had the subsidy that it had lost under the Second Republic returned and it had been restored to its privileged position within the country, largely thanks to a regime that officially stated that it was Catholic. For all of these reasons, the Catholic Church was profoundly grateful to Franco.

The ambassador's analyses of his first months in Spain also reflected the reality of an economic situation that was getting worse by the day and suggested the possibility of increasing tension between the army and the Falange:

> The difficult economic position of the country in the matter of foreign trade and foreign balances, the obstacles thrown in the way of interior industrial and commercial development, and the food shortage existing in acute form in many sections (...) From this latter cause I do not anticipate serious trouble, certainly so long as the Army and Guardia Civil are paid and fed. On the other hand, the Government's apparently unsuccessful economic policies may result in cabinet changes, while the dislike of the military element for the Falange, headed by Serrano Suñer, might lead to open conflict, to the detriment of the latter, who is perhaps losing in popularity.[39]

Although Weddell was certainly right in his economic assessment, he was clearly wrong in his opinions on the general political situation, particularly if we take a look at the parallelisms he drew between the North American and the Spanish Civil War.[40] In a letter to Sumner Welles in August 1939 he wrote the following:

> What the people of the country are gradually coming to recognize is that this recently ended Civil War represents as profound a social revolution as that which occured in our country eighty years ago. Some things that were fair are gone, never to return, and if the ideals of the present Government as publicly expressed are in any measure adhered to, an era of social justice will dawn in Spain such as it has never known before. Browning's familiar lines seem applicable in many respects to the causes provoking the various fumblings and sanguinary strivings toward an improved social structure, "In the great right of an excessive wrong." By this I mean to say that the victors in the recent conflict have, or should have, learned much, and in the extent of this learning lies the future for good or evil of the country.[41]

He seems to be contrasting a supposedly archaic Spain riddled with privileges with the New Spain, and also making an unfortunate comparison with the Civil War in his own country. Apart from this, Weddell was influenced by an image of Spain that had been extremely widespread in the United States since the 1898 war. The danger of totalitarianism existed, he explained. Of course it did. However, it had nothing to do with Franco; rather it was the objective of civilians such as Ramón Serrano Suñer. Thus, Weddell started shaping the fundamentally mistaken dichotomy between Franco and Serrano Suñer that held them to be different politicians. It was mistaken not because Serrano was not a Fascist, but because Franco was: he also wanted to play the card of Fascism. Returning to Weddell's analogies, we should bear in mind that if either of the sides in the Spanish Civil War was like the North in the American Civil War, then that side was the Second Republic, the defenders of the constitution, the vanquished. But not a word about this can be found in the ambassador's writings. In his comparison of the two civil wars Weddell may have omitted the significant fact that Franco had just destroyed Spanish democracy—or at least a system that was considerably closer to it than the Fascistized regime that was to take its place—because like many civil servants of the State Department, he believed the Republic to have been a quasi-Bolshevik regime. This negative view was compounded by the outbreak of the Civil War. Such an enemy meant that the military coup and Franco's subsequent victory were acceptable, as was Franco's alleged desire to do away with the Spain of semifeudal, outdated privileges.

The social reality in Spain at that time and throughout Weddell's term of office—and indeed for many years after it—was dramatic. Despite his rhetoric, which was largely inspired by the single Fascist Party, Franco and his regime applied a policy of price and salary control, considerable intervention in the production and distribution of goods, and autarky in their foreign exchanges. This soon meant that living conditions were so difficult for most of the population that in 1940 and 1941 there was famine, deaths from starvation and malnutrition. As a result, the Falangist welfare organization Auxilio Social, originally an imitation of the Nazi Winterhilfe, which had been set up to cover the needs of the rearguard or the recently conquered areas, was to have a long life under the regime. Thus, almost as soon as the Civil War had ended, the Spanish people had to cope with extremely harsh living conditions and a daily struggle to subsist, which in many cases was an impossible task. All of this was directly related to the regime's arrogant, ultranationalist aspirations. Franco believed that Spain had to fight to be economically self-sufficient and that improving the living conditions of the people was subordinate to this aim. What is more, after the fall of 1939, Spain also had another priority with real economic consequences: preparation to enter the world war.

It was in this context that the Weddells provided humanitarian aid. Mrs Weddell devoted herself to charity work and was at the head of several projects. Shortly after their arrival in Spain, she set up the Comité Americano del Auxilio Social (American Committee of the Social Welfare Organization) made up of women from the United States who were living in the country (many of whom had some connection to the embassy). She worked in close collaboration with the National Delegate of the Auxilio Social, Mercedes Sanz Bachiller. Among other things, this committee funded the restoration of a seventeenth-century hospital in Madrid to accommodate a hundred orphans.[42] It also provided constant help to military hospitals and, in particular, to disabled servicemen in conjunction with the head of the Cuerpo de Mutilados del Ejército (Army Corps of Disabled Servicemen) general Millán Astray. For her efforts in this field she was to receive the congratulations of the archbishop of Madrid-Alcalá. She also helped the refugees of various nationalities who were living in concentration camps after fleeing from their Nazi-occupied countries. In the United States, the Weddells also set up the Mrs. Weddell's Spanish Relief Fund, the aim of which was to collect food and children's clothing and provide an annual grant for a U.S. postgraduate to study at the University of Salamanca. Their task in the United States was directed mainly toward those who were sympathetic to the regime, as was shown by the fact that the celebrations of the third anniversary of the foundation of the Auxilio Social were attended by Commander Nelly, president of the North American pro-Franco Comité de Amigos de la Nueva España (Committee of Friends of the New Spain). In Spain, they carried out their humanitarian work in close collaboration with Franco's authorities.[43]

In the same way that Weddell had been unable to see the truth behind much of Franco's rhetoric on social issues when he first arrived in Spain, he was also unable to see the crude reality of the repression that was now being implemented. The fact was that, on this issue too, the dictator's discourse did not match reality. Although Franco had repeatedly stated in the final months of the war that "he whose hands are not stained with blood has no need to fear the justice of the New Spain," the hundreds of thousands of prisoners of war and Republican civilians in the concentration camps and jails, and the number of executions in the first year after the end of the war indicated a desire for revenge completely unlike the magnanimity that Franco professed in his speeches.[44] The difficulties that Weddell was encountering in securing the release of the former soldiers of the Lincoln Brigade, for whom he had very little sympathy,[45] was a good example of this. Even so, he tended to deny the information circulating in the United States about uncontrolled repression and mass executions. In October 1939 he wrote that "all my investigations give the lie of these stories. No executions are carried out without the previous assent of the Caudillo." And he highlighted Franco's magnanimity by saying that "in at least four instances, two of them affecting persons connected indirectly with the Embassy, reprieves have been granted."[46] Some months later he said:

> I am still pursuing this matter and am still unable to confirm these stories. Furthermore that sort of thing would appear to be contrary to all the political ideals and declarations of the present government. I can assure you that no death sentence is carried out without prior reference to the legal advisor of the Caudillo. In the Embassy itself there have been three or four cases of Spanish employees whose relatives were in danger of death sentence. In each of these cases there has been either exoneration or commutation of the death sentence and in the case of the latter, the father of one of the men concerned told me that his son had been adequately defended by a counsel appointed by the Court and that the trial seemed to him an eminently fair one. I have no wish to hammer the nerve, but I think you can be fairly sure that these execution stories are an aftermath of the extensive propaganda carried on up to the time of the fall of the Republican Government.[47]

Undoubtedly most of the executions took place in the immediate postwar period—unlike what had occurred in the National Zone during the first months of the war—and were the result of established military legal procedures. Of course a military legislation that frequently condemned Republicans to death for the crime of "military rebellion" when in fact they had never actually rebelled, as Franco and his forces had done, was highly questionable. It was also clear that "alegal" repression—that is to say, straightforward murder—was quantitatively speaking not the most important. But it happened. It had begun in 1936 and was still going on in 1939. There is a considerable body of evidence to prove that this was so, although Weddell was undoubtedly unaware of it at the time. Nevertheless, the legal properness of the court martials, the application of internationally recognized standards, left much to be desired: some proceedings were so quick that up to thirty or forty prisoners were sentenced in as little as an hour. Weddell clearly did not know about all this or did not investigate it, so his view of things was out of focus. And it was this view that he transmitted to Washington.

To sum up, the ambassador's perception of Spain was based on his own reality as a North American citizen who had come to know Spain through books on literature and history full of stereotypes; as a person who was genuinely attracted by the country and its people; and as a former ambassador to the richest and most advanced Hispano-American country Argentina, which would have led him to regard Spain as a similar sort of place but with a better pedigree because it was in Europe. His U.S. mentality would also have led him to look down on it somewhat as a Latin country. Likewise, his perception was conditioned by the fact that he was a rich man (whether the fortune was his or his wife's does not come into it), which meant that from the very beginning he was moving in Madrid's high society. Also important was the fact that he was a member of the Democrat Party in the southern state of Virginia, and that both he and his wife took active interest in social issues and particularly charity work.[48] This interest was to be important for the Spanish population because he helped to mobilize the U.S. Red Cross and was directly responsible for other initiatives, which Mrs Weddell often paid for out of her own pocket. For all these reasons, Alexander W. Weddell was to have fundamental difficulties in comprehending the new reality of Franco's Spain and this was to affect his work as ambassador.

In his relations with the Francoist authorities, and particularly with Serrano Suñer, Weddell often felt that he was being misled (and he was right: he was deliberately misled time after time). He was often deceived by officials who did not keep their promises and who were condescending with the United States. In some cases (e.g., Serrano Suñer), they were to end up as enemies. Of course, he was not at all accustomed to such treatment and he responded by showing even greater arrogance than before. This was a strategy that had often been used by the Secretary of State Cordell Hull and the president with foreign diplomatic representatives.[49] However, in Madrid with an ultranationalist, Spanish minister, it did not work.

The continuous conflicts soured Weddell's character and influenced his relations with the authorities. The mutual bad feeling between Weddell and Serrano was to have a particularly marked effect on his work. Signs of this can be found in both of the periods into which we have divided the analysis but they were most intense in the second period. The increasing tension in their relations was also the result of the role played by the State Department, which, at some considerable distance from the scene, tended to react with undue harshness to some of the Francoist decisions, sometimes in support of Weddell's proposals and sometimes not.

AMBASSADOR WEDDELL'S AGENDA ON HIS ARRIVAL AT THE MADRID EMBASSY

Even before Weddell had presented his credentials to Franco, he had been given instructions by the Under Secretary Sumner Welles[50] about the three problems that he had to deal with on his arrival in Spain: namely, the soldiers from the Lincoln Brigade who had been imprisoned by the Francoists and the negotiation for their release; the refusal of the Spanish authorities to allow the president of the Compañía Telefónica Nacional de España and ITT, colonel Sosthenes Behn, to enter Spain; and the Spanish request for a loan to buy cotton in the United States. Although this last problem was to be resolved in the first few months of his term of office— largely as a gesture of good will but also because it made good business sense—*all* the prisoners were not released and Behn was not allowed to enter Spain for at least a year. The subsequent negotiations established the model for the relations between the two states: the Spaniards would only abandon their ultranationalist, proud and, disdainful attitude toward the United States and democracies in general when they were impelled to do so by pressing economic needs. And when they did back down, they were not at all scrupulous about honoring their obligations and were even quite prepared to deceive the Americans.

Despite the personal distaste that Weddell felt for the prisoners of the Abraham Lincoln Brigade who had remained in the concentration camps after Bowers had organized the exchange of a small group for some Italian prisoners, he respected the request of the department and set about working for their release. Matthews had already spoken of this issue with the Under Secretary of Foreign Affairs Domingo de las Bárcenas on two occasions before Weddell's arrival and he had been promised a prompt release of all those prisoners who had no charges leveled against them other than having fought for the enemy.[51] In an interview with the Minister of Foreign Affairs Conde de Jordana on 22 June 1939, Weddell argued in favor of a release that meant very little to Franco and his government but which was an obstacle in the relations between the two countries and a source of considerable concern for the families of the prisoners.[52] He also complained that the military authorities responsible (the Auditoría Militar, entrusted with repression within the army) had not even provided him with a list of the names of the Lincoln Brigade prisoners or of the charges against them.[53] He appealed to Jordana, in his capacity as both minister of foreign affairs and general of the army, to find a prompt solution to this situation. Jordana promised to look into the matter but made it quite clear that those U.S. prisoners who had been involved in other crimes would not be given the same treatment. It was to take him two months to have the eleven prisoners with no criminal charges released and it was only after the event that Weddell and the other American diplomats realized that it had not been the whole group.

The second of these issues, the refusal of the Spanish authorities to grant colonel Behn an entry visa, was resolved shortly after the prisoners had been released. But once again the solution was not entirely satisfactory and the Americans felt that they had been grossly misled. The State Department had received Matthews' warnings and suspected that the Spanish government really intended to nationalize the CTNE because the company had been required to hand over all the documentation on the contract with the state. Their concern increased after the publication on 12 May 1939 of a decree by which the government took control of the board of directors of three private railway companies as the first step in their seizure.[54] Although these companies were not in the same situation as the CTNE because they had owed large sums of money to the state ever since the 1920s, everything suggested a general nationalizing trend. On top of this, the CTNE had been intervened by the state and was now being managed by Spanish civil servants. Therefore, the department decided to give the matter "our maximum support."[55] And they did. For more than a year, the CTNE was the highest priority of U.S. diplomacy in Spain, and the State Department and the Madrid Embassy worked unwaveringly side by side to find a solution. It was an awkward issue because it was an obstacle in the path of normalization in general, and economic normalization in particular, which was one of the aims of the State Department and the Madrid Embassy. As we know, this process of normalization had its critics within the Roosevelt administration.

The Negotiations for the Loan to Purchase Cotton in the United States and the Controversy within the Roosevelt Administration

However, the very real revisionist and nationalizing intentions of the Francoists, and their general attitude toward the United States, were doomed to failure from the very beginning. At the same time as Franco and his leaders were delaying Behn's entry visa, reconsidering the monopoly granted to the CTNE-ITT, taking their time to free the prisoners of the Lincoln Brigade and acting with nationalistic self-sufficiency, they were also asking the United States for a loan to buy the cotton that was absolutely essential to keep the Catalan textile industry afloat. Because of the extreme importance of this industry in Catalonia, the granting of the loan basically meant life or death for the whole of the Spanish textile industry. Alongside the Basque Country, Catalonia was the most industrialized of the Spanish regions and the shortage of cotton and other raw materials had led to a highly critical situation there. Although it had been a bastion of the Republic during the Civil War, many of its businessmen had supported Franco's rebels and fled to such cities in the National Zone as Burgos, San Sebastián, Seville, Saragossa, Salamanca, or Palma in an attempt to escape from the revolutionary period of terror during the first months of the war. During this period, the revolutionaries had mainly taken out their wrath on the clergy and the employers, and had massacred more than 8,000 alleged "Fascists." In political and economic terms, the Franco regime could not afford a semiparalyzed Catalan economy,[56] so when the raw materials in existence at the moment of the military occupation had been exhausted, the ambassador in

Washington, Juan Francisco de Cárdenas,[57] was given orders to request a loan to purchase cotton from the United States.

Let us take a closer look at Cárdenas. Before the Civil War, he had been ambassador to the United States (March 1932–June 1934),[58] and he was subsequently appointed to the post in Paris, which is where he was when the Civil War broke out. He had abandoned his post to take the side of the rebels, traveled to Spain and, once he had been checked and given the all clear, was sent to Washington as Franco's unofficial representative.[59] Once the conflict was over and the Republican Fernando de los Ríos had stepped down, he took charge of the embassy. On 10 May 1939,[60] he presented Under Secretary Welles with an application for a loan to the Export-Import Bank.[61] Two days later, one of the main economic chiefs of Catalonia, the Conde del Montseny, sent a dramatic letter to the minister of industry and trade and personal friend of Franco's, Juan Antonio Suanzes,[62] in which he pleaded for raw material to be sent urgently to the region.

Welles and the department were in favor of granting the loan. It suited them down to the ground because they wanted to normalize economic relations with Spain, and although some thorny issues had been discussed with Cardenas on 10 May, they were not to affect Welle's favorable attitude. One of these issues was a complaint that the names of President's Roosevelt's wife and mother had been on the list of sponsors of an exhibition by the painter Pablo Picasso in New York. Not only had the exhibition displayed the painting Guernica, which was considered an affront by the Francoists, but, according to Cárdenas, one of its aims was to raise funds for the Spanish Republican refugees and make antiregime propaganda. Another issue was Cárdenas's explanation for why the Bank of Spain had brought a lawsuit against the three agencies of the United States' government[63] that in 1938 had helped the Department of the Treasury to purchase fifteen million ounces of silver from the Loyalist government. By means of this lawsuit, the Spanish government hoped to recover the value of the metal, arguing that the silver sold had never belonged to the Spanish Republican government but to the Bank of Spain.

Welles was conciliatory on the first issue: he spoke of the possibility of undertaking an investigation if it were to be shown that the name of the president's wife was being used for propagandistic purposes against the Franco regime, and not for the humanitarian purpose of providing aid to the Republican refugees. On the second issue, however, he was quite firm: he did not believe that the lawsuit would be successful since the government of the United States had been under no obligation to investigate whether the silver being purchased had been expropriated from a bank— which, after all, was a national bank—or not.

Cárdenas agreed and confessed that he had been in favor of finding a diplomatic solution to the dispute, but he had not dared to suggest this to his own government "because they felt so violently about the question."[64] And he added something that made the United States sit up and take notice: if they could overlook an expropriation of Spanish property with no compensation, in the future they should logically refrain from intervening if Spain were to expropriate U.S. properties without paying the corresponding compensation. Despite these verbal skirmishes, the application for the loan was approved by the State Department. Weddell, who was in Washington at the time, played a direct part by meeting with Welles and also with Cárdenas on

10 May.⁶⁵ Another technical problem arose when the United States discovered that Spain was placing more orders for cotton in India and Egypt in conditions that were less favorable than they had imposed.⁶⁶ Despite everything, however, the application finally reached the board of trustees of the Export-Import Bank.

And this is where it ran aground. In a meeting held on 24 May 1939, the representative of the Department of the Treasury refused to grant the loan unless the Spanish government withdrew the lawsuit over the silver. The representative of the State Department on the Board, Herbert Feis⁶⁷—Adviser on International Economic Affairs—was extremely upset, but the Department of the Treasury stood firm.⁶⁸ It was finally decided that the president of the E-I Bank would discuss the issue in person with the president. From the economic point of view, the granting of the loan interested the bank and the state agencies, since the United States had large stocks of cotton and other agricultural products that they were anxious to sell, and the loan was a short-term one.⁶⁹ But it had become the focus of yet another confrontation within the Roosevelt administration. On this occasion, lines had been drawn between those who wished to grant the loan (the State Department) and those who did not (the Secretaries of the Treasury and of Trade, Morgenthau and Hopkins). The State Department was in favor of free trade and the normalization of economic relations with a country where important United States' companies had substantial interests, whereas Morgenthau and Hopkins had strong anti-Franco feelings and were in favor of not making things easier for the victors of the Civil War. The two camps once again took up the positions they had occupied during the Civil War. Or rather, they had never abandoned them.

In the face of the two currents of opinion in his cabinet, and very aware of the need to preserve U.S. interests in Spain, Roosevelt attempted to find a middle way. He instructed Pierson to negotiate a preliminary agreement with Spain on the conditions of the loan and then ask Cárdenas "to withdraw the suits now pending before the Treasury in connection with purchases of silver."⁷⁰ For his part, Jesse Jones, member of the board of trustees of the E-I Bank and chairman of the Reconstruction Finance Corporation, was entrusted with negotiating with Cárdenas and carrying out the president's orders. Jones spoke to Cárdenas of his bank's good will but insisted that the lawsuit should be withdrawn. The Spanish ambassador, however, refused arguing that it was a political issue.⁷¹ Despite this setback, Roosevelt was still in favor of granting the loan but now demanded that Spain keep the issue of the lawsuit and the repayments of the loan quite separate.⁷² Under Secretary Welles had once again intervened in favor of Cárdenas.⁷³

Meanwhile, however, Morgenthau and Hopkins had not been idle. Hopkins had written to Jones a few days before the president let his opinion be known to ask the E-I Bank not to authorize the loan.⁷⁴ For his part, Morgenthau sent Hopkins a report on the lawsuit in an attempt to reinforce their common position within the cabinet.⁷⁵ It should also be borne in mind that the special adviser for the Department of Justice acting in the government's interests was Henry L. Stimson, a Republican and former secretary of war and secretary of state, who was to return to the post of secretary of war in June 1940. His pro-Loyalist sympathies during the Civil War are well known.⁷⁶ He had made a strong defense of the U.S. government's interests in the lawsuit brought by the bank of Spain, and he had shown that both he and the

Department of Justice had little respect for the Franco regime, as can be deduced from the following paragraph:

> In its memorandum on this motion the plaintiff not only attacks the good faith and honesty of the Ambassador [of the Spanish Republic, Fernando de los Ríos] and other officials of the Spanish Government, but also insinuates that our own Government connived with them in illegal acts (...) Plaintiff has made no use of the contention except as a basis for its unworthy and unjustified accusation that payment was made to the Spanish Ambassador on behalf of his Government without any authentic authority and constituted in fact a wrongful diversion, connived at and made possible by the United States.[77]

Nevertheless, since the president had already announced that he was in favor of granting the loan, those who did not agree with him adopted the strategy of making new demands on the Spanish ambassador. When he had provided the E-I Bank with everything that had been asked for and he had agreed that the issue of the loan repayments would remain entirely separate from the issue of the purchase of silver (he even used exactly the same words as Jesse Jones had used in the draft that he had sent him),[78] the representatives of the Treasury on the board of trustees again refused to grant the loan and demanded that the Spanish Ministry of Foreign affairs and the Bank of Spain agree to withdraw their lawsuit in writing.[79] When he found out, an irritated Sumner Welles wrote to the president, asking him to halt the maneuver. He argued that the policy of the State Department, approved by Roosevelt himself, was to show good will toward the loan in an attempt to find a solution to the disputes that were still pending with Spain.

Since the previous 29 May, the State Department had begun to link the issue of the loan with Colonel Behn's entry into Spain. On that day Welles had had an interview with Cárdenas and had reiterated his government's good intentions toward Spain, saying that "this government desired to do what it could to smooth the way for a resumption of friendly and advantageous relations between the two countries."[80] But he was quick to add that

> I could not help but be disturbed by the apparent lack of candor on the part of the Spanish Government in approaching the problem presented by the interests of the Company [CTNE] in Spain (...) all of this doubt and uncertainty and ground for suspicion which now existed with regard to this matter could be promptly cleared up if Colonel Behn were permitted to enter Spain without further delay to discuss with the appropiate Spanish authorities in a frank and friendly manner the matter in which the Company was interested and if the Spanish Government were then prepared to state unequivocally its intention of respecting fully, in accordance with the accepted standards of international law and practice, the legitimate rights of this Company (...) just as I was interested in doing what I appropiately could in furthering the successful conclusion of the cotton transaction, I trusted that the Ambassador would not do what he could in clearing up the problem which I had outlined to him.

He asked him to inform his government of what he had just said. He also instructed Weddell to do the same in Madrid and told him that "the present attitude of the Spanish Government is the less understandable in that it has adopted an intransigent attitude toward a large American interest at the very moment when it is asking the Government of the United States to extend it favor in the form of credit for purchases of needed raw materials."[81] In a subsequent interview with Cárdenas, Welles explained that "some members of the cabinet were suspicious of Spain's possible attitude toward American property given the fact that they insisted on refusing to authorize Colonel Behn's entry into Spain."[82] On 12 June, at the meeting between Welles, Feis, and the Spanish ambassador, Welles reiterated the interest of the United States in renewing economic relations with Spain but warned him that this necessarily meant that "the Spanish Government shared the same wish and purpose, and that accordingly it would grant to American property in Spain and other American interests the same friendly and cooperative consideration which had been received in the past." Herbert Feis went even further and added that

> Perhaps what Mr. Welles had in mind were preoccupations similar to those which I knew were in the minds of various people in the Department, including the Secretary, to wit, that the refusal of the Spanish Government to admit Colonel Behn into Spain so that he could deal with his Company's affairs was creating apprehension lest it signify an intention on the part of the Spanish Government to create difficulties for that Company.

And "the Ambassador would realize that if this Government undertook this financing and then shortly afterwards the Spanish Government used its power or influence adversely to affect American property interests in Spain, or in Latin America, our action in financing this cotton sale would obviously be subject to criticism."[83] After all these pressures, Cárdenas telegraphed Madrid on two occasions to recommend that Behn be authorized to enter the country because "if in the next interview I were able to announce that entry had been authorized (...) the granting of the loan would be made considerably easier."[84] The situation became even more complex when the media got hold of the controversy: on 15 June the "New York Herald Tribune" reported that the negotiations for the loan to purchase cotton were paralyzed because the Spanish refused to grant Behn permission to enter the country.[85]

In this context, on 28 June an angry Cárdenas met with Welles to complain of the delay in granting the loan and the problems that the shortage of raw material was causing in Spain.[86] He even threatened to reconsider purchasing from the United States. Although Welles could not explain the reasons for the delay (hardly surprising since the loan was creating considerable tensions within the administration), he mentioned that he had heard reports that the Falange was about to nationalize the CTNE and other U.S. companies in Spain and he urged him again to get "a categorical statement from his Government with regard to American interests in Spain along the lines he had previously indicated, including the pressing need for permission to be granted to Colonel Behn to enter Spain in connection with the telephone properties."[87] The fact that the State Department required this assurance to assist in their confrontation with the Treasury can be seen in the following words: "If such assurance were forthcoming the impression created here would necessarily be exceedingly beneficial." This pressure to obtain a statement along these lines involved fresh orders from Secretary Hull to Weddell to find "a convenient opportunity to broach again to the Minister of Foreign Affairs the subject of a declaration of the Spanish Government's attitude towards American interests in Spain, including Colonel Behn's admission to (...) [the] country."[88] Throughout the process it was quite clear that the State Department was attaching much more importance to the protection of North American economic interests in Spain than to the issue of the prisoners.

In Madrid, Weddell was unable to get a statement from Jordana, perhaps because the Telefónica question was the competence of Serrano Suñer's Ministry of Governance or perhaps because Franco's government had no intention of making any such statement. In the face of this impasse, it occurred to Weddell to request a formal interview with Franco to break the deadlock.[89] This initiative was immediately approved by the State Department. Meanwhile, he was in close contact with Behn and even traveled to France to see him on 9 and 19 July in St. Jean de Luz.[90] It was there that the colonel spoke of his concern about the possibility of a new, German-inspired telephone and telegraph network being installed in Spain, and the supposed imminence of a new decree that was to remove North Americans from the board of directors of CTNE. And he pointed directly at Serrano Suñer and his ministry as being responsible for all of this.

Meanwhile, back in the United States, there was still considerable pressure to refuse the loan. In July, as has been mentioned above, the president's wife, Eleanor Roosevelt, had invited Jay Allen and the former president of the Spanish Republic, Dr. Negrín, to her home.[91] On the same day, Negrín had also eaten with Morgenthau. The loan was discussed on both occasions. In his letter of thanks to Mrs. Roosevelt, Allen spoke indignantly of those in favor of it (the State Department): "Its proponents say that it is purely a commercial affair. That view is, of course, nonsense. Everyone knows that Franco will never pay and that the credit is highly political in its implications."[92] For his part, Negrín wrote to Morgenthau that he believed the Francoist victory to be only temporary, that the constitution of the Spanish Republic was still in force, and that no future legitimate Spanish government would feel obliged to make the repayments on a loan granted to Franco's illegitimate regime. Eleanor sent Allen's letter of thanks to the president, who in turn asked Sumner Welles to give his opinion. Welles' written response clearly shows the reasons that the State Department had for supporting the request for the loan and, more importantly, the policies on which they were based. After mentioning the commercial interest that the transaction had for the government, Welles gave a long explanation for the political reasons behind his standpoint:

> [T]here is going on within Spain today a bitter rivalry between some of the factions that were supporting Franco at the conclusion of the civil war. If the Falangist element in Spain gets the upper hand, the closest kind of relationship between the Spanish Government and the Governments of Germany and Italy will in all probability be brought about. If the Center republican elements, or the Carlist or the Monarchist elements become predominant, the Franco régime will presumably swing more in the direction of a better understanding with England and France, and in the direction of

those normal relations with the rest of the world, including ourselves, which they are even now advocating.

If, at this stage, therefore, we treat the Franco Government as an outcast, and refuse to negotiate commercial arrangements with that Government similar to those which we are negotiating with many other governments in the world, it would seem to me that we would strengthen the hands of the Falangist element, who are at this moment maintaining that there is no hope of bettering Spain's situation except through a watertight agreement with the Axis powers.

In that connection I may remind you that the Export-Import Bank has authorized cotton credits amounting to four million dollars in Italy in addition to the amounts outstanding on previous commitments. It would seem to me highly illogical for the Export-Import Bank to authorize credits for this purpose to Italy, and yet be unwilling to extend them in far lesser amount to Spain.

The gist of the latter part of Mr. Allen's letter is that this proposed credit to Spain 'is highly political in its implications', and he reverts once more to the old theme that there are some hidden and devious Fascist activities going on in the inner recesses of the Department of State. So far as I am informed, this question of cotton credits to Spain was taken up originally by Spanish agents, as a purely commercial transaction, directly with the Export-Import Bank. It was only later submitted to this Department for its opinion. To the best of my knowledge the opinion of this Department has been formed solely as a result of the considerations set forth in this letter. Believe me.[93]

That is to say, as well as defending himself against the accusation that the State Department was home to "fascists" (and pro-Francoists) and defending the department's policies to promote the economic interests and trade relations of U.S. corporations, its citizens and the country itself with the rest of the world, the under secretary had raised the issue of the two alleged driving forces behind Francoism: the totalitarian pro-Axis forces represented by the Falange and Serrano Suñer, and the alleged group of monarchists and people from the political center—whom he mistakenly describes as Republicans—who were more attracted by Western-type democracies. It was this opinion, together with Franco's alleged desire for neutrality, that was behind the State Department's attitude toward Spain. In the face of such duality in Spain, Welles argued, it was in the United States's interest to support those from the political center in their struggle against the totalitarians. Otherwise, Spain would turn toward the Axis in search of economic aid.

The controversy about the loan continued to be aired in the press in the following weeks. Jay Allen himself had ensured that the press was aware of the ins and outs of the matter and was using it in his attempts to prevent the loan from being granted. In an article published in "The Richmond Times" he showed his opposition in no uncertain terms, and also argued that Spain would not pay back the money loaned because of the lawsuit that had been brought against the purchase of the silver. His exact words, on 14 July 1939, were the following:

> In view of all the aid the United States Government gave Franco through the embargo on shipments of arms and ammunition to Spain, it does not seem excessive that our Export-Import Bank should actually be advocating a virtual gift of 300,000 bales of cotton to Franco's Spanish Government. While it is argued that unless we supply Franco he will get his cotton from India, the best authorities feel that we aren't

going to be paid for it, and that consequently the deal will be of no value to us. That is the view of the Secretary of the Treasury Morgenthau. Certain elements in the State Department are said to favor the "sale," just as they violently opposed lifting the embargo, in order to give the Spanish Loyalists a fighting chance against Hitler, Mussolini and the Moors.

Why does it seem unlikely that we'd ever be paid for the 300,000 bales of cotton? Because Franco has filed a claim for silver obtained by us from the pre-Franco government of Spain, and if he loses, as he is believed sure to do, he will probably refuse to pay for the cotton, on the ground that we haven't paid him for the silver.

It does seem absurd for us to be practically making a gift of 300,000 bales of cotton to Franco, whom Hitler and Mussolini are using to try to penetrate Latin-America, in desperate competition with us. What is the Administration trying to do, anyway? Promote the cause of International Fascism?[94]

In fact, it was generally held by the North American anti-Franco press that the loan was direct aid being provided by the Roosevelt administration to the Franco regime.[95]

THE GRANTING OF THE LOAN FOR THE PURCHASE OF COTTON AND THE FIRST (BUT NOT LASTING) SOLUTION TO THE TWO PENDING DISPUTES

The disagreements within the Roosevelt administration and the opposition of the press led to a deadlock that was only broken when the Francoists backed down and the State Department, with the president's support, achieved a victory in Washington.[96] The difficulties the Francoists had encountered convinced them of the need to find a solution to the disputes concerning Colonel Behn's entry permit and the prisoners of the Lincoln Brigade. When the Weddell-Franco interview provided this solution, the deadlock over loan had already been broken as Sumner Welles and the State Department had come out on top in their struggle with the Treasury and the others who had been against the loan.

Spain's change in attitude, the direct result of their pressing need for the cotton, came about after the New York court had passed a ruling that refused to recognize the Spanish claims in the lawsuit brought against the purchase of silver. Even though it is unlikely that this ruling had a decisive influence on the change in attitude because the Bank of Spain immediately appealed against it,[97] it did make things easier for both parties. Nevertheless, the Spanish concessions were highly deceptive, as we shall see below.

The first indication that the Franco regime was going to change its standpoint had been given to Counselor Robert M. Scotten in Madrid during a series of interviews with the Under Secretary of Foreign Affairs Domingo de las Bárcenas. In the second of these interviews, held on 20 July, the Spaniard had told him that "if you can arrange for the cotton credits the Generalissimo will not only agree for Behn to return but will authorize the release of your prisoners."[98] Four days later, on the 24, Franco was to meet with Weddell but Spain's urgent need to find a solution to this situation was seen on the 22nd when Cárdenas, having satisfactorily concluded negotiations with the E-I Bank,[99] assured Secretary Hull that Spain would give

North American interests in the country a "fair and equitable treatment (…) in accordance with the generally recognized principles of international law and with those governing the friendly relations between the two nations." That is to say, he made the statement that the United States had been asking of Spain. Cárdenas also agreed to include a clause in the loan contract that the State Department had thought up to defend itself from any criticism from within the United States and by which the Spanish government accepted never to mix the issues of the loan repayments and the purchase of Spanish silver by the United States in 1938.[100] And finally, also on 22 July, Secretary Hull informed Weddell that the E-I Bank had provisionally granted the loan to Spain.

At first sight, the interview between Weddell and Franco held two days later was a success.[101] Franco informed him that Behn would be authorized to enter the country within a day or two, and he added that he knew the colonel and thought well of him (which was a lie) "but that he had been reported by several people, it had been necessary to follow up these reports and the investigation had taken longer than expected." As far as the prisoners were concerned, he said that he had nothing against their prompt release. After their meeting, Weddell went to see Minister Jordana, who confirmed that the police was investigating Behn's activities. He added that he was pressing for these investigations to be rapidly terminated and that he hoped to be able to inform him of the results and the authorization of the entry permit later that same day. He also said that the prisoners were at his disposal and asked him where he would like them to be handed over. However, in neither of the two interviews was it specified exactly how many prisoners were to be released. Weddell believed that it would be all of them—those accused of crimes and the other eleven—although he suspected that it may not be the complete group. He wrote that "although I will endeavor to secure the release of as many as possible, the Government may well refuse to release some who have been sentenced on account of specific charges." Later on the same day, Under Secretary Bárcenas phoned to tell him that Behn had been granted permission to enter Spain as from 27 July. Bárcenas himself congratulated him "on his victory" although he also said that he felt that it was "partly his own."[102]

Everything, then, seemed to be going smoothly. Spain had been granted a loan for the purchase of 250,000 bales of cotton (which was made public in the United States on 7 August),[103] Behn had been given permission to enter Spain and the U.S. prisoners were about to be released. The contract governing the loan contained a clause by which Spain agreed that "the cotton shall be exclusively for domestic use in Spain."[104] Even so there were fears that the agreement would be thwarted at the last minute. As Cárdenas explained to Jordana, in his assessment of the outcome of the arduous process of negotiation that had just terminated,

> Mr. Pierson asked me to tell you not to publicize the agreement until the Senate has approved several credits that they hope to obtain soon. Because some parts of the press have fought bitterly against granting loans to Spain, they fear that the announcement of an agreement might create a bit of a stir, which may affect the vote in the Senate. This will give you some idea of the difficulties that we have had in finalizing the agreement, and we should be particularly grateful to the under secretary of

state, Mr. Sumner Welles, since it was his efficiency that procured the intervention of President Roosevelt and enabled us to skirt round the difficulties raised by the friction between different departments within the administration caused by the opposition of the Treasury Department. Likewise, Mr Pierson, the president of the Export-Import Bank has shown good will at all times and the desire to complete the agreement, the finalization of which was also helped by Jones.[105]

However, there were no difficulties in the Senate and on 28 August Pierson himself arrived in Spain to interview the Spanish minister of foreign affairs and other members of the government.[106] The Franco regime had got what it had been striving for and, apparently, so had the State Department.

Encouraged by all these happenings, the department believed that a general trade agreement was possible with Spain, picking up from where they had left off in 1935. This undoubtedly contributed to the excellent atmosphere that had reigned during the interview between Cárdenas and Welles, in which Cárdenas had informed Welles of Spain's full acceptance of the terms of the loan and Welles had stated "that he hoped that the conclusion of this agreement would have specific benefits for the commercial interests between both our countries." Cárdenas had responded that "he had been especially entrusted by his government to tell the United States that Spain intended to give the rights and interests of the United States in Spain a fair and equitable treatment in accordance with the generally recognized principles of international law." Welles replied along the same lines, saying that "this government intended to give Spanish rights and interests a fair and equitable treatment in accordance with the principles of international law."[107] The Madrid Embassy was asked to report on Spanish commercial policy toward the United States.[108] After contacts had been made between the U.S. commercial attaché in Madrid Ralph Ackerman and a high-ranking civil servant from the Ministry of Industry and Commerce, Emilio Navascués, Weddell recommended that they should take advantage of the good relations between the two countries to begin a negotiation process.[109]

But things went wrong. Very soon Weddell realized that Spain had had no intention of respecting the agreements that had been entered into. The matter of the prisoners soon became a bigger problem than he had feared: in the city of San Sebastián, where the government was housed in the summer, only the eleven who had not been charged with any other crimes were handed over, leaving at least eight still in prison. We say "at least" because even by this stage the embassy had not been able to determine exactly how many prisoners there were. The eleven who had been released were sent across the International Bridge in Irún to France where they were entrusted to the Friends of the Abraham Lincoln Brigade.[110] Immediately after the release, on 23 August, Weddell met with the new minister of foreign affairs, colonel Juan Beigbeder, who had been appointed after a cabinet reshuffle two weeks earlier, to make a formal complaint. The colonel argued that those who had not been released had committed other crimes, to which Weddell responded that Franco's promise had been "unconditional" and that in the New State it was Franco who had the power to grant pardons.[111] Beigbeder promised to look into it.

But this was not all. Once in Spain, neither Colonel Behn nor any of the other U.S. managers were allowed to take up their former duties. And, of course, that he should act as main owner of the company was out of the question. That is to say, the regime continued their official intervention of the company.

Weddell was highly indignant about this situation, because he believed it to be the result of deliberate deception, and because the United States had honored its word to grant the loan. His indignation was shared by the State Department to such an extent that recovering the management and control of CTNE was to be the mainstay of U.S. policy in Spain for more than a year, until August 1940. And their indignation would have been greater if they had known that on 4 August, just after Behn had entered Spain, orders had been given to investigate the activities of Behn, Caldwell, and three other directors in the Red Zone during the war,[112] and that Serrano Suñer in his capacity as minister of governance was going to take advantage of these investigations to politically cleanse the CTNE, a process that was already underway.[113]

The struggle to recover the management of the CTNE and to release the remaining prisoners of the Lincoln Brigade (or at least the survivors since one of them died of pneumonia during the wait) was to become the main area of concern of the Madrid Embassy. The definitive release was to take place in February 1940, six months before an agreement was reached about the CTNE.

THE TELEFÓNICA AFFAIR AND THE RELEASE OF THE LINCOLN BRIGADE PRISONERS

The two new disputes were resolved by repeating the formula that had worked before: whatever the issue, returning the CTNE to its leading shareholders or releasing the prisoners, Spain would only back down when it was essential and inevitable for an economic agreement to be reached with the United States. A new factor that had to be taken into account, however, was that the relations between the United States of America and Franco's Spain now had to be approached in the context of the first year of the world war. Franco's Spain felt more self-assured and stronger in its foundational principles because of the conviction that Germany would be successful in its struggle against the democracies, and the United States was increasingly committed to assisting the democratic cause. However, what was not new was that the ministers and high-ranking officials that the North Americans had to deal with all had their own personalities and different attitudes. And of course, above all else, Franco's will and that of his main political adviser, Ramón Serrano Suñer, prevailed.

Let us begin with the Telefónica affair. After Colonel Behn had arrived in Spain on 30 July 1939 not only had he not been able to take charge of the company he owned but also that he had not even been able to meet with Serrano Suñer, the minister responsible for communications, the seizure of the company, and its subsequent political clearance. Serrano did not grant him an audience until four months later, on 29 November 1939,[114] and this only after Franco had suggested that it would be advisable to do so. The problems that awaited the CTNE were serious. In the first place, there was the danger that the whole of the telephone monopoly would be reconsidered. This was a real possibility since Franco, Serrano, and many of the other leaders believed it to be an affront to national independence. However, of more immediate concern was the basic question of recovering the management of the company for Behn and the North American employees, the main obstacle to which was that, like all public and private organizations in the former Loyalist zone, its employees had to be subject to a process of political clearance. Whether the U.S. executives were allowed to return to their posts or not depended on a "positive" outcome to this process. This meant that things did not look too good since the Francoists were suspicious of some of them for the alleged relations they had had with the reds in Madrid during the war. Let us not forget that a lawsuit had also been brought by the military jurisdiction against a group of five managers—headed by Behn—that could lead to serious criminal charges.

Serrano, Franco's brother-in-law, not only took four months to grant Behn an interview—which in itself shows the intent clearly—but the interview itself was to serve no purpose. He promised Behn that the U.S. managers would soon be restored to their posts with only one or two exceptions, but in a subsequent meeting two weeks' later he informed him that he did not intend to reinstate any of them until they had received clearance.[115] Thus began a period of cut and thrust that was to last several months.

For his part, Behn, and more importantly the Madrid Embassy and the State Department, began to take steps to win back control of the company for its North American owners very shortly after he arrived in Spain. Some of the steps taken reveal the hostility that Franco himself felt for Behn and, above all, the extent to which both the embassy and the State Department were involved in the Telefónica affair (at times verging on full-time dedication). On 18 October, Ambassador Cárdenas told Pierrepont Moffatt, chief of the division of European Affairs, that Franco was hostile toward Behn because he felt betrayed by him during the Civil War.[116] Apparently, in 1934, two years before it broke out, Behn had promised him that "if at any time Spain needed his help, he would give it." However, according to the Generalissimo, he had sent him several messages requesting his help during the war but had received no response. This apart, and also according to Cárdenas, Franco's leaders felt that Behn had stayed too long in "red" Madrid, in contact with Loyalist generals, and they knew that the central Telefónica building in the capital had been used by the Republicans as an artillery look out point in their bombardments of the nationalist lines. However, the background to all this was that the Francoists were considering changing the contract with CTNE-ITT, because its clauses on management, profit, and payment in gold meant, in Cárdenas' words, that the whole of Spain was working for their benefit. On top of this, the CTNE was extremely unpopular in the country. Cárdenas himself confessed that he was in favor of making the necessary changes through friendly agreements and stated that the Minister of the Treasury Larraz and the under secretary of the presidency of the government, Colonel Galarza, as well as the under secretaries of foreign affairs and the treasury felt the same way. However, although he gave no further details there was another current of opinion that was more hard line.

However, for several months before this revealing interview, the U.S. diplomatic machinery was working in favor of Behn, who in September had met with the ministers of foreign affairs and the treasury, the minister of industry and trade, Alarcón de la Lastra, and the under secretary of foreign affairs, Bárcenas. In these interviews he did not merely fight for the management of the company to be restored to him, he also offered to expand the capacity of the production plants,[117] which was of particular interest to the minister of industry and trade. At the same time, Weddell began to exert what was to prove to be a long period of pressure on the Minister of Foreign Affairs Beigbeder by telling him to his face that if a solution was not found then, once the imported cotton had run out, Spain would be granted no further loans.[118] It was at this point that Moffatt arranged to speak to the Spanish ambassador in Washington.[119]

Behn's strategy of searching for support within Franco's government had some success, and this had the immediate effect of increasing the tension between Serrano and the ministers involved in the conversations. As some of these ministers had other affairs pending with the United States, they saw their chance to find quick solutions. This was the case of the Minister of the Treasury Larraz, who wanted the United States to manufacture nickel coins, and Alarcón de la Lastra, who wanted to strengthen trade relations with the United States because there was a shortage of raw materials and fuel and since the outbreak of war in Europe Spain had increasingly come to depend on other nations. Other leaders were also in favor of an agreement although even today the reasons for this are not clear and private interest cannot be excluded. One of these leaders was Colonel Galarza, under secretary of the presidency of the government. He was very close to Franco, notoriously anti-Serrano and one of the leaders of the most anti-Falangist faction of the army. He may have been motivated simply by hostility for Serrano Suñer. In fact, one possible interpretation of the affair that we are analyzing is that it was one more element in the progressive poisoning of the relations between Galarza and Serrano, which reached its peak some time later in the so-called Crisis of May of 1941 and which, as we shall see at the end of the chapter, was to end up by weakening the position of the ironically nicknamed *Cuñadísimo*[120] in the eyes of Franco.

However, in 1939, it was Ramón Serrano Suñer who was responsible for communications and for this particular issue; and he consulted everything with Franco. Perhaps at this point we should point out that the Generalissimo always tended to respect the competences of his ministers. In fact, three months after the beginning of the controversy Galarza warned Behn not to request an audience with Franco to speak of the affair because the issue was the responsibility of the Ministry of Governance and he would not be received.[121] The Minister of Foreign Affairs Beigbeder received most of the direct diplomatic pressure from the United States but he was well aware that he owed his ministerial appointment to Serrano Suñer, whom he had met in July 1938 when he was the high commissioner in the Protectorate of Morocco, and he was therefore very cautious. Serrano's influence, then, pervaded the whole issue. Under Secretary Bárcenas had also warned Behn that it was a highly delicate matter that "he should tread with the utmost care."

Neither Weddell nor the State Department, however, were inactive and in December 1939 their verbal requests that the management and control of CTNE should be restored to Behn soon passed to official written demands. As early as November of the same year, Under Secretary Welles had sent a letter to Weddell saying that

> it is hard to understand the delay of the Spanish Government in carrying out the promise which General Franco gave you personally to release the remaining American

citizens who are still under detention as prisoners of war (...) Given what we have done for Spain in the way of credits, et cetera, it seems to me that the next move is definitely on the Spanish side. The release of these men, the trial of American citizens under detention on various charges not connected with hostile military service, and a prompt and equitable agreement with the American owners of the telephone company would seem the least we could expect.[122]

In a further display of collusion between the colonel, the Madrid Embassy, and the State Department, Behn suggested that Weddell should send a note of complaint to the Spanish minister of foreign affairs. Considering that Behn was not a member of the U.S. diplomatic corps his active role in events is particularly surprising. Just as he suggested, the note was written by the embassy on 22 December 1939 and approved six days later by Washington.[123] In it[124] the ambassador complained that no solution had been found for the management of the CTNE "notwithstanding the fact that for more than 4 months the representative of the American majority stockholders, Colonel Sosthenes Behn, has patiently endeavored to reach a settlement with the various Spanish authorities to whom he has been successively referred." As a result, he added:

> My Government directs me [...] to express to Your Excellency its deep concern at this situation and to express its hope that in view of the Spanish Government's previous assurances of its desire to treat American interests in Spain justly and equitably the Spanish Government will give its early attention to the question of a settlement of the status of the management of the Telephone Company which fully protect the American interests involved.[125]

He also expressed "our surprise that while one hand was being extended to solicit a credit, the other was holding a big stick over important American interests." On receiving the note, Beigbeder telephoned Galarza and he agreed to deal with the issue in the cabinet meeting that same afternoon or in a special interview between the minister for foreign affairs and Franco.

However, Beigbeder's official response on 8 January 1940 was such that United States' tempers became even more frayed. The text, which he had agreed on with Galarza, stated that "the previous situation [the status quo prior to the CTNE][126] was in no danger" and that "the situation of the North-American staff in Spain is affected by the general political clearance of the staff of the company, which has been involved in activity under red rule." And he added: "If any measure of this sort affects any particular members of staff, this is not a variation in the representation and functions that foreigners had and can continue to have (...). All other measures of an internal nature that are not affected by state action should be discussed with the company itself." Finally, Beigbeder pointed out the option of dealing with any further claims through legal channels. On the same day he received Weddell and discussed the general question of the process of political clearance. The ambassador was not prepared to accept that U.S. citizens should be subject to the process, as can be seen from the following dialogue that he had with the minister and which he discussed with the State Department: "He [the minister] said that this [political clearance] meant that if Señor X had to leave, that Señor Y would be permitted to carry on exactly the same functions (...) and I finally remarked that I could not see that it made much difference since the Telephone Company was not master in its own house."[127] Weddell also complained about the reference to legal channels since there was no dispute between ITT and CTNE; rather the conflict had come about as the result of the Spanish government's attitude but, even so, Beigbeder still insisted on these channels as a means of finding a solution. Sick and tired, Weddell wrote that Beigbeder seemed to be "a Spanish edition of Saavedra Lamas," the Argentine minister for foreign affairs.

In response to this complex process of political clearance, lack of headway in restoring control of the CTNE to its U.S. managers and the deadlock in Madrid, the U.S. ambassador consulted Scotten and the CTNE's North American number two Fred Caldwell. After getting approval from Behn, who was in London, he recommended that the State Department adopt a hard-line approach toward Spain and the granting of any further loans, particularly with respect to the loan the Spanish Treasury had already requested to cover the costs of manufacturing nickel coins. This loan had been requested by Ambassador Cárdenas in an interview with Sumner Welles at the end of January 1940,[128] and was the perfect excuse for Welles to read him the riot act. He gave him a severe reprimand and stated that the United States had shown signs of good will toward Spain eight months earlier by granting the loan to purchase cotton. Meanwhile, Franco's government had still not returned the CTNE to its rightful owners or released the Lincoln Brigade prisoners, one of whom had died of pneumonia while languishing in prison.[129] Cárdenas withstood the barrage as best he could. According to Welles, at that time some of the tasks that the Spanish ambassador, a diplomat of the old school, had to cope were making him "distinctly embarrassed."[130] It was a real tirade along the lines of those that Secretary Hull and the president himself liked to deliver, but this time it was delivered by Welles to a diplomat who was also a personal friend of his.

In the middle of January 1940, after fresh contacts between Colonel Behn, Caldwell, and Weddell,[131] a new proposal was made. The Secretary of State Hull should send a new note to Beigbeder, this time taking him at his word and interpreting his response to the previous note in the strict sense: that is to say, the CTNE affair was strictly private and free of any political constraints. He would therefore directly inform him that the North American managers were going to be reinstated to their posts *motu propio*. The note was written and was sent to Beigbeder.[132] It said the following:

> My government has received with satisfaction the news that the Spanish government has reiterated its statement that American interests in Spain, and particularly those of the Compañía Telefónica Nacional de España, shall enjoy their previous *status quo* and that there is no danger that they should not legitimately enjoy this situation.
>
> My government therefore also understands that the Spanish government does not prohibit the reinstatement of American civil servants and employees, that these may be elected and appointed to the National Telephone Company, and that those against whom there are no charges or who have been cleared of charges can take up their respective posts again. My government assumes that Americans can also be temporarily appointed or reinstated, occupying their posts while the accusations against them are being discussed, as is the case with a considerable number of Spanish employees in the Compañía Nacional.

We would be very grateful if, at your earliest possible convenience, you could confirm whether my government's interpretation of your government's attitude reflects the reality of the situation.[133]

On 16 January Beigbeder responded by simply affirming that the process of clearance "will not exercise any discrimination to the prejudice of the foreign personnel."[134] Weddell insisted in his request for confirmation but, for the moment, he was to receive no further answer.[135] It should also be borne in mind that Franco had passed a decree law in September 1939 that stipulated that the appointment of members of the board of directors and managers of all companies with a capital greater than five million pesetas required government approval, and that it was illegal to operate otherwise. That is to say, the situation had been brought to a complete standstill.

Nevertheless, both Minister Beigbeder himself and the Under Secretary to the Presidency Galarza began to take steps to reach an agreement about CTNE and the prisoners. This was undoubtedly partly due to Spain's economic needs and the attitude of "friendly hardness" that Under Secretary Welles adopted to the demands that Cárdenas made in Washington. After approaching him about the problem of paying for minting the coins that the Spanish Treasury had ordered, Cárdenas said that

> The government of the United States was very upset to see that we have not returned their friendly gesture [in reference to the loan to purchase the cotton] since they have received no satisfactory response to their requests about the prisoners and the Compañía Telefónica. [Welles] added that he was quite sure that this was not due to bad will and therefore expected that a solution would soon be found. He hoped that this would be as soon as possible so that he could continue helping us, as he had done in the cotton negotiation.

Cárdenas was convinced that "it would be impossible to obtain loans or other credit facilities until a formula was found that was satisfactory to them."[136] Beigbeder sent this communication to Serrano and asked him "if he considered it possible, to provide the desired formula so that the government and the financial institutions in Washington would have the attitude that the current circumstances required."[137]

As a result of the steps taken by both ministers and Weddell's insistence with the Minister for the Army General Varela, the eight remaining prisoners of the Lincoln Brigade with charges pending were released at the end of February 1940.[138] The embassy sent them back to the United States and at least one of them, Dahl, was arrested as soon as he arrived in New York.[139] Cárdenas was jubilant when he received the news, but he said that although "the effect had been good and the situation had improved" he did not believe that Spain would "obtain what we so desire without satisfying the American government's other aspiration."[140] At that point in time, the aspiration was to renew the 1939 loan for the purchase of cotton. What is more, new channels for obtaining loans had been opened, which the dispute over the CTNE effectively closed. On this issue, Beigbeder wrote the following:

> Mr Hammond, former United States ambassador to Spain and a good friend of the Cause who has always been ready to help, and a group of his friends, all leading bankers or businessmen, would probably find ways of helping us to obtain the necessary

loans for purchasing corn, cotton, etc. In fact, as far as corn is concerned, I have been informed that as well as being granted the long-term loans to meet the payments, if we were to purchase here between 150 and 200 thousand tons, we may be eligible for the subsidy that at the moment is only awarded to purchases from the East to compete with Australian corn. As far as the purchases of cotton are concerned, I have also been assured that credit facilities would be greater (…) If some of these ideas were to take shape it would be advisable for Mr. Hammond or another representative of his group to go to Spain to present his projects to the government. As I have already said, given the seriousness and solvency of the people involved, I believe there is a solid base for getting results (…) Some of the most important banks, such as the National City Bank and others, would be prepared to work with us on this project, which I have only briefly outlined here to see whether it is of any interest to the National Government or not.[141]

For their part, the Americans of the CTNE had sent a memorandum to the Ministry of Foreign Affairs with the names of those they believed had to stay in Spain. In addition to Colonel Behn, chairman of the board of directors, who did not live in the country, the list included Caldwell (director general, executive vice chairman and member of the board of directors), Clement and Wendell (members of the board of directors), Dennis (head of accounting), an engineer as head of construction and maintenance, and seven others.[142]

However, things started to go wrong almost at once because on 9 March Serrano Suñer presented the results of the clearing process of the United States personnel: it had been decided to remove eight of the sixteen managers that the company had been relying on, including the Vice Chairman Fred Caldwell,[143] but none of the others who were on the list. Colonel Behn was not among those to be removed, probably because it would have been ridiculous to relieve him if his duties with the CTNE and also because he did not live in Spain. But Serrano also refused to authorize a shareholders' meeting scheduled for the 30 of the month until a balance sheet had been prepared.[144] Given the CTNE's situation during the Civil War, this was by no means a trivial task because, among other things, the company had been split into two parts. This response by the minister of governance put paid to Behn's hopes of forcing the prompt return of the CTNE management by holding the shareholders' meeting.[145] And of course Behn's arguments that it was impossible to prepare the balance sheet because of the inefficiency of the Spanish accounting system after the seizure were to no avail.

Ambassador Weddell responded to the result of the clearing process by immediately requesting information about the precise nature of the charges. He was given a ruling from the proceedings that the military jurisdiction had instituted against the managers, with Behn at the top of the list, on 4 August 1939. The military judge had subsequently filed a lawsuit on 10 January 1940 but it had not yet concluded.[146] The ruling also mentioned information that had been acquired by the Ministry of Governance itself and, although it did not specify exactly what this information was, it stated that it gave rise to "analogous charges."[147]

The force with which Serrano Suñer had acted—and Weddell saw only the hand of the cuñadísimo here and not that of Franco, even though he was also involved as the head of state and head of the cabinet—finally convinced Weddell that Serrano was more powerful than Beigbeder.[148] He decided to adopt a twofold strategy. In the first place he would try to persuade the State Department of the need to use the loans as a weapon to force Spain to back down. The embassy had recently found out that Spain was about to request another loan from the private bank J.P. Morgan, so this tactic would be of immediate relevance.[149] And in the second place he would make a direct appeal to Franco. Thus, on 28 March 1940, he asked Secretary Hull to authorize an official request for an interview with the Generalissimo, with the specific intention of dealing with the Telefónica affair.[150] The department was determined to defend the interests of ITT so not only did it give authorization at once, it also sent him the text of the *aide-mémoire* he should use to make his request. It went straight to the point by asking "the Caudillo to make effective the assurances which have been given in the past and to issue the necessary instructions to restore the management and control of its properties to the National Telephone Company of Spain without further delay."[151] That is to say, the intervention should end and the management of the company be restored to its U.S. owners.

The response to the request came on 9 April and it left Weddell completely bewildered.[152] It had been written after a government meeting and Beigbeder informed him that the Generalissimo would be delighted to meet with him, but under no circumstances was he prepared to discuss the company's administrative problems. The Spanish government, he went on, only intervened in matters of the morality and conduct of the managers of the CTNE: that is to say, political clearance. He pointed out that

> The American economic interests in Spain are guaranteed by Spanish law and in accordance with international procedure. The following case is proof of the interest with which American matters are considered: The International Telephone and Telegraph Company attempted to collect dividends in arrears from the Telephone Company. The representatives of the state alleged the possible prescription of the right to collect and consulted with the Minister of Finance concerning the matter. The latter will reply recognizing the right of the International Telephone and Telegraph and stating prescription does not exist as regards the collection of dividends in arrears. The state cannot consider the nationality of shareholders of corporations who have a juridical personality in conjunction with such Spanish corporation; the personality of a shareholder of another nationality not constituting a factor to be given consideration. Therefore it is a question of interior relations within a company and notwithstanding contracts between companies not subject to state intervention.

The minister of foreign affairs also told him that accepting the ambassador's note would have meant that Franco considered that the relations between the countries were not good, which was untrue. Weddell replied that he wanted to have an interview with Franco to inform him of a few things that he was apparently unaware of: for example, the release of the prisoners, promised by the Caudillo in July 1939 but not fully carried into effect until just a few weeks before; and Behn's entry permit, which he had understood to be not just physical entry into the country but also repossession of all his business obligations. In both cases he believed that the head of state's orders had been distorted without his knowledge. He also mentioned that there were elements within the cabinet that did not want the relations between

Spain and the United States to improve and that these elements belonged in the main to the Ministry of Governance and its head Serrano Suñer. Beigbeder took little notice and told him that the company could hold its shareholders' meeting within three weeks as long as it had prepared its balance sheet. If it had not, the meeting would be illegal and would create a problem of public order for the authorities. After asking him who had told him all this and confirming that it had been Serrano Suñer, an increasingly agitated Weddell told him that the deadline was too tight, largely because the North American managers were prevented from auditing their own company, and asked for permission to hold the meeting without the balance. Beigbeder refused. Finally an uncomfortable Beigbeder agreed to transmit his wishes to Franco.[153]

Weddell communicated everything that had been said during the interview to Washington and, unusually, to Colonel Behn, who was in Paris. Secretary Hull's reaction was devastating: he ordered Weddell to make an official request for an interview with Franco, but this time in writing, so that he could give him the *aide-mémoire* concerning the problem of Telefónica[154] and tell him to his face that the U.S. government did not believe Beigbeder's arguments. The ambassador, however, tried to correct his superior's interpretation of events by arguing that Franco already knew of the aide-mémoire, that the standpoint expressed by Beigbeder had previously been discussed by the Spanish cabinet, that the whole affair was being used as a means of exerting pressure and obtaining new loans, and that the United States needed to adopt a more hard-line policy. He suggested that he should travel to the United States and make the journey seem to be an official summons from the department to inform personally on the CTNE affair. The trip would also serve to discuss all other questions concerning relations with Spain. Weddell also suggested that the department should call Ambassador Cárdenas and make it clear that the CTNE affair had become a test of the state of relations between the two countries and that, in the light of what had been happening, the Spanish assurances that "the American economic interests in Spain are guaranteed by Spanish law and in accordance with international procedure" were hardly credible.[155] In short, he was prepared to keep the relations between the United States and Spain tensed to the utmost in order to find a solution to the Telefónica affair.

He had also requested permission in a letter he had sent to Under Secretary Welles ten days earlier to travel to the United States. In this letter, Weddell shows that, as well as struggling tirelessly to find a solution to the Telefónica dispute, which had been dragging on since the summer of 1939, both he and the under secretary hoped to normalize the general and economic relations with the Franco regime. And he was also considering the need for the United States to have a specific Spanish policy in case the war in Europe should spread, as it was to do in the very near future. He said that

> I had been forced to the conclusion that we had come to the parting of the ways with the Spanish Government in regard to this (...) latter case [Telefónica], and that the whole problem resolved itself into the simple question of the good or bad faith of this Government. Should these people really want to play ball with us and should they be willing to demonstrate their good faith in the matter, I agree with you that "it should

be possible really to do something constructive in the matter of Spanish-American relations" (...) In any case it seems to me that a decision in this case, either favorable or unfavorable, will mark a definite phase in the developing relations between the two countries.[156]

And with respect to the normalization of relations, he pointed out that

> There remain a number of problems and phases which will require the closest teamwork between you in the Department and one of us here; these embrace the clearing of the blocked pesetas, the possibility of beginning negotiations for a trade agreement, the possibility of a new commercial treaty which will remove some of the restrictions which are now impending American commerce, the increasing importance of our air communications with Europe via this Peninsula (...) and the attitude and policies of Spain in the event of the extension of the European conflict. These are some of the things that I have much in mind, as I am sure that you have also, and which will sooner or later present themselves to us for a solution.

But he also bore in mind the need to provide help in a situation that was now delicate but steadily worsening: food and supply. He said that "another question of urgent and primary importance which may well present itself in the near future is the character, extent, and direction of the aid which we may eventually feel it practicable or desirable to give to this country."

Weddell's proposal to Hull was partly accepted: he was told to request another interview with Franco; he was given permission to travel to the United States, although he was told not to communicate this decision to the Spanish authorities for the time being so that the announcement of the journey could be used as a means of bringing pressure to bear if the other measures did not work; and Cárdenas was summoned to a meeting.[157] When the Spanish ambassador appeared before Welles, he was apparently subject to another historic tongue lashing. Following Weddell's script, Welles told him that the United States considered the ITT-CTNE controversy with the Spanish government as a test to see how North American interests were going to be treated in Franco's Spain. And he pointed out that the United States did not intend to negotiate or back down on anything in their efforts to restore the CTNE to its rightful owners. He added a general lesson on the rights of diplomatic representatives to be received by the heads of state of the countries in which they were accredited and Cárdenas, by now an aging diplomat of the old school, was left feeling embarrassed and with no response other than remorseful assent.[158]

The strategy adopted by Weddell and the State Department worked. And it had a profound effect on a Spain that was suffering from the economic ravages of the war. It should not be forgotten that the Anglo-French naval blockade that had been established at the beginning of the conflict was preventing Spain from exporting to their German and Italian markets.[159] The fact that Spain shared no common land borders with their prospective buyers and that the British and French fleets were guarding the seas and beginning to apply a system of *navicerts* (Navy Certificates that served as trade passports for all ships and shipments within Europe)[160] meant that exporting had become a nightmare for Spain. Between April and November 1939, Spain had exported merchandise to Germany for a total value of 60 million gold pesetas; in 1940 this figure dropped to 14 million. Neither did exports to Italy increase significantly, remaining at around 14–15 million. However, in the same period, exports to the United Kingdom increased from 60 to almost 90 million gold pesetas,[161] and it was the United Kingdom that controlled the seas and the key to many of Spain's supply routes. As far as corn was concerned, Spain had been suffering shortages since the failure of the harvest in 1939 and the application of the interventionist policy. In 1939 and 1940 Spain had constantly resorted to importing corn from Argentina although the extreme misery created by the shortage of this basic cereal was never really alleviated.[162] Spain's dependence on the United States and the United Kingdom for oil was also total because the only other option was the more expensive Rumanian oil. As we shall see below, Spain did actually contemplate this option but never actually made the change. The growing misery in Spain was actually quite useful for Great Britain and France, who desperately needed Spain to stay neutral in the war. For this reason, and after giving the Spaniards a brief taste of what deprivation was like, they had signed some trade agreements in March 1940, the most important of which was with the United Kingdom. Spain was granted certain concessions in the repayment of an outstanding debt and a loan of two million pounds to purchase products in the Sterling Area, which were guaranteed passage through the blockade on the condition that they were not subsequently reexported to the Axis powers.[163] That is to say, Spain needed the democracies and, much to its regret, also relied increasingly on the United States of America. Not only did the United States have more reserves and fields of oil, cotton, and corn but also its resources were needed by the United Kingdom.

Spain, then, finally took the initiative in an attempt to solve the CTNE-ITT affair. Serrano Suñer and Franco decided to bow to U.S. pressure and scheduled the Weddell-Franco interview for 23 April 1940. And although to Weddell's desperation it was postponed at the last minute, it was held shortly afterward. Meanwhile, and as a sign of the urgent need to alleviate the food shortages throughout Spain, the Franco government had ordered Cárdenas to request another loan, this time for the purchase of 100,000 tons of corn.[164] When the Spanish minister of foreign affairs informed Weddell, he said Spain was making the request because "the problem of Telefónica had now been solved." An indignant Weddell immediately asked the State Department to come to no agreement with Spain until he arrived in Washington.[165]

But now it was the Franco regime that was in a hurry to reach an agreement. In the course of the interviews that were held first with Serrano Suñer and then with Franco himself on 26 and 29 April 1940, the Spanish ambassador was again told that CTNE would be allowed to hold its shareholders' meeting as soon as the balance sheet had been prepared. He was also told that the North American substitutes for the eight who had not been politically cleared (and who were about to be expelled from the country) could take up their posts immediately and begin to prepare the balance sheet. Weddell's attitude during his interview with the Caudillo was one of great determination and he took initiatives that went above and beyond department orders. He was extremely rigid, probably as a reaction to all that he felt he had had to put up with from the Spanish government and also because he was convinced that the time was ripe for all his demands to be met. His reaction was also one of a person who was extremely involved in the affair and who was very close to Colonel Behn and the other managers of the CTNE. In fact, he told Franco that those who had not received clearance had not been given the chance to defend themselves and did not even know what they had been accused of. Franco insisted that they had been given the chance to defend themselves and that they had been aware of the charges. But when Weddell said that he would appeal against the charges, Franco merely nodded.[166]

The U.S. ambassador, then, set out to save those who had not received political clearance. This decision was based on his personal involvement in the whole matter and a stubbornness that was rooted in his conviction that the charges that had been leveled against these men had been trumped up. The State Department did not give him its full support, although he was finally allowed to go ahead. The attitude adopted by the State Department was hardly surprising since the end of the dispute was in sight and the goal of defending the economic interests of the leading U.S. company in Spain was about to be achieved. There was no point in continuing the struggle, then, and although Weddell was not stopped, in Washington Pierrepont Moffatt met with Frank Page, an ITT director,[167] and argued that once Franco had guaranteed that the management and control of CTNE would be restored to Colonel Behn, there was no need to fight on for eight managers, who, whether the charges were trumped up or not, Franco's government had every right to remove and expel.[168] Page agreed and told him that Colonel Behn would too.

In Madrid, however, Weddell stood his ground and on 4 May 1940 he presented the appeals against the accusations that had led to the removal of the managers.[169] The subsequent administrative procedure gave rise to an incident. Beigbeder passed the appeals on to the Ministry of the Army, which was responsible for imposing military law during wartime and Military Court No. 16, which had brought the lawsuit against Behn and four other managers. He should, however, have passed them on to Serrano Suñer's Ministry of Governance.[170] As far as we know, Weddell's efforts were to lead to at least one success—the reinstatement of Caldwell as vice president—but, more importantly, the path to an agreement was becoming increasingly clearer. The next day Serrano Suñer announced that he no longer felt that it was necessary for the company to present a balance sheet to be able to hold its shareholders' meeting.[171] Even so, Weddell again recommended that the department should not accept any requests for loans to Spain before he arrived in Washington. He immediately set off with his wife for the United States.[172]

Finally pragmatism prevailed, if not for Weddell, certainly for Colonel Behn and the Spanish authorities, who were prepared to do anything necessary to get a loan from the United States. And on 13 and 15 May 1940 the colonel reached the beginnings of an agreement with Serrano Suñer and then with Franco. Apparently, then, the case was closed. According to Counselor Bucknell, who had replaced Counselor Scotten and had been left in charge of the Madrid Embassy,[173] the most important clauses of the agreement were the following:

1. The International Telephone and Telegraph will be reinstated in the management and control of the National Telephone Company of Spain thus re-establishing the "statu quo ante" of July 18, 1936

(...)
4. The Americans who have been separated from their positions as a result of proceedings whose revision has been requested of the government, or who leave the company for any other reason, can be substituted by other Americans to whom the authorities shall grant the necessary permits without any obstacle whatever, as well as to the remainder of the American personnel which is appointed.
5. There is no question whatever with respect to the contract with the State and the contacts between the Compañía Telefónica Nacional de España and the International Telephone and Telegraph Corporation.
6. Without this paragraph constituting a limitation in view of the provisions of the contract with the state the International Telephone and Telegraph Corporation proposes for the present to appoint 6 Americans of the 18 directors elected by the stockholders, the 3 Government delegates completing the total number of 21 directors provided by the company's statutes.[174]

The agreement was extremely beneficial for ITT because it formally accepted that the general contract it had with the CTNE would not be questioned. What is more, although Behn was prepared to accept the removal of eight managers, the Madrid Embassy was convinced that at least Caldwell would be reinstated.[175] As we have mentioned above, this was to prove to be the case.

THE DEFEAT OF FRANCE IN JUNE 1940 AND ITS INFLUENCE ON U.S. POLICY TOWARD FRANCE

The Spanish government's need for supplies had solved the dispute and been the way round its pride and ultrapatriotism. This need was immediately seen to be pressing because on the same day as the preliminary agreement was signed, Ambassador Cárdenas made a new request to Under Secretary Welles for a loan of between 150 and 200 million dollars to purchase cereal and cotton.[176] At first, Sumner Welles was not overenthusiastic but just one week later, affected by the dramatic situation of the war in Europe, he felt that the loan should be granted. At the end of May 1940, the situation was that France had been overrun by the German advance, initiated just two weeks before; Belgium, despite declaring its neutrality, had been invaded by the Germans and was on the point of surrender; and Italy was rumored to enter the war with Germany. In this context, Welles wrote to Weddell, who was then on holiday in his home in Richmond, and asked him to inform the Spanish authorities on his return to Spain of the U.S. government's readiness to grant the loans they had requested.

However, the under secretary, in a complete departure, also asked the ambassador in Madrid to make it clear to Franco's government that the United States was only prepared to grant loans if Spain stayed neutral. In his own words, the granting of new loans "in any form by any agency of this government will be contingent upon the definite maintenance by Spain of its neutral status in the present European war."[177] Thus, Sumner Welles introduced a new element that from that moment on would always be a characteristic feature of the relations between the United States of America and Franco's Spain.[178] And he did so at the same time as the United Kingdom was adopting a new policy toward Spain. On 15 May, the

British Ambassador Sir Maurice Peterson was replaced by the distinguished conservative politician sir Samuel Hoare who was to have a "special mission," determined by the chiefs of the General Staff and accepted by the new Prime Minister Winston Churchill: "attempt to improve relations with Franco, counteract the Italo-German influence on him and prevent Spain from entering the war on Germany's side (or at least to delay this entry for as long as possible)."[179] Alexander W. Weddell was to remain in the United States until the beginning of June 1940 when he took up his post in Madrid once again. We know that during his stay he had an interview with President Roosevelt,[180] although we have found no information about what they spoke about.

SPAIN STEPS UP ITS PLANS TO TAKE PART IN THE SECOND WORLD WAR: THE SPANISH OCCUPATION OF THE CITY OF TANGIER AND THE INTERNATIONAL ZONE ON 14 JUNE 1940 AND THE ABORTED ATTACK ON THE FRENCH PROTECTORATE OF MOROCCO. THE HARDENING OF THE SPANISH POLICY TOWARD THE UNITED STATES AND THE NEW SLANT IN THE POLICY OF HISPANIDAD

The evolution of the European war in May and June 1940 affected Franco's foreign policy to such an extent that Spain was on the verge of entering the conflict. The surprising German success in France prompted Spain to step up its plans to take part in the war in the fall of 1939. These plans not only involved making a "last-minute" appearance with the aim of taking advantage of the weakness of the French but also considered the possibility of a "long war," contrary to what some of Franco's leaders at the time were to explain subsequently.[181] In the end, it all amounted to a completely bloodless event: the occupation of the city of Tangier and its International Zone on 14 June 1940. But Spain had been on the verge of unleashing a fully fledged attack on the French Protectorate of Morocco.

Spain's change in attitude, however, also affected its relations with the United States. The surprising thing as far as the Americans were concerned was that, just when the last of the disputes with Spain had been solved and that progress was about to be made in furthering trade relations between the two countries, Franco began to show signs that his interest in the CTNE agreement was waning and that he even might consider withdrawing from it. In response to this situation, British demands, and initiatives from the anti-Franco sector of the Roosevelt administration, the United States decided to take action that would have adverse effects on the regime and thus help to bring the CTNE dispute to an end. At the same time, however, Franco's government began to give a new slant to its policy of *Hispanidad*.

The regime mobilized when France was staring defeat in the face. First, on 12 June 1940 Spain announced that it was changing its status from neutral to nonbelligerent. That is to say, it was adopting a new status in international politics that had been invented by Italy at the outbreak of the war and which just two days before, on 10 June, had changed from nonbelligerence to aggression. On 14 June, as German troops were entering Paris, a Spanish unit left its base in the protectorate and occupied the city and the International Zone of Tangier, thus violating its international statute. Tangier was the main port in the north of Morocco and although it was deep in the heart of the Spanish zone of the protectorate it did not belong to it; rather it had enjoyed a special status since 1923 and had therefore become the main focus of Spanish irredentism in the region.

But before Franco undertook the occupation, he sent an envoy, General Juan Vigón, to explain Spain's territorial claims to Hitler. He realized that France was on the verge of defeat and decided to go to Europe's new master and assert Spain's imperial demands. His aim was twofold: to have territories in North Africa and the Gulf of Guinea recognized as being Spanish possessions at the expense of France, and to acquire armaments (some of which had recently been captured from the Allies)[182] to carry out his program of territorial expansion and to defend himself against a possible U.S. disembarkation in Morocco or Portugal. However, he did not merely make his demands known to the Führer; he also began to take action (as was seen in Tangier). Vigón explained all this to Hitler and Von Ribbentrop in the chateu d'Acoz on 16 June, after spending six days searching for the German leader along the length and breadth of the Western Front. He gave them a letter signed by Franco on 3 June, the content of which was confirmed in a telegram from the Minister of Foreign Affairs Beigbeder to the German (and also the Italian) government the next day. The letter made it clear that

> Should the defeat of France have the natural consequence of a fair redistribution of African territories, Spain lays claim to the part of Morocco that is already under the Spanish protectorate, the Algerian territory colonized by Spain, on the neighboring stretch of coast, the enlargement of the Sahara with minor modifications, and the extension of Spanish possessions in the Gulf of Guinea with villages that provide seasonal black farm laborers, which at the moment we completely lack (...) If England continues to fight, [Spain] would be prepared to gradually become a belligerent nation, as long as we have time to prepare public opinion and are given assistance with the supplies, materials and armaments we shall require to attack Gibraltar and defend our archipelagos, and the appropriate naval and air support.[183]

Spain's offer to enter the war could not have been clearer in the message. Apparently, however, the offer was not so clear in the conversation between Vigón and Hitler, and the German leader had been noncommittal. He congratulated Spain on the decisive action taken in Tangier, promised to provide help, stated that he would not tolerate a U.S. disembarkation, showed interest in reestablishing land links with Spain (through the defeated France), and was in favor of Gibraltar being returned to Spain. However, he also made it clear that Italy had expressed an interest in Morocco.[184] At that time, Hitler believed that the war was about to end and in the following weeks he showed little interest in Spain's offer to join the war. His attitude was to change later on, but at that time it was a surprise for the Spanish leaders who, as they had done in Tangier, were prepared to take the initiative once again and attack the French Protectorate of Morocco.

By taking Gibraltar, Spain wanted to exact revenge on the United Kingdom for an affront with a history of more than 200 years, and attacking the French Protectorate of Morocco was an attempt to settle a debt with France that had been outstanding since Morocco had been divided into two protectorates in 1912. The division had been unequal and Spain had been apportioned, in the words of the king of Italy Victor Manuel III, "the Moroccan rib bone": that is to say, the poor mountainous territories in the north, quite unlike the more prosperous and more populated central and southern regions that had been handed over to France. Spain, then, had a debt to settle with France, and the tension between the two countries had increased when small portions of the Spanish protectorate had been illegally occupied in 1925 as a result of the war against the Rif rebels.

In fact, ever since April 1940 Franco had been preparing a partial occupation of the International Zone of Tangier but not of the city because he feared that the French and the British would do the same. On 15 April, the Minister of Foreign Affairs Colonel Beigbeder had written to the high commissioner of the Spanish protectorate, General Asensio, saying that

> The National Defense Committee and the cabinet have met to discuss the international situation and the possible consequences that the intensification of the war and the increasing hatred may have for us. We have concluded that, should there be a conflict in the Mediterranean, Spanish neutrality would be in danger because of possible attacks on the Balearic Islands, Gibraltar, Tarifa, the Spanish Protectorate of Morocco and Tangier (...) This is the most delicate part of your responsibilities, because I suspect that our neutrality shall first be endangered by a Franco-English disembarkation in Tangier. This is constantly being confirmed by the reports I have been receiving.[185]

He ordered him to take steps—in conjunction with other steps that were to be taken in other possible theaters of conflict—to occupy not the city of Tangier but its International Zone "which we have to occupy in a friendly way without friction with the French or the English, because if they violate a Statute, then so shall we, and we shall then make contact with them to establish a *modus vivendi* for temporary occupation."[186] The same instructions considered the possibility of intervening in the war. Beigbeder also said that

> Of course this is not war because if they were merely to occupy Tangier and we the International Zone, we could sustain the situation. If the conflict were to become more serious and the storm were to burst, you would be given instructions, which would surely be to arm the country [in reference not only to a previous shipment of military equipment but also to the arming of the "harkas" of indigenous settlers] and enter the French zone, but this is still a long way off. What is urgent now is Tangier, so that they do not get in ahead of us.[187]

Beigbeder was mistaken; the war had not reached the protectorate but France had had an unfortunate stroke of bad luck. This meant that Spanish irredentist expectations had suddenly become urgent and it was decided to occupy not only the zone but also the city on 14 June.

But no further steps were taken. Germany did not respond to the telegram of 17 June. Spain had deployed its troops along the border between the protectorates during the night of 17–18 June[188] with the intention of attacking and General Asensio waited for the order to march to be sent from Madrid. But the attack was not launched. For his part, General Nogués, resident-general of the French protectorate, reinforced his defense in a somewhat contrived way by making the Spanish believe he had more troops than he actually had and he made it quite clear that that he was going to defend himself.[189] He had more troops and equipment, including aviation, than Franco's forces so if the Spanish had attacked, the result would by no means have been a foregone conclusion and may well have gone against the Spanish army. In fact, Nogués had been planning to invade the Spanish protectorate ever since 1939.[190] What he really feared was that German troops would be allowed into the protectorate by the Spaniards to carry out the attack, and that the Italians would advance on Tunisia from their possessions in Libya.[191] However, the Spanish troops did not move. They continued to wait for Germany's response. On 25 June, Ribbentrop told them that he would give an answer very soon.[192]

Before this, though, Spain had adopted another strategy in parallel to that of armed conflict. On 18 June, Beigbeder had ordered Ambassador Lequerica to present the new French government with a short list of territorial claims, mainly of the Moroccan territories that France had annexed in 1925. Conversations were held on frontier rectifications and involved the leader of the new collaborationist Vichy France, Marshal Pétain, former ambassador to Franco during the Civil War. Spain, however, was to achieve nothing by these means because of General Nogués' firm opposition.[193]

However, on 3 July, the day of the British attack on the French fleet anchored in the port of Mers-el-Kébir, the possibility of using if not force then at least a threat to extend the Spanish protectorate at the expense of the French was entertained. The aim of the attack was to prevent the squadron from being captured by Germany or taking hostile action against the United Kingdom and which Vichy responded to by threatening to attack British interests in Egypt. So a war was on the verge of breaking out between Vichy and Great Britain. It was at this point that Beigbeder wrote to Franco saying that

> Things are changing as quickly as a chameleon. France could end up allied to Italy against the English. They may have reached the following devilish agreement: France hands Tunisia to Italy, takes Egypt and also gives it to Italy. France thus avoids any amputations and Italy gains Tunisia and Egypt. This is highly dubious for us because we are left out on a limb. We should therefore be prepared for our task in Morocco with Germany, with whom we should have increasingly closer ties. Would it not be appropriate to advance at once to the Uarga [the river Uarga, located in the border zone between the two protectorates claimed by Spain]? We are getting rusty and I cannot see how to break the stalemate. An ultimatum may be one way. They would have to give way and they'll breathe a sigh of relief thinking that we are satisfied with that.[194]

But things remained on hold with everybody awaiting events. As Beigbeder wrote to the high commissioner one month later, on 25 July:

> We must always be prepared to intervene in the French Protectorate when the opportunity arises. We must have studied the operation and maintain the small nucleus of harkas that you have organized, which could be increased to 35 or 40 thousand men if necessary. For the moment, no armed intervention is required: we need to wait and

see how the neighboring zone decomposes and then see what developments there are in the European war and particularly in the offensive against England, which will be an indication of the attitude we should adopt.

And he tried to calm Asensio's impatience for action by saying:

These times are full of opportunities that are apparently propitious, but which conceal a trap. We believe that if French Morocco resists, it will sooner or later find support from England, if England manages to survive the German attack. We are all well aware of the difficulties of your mission, with which you are dealing with great tact and skill, but which still require a period of waiting. For a start, I would like to point out again that the time does not seem to be ripe to enter French Morocco and that the circumstances oblige us to continue to wait expectantly.[195]

In fact the Spanish leaders were optimistic about future imperial expansion at the expense of France, but when Hitler failed to respond they began to grow concerned because it was clear that the Axis powers had their eye on North Africa. In the words of minister Beigbeder,

I am worried about the Italian and German pretensions, and this is a matter that the Head of State is directly responsible for in top secret negotiations, which cannot be discussed. I am fully aware that Germany can acquire considerable prestige in Morocco and this will necessarily lead to a loss of prestige for us. This, then, is the problem that I entrust to your skill, tact and discretion; that is to say, the natives should know that they will inevitably fall under the influence of Spain on the day that peace is declared. We do not know when this will be, or how it will come about but the greater or lesser chunk that we can obtain in Morocco and in the colonial empire will depend on it.[196]

Franco was to try and resolve all these questions in the following months of September and October, when Serrano Suñer traveled to Berlin and Rome, and when he had a meeting with Hitler in Hendaye (see below).

Spain, then, had started to take crucial steps toward extending its colonial territories as soon as the defeat of France had seemed to be imminent. In addition to the action taken in Tangier, Spain had been on the verge of invading some areas of the French protectorate and these plans were still on stand by. Franco did not, however, stop making claims and he was constantly attempting to get a cession agreement from Germany. This seemed to be the right moment: the war appeared to be nearing its end and it was feasible to think that Great Britain would not continue the struggle by itself. Up to that time, in European wars, a country did not have to be totally invaded before it requested an armistice, and Franco's leaders believed that if they did not take part, they could end up with no war and, therefore, with no gains in Gibraltar and North Africa.

The problem, however, was that Hitler was not considering Franco's offer. He was on the verge of returning the whole of France's colonial empire to Pétain because he believed that this would enable him to make peace with the United Kingdom sooner and thus finish the war. Once the war had ended, he thought, he would discuss the

North Africa question with Spain, which involved not only Germany's own interests but also those of Italy, Spain, and, of course, France.

The fact that Spain did not enter the world war in the summer of 1940 does not mean that it was not prepared to help the Axis powers in other more secretive ways. On 10 June, Italy asked Serrano Suñer for permission to refuel their bombers on missions to Gibraltar on Spanish territory and he responded "not only once but as many times as you like."[197] These missions were to be repeated on fourteen occasions before 1944, and always involved some form of Spanish collaboration.[198] What is more, in 1940 and 1941, before the British had managed to locate and eliminate them, German oil tankers based in the Spanish Atlantic ports of Vigo and Cádiz[199] supplied their submarines on twenty-three different occasions; small quantities of gasoline from these tankers were exchanged for Spanish diesel fuel on two occasions;[200] between June 1940 and June 1942 Italian submarines were supplied at least five times; and Italian commandoes operating out of Spain attacked British ships in Gibraltar nine times before August 1943.[201]

However, after the supply of oil to the Axis powers was cut off in June 1940, it does not seem that Spain diverted the oil obtained from the United States or the Western Hemisphere on a massive, systematic basis although small quantities were occasionally exchanged. On this matter, the vigilance and pressure of the British, first, and then the Great Britain–United States alliance were crucial. The quotas that Great Britain imposed on Spain in September 1940 after oil supplies had been cut off (see below) were extremely effective.

Spain, however, collaborated in the war effort of the Axis powers in many other areas: the Spanish merchant navy was constantly at their service; they were provided with assistance in police control and repression, particularly in German-occupied France where such leading Republican figures as Lluís Companys were to be victims and thousands of others were to end up in Nazi concentration camps; their spies and saboteurs were given every facility and, among other things, were allowed to use radio and observation stations in the peninsula, the islands and the protectorate; and their press services were given a privileged position within the Spanish press.[202]

Another sign of Spanish enthusiasm was the change in the policy of Hispanidad. Beigbeder had revitalized the policy that had been applied under the dictatorship of Primo de Rivera; that is to say, he encouraged Catholicism and the promotion of Spanish culture by creating organizations such as the Consejo Superior de Misiones (Higher Missions Council) and the unofficial Asociación Cultural Hispanoamericana (Hispano-American Cultural Association).[203] This latter organization had been created in January 1940 to counteract the antitotalitarian campaigns instigated by Great Britain, France, and the United States, the antiregime propaganda of the Republican exiles who were arriving on the American continent during 1939 and 1940, and the Pan-American policies adopted at the Panama Conference. What is more, the pro-*nacionales* atmosphere in many Latin American countries during the Civil War had gradually turned to suspicion of the regime, its diplomatic legations and the Falangist organizations abroad, which were seen as fifth columns of the Axis powers in America, even though Beigbeder had not agreed to following a common propaganda policy with Germany and Italy in Latin

America. This policy, however, took on a new complexion with the defeat of France. Relations were briefly broken off with Chile (July–October 1940) because a Chilean politician (not a member of the government) had insulted Franco; the possibility of cooperating with Germany and intensifying trade relations had been looked into; and Spain became increasingly hostile toward the United States after the Havana Conference of July 1940.[204] Spain's hostility was directed against the idea of an "America for North Americans" and involved caricatures of Roosevelt and even articles in favor of his Republican opponent, Wilkie, in the November elections of 1940. One year before, Franco had spoken to the Germans of these elections and stressed the need of preventing Roosevelt from being reelected.[205]

So in the middle of 1940 the regime's leaders were openly enthusiastic toward the Axis powers. This positive, prewar atmosphere was in stark contrast to the country's increasing economic difficulties, which many thought would soon be solved by the aid they were expecting from the Axis. On 22 June 1940, in the middle of this novel and euphoric atmosphere fired by the regime's desire for greater imperial glory, a heated Serrano Suñer told Weddell that the agreement with Colonel Behn was not official, merely personal.[206] He accompanied his statement with a tirade about how unbearable and humiliating it was for Spain that foreign interests should control vital aspects of the country's economy. In compliance with the express orders he had been given by the department after Spain had adopted the status of nonbelligerent, Weddell had requested this particular interview in an attempt to determine what the regime's intentions were with respect to the war.[207] But he got nothing out of Serrano or the Generalissimo, who he saw later that day.

Franco was not as aggressive as Serrano but he was also distant. He spoke of the great moral debt that Spain owed Italy because of the aid provided during the Civil War and the Italian dead buried on Spanish soil; he referred to Hitler as a "very humane man" and a statesman who would take into account Spain's demands in any future division of the French and British colonies; and he also deliberately deceived him by saying that Spain was not about to take part in the war and that "The United States [were] (...) nearer to war than we are." He was a little less misleading, however, when he said that nonbelligerence meant a "state of lively sympathy and wakeful attitude." And he disagreed when Weddell told him that in the following months the food situation in Europe would be dramatic and that U.S. aid would be necessary. In fact, he merely responded with a "feeble smile" when Weddell spoke of his country's interest in sending food to Spain via the Red Cross. However, he spoke at length about his social program, the construction of 24,000 small houses for workers, and the welfare work of the Auxilio Social, complaining bitterly that none of this was appreciated in the United States. He gave no sign, then, of his real aims or what he was really doing with respect to the war. For Franco, the defeat of Great Britain was a matter of time, of a few months, and Spain had to take advantage of the opportunity. In this context of feverish expansionist anxiety, relations with the United States took second place. We should not forget that the Caudillo considered the United States to be one of Spain's democratic enemies

This new aggressive anti-U.S. propaganda, however, now met with a more considered response from Washington. Weddell warned of the growing feeling against the United States within the regime and of the danger that Germany would use Spain to infiltrate America with its political and economic ideas. And the result was that the FBI began to investigate Francoists throughout the American continent.[208] Most importantly, in June 1940, the U.S. Congress approved funds of $500,000 to combat totalitarianism and, from that moment on, the real threat of Spain's entry into the war meant that Washington was to consider all the regime's propaganda in Latin America to be dangerous because it went against the official U.S. line. What is more, Spain managed to avoid being condemned by the Havana Conference for severing relations with Chile, but was affected by the measures for controlling foreign diplomats and fighting against subversive and antidemocratic activities.[209]

However, Ambassador Weddell continued to believe that Franco did not wish to involve his country in the war. He had believed this from the beginning of the war in Europe, although he also feared that German and Italian pressure might end up by forcing Spain to take part.[210] This fear of German pressure increased when western France was occupied and German troops arrived on the other side of the Pyrenees. Thus on 3 July 1940, he wrote to Welles that "Franco is sincerely trying to keep the country on an even keel and to avoid committing the inevitable suicide which this country's entry into the war would undoubtedly bring about. But the pressure from German and Italian sources is very great and I much fear that Hitler is almost as powerful here as he is in Berlin."[211] The fact was, however, that the pressure to enter the war at the time was not coming from Berlin but from Madrid.

Sir Samuel Hoare, New British Ambassador to Spain and His "Special Mission"

Weddell's conviction that Spain desired neutrality was shared by his British counterpart in Madrid, Sir Maurice Peterson, who had said in London on 19 May that "Spain will not enter into war against us (...) The country cannot afford to do so: its people are dying of starvation.[212] But His Majesty's Government, as we have mentioned above, was not so sure, relieved him of his duties and sent Sir Samuel Hoare, one of the Conservative Party's heavyweights on a "special mission."[213]

Former first lord of the admirality, home secretary, foreign secretary (a post he had to resign because of public uproar against the Hoare-Laval Agreement[214] with his French counterpart that would have granted Italy considerable territorial concessions after the invasion of Ethiopia) and, finally, lord privy seal and secretary of state for air with a seat in the war cabinet,[215] Hoare had been a passionate appeaser in the Chamberlain government and one of Churchill's political enemies. More importantly, from our point of view, like many other Conservative leaders including Churchill himself, he had supported Franco during the Spanish Civil War.[216] Hoare was now an ambassador in the Foreign Office, led by his friend and former appeaser Lord Halifax, and he was entrusted by Churchill and the War Cabinet with the "special mission" of stopping Spain from entering the war in support of Germany (or at least delaying their entry for as long as possible), improving Anglo-Spanish relations, and counteracting the influence of the Axis powers in Spain.[217] Hoare implemented this policy in such a way that it was immediately qualified as appeasement by his British and U.S. critics. His staff in Madrid was the same as Peterson's: Counselor Arthur Yencken, Commercial Attaché Hugh Elis-Rees, Military Attaché Brigadier Torr, Naval Attaché, and Ship's Captain Alan Hillgarth.[218] The last of these was also the head of the Secret Intelligence Service and had direct access to Churchill, who had asked him to use his Spanish contacts to keep Spain out of the war.[219] David Eccles, delegate of the Ministry of Economic Warfare (MEW) in the Iberian peninsula, also played a leading role in Spain.[220] Hoare was appointed on 15 May and arrived in Madrid via Lisbon on the following 1 June. Eccles provided the following account of Hoare's arrival in the Peninsula:

> Hoare thought that a well-connected and superbly intelligent man like himself had a duty to tell inferior mortals what to do. His contempt for the lower classes was matched by his admiration for authority, which led him to take a kinder view of Mussolini than his predecessor at the Foreign Office, Anthony Eden, had done. He made the notorious "Hoare-Laval pact" which earned him a place among the "Guilty Men". These were a list of public men held responsible by a large section of British opinion for appeasing the dictators and failing to re-arm Britain in the 1930s. Hoare came to the Embassy in Madrid handicapped by the label of a "Guilty Man." However, his mission was a success and he lived down his bad reputation.
>
> Sir Samuel and Lady Maud [Hoare], on their way to take up his post in Madrid, suitably dressed for a garden party at Buckingham Palace, arrived in Lisbon on 30 May 1940, and stayed two nights in the Embassy. I was living in the house and was present at the talks which Hoare had with Sir Walford Selby [British ambassador in Lisbon]. Hoare opened the conversation by assuring us that only with reluctance and under extreme pressure from Churchill and the King, had he accepted the post of Ambassador to Spain. He could only spare a month or two as he was going to be appointed Viceroy of India. He was confident that in this short time he could obtain from Franco a firm guarantee that Spain would remain neutral for the duration of the war. Selby, instead of being exasperated by his self-assurance, was struck dumb, and only just managed to ask me to describe the situation Hoare would find in Spain. I told him that in the cities the people were near starvation and that we heard from good sources that Hitler's efforts to persuade Franco to come into the war against us might be on the point of succeeding. Hoare turned pale, cried out that he had been deceived, said his mission was useless and he would go back to London in the morning. This was the first of many times when I was to see him panic. Selby and I rallied him as best we could, but when he reached Madrid he kept his private aircraft waiting ready to take him home and he had to be persuaded to unpack.[221]

However, he was to remain in Spain for almost five years. And by the time he had been in the country for two months, and just like his predecessor, he did not believe that Spain was going to enter the war, at least in the short term. He also designed a whole plan for implementing his policy. In a meeting with Weddell on 30 July, he told him that "he had attempted to run [these rumors of German intervention] down" and that he was "convinced of their essential lack of foundation." Weddell added that he believed that "Spain's neutrality at the moment was due to the fact that there was no pressure from Germany to alter this." Hoare agreed and added that "Franco and his generals are too well informed of their own lacks to desire to alter the 'status quo'"[222]

THE REACTION OF BRITAIN AND THE UNITED STATES IN THE SUMMER OF 1940: THE CUT IN THE OIL SUPPLY

The Francoist euphoria very soon came up against the extremely uncomfortable reality of the almost complete embargo on the supply of oil that was imposed throughout most of the summer of 1940. This embargo had been established as a result not only of French and British demands but also of the insistence of President Roosevelt and his administration (although the issue had created considerable internal friction). In June, then, the French and British ambassadors in Washington had asked the United States to restrict the number of oil tankers being sent to Spain, which they considered to be much higher than previous years.[223] In particular, the French ambassador had told the State Department that at that time the Texas Oil Company had no fewer than twenty-one tankers—most of which were sailing under the U.S. flag—bound for Spain and carrying oil that was eventually going to end up in Italy.[224] Three days later the British ambassador in Washington, Lord Lothian, delivered a memorandum to Secretary Hull in which he expressed his government's concern about the amount of oil that was being sent to Spain by U.S. companies. Great Britain suspected that these enormous amounts of oil concealed the fact that the companies were helping the Axis powers. In the words of the ambassador, this "ran counter to the expressed desire of the United States Government to lend all possible material aid to the allies."[225] In the three previous months, again according to the ambassador, 115,000 tons had been sent from U.S. ports in the Gulf of Mexico by Spanish tankers and a further 180,000 tons by neutral tankers. Spain's monthly consumption was calculated to be 85,000 tons so it was suspected that a considerable surplus was accumulating.[226] In fact, it is quite plausible that Spain was attempting to stockpile provisions because of the prevailing climate of world war.[227] And it is even more plausible that the country was preparing for war. Whatever the case may have been, Great Britain was concerned and asked the United States to restrict not only the amount of oil transported to Spain in their tankers but also the amount of lubricants and aviation gasoline.[228] On 14 June, Britain made a more general request for "the interruption at their point of origin of all the supplies to enemy countries and territory under enemy control, and full cooperation in our control of contraband to all other European countries, including soviet Russia."[229]

The State Department ruled out any official control of oil exports to Spain, fearful as always of public controversies and that the administration might be accused of taking part in the war, because as yet there was no specific legislation to justify such a decision. Instead it decided to take discreet action. Contact was made with the Maritime Commission, which decreed that sending oil to Spain was dangerous and that U.S. tankers should not be involved. Therefore, permission for oil tankers to put to sea under the U.S. flag was refused. An agreement was also reached with the Treasury Department that all vessels destined for Spain would be inspected to ensure that they reached their proper destination.[230]

All these events had immediate effects on supply because the Spanish oil fleet was completely insufficient (only twelve vessels) and Spain had traditionally chartered from Norway, Holland, and Denmark. However, since these countries had been occupied by the Nazis, Spain had resorted to using U.S. tankers, and it was precisely these tankers and those of the North American oil companies that the Maritime Commission was refusing permission to carry oil to Spain.[231] Particularly affected were the Texas Oil Company (which provided all of CAMPSA's gasoline) from its refineries in the Gulf, and the Socony Vacuum Oil Company, which sold gasoline to CEPSA from its fields in Colombia. The Standard Oil Company of New Jersey, on the other hand, which sold crude oil to CEPSA from Venezuela so that it could be refined in Tenerife, made its shipments in vessels under the Panamanian flag, so it managed to get round the restrictive measures imposed by the United States.[232] Secretary Hull felt that these measures would begin to resolve the problem of the surplus stocks in Spanish hands,[233] particularly after the increase in purchases in 1939 and the first half of 1940.[234] And he also felt that the measures had been taken discreetly in the United States' interests.

But this was not all. On 27 June 1940, and as a result of the Espionage Act,[235] the president made the Secretary of the Treasury Morgenthau responsible for the movement of all vessels in U.S. waters, including the granting of sailing permits.[236] Morgenthau exercised his new authority two weeks later by refusing to allow three oil tankers to set off for Spain, two of which were flying the U.S. flag and one the Swedish flag, because he was convinced that the oil would end up in the hands of the Axis powers. This decision had originated within his Treasury Department when Basil Harris, in charge of sea transport, compared the figures for fuel exports to Spain before and during the current war. He had found that during the war there had been a surplus to date of 300,000 tons of gasoline sent to Spain, and he immediately informed Morgenthau, who in turn informed the president.[237] Because both Harris and the secretary were sure that this surplus was ending up in the hands of Germany and Italy, they decided to stop it from leaving the country. Harris was also aware that oil was being sent by North American companies from Central and South America and he proposed approaching them and asking them to stop. Morgenthau was enthusiastic about the idea and, a few days later, he and Secretary Knox managed to convince the president to order Hull to approach the companies that operated in Colombia and Venezuela and get them to cease sending oil to Spain. Morgenthau also immediately asked the British for their cooperation, their "one-hundred per cent cooperation," and added that

> We don't want to find out that we stop this thing and the good old English businessmen continue to do the same thing [(...)] As for tonight, no American flag ship is going to sail for Spain and the Canary Islands. We're going to ask the American companies to stop shipping oil out of Central and South America to Spain and we're even holding a Swedish ship. We have gone that far. This is as good a chance as I know—the English ought to jump at it and kiss it on both cheeks.[238]

However, the ban on shipments posed a legal problem in the case of the vessel flying under the Swedish flag. The law made it possible for the United States to prevent its own vessels with loads that were "detrimental to the national interest"[239] from setting sail, but this law was not applicable to vessels flying the flag of another country. In this case, however, both Hull himself and Admiral Land of the

Maritime Commission supported the secretary of the treasury[240] who maintained the prohibition as long as he could, although in the end he was obliged to allow the Scandinavian tanker to set sail.[241]

This incident and the events of the following two weeks led to greater deterioration in the relations between Morgenthau, Hull, and Welles on the question of Spain and, even more importantly, Japan. Morgenthau was not satisfied with the restrictions that had been imposed on oil transport to Spain by the State Department in June and he demanded stronger action. The department, however, was concerned about the effect that this action might have on Congress and Spanish policy. In fact, the economic adviser of the State Department had had no success when he asked the U.S. oil companies to send less oil to Spain.[242] Conflict with the Treasury Department, then, was in the offing and it was shortly to come to a head.

The cut in the oil supply from the United States bewildered the Spanish government. They did not understand why the Maritime Commission had not allowed Spain to charter tankers flying the U.S. flag[243] and they reacted by sending Ambassador Cárdenas to meet with the under secretary. They rightly suspected that Great Britain was at the bottom of it, but Welles denied this and attributed the Commission's decision to concern for the safety of North American vessels.[244] So Cárdenas and the Texas Oil Company, which supplied CAMPSA, decided to find tankers belonging to other nations.[245] For its part, CAMPSA considered contracting some extra gasoline cargoes from Rumania,[246] despite the considerable difference in price,[247] but the Rumanian company's refusal to take its tankers to the Mediterranean meant that the operation came to nought. Even if the company had not refused, however, the problem would not have been solved.[248]

Not only was the situation not improving, it was in fact getting worse because Great Britain continued to refuse to grant navicerts to any tankers bound for Spain.[249] A law passed by Franco's government on 28 June recognized "that the increasing difficulties in the supply of oil and in the freight market make it necessary to intensify the restrictive measures on fuel consumption." On 8 July a new Comisaría de Carburantes Líquidos (Liquid Fuels Commission) was set up to manage these measures.[250] This may have been a sign of Spain's desire to preserve its stocks for use in case of war, but the supply from abroad had dried up and the situation was unsustainable in the short term. As the weeks went by, Spain became increasingly convinced that the root of the problem was the United Kingdom but remained unaware that some sectors of the Roosevelt administration were also against supplying them with oil. In fact, when the president of the Texas Oil Company Thorkild Rieber had a meeting with the official in charge of sea transport at the British Embassy in Washington, he got the impression that "England is trying to suppress or severely reduce the number of vessels bearing oil supplies to Spain."[251] And on 16 July, Cárdenas informed that

> The English (...) [are making it difficult] for us to receive large amounts of oil and other supplies because they believe that we have considerable stocks, which they want us to use up. They may have warned the Americans that they will detain their oil tankers bound for Spain and, to avoid incidents, the Americans have decided not to allow vessels carrying oil to set sail for Spain under their flag.[252]

Shortly afterward, the *New York Times* and the British press revealed the reason for these restrictions: that some of the oil sent to Spain was subsequently reexported to Germany. Cárdenas believed that the source of this information was an item published in June (in fact it was 3 July) by the *National Petroleum News* and which the Francoists believed to be Communist-inspired.[253] The Spanish government was becoming increasingly concerned and ordered the ambassadors in Washington and London to deny what it considered to be entirely false accusations. Spain also invited Britain to compare the amounts of oil in Spain with the amounts that had been imported. They also categorically denied having imported—as Cárdenas had been told by the State Department—a single liter of aviation gasoline since the end of the Civil War. In response to the accusation that Spain had accumulated "considerable reserves," Beigbeder explained to Cárdenas that "during 1939 and 1940 Spain has not imported a single liter of aviation gasoline because we have been using the surplus from our war. All the aviation gasoline for our war was supplied by the Texas Oil Company and Capitain Riever [sic]."[254]

Franco's government, however, was aware that things were beginning to change and that, as had been happening since June, free trade was no longer a possibility. For its part, the Madrid Embassy felt that "the situation is very serious."[255] One of CAMPSA's executives believed that "the United States want to limit the shipments and (...) this limit will not be exceeded.[256] This was not true: it was the British who wanted to set a quota. Beigbeder, however, believed it to be so and on 23 July 1940, he told Cárdenas that

> The measures against oil tankers setting sail for Spain have had a serious effect on our economy. The policy of this country to set quotas for Spain has been announced in such vague, imprecise terms that it has created real uncertainty. Notwithstanding the establishment of a fair quota and taking for granted that the shipments this year are comparable to the 1935 figures, we need to clear up the following doubt: can CAMPSA immediately send five vessels under the Spanish flag to be supplied with a total of 28,000 tons by the Texas Company? The Spanish government needs to know urgently whether guarantees can be given that these vessels can be loaded on their arrival and sent to Spain. Should the response be negative, suggest that Spain might take measures. We trust that you will take due care in how you express this.[257]

While Madrid was waiting for a response, and Ambassador Weddell was explaining to his government that he was extremely concerned about the critical situation in Spain,[258] things almost took a definitive turn for the worse because a total blockade was on the verge of being approved.

Meanwhile Morgenthau had not been idle. He managed to mix the two questions of oil bound for Spain and for Japan. During a dinner attended by the secretary of the treasury, the Secretaries Stimson and Knox, and the British Ambassador Lord Lothian on 18 July, the latter was reproached because Great Britain had given in to the Japanese demand that the Burma Road should be closed, thus cutting off the supply route to China. The ambassador responded by reminding the Americans that "After all, you are continuing to ship aviation gasoline to Japan." And he also made a suggestion: if the United States were to cut off supplies to Japan and the United Kingdom were to destroy the oil fields in the Dutch Indies, the Japanese would be left without gasoline for their war machinery[259] and that particular danger would be deactivated." Morgenthau[260] liked the proposal, adapted it, and presented it to the president.

Before going on, we should point out that Roosevelt often gave responsibilities to his secretaries that often had little to do with the post they held, not only because he needed people he trusted absolutely in key positions but also because he was reluctant to resort to dismissal.[261] That is to say, rather than dismiss secretaries he preferred to keep them in their posts and entrust some of their duties to others. This habit meant that the internal operation of his administration was somewhat unusual. As we have seen, Morgenthau was given his new responsibility as a result of the Espionage Act. It was yet another indication that the president trusted him implicitly and was related to other responsibilities that he already had such as the Secret Service or the Bureau of Narcotics.[262] But let us return to his proposal. Morgenthau told the president that if the United States were to stop exporting oil (while at the same time ensuring that the United Kingdom was supplied from Venezuela and Colombia) and the British were to destroy the Dutch fields in Indonesia and the German plants that produced synthetic gasoline, the war would soon be over.[263] Roosevelt was extremely interested in the proposal, and he discussed it with Stimson and Knox. But when Sumner Welles told him that if it were to be put into practice it would provoke a Japanese attack on British possessions, he backed down. Roosevelt did not want to implement the measure because he had been nominated for a third term with a program of nonparticipation in the war (unless the United States were attacked) and he feared that the outbreak of a new conflict in Asia would weaken the United Kingdom in its struggle against the Axis powers. The secretary of the treasury complained of the "beautiful Chamberlain talk that I listened to Sumner Welles give (...) Everything is going to be lovely. And after that then Japan is going to come over and kiss our big toe.[264] All this was another sign of the differences within the government and the administration on issues affecting Spain: Morgenthau, Ickes, Stimson, and Knox were still clashing with Hull and Welles, who were much more accommodating and not inclined to implement measures that may have led to reprisals and "push Japan into war" or "force [Spain] into the arms of the Axis powers."

But neither Morgenthau or Stimson would abandon their idea. Now the secretary of the treasury focused on the fact that Japan was importing considerable amounts of high-octane gasoline for its aircraft.[265] Stimson told Roosevelt that this went against U.S. interests and suggested that he put gasoline and scrap metal on the list of strategic materials that would be subject to embargo under the recently passed Export Control Act, which gave the president the power to ban or restrict the exportation of military equipment, munitions, tools, and materials when he believed it to be necessary for defense purposes.[266] The proposal was directed against Japan but also against Franco's Spain[267] and once again it interested Roosevelt. On 26 July 1940[268] he signed an order that prohibited the exportation of all oil and scrap unless a specific export license had been granted.[269]

When the order reached the State Department there was widespread alarm because of the enormous implications it could have on relations with Japan and Spain. It was thought that it would provoke Japan into declaring war and push Spain further toward the Axis powers. At the time, Secretary Hull was out of the country so Under Secretary Welles took charge of the counteroffensive.[270] He prepared a new text, which he presented to a cabinet meeting in an attempt to confine the embargo to "high-octane gasoline, airplane motor oil, and tetraethyl lead, as well as number one heavy meeting-grade iron and steel scrap." He argued in favor of a new text saying that "A total embargo of oil would be 'administratively tremendously difficult'" while his proposals "would still seriously hamper the Japanese air force."[271] The revised order was approved by the president after an arduous debate during which Morgenthau and Knox reminded those present that, in the meeting held two weeks before, the State Department had been told to approach the U.S. oil companies and ask them not to ship oil out of Central and South America. They pointed out that Hull had apparently done nothing about it. This was not entirely true because Feis had asked the companies to make a general reduction in their shipments. Welles response must have upset the two secretaries and, as was to be seen, also the president. The Secretary of the Interior Harold Ickes recorded in his diary that he had said that Mexican, Venezuelan, and Colombian oil in the hands of U.S. companies was ending up in German hands, but that these companies had no reason to lose this market share.[272] At this point Roosevelt interrupted and told him in no uncertain terms that the United States was helping Great Britain in the war against Germany and that this was a matter of conscience. He then obliged Welles and Morgenthau to leave the room and come to an agreement. This they did: Morgenthau accepted the restricted order, which was a partial success for Welles. The president signed the new order on the same day, 26 July 1940. It was limited to aviation gasoline with an octane rating of more than 87 and high quality scrap iron, among other products that could be used in war time or by industries that manufactured war material.[273] This meant that an embargo that would have been fatal to Spain, which was already experiencing severe supply problems, was prevented. Given the products that were affected by the order, Spain was affected much less than Japan. Even so, as mentioned above, the Japanese were not seriously affected by the gasoline restrictions because their planes used gasoline with an octane rating of 86.

One of the results of the Welles-Morgenthau confrontation on 26 July was that the State Department mobilized and Welles summoned the heads of the U.S. oil companies to Washington on 1 August 1940 to ask them to reduce exportations to Spain to the 1939 figures and to ensure that supplies did not fall into German or Italian hands. The main suspect was the Texas Oil Company because it had supplied Franco's rebels during the Civil War and because its president was known to be close to the Germans. Great Britain and France had denounced that one of its tankers had transported crude oil to Tenerife on 24 June where it had been transferred to three Italian tankers.[274] In fact, in the same month, a press campaign against Rieber forced him to resign.[275]

The companies responded to Welles' request and in the month of August Spain imported no oil at all.[276] The reduction in supplies in the summer of 1940 and the interruption just mentioned came about as a result of the initial Anglo-French request, subsequent British pressure on the U.S. administration, Roosevelt's response to this pressure and the decision to involve the companies. But it was also the result of the tight rein that the United Kingdom had been keeping on the Spanish navy since the middle of June, which meant that few navicerts were granted and that the list of forbidden products was forever getting longer.[277] All of this was part of the set of measures approved on 13 June by the minister of Economic Warfare, the labor politician Hugh Dalton;[278] as a result, those vessels carrying goods to Spain that did not have the required navicert were detained on the high seas or not allowed to weigh anchor. After 1 August, the navicert system was extended to include cargoes of corn purchased in Argentina, scrap iron, phosphates from French North Africa, cork, cotton, rice, and other products[279] as well as oil tankers. This mechanism became one of the most effective instruments in Britain's attempts to keep Spain neutral. Spain was dependent on supplies from abroad, so the navicert system meant that Britain had the country at its mercy. At this point in time it was important to keep the pressure on but not to go too far, so the British directives allowed for supplies of "reasonable quantities of goods required for consumption in Spain."[280] That is to say, after a show of force the United Kingdom gave a peace offering. As Enrique Moradiellos has explained, during the second half of June and the whole of the following month there was considerable debate between Dalton and Hoare about the severity of the blockade on Spain.[281] Dalton was still very aware of the policy of providing supplies to Italy in an attempt at appeasement and he had no wish to repeat the experience. But in the end he gave way. David Eccles had been negotiating a triangular agreement between Great Britain, Portugal, and Spain shortly before the fall of France so that Spain could purchase products from Portugal and its colonies for internal consumption with a British loan. The agreement was signed in Lisbon on 24 July 1940.[282] And at the same time, British officials and the Franco authorities checked the oil consumption figures and found, in Beigbeder's words, "perfect normality and exclusive internal consumption of the oil received."[283] The role of Eccles,[284] the Embassy Minister Yencken and, of course Hoare, who was becoming increasingly involved in achieving supplies for Spain because he believed that it was the key to Spanish neutrality, was fundamental in all this. During August, an official from the British Ministry of Economic Warfare, Mark Turner, traveled to Spain. According to the Spanish, "after an objective examination of the situation, he has remained fully convinced of the absolute normality of the Spanish requests and the advisability of satisfying them."[285] Conversations were initiated between the Minister of Foreign Affairs Beigbeder and Ambassador Hoare in August in attempt to reach an agreement on the issue of the oil supply.

The British offer was to "set a monthly import quota that should not exceed the equivalent of Spain's needs for two and a half months."[286] These amounts would be provided with the requisite navicerts and would therefore be allowed through the naval blockade. In exchange, Spain agreed to keep the British informed of the rate of supply and consumption, and not to sell any on to the Axis powers. The British, then, would give the permits and the Americans would sell the oil. As soon as a draft agreement had been reached, some of CAMPSA's oil tankers were allowed to set sail for the United States but, because of the shortcomings of their own fleet, Spain continued to insist on the need to provide navicerts to chartered vessels flying under other flags.[287] Before the Anglo-Spanish Oil Agreement was signed on 6 September, the State Department was consulted.[288] The signature of this document signified the introduction of a mechanism for regulating the supply of oil products that was to be the corner stone of British strategy toward Spain. And it required the cooperation of the United States, which did not define its own trade policy toward Spain until a year later, shortly before Pearl Harbor. The result of the agreement was that, in the end, the importations of oil products into Spain in 1940 were 88 percent of those of 1935,[289] while consumption was 94 percent.[290] The situation would get ostensibly worse for Spain during 1941, as we shall explain in the next chapter.

In addition to keeping Spain supplied, presumably so that "it would not fall into the arms of the Axis powers," the United Kingdom used other arms. One of these was bribery[291] of a whole group of generals and chiefs of the Spanish army (for which they used the Majorcan banker Juan March Ordinas); another was that Hoare suggested to Beigbeder that Britain might be prepared to enter into discussions with Spain about French possessions in North Africa and even the future of Gibraltar. Fundamental to the design and execution of the program of bribery was Captain Hillgarth's network of contacts among the Spanish military and with March that had been forged in Majorca during the Civil War and subsequently during his time as Naval Attaché.[292] The operation consisted of paying large amounts of money, supposedly patriotic contributions from a group of Spanish banks and companies,[293] to a group of thirty high-ranking officials for keeping Spain from entering the war in support of the Axis powers. Among them were the Generals Aranda, Orgaz, Kindelán, Martínez Campos, and, after his dismissal as minister of foreign affairs in October 1940, Colonel Beigbeder himself.[294] Another way was Hoare's offer to provide the Spanish with solutions to the questions of Morocco and Gibraltar in exchange for neutrality, even if this meant giving up the Rock. Churchill, however, refused to discuss this issue and discounted the option immediately.[295]

Nevertheless, British policy toward Spain during the summer of 1940 was not based only, or even primarily, on the initiatives of the ambassador. Plans were made to react immediately to any Spanish attempt to enter the war on the side of the Axis powers, including offensives against the main Spanish Atlantic naval bases (Vigo, El Ferrol, and Cádiz), and the occupation of the Portuguese Azores (Operation Brisk) and cape Verde (Operation Shrapnel).[296]

THE DEFINITIVE SOLUTION TO THE TELEFÓNICA AFFAIR IN AUGUST 1940

The considerable cut in the oil supply of oil products that had begun in June 1940 and continued until the signing of the Anglo-Spanish agreement in September of the same year affected the last dispute that had been pending between the U.S. and the Franco regime since the end of the Civil War: the CTNE-ITT. The interruption of oil supply from the United States in the summer of 1940 was just what was needed to force a solution. When the first rumors about the cut in the oil supply reached Madrid in June, Franco's government innocently thought that they could use the Telefónica affair to halt it. For his part, Weddell had been quite jubilant and immediately advised the State Department to take advantage of the situation to reach an agreement. When the supply was cut off in August, he told Beigbeder that it could only be resumed if a solution was found to the Telefónica affair. Cárdenas protested to Welles in Washington[297] but the diplomatic reply was that "the ambassador merely wished to say that if the Telefónica issue were to be solved along the lines already agreed on, the relations between both governments would improve enormously and the United States government would look on Spain very favorably."[298] Welles must also have complained about the Spanish press and its constant attacks on Great Britain and the United States for their part in the problems of the oil supply since Cárdenas sent a telegram to Beigbeder saying that

> The articles published in our newspapers in favor of war, some of which are quite violent, are summarized here and give the impression that we could be entering the war at any minute. This has created considerable confusion and been extremely damaging to our commercial interests (yesterday an insurance company refused to insure a cargo of goods bound for Spain). These articles make it difficult for me to carry out the tasks entrusted despite all my efforts.

The Spanish minister agreed and, before passing the telegram on to Franco, wrote in the margin that "it may be advisable to mellow the press campaigns against England and the United States until the oil conflict is over: I sincerely believe that it would be advisable."[299]

So the department and Weddell used the oil issue to reach an agreement. And they were successful. On 19 August 1940, Weddell informed Washington[300] that after a series of conversations between Colonel Behn and Serrano Suñer the Ministry of Governance had set the date of the company's shareholders' meeting for 14 September. He also revealed that a new list of North American managers to replace those who had fallen victim to the process of political clearance had been approved and that Fred Caldwell would be appointed executive vice president, which was a personal triumph for Weddell and his persistence. In response to these concessions, he asked the department to authorize him to make an official communication to the Spanish Ministry of Foreign Affairs that the U.S. government would not stand in the way of any sales of gasoline to Spain as long as they acquired the British navicerts and were shipped in vessels that did not fly the U.S. flag. He also recommended:

> that no reference be made on this occasion to the satisfactory solution of the telephone company case for the reason that this would inevitably be construed as an admitted return on our part for Spanish concessions in connection with this American property. The fact that gasoline suddenly became available without explanation will perhaps be sufficient to convince the Spanish authorities that we are only prepared to deal generously with them when American rights and interests are respected.[301]

Weddell also assured that, as the United Kingdom already had a representative of the Ministry of Economic Warfare in Spain checking oil supplies in order to prepare the Oil Agreement, it would be impossible for the Spanish to acquire an excess of *navicerts*. With respect to other products that Spain was interested in acquiring from the United States, such as corn and cotton, he recommended that Spain should be made to repeat their request for supplies. He no longer trusted the good faith of the Francoists and he realized that they would only bow to pressure. Secretary Hull's answer on 30 August authorized him to make the official communication and congratulated him on behalf of ITT in New York for having successfully resolved the

Telefónica issue. Hull also informed him that regular gasoline was once again being shipped to Spain.[302] The fuel was flowing, then, subject to the quota established in the Anglo-Spanish agreement.

Thus ended a problematical period that had soured the relations between Spain and the United States since the final stages of the Spanish Civil War. So there was now a glimmer of hope that these relations could be improved, although little was to happen until more than a year later, shortly before Pearl Harbor. Finally, we should mention that the Francoists had not abandoned their hopes of nationalizing the CTNE and in October 1940 they examined a proposal that a Bulgarian representative had conveyed to Cárdenas immediately after the Telefónica agreement had been reached. It was essentially an offer to secretly finance the purchase of the Company's stock for the Spanish state and was based on ITT's very real dissatisfaction that the company could not get its profit out of Spain or convert it into dollars. Although the offer was not accepted, the Ministries of the Treasury and Foreign Affairs at least took the trouble to examine it.[303] The dissatisfaction of both Franco's government and ITT itself—as we shall see in the next chapter—was made evident in April 1941 when Colonel Behn expressed an interest in selling the company. However, he had to wait until 1945 and the end of the twenty-year concession that ITT had been granted on 25 August 1924 before the CTNE was bought from ITT and became fully Spanish. Strangely enough, the operation with the Ministry of Industry and Commerce was negotiated by Fred Caldwell, ITT's vice president.[304]

CHAPTER 4

THE SECOND STAGE OF ALEXANDER W. WEDDELL'S EMBASSY (AUGUST 1940– MARCH 1942)

THE RELATIONS BETWEEN THE UNITED STATES OF AMERICA and Franco's Spain in the period we are discussing here were one more expression of the general U.S. policy to support the United Kingdom. In many respects, the Americans were pulled along by the British and it was not until shortly before Pearl Harbor that Washington designed a specific policy based on U.S. interests. But despite their desire to cooperate with the United Kingdom, their relations with Spain were complicated and controversial. Washington was suspicious of a country that they believed to be in cahoots with the Axis powers (although Spain was still not prepared to take the step of entering the war). This suspicion was fueled by the trips made by Franco and Serrano Suñer to speak with Hitler and Mussolini, Spain's more aggressive and fascistized policy of Hispanicity toward Spanish America now that Serrano Suñer was minister of foreign affairs, Franco's policy of repression and his declarations of friendship with Germany and Italy, and the hostility displayed by Franco's leaders—particularly Serrano Suñer—and the Spanish press toward the democracies and the United States.

U.S. public opinion, on the other hand, proved to be receptive to the anti-Francoist news published in many of the newspapers. In addition to describing what Franco's leaders were doing, the papers immediately published the antidemocracy and anti–United States declarations of the Francoists and sometimes the news was erroneous, exaggerated, and/or sensationalist. The only dissenting voice within the Roosevelt administration at this time was that of the Madrid Embassy, which was attempting to convince the United States to support General Franco, who they believed was resisting Hitler's pressure to enter the war.

However, the fact that U.S. supplies were reaching Spain was not so much because of the efforts of Ambassador Weddell and his staff, but rather thanks to Britain—another country—pressurizing Washington. The arrival of the supplies, however, was not constant: it fluctuated in response to the political and military consequences of British policy, the activity of Franco's government (e.g., Franco's speech on 17 July 1941), or the conflicts and disagreements between the United States and Spain.

In March 1941 everything seemed to suggest that the two countries were about to enter into a trade agreement and it is for this reason that this chapter has been subdivided into the periods before and after this date. Nevertheless, it only seemed this way: new problems arose when Serrano Suñer and Franco again considered the possibility of Spain's entering the war in support of the Axis powers. These problems were resolved only shortly before Pearl Harbor. In March 1942, as a result of the rearmament of the United States and the country's entry into the Second World War, a trade agreement was finally reached. It was at this point, for the first time since 1939, that the United States drafted its own, coordinated policy, which partially coincided with British policy but did not depend on it. In Madrid, however, there was to be a new ambassador who would be entrusted with implementing it. Weddell had been disillusioned by the extremely difficult period he had had to struggle through and his own mistakes, and he was relieved of his duties in March 1942.

From August 1940 to March 1941

At the end of August 1940, once the Telefónica affair had been satisfactorily resolved, everything seemed to suggest that the time was ripe for the Unites States and Spain to start negotiating a trade agreement. From the Spanish viewpoint, the economic prospects for the winter were far from good and the need to obtain provisions from abroad was greater than ever. Despite the agreements signed in March and September with Great Britain, and the ones that were to be signed in the following November and December, Spain still needed to resort to Argentina and the United States because of increasingly severe food shortages (particularly wheat). The oil supply seemed to have been ensured, although it still depended on the quotas that continually had to be negotiated with Great Britain in order to obtain the prized navicerts.

The United States and Spain during Franco's and Serrano Suñer's Negotiations with Germany to Enter the War in September and October 1940

At the same time as Franco was anxious to negotiate with Washington, however, he was also preparing the country for war and attempting to obtain many of the supplies that Spain needed from Germany. Serrano Suñer, Von Ribbentrop, and Hitler dealt with these issues for the first time in September 1940. Spain, then, was playing a double game in an attempt to acquire all the supplies it needed and to extend its empire by entering the war, which after the defeat of France and at the height of the Battle of Britain seemed to be nearing its end. In view of the activity of the regime's leaders during September and October 1940 it is difficult to accept that the lack of oil since August was dissuading them from making plans for war. As early as the beginning of July, Serrano Suñer had wanted to travel to Germany but the Germans were not interested. By the beginning of August, however, they were. Hitler had just planned his attack on the USSR for May 1941 and he wanted to make sure that northwest

Africa was safe from a future U.S. or British attack, and put an end to the base in Gibraltar. He had paid little attention to Spain's offer to enter the war in the middle of the previous June because he believed that if he granted their territorial demands the collaborationist Vichy government, whom he was relying on to defend the region, would turn against him. But when Vichy refused to allow him to use their bases in the French Protectorate of Morocco on 19 and 20 July he reconsidered Franco's offer. He was aware that having Spain as an ally would be a considerable economic burden but he was prepared to pay the price. What is more, in exchange for Gibraltar, Tangier, all Morocco, and the Algerian district of Oran, Hitler hoped to gain large mining concessions in the protectorate, military bases on the North African Atlantic coast and two Spanish islands: one of the Canary Islands and Fernando Poo in the Gulf of Guinea. The Spanish leaders were aware of none of this at that time although they did see a change in Germany's attitude and, in August, the negotiation of the economic aspects began. On 15 of the month, Franco wrote to Mussolini asking for support in his African demands. And he reaffirmed that Spain would enter the war if his economic, military, and territorial demands were granted. This was the background to the trip that Franco's right-hand man Serrano Suñer, not the Minister of Foreign Affairs Beigbeder, was to begin on 13 September and which was to take him to Germany and Italy for more than two weeks so that he could meet with these countries' leaders.[1]

Neither Washington nor Madrid was aware of Spain's interest in entering the war or of Franco's and Serrano's maneuvers to reach an agreement to this end. On 28 August Weddell[2] wrote to President Roosevelt from Zarauz, a town on the Basque coast that had used to be the summer residence of the royal family and was still popular with the nobility and the wealthy. He once again pointed out what he believed about Franco and the world war, and the difference of opinions among the Francoists in this respect. He said:

> The situation here shows no significant changes in recent weeks. I sincerely believe that Franco wishes to keep his country out of European conflict; and equally, I think his desire is shared by the military elements in the Cabinet; not so by Phalangist leaders, who are doubtless obsessed by belief in Germany's eventual overwhelming victory.

For the ambassador, the threat was not only Serrano and his Falangist henchmen: he was also concerned about possible German pressure. On this issue, he said:

> There can be no doubt that Hitler, who paid the piper in the Spanish Civil War, possesses the power to call the tune, and that the reason this country yet remains outside the conflict is because Germany does not now wish its entry. However, a sharp reverse in the attack on England may alter Hitler's present attitude and induce in him the desire to add Spain to the Axis powers.

In his analysis of the consequences of a possible Spanish entry into the war, Weddell pointed out the need to block the Straits and openly use the peninsular ports. He also said that

> With such a devoutly Roman Catholic country as an ally the charge of anti-Roman Catholicism, if not of anti-religion, brought against Germany by certain elements,

and which has a powerful effect among the Faithful, would be silenced. (...) The Spanish press has recently played up strongly the alleged loyal support of Hitler's cause by German Catholic bishops and has also given wide publicity to the gift to Spain by the German Catholic churches of a large quantity of religious art objects.

However, he also pointed out that there were numerous internal factors against Spain's entering the war;

Further militating against war, which the people dread, is the fact that the actual Government certainly does not represent the majority, although many of its opponents by no means would like to return to a Republic. There are many things that indicate that the reestablishment of the Monarchy would more nearly meet the situation; there is much talk recently indicating that Franco would be willing to accept as king the infant grandson of Alfonso XIII [a mistaken reference to the young son of King Don Juan de Borbón Battenberg, who was the Alfonsino monarchists' candidate to occupy the throne once Alfonso XIII had officially announced him to be the heir, which he was to do shortly afterwards, on 15 January 1941], Franco then to become Regent.

He also added:

Although my knowledge of the Almanach de Gotha is limited, I believe the infant in question unites in himself both the Carlist and what might be called the Legitimist branches, and hence a heretofore powerful disruptive force is removed. But this possible solution is not viewed with favor by the monarchist group, it is said.

Neither was it favorable that

There seems to be still between two and three hundred thousand so-called political prisoners in Spanish jails, whose families and friends bitterly resent this; and while a certain number of these are being released,[3] the processes of the military tribunals which attempt to pass upon each case are heartbreakingly slow.

What Weddell believed to be crucial for Spain was the economic agreement with the United Status, which would put Franco in a stronger position and enable him to keep Spain out of the war despite the pressure exerted by the Axis. This policy tied in with the policy of the State Department—led by Sumner Welles—to reinforce the more moderate of Franco's ministers who were against intervention and Serrano Suñer. Thus, at the beginning of September, when Weddell was ordered by the Ministry of Trade and Industry to initiate trade negotiations between the two countries, he set to work immediately, determined that they should be fruitful.

In the first stages of the talks, the Spanish government employees told him about the catastrophic economic situation:[4] the wheat harvest in the summer of 1940 had been much lower than expected and a deficit of 1,300,000 tons was anticipated. To alleviate the situation, 200,000 tons of wheat had been purchased from Australia, but the amount was insufficient and the distance from the supplier a problem. He was not told, however, that at the end of July Spain had imported a further 500,000 tons from Argentina.[5] To redress this and other shortcomings, they now attempted to acquire a loan from the United States of 100,000 dollars, considerably less than the 150–200 million they had requested the previous May, probably because of the deteriorating economic situation. Of the 100 million dollars, they planned to spend a total of 70 on wheat (22 million), gasoline (20 million), cotton (20 million), and other essential products such as scrap iron and cork. They proposed to make the repayments over twenty years by sending batches of olive oil to the value of five million dollars per year.

Weddell was convinced by the proposal and immediately sent a favorable report to the State Department. It is worth taking a look at the arguments he used, not only to see the foundations of his strategy but also to see how completely he had been taken in by Franco and Serrano and their intentions with respect to the World War. He said that[6]

> In considering the whole matter it is becoming more evident that internal conditions in Spain are rapidly approaching a most dangerous stage and that the only points from which relief can be expected are either from the sterling area or from the United States. It is also becoming more evident that *the present Government in Spain is endeavoring to resist pressure to enter the war and that they will probably continue to do so unless and until Axis pressure becomes so strong as to force them in without regard to they own desires.* It is also believed that the time element is of great importance and that every month that Spain remains out of the war strengthens the possibility that with a change in the current of events the present Spanish resolution to maintain the country's attitude of at least "non belligerency" may be progressively fortified. (Italics mine)

He also added:

> Unless some relief particularly in the way of foodstuffs is forthcoming from some quarter, conditions may be expected to become so chaotic that internal uprisings in Spain will become a distinct possibility with the result that the present regime, which appears to be steadily more inclined against entering the war, may either be forced to accept complete Axis domination or be supplanted by other elements who might seize any opportunity to relieve themselves of internal dissatisfaction by a foreign adventure however hazardous to the future of Spain.

That is to say, Weddell was unaware that Franco was interested in negotiating Spain's support of Germany in exchange for the longed for North African empire and supplies; in fact he believed that Germany was a great danger to Spain. Therefore, the Spanish government, which was determined to remain neutral, needed to be reinforced. If this was not done by means of economic aid, the situation could degenerate into chaos and the government could be forced to change its attitude and join the Axis. Although he did not mention him by name, the specter of Serrano—allegedly the man behind the warmongering—was present. Weddell, then, believed that it was time to help and he recommended that the loan be extended. According to him, the possible "intangible" (political) benefits of the operation were enormous and, although 100 million dolars was not an inconsiderable sum "its influence upon the future course of Spain's foreign policy might be well worth the investment even if repayment were delayed over a considerable period of years." To reinforce his recommendation he added that he had just been told by Sir Samuel Hoare that Great Britain had decided to give a substantial amount of aid to Spain. This aid soon materialized in the form of new agreements between the two countries. The British objective was for Spain to persist in its attitude of nonparticipation in the war at least for a few more months.

The first reaction to his recommendation reached him almost two weeks later and came directly from Secretary Hull.[7] It was, however, not at all what he had been expecting. In the first place, in view of recent dealings with Spain, the problems that had only recently been solved and the bad reputation that the Franco regime had in much of the country, and despite the fact that the United States was prepared to increase its economic relations with Spain "we could only justify [to the country] action if there is sufficient assurance that it would be in accordance with those general principles of international relationship for which this Government stands." These principles were free trade and respect for foreign-owned property, among others, which the Francoists had given no signs of sharing. But Hull also introduced another factor: the meetings that Serrano Suñer had had in Berlin and Rome between 13 and 27 September. Concerned about the economic impact of these talks, he felt that if Spain were to enter the war the risk of the loans not being repaid was high. And in accordance with the policy that had been adopted with Spain and expressed by Sumner Welles in May, he made it clear that guarantees had to be provided that the products purchased from the United States would not be re-exported to the Axis powers.

Hull could hardly be described as receptive but he made another suggestion: the possible sending of food as humanitarian aid. This possibility had in fact already been put forward by Weddell himself in his interview with Franco in June and had provoked a "feeble smile." He said that the president of the United States Red Cross, Norman Davis, had expressed interest in urgently shipping food to Spain and that these shipments would only be sent if guarantees were given that they would not be reexported.

Nevertheless, what Weddell was told and the heated arguments of the secretary of state apparently did not reflect the debate within the State Department, which was ended by President Roosevelt's decision to ask the Red Cross to send humanitarian aid. The debate was between Hull—encouraged by James C. Dunn, the adviser for political relations described by Eleanor Roosevelt as an ardent Francoist—who was in favor of granting the loan, and Under Secretary Sumner Welles who asked Roosevelt who was responsible for radically modifying the proposal.[8] Politically speaking, the use of the Red Cross was less awkward and it was made easier because of the proximity of its president to Roosevelt and Hull. Like Hull, he was a Democrat from Tennessee and former secretary of state with President Wilson, and he had been appointed head of the Red Cross by Roosevelt. As we shall see below, the announcement of this controversy in the press two months later was to make a decisive contribution to widening the personal rift between Hull and Welles.

In Madrid, Weddell took little notice of Hull and asked the Export-Import Bank and other government agencies exactly how much they would be prepared to loan to Spain. As a result, he received another message from Hull on 26 September. It was expressed in no uncertain terms and must have come as quite a shock. The message affirmed yet again that, before initiating any negotiations and because of the economic risk involved in a transaction with a country at war, the administration required guarantees that Spain would not be entering the world war. In particular, Hull said that "it would obviously not be possible to give consideration to the extension of credits to Spain if it appeared that that country did not intend to remain outside of the present war, since aside from any other consideration such a development would create a prohibitive credit risk."[9]

Hull and the State Department had adopted this attitude because they had perceived much more clearly than the Madrid Embassy that Spain may have been on the point of entering the world war on the side of the Axis powers. Logically, Serrano Suñer's trips[10] and his interviews with Hitler, Von Ribbentrop, Mussolini, and Ciano were the cause of some considerable concern in Washington. In this context, providing unconditional aid to the Franco regime was unacceptable, so they could not share the Madrid Embassy's attitude. And it seems that Hull, Morgenthau, Ickes, Stimson, and Knox were all in agreement. What is more, in the same message Cordell Hull ordered the ambassador to take the demand to the Minister of Foreign Affairs Beigbeder for Spain to stay out of the war.

The secretary's concern was fully justified. Despite the fact that Serrano's conversations in Berlin had not ended in an agreement to enter the war, both Spain and Germany were still showing interest and they had agreed to take a decision in a future meeting scheduled to take place between Hitler and Franco in Hendaye. In his meetings first with Ribbentrop, on the next day with Hitler and then again with the Nazi foreign minister on 16, 17, and 18 September, the Germans had provisionally accepted Serrano's military, territorial, and economic demands (which included supplying Spain with 56,000 tons of gasoline every month). The situation cooled off rapidly, however, when Serrano was informed of what Germany required in return: one of the Canary Islands and German bases in Agadir and Mogador (Atlantic ports in the French zone, which would become Spanish).

Even so, both countries were still anxious to reach an agreement, as the correspondence between Franco and Hitler in the subsequent days indicated. However, Hitler began to ponder on Spain's refusal to hand over islands or grant bases to Germany, and the effects of the failed Anglo-Gaullist attack on the Vichy-controlled French base in Dakar, Senegal, on 23 September. In the following weeks, the resistance the French troops was to affect the Fuhrer's decisions, but when he saw Serrano Suñer again on 24 September he was still thinking in terms of ceding all Morocco and Oran to Spain in exchange for an island and the bases.[11] Serrano stood his ground and returned home at the beginning of August. He was upset (in Rome he had complained to Ciano about Ribbentrop's threatening attitude[12]) but, like Franco, was anxious to reach an agreement, so they both set to work and started preparing the meeting scheduled for a few weeks' time in Hendaye. What is more, three days after Serrano's last interview, Hitler had signed the Tripartite Pact with Italy and Japan to form a common front against the United States and to prevent their intervening in the war. And, of course, to attack North Africa.

So when Hull ordered Weddell to ask the Spanish for guarantees that they would remain neutral, he knew precisely what he was doing, even though he was unaware of what had been discussed in Berlin. Weddell prepared to carry out the order and on 30 September,[13] Bucknell, Ackerman, and himself met with Beigbeder, colonel Alarcón de la Lastra the minister of industry and commerce, and Larraz the minister of the treasury, which shows how important the loan was to them. During the meeting, and in response to Weddell's demand for guarantees, Beigbeder said that it was impossible for the Spanish government to make a public statement or sign a protocol about its intentions with respect to the war, but he could promise on behalf of the cabinet that the country would not enter the conflict unless attacked. The three ministers insisted that the loan would reinforce the Spanish government's determination not to enter the war. This coincided exactly with Weddell's appreciation of the situation and he must have been delighted to hear them say so. Beigbeder explained that Serrano Suñer had gone to Germany and Italy strictly for reasons of diplomatic courtesy and that Spain had not signed the Tripartite Pact. In short, the United States had nothing to fear. He also told the ambassador that the general economic situation had worsened. According to his calculations, before the next harvest in June 1941 Spain would require 800,000 tons of wheat (he must have included the half million tons of Argentine wheat), and he confessed that the following week the bread ration was to be reduced by a third.

Sixteen days after this meeting, two of the three ministers present, Beigbeder and Alarcón de la Lastra, were dismissed and Serrano Suñer was appointed minister of foreign affairs. To what extent did the meeting influence the decision to dismiss him? As we shall see below, Beigbeder himself believed it to be the direct cause, although this does not seem likely. In any case, on the day of the meeting, 30 September, Beigbeder was no longer the warmonger he had been a few months before and was against Spain's entering the conflict. He must also have resented not having been involved in the contacts with Germany and Italy. On 27 September,[14] when Serrano Suñer was still away and only three days before the meeting with Weddell, he had made secret contact with the British Ambassador Hoare to propose measures to counteract the influence of Franco's brother-in-law.[15] This contact had led to the Serrano-controlled police to keep him under surveillance.

Be that as it may, Weddell believed the arguments of the three ministers. In the report that he sent to Hull, he said that the verbal guarantees given by Beigbeder that Spain would not enter the war were all that the United States could possibly expect and that Spain's predicament as far as the economy and food supplies were concerned was extremely serious. He proposed that the loan should be granted and that 800,000 tons of cereal be sent, followed by cotton and other materials. He made this proposal because he was "more and more convinced that it is the intense desire of these three Ministers and of the majority of the Cabinet as well as the overwhelming majority of the Spanish people to maintain their present position or at least non-belligerency."[16] It now seems feasible that he was right in the case of Beigbeder and perhaps even the other two ministers (which does not mean that they were politically liberal or prodemocracy), but he persisted in his mistaken appreciation of the attitude of Franco and that of most of his government.

Surprisingly, Beigbeder's prowar stance of the previous months had undergone a radical transformation and he was now steadfast in his determination that Spain should not enter the war in support of the Axis powers but draw closer to the United Kingdom and the United States. On 3 October 1940, when Serrano was in Rome, he saw Weddell again and told him "with the utmost gravity of manner" that "your president can change the policy of Spain and of Europe by a telegram announcing that wheat will be supplied to Spain (...) the psychological moment has arrived."[17] His request betrayed his extreme concern about the danger of entering the war, and the need for his stance to be reinforced by North American aid. Weddell interpreted this as meaning that Serrano Suñer was asserting himself, although in fact Franco, the army, and the Falange were all anxious to join the conflict, and that Beigbeder was isolated from Franco and Serrano, which was absolutely true. Weddell forwarded Beigbeder's request but, considering Serrano's recent visit to Rome, the department quite logically took no notice.

The channel that Washington continued to use was the shipment of humanitarian aid by the Red Cross, paid for by the administration. This would have the same effect on Spain's nonentry into the war and was understood by public opinion in the United States unlike the granting of a loan that would involve the Roosevelt administration with a government that had dealings with Berlin and Rome and that was making preparations for war. Hull told Weddell that the president was prepared to ask the Red Cross to ship emergency food supplies to Spain on behalf of the U.S. government but that the loan was another matter entirely and would be dealt with quite separately.[18] The conditions for providing such aid were that it would have to be publicized in the Spanish press, the North American Red Cross would be involved in the distribution, and, above all, that nothing should be reexported to other countries.[19] What is more, Weddell would have to be allowed to give Franco all the details about the aid package personally.[20]

In fact, Weddell's stance was given greater support by the British government than by the United States, largely because the British were implementing measures that were similar to his proposals, both as regards loans and supplies. The British, however, also wanted the United States to adopt a similar, coordinated policy because they could not send all the gasoline, wheat and other products that Spain needed. The British policy of providing Spain with aid had become official after Churchill's intervention in Parliament on 8 October 1940, when he had expressed the desire to respect Spanish neutrality and to send supplies on the condition that nothing would be reexported to the Axis. All this was accompanied by the promise that he would not interfere in the affairs of Spain,[21] which was a veiled message to the regime about the exiled Republicans.

It was in this context and with this objective that the British ambassador in Washington met with Hull on 7 October 1940. He agreed with the American proposal to send humanitarian aid by the Red Cross and he used the same words as Beigbeder had used with Weddell to say that "it was the psychological moment to do so."[22] He also insisted on the United States granting the loan that Spain had asked for. At the same time as this was taking place, in London a state body had been set up to make preventive purchases in Spain: that is to say, to purchase strategic material that they did not want to fall into the hands of the Axis. This strategy had the additional advantage that it provided the Spaniards with foreign currency so that they could acquire what they needed in foreign markets. The name of the company was United Kingdom Commercial Corporation, it was founded on 14 October, and it had £2 million to spend over a five-month period.[23] Taking into account the economic difficulties of the United Kingdom, then, Churchill was making a considerable effort to prevent Spain from joining the Axis.

Meanwhile, in Madrid, and in compliance with the orders received from Washington, on 8 October 1940 Weddell had an appointment with Franco,[24] who accepted each and every one of the conditions for the Red Cross to begin shipping foodstuffs to Spain. He said that the economic situation of the country was desperate because of the bad cereal harvest, the difficulties of exporting in the middle of a world war, and the shortcomings of the internal communications system caused by the Civil War. Apparently, he did not speak of the loan. Weddell left the meeting fully convinced by Franco's arguments. He thought that it was necessary not to give the impression that Spain was receiving North American charity because this would make good propaganda for the Axis, and that the humanitarian aid being provided should be presented as an agreement between heads of state. He also believed that there was no need to wound Spain's pride by insisting that the North American Red Cross supervise the distribution of the supplies once in the country. For the ambassador, the fundamental objective of the operation was to reinforce the "moderate elements of the present regime in Spain," among whom he included Franco and the three ministers with whom he had spoken previously. He even hoped to channel the aid through these ministers, thus intervening in the internal politics of Spain, a tactic that he was to repeat on other occasions although never entirely satisfactorily.

Once Franco had given his approval,[25] President Roosevelt officially requested the Red Cross to make preparations to ship the humanitarian aid to Spain, and he prepared to announce the operation simultaneously in Madrid and Washington. The announcement specified that the US government would pay all the costs of the operation in accordance with the Act of Congress of 26 June 1940 on assistance to destitute civilians as the result of hostilities abroad. On the issue of the loan, however, Roosevelt's attitude was unwavering:[26] the department informed Weddell that the political conditions that had been imposed still stood. And, meanwhile, Weddell was being pressurized by the minister of foreign affairs and the minister of industry and commerce. Beigbeder in particular was euphoric about the imminent announcement of humanitarian aid because he believed, rather innocently, that it would be a "political bombshell" in Spain. In fact he was telling Weddell how important it was, on 16 October just a few hours before he was relieved of his duties.[27] Spanish politics was clearly going in quite another direction and Beigbeder found that he was not wanted as a traveling companion.

The dismissals of Colonels Beigbeder and Alarcón de la Lastra on 16 October were connected with what we have been dealing with. Beigbeder had been sidelined in the negotiations with Germany and had been seen to be plotting with Great Britain at the last minute, but Serrano Suñer was also anxious to take over from him as minister of foreign affairs, particularly now that the interview between Franco and Hitler was scheduled for one week hence. By the time the interview took place, Serrano wanted to have been appointed minister so that he was on equal terms with Ribbentrop. Beigbeder's dismissal must also have been influenced by the fact that he had an English lover, Mrs Rosalind P. Fox, a well-known British spy. It was by no means a new problem and Franco had personally warned him about it in 1938.[28] Now, his conspiratorial activities meant that this relationship must have been seen in a new light. For his part, Beigbeder disclosed immediately after his dismissal that he and the other two ministers had been relieved of their duties as a result of the interview with Weddell and German pressure to prevent an economic agreement between Spain and the United States. According to a note from the police that was found among Franco's personal papers, Beigbeder was saying that

> He and Alarcón de la Lastra had entered into an agreement, by which the United States had agreed to send Spain 600,000 tons of wheat, which the Spanish state would pay for in the conditions that he wished, with the only condition that the Spanish press should publish a note that faithfully reflected the favorable conditions in which Spain was to acquire the cereal. When the Germans found out about the agreement (...) they forced Franco to cancel the operation that would have been so beneficial for Spain, thus creating a political crisis because they, Alarcón and Beigbeder, rebelled against the foreign imposition.[29]

It would seem, however, that Beigbeder's version does not reflect reality because the Spaniards were playing a double game in their attempts to get supplies and they were keeping Germany informed. On 10 October, for example, Serrano sent a letter to Ribbentrop informing him of Spain's attempts to reach an agreement on supplies from America.[30] In any case, Beigbeder's interpretation of events meant that he drew closer to the ambassadors of the United Kingdom and the United States and it was probably at this point that he joined the group of high-ranking Spanish military officers who were indirectly being bribed by Great Britain.

All this aside, Beigbeder's dismissal put an end to a highly unusual situation, in which a minister of foreign affairs had not acted as such on the main issue of Spanish foreign policy at the time: negotiations with the Axis powers. This was even more surprising because he knew Germany from his time as military attaché there during the Second Republic,[31] he spoke German, and he had a military career on the General Staff, which was important in negotiations about entering a war. What is more, the person entrusted with acting as the negotiator had been the minister of the interior (or minister of governance, to use the Francoist terminology) who did not know Germany or its language, but who was Franco's right-hand man and closest adviser. He was qualified, however, to negotiate with Italy, not only because of his political affinities and good personal relationship with the foreign minister, Conde Ciano, but also because he knew the country and its language well (as a young man he had done a postgraduate course in Rome).

Alarcón de la Lastra's dismissal had been influenced by Serrano Suñer's desire to promote Demetrio Carceller Segura, the businessman who had accompanied him on his trip to Germany and with whom he got on well not only because he was a former member of the Falange but also because he too had been a former friend of José Antonio Primo de Rivera. Carceller's career was impressive. He came from a humble background, and he was a self-made man in the world of Spanish oil and one of the owners of CEPSA, the only official company apart from the state monopoly CAMPSA, which worked out of the Canary Islands and the Protectorate and was the owner of the only Spanish refinery. Carceller acted with a considerable amount of duplicity in his position as foreign minister and he negotiated with the Allies and the Axis at the same time, convincing them both that he was on their side. He had done the same when, as first assistant technical manager of CAMPSA after it had been founded in 1927, he had taken advantage of a business trip in 1929 to start negotiations with a Venezuelan company and, some months later, to set up a new company, CEPSA, of which he was a shareholder. This company was to become one of CAMPSA's suppliers. Although this had obliged him to resign as assistant manager of CAMPSA in 1930, the business relationship between the two companies flourished. Throughout the Republic, Carceller had maintained his connections with the two companies, met José Antonio Primo de Rivera, and, apparently, become a member of the Falange. José Antonio himself had been impressed by his character, his daring, and his business sense, and even considered him for the post of minister of the economy when in 1935 he drew up the list of his hypothetical government. After the Civil War had broken out, he escaped from the Republican Zone and traveled to the Nationalist capital in Burgos, where he became a member of the Commission for Industry and Commerce of the Junta Técnica del Estado (State Technical Board), the first political-administrative structure created by Franco before forming his first government in January 1938. Another of the CAMPSA managers who had fled was appointed minister of the treasury.[32]

It should also be pointed out that although Serrano Suñer was now foreign minister he did not abandon his responsibilities as minister of governance. The Under Secretary Lorente Sanz—one of Serrano's men—became the de facto minister although nominally the post was Franco's responsibility. After 16 October 1940, then, Serrano's power was greater than ever. Both he and Franco attached enormous importance to the interview in Hendaye between the heads of state of Germany and Spain because this is where it would be decided whether Spain would participate in the war in exchange for the Rock of Gibraltar (one of the first military operations that the Spanish wanted to launch with the logistical support of the Germans), whether supplies would be provided and whether Spain's tiny empire in North Africa would be increased in size at the cost of the French.

Weddell's reaction to this real political bombshell of the two dismissals was naive.[33] He justified Beigbeder's dismissal by saying that it had been a foregone conclusion and fully believed that "Franco would not permit any changes in foreign policy," as he was told by a member of the Political Committee of the Falange. He was aware of the favorable comments that were circulating in Madrid about the management ability of the new Minister of Industry and Commerce Carceller, and he was concerned about the fears that Serrano's move to the Ministry of Foreign Affairs would mean an increase in German pressure for Spain to enter the war. And he passed all this information on to Hull precisely when the Spanish were trying to convince Germany to allow them to take part! His final recommendation was to continue with the same policy that they had been following: they should continue to make preparations for the Red Cross to ship the wheat and they should continue to study the possibility of granting a loan (although they should let the Spanish government take the initiative and not bring the subject up themselves).

The reaction of the British Embassy, on the other hand, was not so naive. Great Britain was negotiating new trade agreements with Spain and it was decided that the talks should be temporarily suspended until the Spanish gave guarantees that there was to be no change in their foreign policy. This prudent policy of "wait and see" had been suggested by David Eccles as Hoare was terrified and could not think straight.³⁴ London was also asked to advise the United States to stop sending supplies and even the Red Cross aid.³⁵ Nevertheless, without underestimating in the slightest how dangerous the situation was, Hoare believed that the economic situation and the food shortages were so extreme, and Franco so dependent on Great Britain and the United States that realism would win the day.³⁶ As we have already mentioned, Hoare was particularly weak at this time³⁷ and he had even asked for permission to leave Spain.³⁸ He had been feeling frightened—and to some extent justifiedly so—ever since 17 October when London had ordered the negotiators from the Ministry of Economic Warfare in Madrid to leave Spain and remain in Portugal until they received the guarantees already mentioned.³⁹

In the following days, Hoare was spurred on by the recently dismissed Beigbeder, who was so determined to conspire against the regime that it is surprising that he was not arrested. On the day before the meeting in Hendaye, he advised London to support a hypothetical military movement by the Spanish that would try to prevent German troops from entering the peninsula. This movement was particularly strong in the south of the country and Morocco, and was led by Beigbeder himself. Beigbeder had also suggested, and Hoare had agreed, that the former Republican Prime Minister Juan Negrín should be expelled from England so as not to give the impression that the operation was linked to the Republicans in exile. Hoare made this request on as many as four different occasions in November and Clement Attlee, the deputy prime minister of the British government, refused point blank.⁴⁰ Although Beigbeder's plan was studied by the military high command, it was finally shelved. As we shall see below, however, Churchill insisted that other plans be sought.

In Washington, the State Department reacted cautiously to the dismissals of the two ministers. Weddell was told to speak with Franco to find out what his attitude to the new situation was.⁴¹ He was to make it clear to the Spanish leader that the shipment of supplies by the Red Cross depended on him,⁴² but that for the moment it had been halted, not only as a result of the British request not to go ahead with the shipment but also because the two camps in the Roosevelt administration that had different views on how to deal with Franco's Spain both agreed that it was the right thing to do. Although Under Secretary Welles wrote to the president proposing to cancel the shipment of supplies after Hendaye (his exact words were "I can certainly imagine no useful purpose to be gained under the present conditions by asking the Red Cross to continue the consideration of this question"),⁴³ the Secretary of the Interior Ickes had already made his opposition to the aid packages clear on 23 October, the day he had found out about the project from Jay Allen,⁴⁴ without realizing that Franco and Hitler were speaking at that very moment in Hendaye. But this was not all. The press soon got hold of the story and in the coming weeks a considerable body of opinion came out against sending humanitarian aid.

In Madrid, Weddell was unable to get an appointment with Franco until five weeks later and the new Minister of Foreign Affairs Serrano Suñer did not receive him until 31 October, almost two weeks later. These were decisive times for Spain's expectations of a prompt entry into the war and in the days immediately before and after Hendaye both Franco and his brother-in-law were extremely busy. They had both been disappointed by the meeting with Hitler, given his change in attitude and the fact that he was reluctant to discuss territorial compensations in any detail. The Fuhrer had gone to the meeting to persuade Franco to take part in the war in exchange for receiving some unspecified territories in North Africa after the victory. He was loath to be specific for two reasons. First, he did not wish to alienate Vichy and lose their support in the defense of northeast Africa, which had proved to be so valuable in Dakar. And second because, apart from Gibraltar, he only planned to give the Spanish a small part of French Morocco, not all of it as they had demanded, and neither was he prepared to cede Oran or French Catalonia, which Serrano had been quick to lay a claim to in Berlin. Hitler was obsessed with the possibility of an Anglo-American attack on French northwest Africa and, more immediately, with the possibility that the region might defect to De Gaulle. Therefore, it was essential for Vichy to be involved in the defense of its possessions and this it would not do if some of its colonies were taken and given to Spain. As far as the United States was concerned, the recently signed Tripartite Pact meant that that its fleet would remain in the Pacific. In this context, the conquest of Gibraltar acquired particular importance, not only because it eliminated a base but also because it could be used to send German troops to North Africa should there be an attack.

Franco was extremely disappointed when he heard Hitler's plan, and particularly when it was made clear to him that he would only be provided with arms and other supplies once Spain had entered the war. He responded—surely because he had not fully understood what he had been told—with a lecture on Spain's rights in Morocco, which bored Hitler to death. The next day, Hitler explained the same plan to Pétain. Thus he was attempting to drum up support from both Spain and Vichy but without making it clear what they would get out of it, in what has become to be known as the "grand deception."[45] On the same day in Hendaye there was another meeting between the two foreign ministers in which Ribbentrop gave Serrano a document that Hitler had previously shown to Franco and that has come to be known as the Hendaye Protocol. It was six articles long and specified that Spain would enter the war (although no mention was made of when, which would be decided by an agreement between Berlin, Rome and Madrid), that Spain would sign the Tripartite Pact, that Germany would provide arms and economic aid (although no details were given), and that Gibraltar and other unspecified territories from the French empire would be Spanish, but only if France could be compensated with other territories. The talks focused on this point (article 5). Serrano complained about the preferential treatment given to France and the German minister replied that North Africa had to be prevented from turning to De Gaulle. Serrano concluded by saying that the issue of the compensations could be decided at a later date by correspondence.

Von Ribbentrop waited in Hendaye for the Spanish to sign the protocol, which they took to San Sebastián where they were to spend the night. The Spanish ambassador in Berlin, General Espinosa de los Monteros, was sent to fetch the signed document, which Franco gave him but not before he had tried to deceive the Germans. To a sentence in article 5 about the the raw materials that would be given to Germany as compensation by French Morocco he added that this part of Morocco would subsequently become a Spanish possession.[46] Franco's signature also meant that Spain was to join the Tripartite Pact although this, and of course the very existence of the protocol, was a closely guarded secret. Franco and Serrano were outraged. Franco said, "These people are intolerable. They want us to enter the war for nothing. We cannot trust them if they do not formally and categorically agree, as soon as we sign, to hand over the territories that, as I have explained, are our right."[47] They were outraged but quite prepared to carry on pressurizing to obtain the right price for entering the war. In this respect, Franco wrote a personal letter to Hitler one week after the talks, on 30 October. The German leaders, for their part, were convinced that the signature of the protocol meant that Spain was going to enter the war within a very short period of time.

The Repercussions of the Execution of the Former President of the Catalan Government, Lluís Companys Jover, and the Visit to Spain of the Reichsführer of the SS Heinrich Himmler

In Washington, suspicion about Spain's attitude grew when the United States found out about the talks at Hendaye. And if the situation was not awkward enough, it was to be further complicated by another event that took place while Weddell continued to wait for his audience with Franco. On the morning of the day before the ministerial changes—15 October 1940—the Francoists had executed by firing squad Lluís Companys Jover, the former president of the autonomous Catalan government (the Generalitat) during the Republic and the Civil War. Companys had been arrested on 13 August in German-occupied France at the request of the Spanish authorities and immediately handed over to Franco's police who were searching for exiled Republican leaders in France.[48] It was a coordinated operation in which a high-ranking official from the Ministry of Governance traveled to occupied France to help in tracking them down. Other prisoners handed over included Julián Zugazagoitia and Cipriano Rivas Cherif, brother-in-law of the former president of the Republic Manuel Azaña, who had not been located. No more prisoners were directly handed over after August because the Vichy regime had protested to the Wiesbaden Armistice Commission, arguing that it was the Vichy government that should deal with such issues after Spain had sent a request for extradition.[49] The outrage over the execution of the former president obliged Roosevelt—encouraged by his immediate family and the anti-Francoists around him—to consider taking action in favor of the refugees at the beginning of 1941 (see below) although, for legal reasons, he never got beyond the planning stage.

Nevertheless, at this time, the second half of October 1940, the reaction was somewhat cooler and focused on attempting to save the other Republican leaders handed over by the Germans from the same fate as Companys. The president and the State Department were receiving telegrams[50] asking them to intercede with Franco to prevent some of the prisoners who had just been handed over from being put to death.[51] Secretary Hull's attitude on this question was, as usual, extremely cautious and legalistic. When the president asked him for advice, he replied that he was not sure whether "it would be advisable to attempt to intercede with the Spanish Government in this matter, since it involves the treatment by that Government of its own nationals. Consequently it is not a matter in which we can claim a basic interest or present a legal justification for our action."[52] But he added, "In the event that you may feel that some action should be taken upon humanitarian grounds" they could call the Spanish ambassador and make a cautious request for clemency. Roosevelt accepted the suggestion and the following day Under Secretary Welles had an appointment with Cárdenas, who hinted that he was not on the same terms with Serrano Suñer as with Beigbeder and that the issue was a complex one. However, he said that he would try to do something about it as soon as possible.[53] Whether he did that is not very clear. Neither has any evidence been found that the Spanish authorities were approached by Weddell, who the department had asked to raise the issue more informally. Julián Zugaagoitia was executed by firing squad in Madrid on 5 November whereas Rivas' sentence was changed to thirty years' imprisonment.

There was one further, highly visible, issue connected to Hendaye that was to complicate relations with the United States: the visit that Heinrich Himmler, the Reichsführer of the SS and the German police, made to Spain between 19–24 October 1940 as part of a more general trip to oversee the security of the talks to be held in the French town. He spent some time in Madrid and in the city and province of Barcelona, including a visit to the mountain and Benedictine monastery of Montserrat, which some people have related to Wagner's *Montsalvat* and the tradition of the Holy Grail.[54] Weddell said the following about Himmler's stay in Madrid in a letter to Welles:

> When I remarked to a Spanish friend that he must be delighted at the attention being paid to this Twentieth Century Marquis de Sade, he retorted with a measure of violence that left no doubt as to his feelings. The town was beflagged to honor this infamous guest and Alba's [del Duque de Alba] sister remarked to me with some bitterness that she wondered what was left to do if they entertained a royal visitor. In several of the numerous photographs published showing the ceremonies in honor of this pervert, were to be seen an effeminate looking young man who de la Baume [the Vichy ambassador] remarked with a shudder, played the role with Himmler similar to that of the young Antinous with his master.[55]

Neither Weddell nor his government were aware that one of the main reasons for his trip was to discuss the main points of a German-Spanish plan to create a joint spy network for Latin America. The plan had been entrusted to General Faupel, the president of the Ibero-American Institute and former Nazi ambassador to Franco's Spain. Serrano suggested that Spain's contribution should be made by the new Consejo de la Hispanidad (the Hispanicity Council) that he was going to found, and Himmler agreed. However, the funds promised by Germany were not forthcoming and the plan was to come to nothing.[56]

Serrano Suñer's Statement to Weddell of Spanish Political Solidarity with the Axis and Its Political Consequences

Washington, however, was more concerned about what Franco and Hitler had discussed in Hendaye and, one week after the talks, the State Department was still on tenterhooks. Cárdenas had answered Welles's questions on 31 October but provided little of any value.[57] Neither had he been able to explain the reasons for Himmler's visit. In fact it is quite feasible that he knew very little about either of these issues given the secrecy with which Franco, Serrano, and his closest collaborators had shrouded the question of Spain's participation in the war.[58] As it happened, Weddell had also managed to get an appointment with Serrano Suñer on 31 October and what he was told created yet another problem in the relations between the United States and the Franco regime.[59]

As mentioned above, the North American ambassador had been made to wait two weeks for an appointment, which in itself was quite a political statement because the German and Italian ambassadors never had to put up with such delays. During the meeting, Serrano was cynical enough to complain about how long Weddell had taken to come to speak to him. In response, Weddell recited the long list of all his frustrated attempts to get an appointment. When Weddell asked about Spain's attitude to Germany, Italy, and the war, Serrano gave a vague yet specific answer: in his visits to Berlin and Rome he had made Spain's position clear and both countries had provided him with a "full statement of their program and aims." Therefore, he said, "he could assure me of the political solidarity of it with Germany and Italy." In an attempt to clarify things, and guided by his own theory on the matter, Weddell asked him three times whether Spain had received any pressure from the Axis to enter the war. Serrano obviously denied that Spain had received any such pressure and pointed out that relations with Germany and Italy were excellent, quite unlike the lack of cordiality that characterized relations with England and France that had supported the Spanish Republic during the Civil War. And he also made a complaint that caught the ambassador off his guard: he said that Franco was very surprised that the shipment of wheat by the Red Cross that had been agreed upon had still not arrived. Weddell replied that the plans to send the humanitarian aid had been brought to a halt during the two weeks that he had been unable to contact him (which was partly true, as we know). But he also added that, before sending the aid, the U.S. government wished to know how Spain stood in relation to the world war. To this effect he left a memorandum, which Serrano promised to look at immediately. And finally, Weddell made an official request for a meeting with Franco, in which he hoped to obtain guarantees about the future direction of Spanish foreign policy.

Unfortunately for Weddell, although the recommendations he sent to the department after the interview with Serrano were more realistic than the previous ones, the response to Serrano's arguments was categorical: the State Department literally believed his statement of political solidarity with the Axis and decided to exert direct pressure so that Spain would keep out of the war. Both the department and the anti-Franco sector of the administration agreed on this attitude. They were influenced by British policy and public opinion in the United States that, according to Hull, was "almost unanimously opposed to the undertaking by the American Red Cross" of shipping the wheat and also "to the furnishing by the Government of the United States of the funds necessary for such purpose."[60] Weddell was informed of all this by the secretary on the very day of the elections that were to give Roosevelt his third term. Thus, little notice was taken of Weddell's arguments that the Red Cross aid would "strengthen Spain to resist German pressure" and that now Spain would be encouraged "to enter the war or to permit the passage of German troops"[61] to North Africa. However, the ambassador believed that "the actual shipments to Spain should be limited to a point where such stocks can be built up leaving the hope always before them however of greater supplies in the future in the event that they remain outside the conflict." Of course, all the aid would be cancelled "immediately should a drastic change in the situation occur." Meanwhile, he recommended that trade negotiations with Spain be entered into "with more abandon that would be possible under normal circumstances with the realization that the greater part of such supplies may never reach this country."

The State Department, however, did not agree and instructed him to make no further requests to meet with Franco.[62] Were the meeting finally to take place, Weddell was told to make it clear that any shipment of wheat received from the Red Cross was to be purchased with funds of the North American government, which was totally committed to the British and their struggle against the Axis powers. These funds could not be made available if the "political solidarity" mentioned by Serrano Suñer meant that Spain would be providing the Axis with direct or indirect support in the form of naval bases or other installations. Weddell was also told to make it clear that the issue of sending food supplies had been discussed at a time that Spain had been neutral, but that Serrano Suñer seemed to be suggesting that the country had "no intention of maintaining such an attitude." The department's hard-line attitude took Weddell by surprise and he made one last, almost desperate, attempt in favor of the shipment of wheat. He pointed out that Serrano's statement about Spain's solidarity with the Axis powers[63] did not mean that he was providing the Axis powers with military bases or logistical support, and he argued the need to reinforce the stance adopted by Churchill, who had just reinitiated trade talks with Spain in the belief that in this way Spain could be prevented from making a radical change in its attitude to the war.

Of course, Weddell was mistaken: not only because the Spanish kept trying to enter the war but also because they were already secretly supporting the Axis. Italy and Spain had even signed an agreement of principles with Serrano and Carceller for strategic materials such as rubber and tin to be purchased by Spain from the British and then sold on.[64] For his part, after his conversations with Serrano, Sir Samuel Hoare was still in favor of assisting Spain and had assured Weddell that "the British position in Spain can be most strengthened by assistance particularly in the way of foodstuffs from the United States."[65] Weddell believed not only that aid should be sent but also that it should be made public immediately after his meeting with Franco, which had been set for 7 November. Therefore he needed the department to give him a response as soon as possible[66] and, because he was aware that time was short he also said that he would try "to be 'ill' until such time as I receive the Department's instructions."[67]

But the department refused to back down. Hull told Weddell in his reply[68] that public opinion in the United States was against helping a country that was executing its political enemies, including some of the leading Republicans recently captured in France, particularly because this help could directly or indirectly end up by benefiting the Axis. He reiterated that the only solution was for the Franco regime to officially state that it would continue to be neutral and that it would under no circumstances provide Germany and Italy with any support in their struggle against the United Kingdom. In the instructions that were sent for Weddell's interview with Franco, Hull told him that unless the Spanish leader

> were to find it possible to make publicly known that the policy of the Spanish Government not only does not envisage any change in the present neutral position of Spain, but also does not envisage any assistance to Germany and Italy in the war upon Great Britain, the Government of the United States could not justify the assistance which it had proposed to render to the Spanish people and to the Spanish Government

If the aid were to be sent and Spain were to enter the war, Hull said, the Roosevelt administration would be made to look pretty foolish, and would be severely and justifiably criticized. He also broached the subject of the executions of the Republicans handed over by the Germans, saying that "should your conversation with General Franco take such a course as to make it in your opinion desirable and expedient" Weddell should point out that "if the Government of the United States undertakes to render assistance of the nature proposed and undertake an act of mercy to the Spanish people in their distress," the Spanish government should also show some clemency to their prisoners, and particularly those who had recently been handed over by the Germans.[69]

In this context and with the shipment of food supplies held up in Washington, the British came to Weddell's aid. On 9 and 11 November 1940, the chargé d'affaires in Washington, Butler, visited Under Secretary Welles.[70] He said that the British policy with regard to Spain had been designed by Ambassador Hoare and he hoped that they could rely on the support of the United States. This policy, he added, had three mainstays: the urgent shipment of wheat from the United States; a future trade agreement between the United States and Spain; and the new Anglo-Spanish trade agreement that was currently being negotiated. The wheat, he said, needed to be sent at once "as famine is imminent this month and might cause General Franco's government to throw in its lot more entirely with the Axis."[71] There was no point in asking the Spanish for more guarantees than those that Franco and Serrano had already given. The British and American supplies would be thoroughly controlled, stockpiling would not be allowed, and the shipments would immediately be stopped if there were any change in Spanish foreign policy. He also said that the government of the United Kingdom agreed with Hoare that if the United States withdrew its offer to send food supplies, Spain would be forced into the arms of Germany, which would have serious consequences. As we know, this was also Weddell's point of view.

At this point in time, London and Hoare were in possession of a version of events at Hendaye that prompted them to continue with this policy.[72] As it happened, the version they had was mistaken but it led them to believe that Hitler had not accepted Spain's demands about French Morocco. This and the defeats that had been inflicted on the Italians in Albania and Greece had reinforced Franco's desire not to participate in a long war.[73] Meanwhile, the United Kingdom continued to hold economic talks with Spain but, at the same time, the military high command was preparing an "Operations Plan in Spain" in case Spain were to enter the war in support of the Axis. By 8 November, the plan had been completed and essentially aimed to make sure that Gibraltar remained in British hands and to take over the Balearic Islands, the Canary Islands, and Spanish Morocco. Finally, however, it was rejected because of its inherent complexity, although throughout November and December other plans for intervention in specific areas—Blackthorn, Grind, Sapphic, Ballast, Challenger, and Humour—were prepared.[74] The British, then, were still using the two options of the carrot and the stick in their dealings with the Franco regime, although they tended to favor the former.[75]

The possibility of providing Spain with aid, however, hit trouble when the *New York Times* began to publish news about the conversations that the Roosevelt administration and Great Britain were holding on Spain. For the first two weeks in November several newspapers reported that the administration had agreed to give Franco loans of between 100 and 260 million dollars to purchase food and gasoline in exchange for remaining neutral.[76] Secretary Hull confirmed that conversations had taken place but that nothing had been decided yet, which may suggest that British pressure was having some effect. The situation was to become even more complex on 20 December when the anti-Franco journalist Drew Pearson published an article in the *Washington Merry-Go-Round* on the differences between Hull (and Dunn) and Welles on the issue of the 100 million dollar loan that Roosevelt had resolved by proposing the involvement of the Red Cross. He had got his information from the anti-Franco elements of the cabinet and such sources close to the president as Vice President Wallace, Secretary Ickes, and Hopkins. And Sumner Welles had confirmed it all.[77] Hull not only indignantly denied that he had any differences with Welles but also, in direct contradiction with what he had said shortly before, that the loan had not even been considered. He demanded an instant rectification. Pearson could be an extremely awkward reporter and in 1938 had embarrassed Hull by revealing that the United States was selling munitions to Nazi Germany. For his part Welles was concerned about whether he would be allowed to remain in his post and so supported Hull's version by making public statements such as the following: "I think it would have been impossible for two people, over a period of eight years, to agree more consistently and thoroughly than Mr. Hull and I have done."[78] Even so, there were rumors that he was about to be sent as ambassador to London. Although this incident was particularly important because of its public significance, it was simply one of a long line of disagreements between the two leading figures of the State Department, which were not finally resolved until three years later when Welles was dismissed by the president as the result of a much thornier affair (see below).[79] As far as Spain was concerned, the result of the incident was that now, at the end of December, the loan was even less likely to be granted.

Back in November, however, and while the British Embassy and the department were beginning discussions in Washington, in Madrid Weddell continued to insist that it was a mistake to interpret Serrano's famous sentence about solidarity with the Axis literally. In an attempt to get evidence in favor of his interpretation, he went to see Franco's brother-in-law again on 11 November and asked him directly about the sentence. Serrano replied that the relation between Spain and the Axis was almost identical to that between the United States and Great Britain, with the only difference that Spain could do nothing for the Axis whereas the United States could do everything for Great Britain. It was hardly a reassuring answer, but Weddell felt that it could be useful for his purposes. In one final question, Weddell asked him whether Spain would resist a hypothetical arrival of German and Italian troops on Spanish soil. Serrano said that Spain would fight to the last man. Weddell immediately transmitted the conversation to Washington and said that he thought that the Spanish economic and political situation was so serious that he did not believe that the country could support the Axis. In particular, he said that "the impression left on me by the Minister's remarks was that 'political solidarity' with the Axis under present circumstances is a matter of sentiment and ideologies and hardly translatable into actual aid."[80] Six days later he reported that he had been unable to see Franco and that in ministerial circles it was thought to be virtually impossible for Spain to fulfill the conditions required by the United States for the food supplies to be sent (that is to say, an official statement that Spain would not support the Axis in a war).[81] The next day he wrote a personal letter to Welles in which he reaffirmed his conviction that neither Franco nor the army wanted to go to war. He said: "I think (...) as something unchanging, you might keep in mind what I consider to be the high personal character of Franco and the personal loyalty of the military member of his Government." In reference to Serrano and the Falangists, he added, "I cannot speak for others." He insisted on the importance of providing Spain not only with food supplies but also with the loan:

> The interior situation here grows steadily worse and I can only hope that help may be forthcoming from us in time to avert chaos. I believe with all my heart that—humanitarian aspects apart—it would be worth many millions to us, certainly to the British cause with which ours is associated, to keep this country neutral as long as possible. To express this in bald terms: It would pay us, I sincerely believe, to give one wheat ship if that meant holding this country to its present status for a month.[82]

He expressed this same reasoning in several personal letters that he sent at this time. For example

> Any help which we may offer would be with the idea of keeping Spain out of the conflict thereby aiding Britain, thereby aiding ourselves, and finally and incidentally, performing a humanitarian task. Our risk in any given moment is one ship-load of wheat, and it is a gamble worth taking. I am making every effort to promote the policy indicated above and in this I am working in close harmony with my British colleague.[83]

Other private letters of his reveal that he persisted in his mistaken understanding of Franco and his intentions. He not only believed that one of the "more encouraging" aspects of the Spanish situation was "the personal character of Franco and (...) his desire to save his country from the horrors of another war"[84] but also that Franco was "an ardent Roman Catholic who has been wounded in his most sacred feelings by the attitude of the Huns toward the Church." This was debatable, to say the least, given the admiration that he felt for Hitler and the limitations of his own personal Catholic faith. What most distressed Weddell, however, was the dreadful dilemma facing Spain. Despite the attitude of the U.S. press, including that of Pearson, the only way out was for the United States to send aid. Weddell wrote that

> leaving aside the question of gratitude, which may possibly be felt because of German aid in the [civil] war, the country finds itself between the anvil of actual or impending famine and the hammer of the German menace. Franco and his Generals realize that a false step on their part may release at any moment the German horde to the north of them. At the same time they equally realize that Germany cannot help them with foodstuffs. They are therefore looking to us. And I am sure you know the viewpoint of those great internationalists like Drew Pierson [sic] and Jay Allen [a reference to two well-known anti-Franco journalists]. Two battleships cost one hundred million dollars; half that sum in the shape of surplus foodstuffs might save this country, not necessarily to the British cause, but at least to the cause of neutrality with all its humanitarian implications. I am doing my very best, but am concerned about the outlook.[85]

Personally, Weddell was so overwhelmed by the situation that after he heard rumors that the president would be making changes to the diplomatic assignments after his reelection—which were subsequently proved to be false—he put himself forward as a candidate for the post of ambassador to Mexico.[86] This decision must have been influenced by the fact that he felt isolated in Europe: at that time he was the only U.S. ambassador to remain in his post, apart from those in Moscow and Ankara[87] and most of the legations were presided over by the chargés d'affaires.[88] He was still unaware that the president was about to appoint Admiral William D. Leahy as ambassador to Vichy France.[89]

Meanwhile the British had received yet another request for a loan of £2.5 million[90] and were unceasing in their attempts to get Roosevelt to change his mind. Butler visited Welles again on 19 November and asked him to withdraw the condition imposed for the sending of humanitarian aid and to initiate talks with Spain about the loan. Great Britain, he told him, had been informed by Carceller that the Spanish had no intention of making the required statement and that the Germans had offered them wheat. There was also a strong movement in the Spanish army against Serrano Suñer and "the policies which he is advocating which threaten the involvement of Spain in the war."[91] We now know that this movement was led by General Antonio Aranda, one of the army officers who was being bribed. Welles told Butler that he would inform Roosevelt of all his requests but that he doubted that the U.S. government would change their attitude until Ambassador Weddell had been received by Franco to discuss the whole business.

The Spanish generals who opposed Spain's entering the war in support of the Axis had become increasingly concerned because of Serrano's new trip to Germany. Serrano and Von Ribbentrop had been in contact since 11 November and they had agreed to meet on 18 November. The aim of the meeting was to continue negotiating and Serrano was hopeful of being given a positive response to the requests for territory and supplies that Franco had made in his letter to Hitler on 30 October. Given the importance of the encounter, Franco and Serrano had held a meeting in Madrid with the minister of the army General Varela, the minister of the navy admiral Moreno and the chief of the general staff General Vignon,[92] during which they had discussed a report from the chief of operations of the general staff of the navy, the frigate captain Luis Carrero Blanco. The report maintained that Spain should not enter the war until the Axis had taken control of the Suez Canal and this is what was decided: Spain would continue to delay until the Canal had been taken.[93]

The Serrano-Hitler interview took place on 18 November 1940 in Berchtesgaden, in the Führer's Alpine refuge. Hitler had decided that they would set the date for Spain's entry into the war and on the previous 12 November he had issued War Directive No. 18 that included Operation Felix, Germany's attack on Gibraltar. However, he came up against Serrano, who insisted on his territorial claims, his demands for supplies, his reproach that Hitler was sacrificing Spain in favor of Vichy and his new proposal to delay Spain's entry until the gateway to the eastern Mediterranean had been shut. The Führer told him that he could not agree to give him all that he was demanding in Africa at France's expense because the region would go over to De Gaulle. He even added that he would prefer Pétain to control everything and Gibraltar to remain British than for North Africa to defect to the Allies.[94] Hitler explained the urgency of the attack on Gibraltar and the need to set the date for Spain's entry into the war. Serrano prevaricated by saying that he would inform Franco and he maintained the same standpoint in his interview with Von Ribbentrop.

The Führer was not to be put off so easily and two days later Admiral Wilhelm Canaris, the head of the German military secret service, visited Franco with a proposal for Spain to enter the war on 10 January 1941.[95] Franco argued that it was impossible for Spain to enter the war in the short term given the enormous shortages of supplies and arms, and he invited him to send an economic commission to see the situation for themselves. Both Franco and Serrano were now aware of the impossibility of gaining a North African empire in the short term and their interest in entering the war had waned somewhat. All these events were taking place while food was in short supply all over the country. They did not discount entering the war in the future, as was to be seen in the following months, but the enthusiasm of June had turned into bitter disappointment.

The situation in Spain was so severe that on 19 November 1940 ambassador Weddell was again invited to talks with ministers,[96] just as he had been on 30 September with Beigbeder, Alarcón, and Larraz. On this occasion, the two ministers present were those in whom Serrano trusted absolutely: Demetrio Carceller—of Industry and Commerce—and Pedro Gamero del Castillo—minister without portfolio and vice-secretary of the party (Serrano's right-hand man and chairman of the Political Board). They both did their best to convince him that it was impossible for the Spanish government to make an official statement of its intentions as regards the war "with Germany at the frontier."[97] Weddell was unable to get any information out of them about Serrano's recent movements in Germany but was so impressed with their arguments that he asked the department once again to send aid forthwith to Spain. He dramatically wrote that "failing relief along the lines suggested I anticipate a situation approaching chaos (...) a situation which Britain is bending every effort to prevent. Withholding relief therefore might easily defeat our Government's avowed purpose of extending all possible aid to Great Britain." To overcome this impasse and what he believed would be its disastrous consequences, he suggested that it would be sufficient for Franco himself to give "personal and private assurances (...) along the lines of the public declaration."[98]

And surprising though it may seem, this time Under Secretary Welles and President Roosevelt themselves accepted Weddell's suggestion on this point.[99] The ambassador was sent new instructions authorizing him not to demand a public statement that Spain would remain neutral.[100] This change in attitude and the acceptance of possible "personal assurances" from Franco instead of a public statement had been considerably influenced by British pressure exerted at the highest level on Johnson, the chargé d'affaires in London, and on Welles and Hull in Washington.[101] Three days after his change of attitude, on 23 November 1840, Winston Churchill wrote to Roosevelt[102] about the danger of Germany controlling the Straits of Gibraltar and Great Britain's need to gain time. "Small things do not count now (...) an offer by you to dole out food month by month so long as they [the Spanish] keep out of the war might be decisive." This move by Churchill had been influenced by Sir Samuel Hoare who, on 19 November had made it clear to the cabinet that pressure on the United States needed to be increased. Two days later he had repeated his message, insisting that Spain would soon collapse and be absorbed by Germany if nobody provided economic aid. The fall of Spain, he argued, meant that Portugal would be sure to follow and the result was danger for Great Britain. All this could be prevented by providing 10 million pounds in aid: that is to say, the cost of one or two days of war. He urged that pressure on the United States should be increased and advised that the United Kingdom should act alone if the United States was not prepared to send aid to Spain. Two days later, on 23 November, the Chiefs of Staff had come out in support of Hoare's requests and in favor of sending supplies of wheat if the United States were not to respond. In particular they said: "The retention of Gibraltar as a naval base is vital to us for the rapid prosecution of the campaign against Italy, since, without the use of this base, it would not be possible for us to maintain the blockade or to pass reinforcements through the Mediterranean."[103] And, "If Sir Samuel Hoare is correct, Portugal will follow Spain. If this is so, the Germans will acquire in Lisbon a naval base, which can accommodate all classes of ships, and from which they can directly threaten the Western Patrol. They will thus be in a very favorable position for making a still further breach in the blockade."[104] On this same day, impressed by Hoare's arguments, the prime minister had written to Roosevelt. But what is most important is that, after receiving the letter from Churchill, the president agreed to send the Red Cross aid and also to negotiate possible loans and agreements with Franco.

The United Kingdom took immediate action and immediately signed two new economic agreements with Spain. The first allowed Spain to purchase wheat, phosphates, and manganese up to a value of £350,000 from French Morocco on the condition that these products would not then be reexported to the Axis. The second was known as the Anglo-Spanish Financial Agreement, which "extended to all fields and products the control mechanisms for paying with sterling pounds established in the agreement of March 1940."[105] This immediately allowed Spain to purchase 100,000 tons of Canadian wheat.[106] Despite all this activity, however, it was not enough and by the end of December Carceller was already asking the United Kingdom for more loans to pay for essential imports. These extra loans were finally granted in the following April.[107]

The Agreement to Send Humanitarian Aid to Spain by Means of the United States Red Cross

Ambassador Weddell had an interview with Franco on 29 November 1940, nine days after Roosevelt had adopted this new attitude. He went straight to the point by saying that the United States was interested in Spain's economic recovery but that, in the light of the recent contacts between Spanish and German leaders, he wished to clarify Spain's relation with the Axis. This was necessary, he added, so that his government could justify using the Red Cross to send wheat or of possibly granting loans for the purchase of raw materials in the United States.[108] Franco was most cordial throughout and he explained that Serrano first went to Germany to discuss various issues, one of which was Africa, and this meeting had given rise to the idea of a meeting with Hitler on the border. Serrano's second trip, he went on, was to clear up misunderstandings over conflicting statements made by Ribbentrop to the ambassador in Berlin and Pierre Laval, vice president of the Vichy government, to the Spanish ambassador in Paris. He gave no further details. Weddell asked him whether he had signed the Tripartite Pact, to which Franco lied and said he had not, adding that it did not affect Spain and that it was a "pact of peace." Weddell then went on to justify the aid policy that the United States was implementing with Great Britain and insisted once again on the need of a democratic country such as his to justify any aid provided to Spain in the eyes of public opinion. Franco said that it seemed to him that the U.S. policy was directed by the belief that Great Britain would win the war while he believed the opposite. He also believed that the war would be a long one. And he made particular reference to Spain's gratitude to Germany and Italy for their support in his victory over the "red" regime and the fact that "Germany had some 250 idle divisions, a considerable number of which (...) were on the Spanish frontier 'through no fault of Spain.'" His conclusion was that "no one can foretell the future."[109]

When Weddell spoke of the need for the two heads of state to reach an agreement with personal and private guarantees, he assented and, considering everything that he was concealing, cynically added that "it would be impossible for him to deceive a man such as President Roosevelt." At this point the ambassador asked him whether he could inform his government that Spain was not considering any change in its international attitude or any sort of support to the Axis. Franco replied that this was so, but was quick to point out that "Spain could not help the Axis Powers if it wished and that no one could foresee what the future might bring forth." Quite satisfied with the guarantees that he had been given, Weddell told him that he would inform his government of the conversation forthwith.

The conclusions that he drew were that neither Franco nor Serrano Suñer believed in an Axis victory any longer. We now know that this was partly true and that the enthusiasm of the previous June had waned because of their frustrating attempts to get territorial compensation from Hitler or, at least, a written commitment that compensation would be forthcoming once the conflict had terminated. We also know, however, that this did not mean that they had stopped considering entering the war in support of the Axis at a future date. The ambassador had also been convinced that, as far as statements and assurances about Spain's attitude, it would be difficult to get more out of Franco, and that what had been said met the department's conditions, so he advised that they be accepted.[110]

Nevertheless, Franco had felt personally offended by Weddell during their interview. A few months later, he told the British Ambassador Hoare that Weddell had said "monstruous things,"[111] surely a reference to his insistence on prodemocratic statements and his tone. Weddell seemed to have this effect on the most important leaders of the regime because he managed to end up by offending them both. This was particularly unfortunate for Weddell because he felt a real fondness for Franco. Everything seems to suggest, however, that from this point on Franco felt resentful toward the ambassador. This personal dislike, on top of the dislike he felt for the United States, was to rear its head in a speech he made on 17 July 1941 that was to have a profound impact on the relations between the two countries (see below).

Three days after the interview, on 2 December, Weddell had an appointment with Serrano Suñer, who now seemed to be overwhelmed by the severity of the food shortages and who told the ambassador that some bakeries in Madrid had been put under police protection to prevent them from being overrun by the starving populace.[112] According to Serrano, Spain now needed a million tons of wheat, and he pleaded for aid to be sent immediately, promising that any conditions set by the U.S. government would be met. At that time, the conditions for providing free wheat were that Spain should make a public statement about the aid received, distribution within Spain would be supervised, and that guarantees would have to be given that the wheat would not be reexported. The food shortages were undoubtedly extremely severe and it is significant that the winter of 1940–1941 is still referred to today as "The Year of Hunger."

On the next day, after receiving the required assurances from Serrano[113] and in the light of the severity of the situation, Weddell recommended that when the shipment of wheat by the Red Cross was announced simultaneously in Washington and Madrid, it should also be announced that trade talks were about to begin.[114] In a private letter to Under Secretary Welles he showed his satisfaction by saying that "things here came yesterday to what I hope is a happy climax when I received around midnight the Foreign Minister's note meeting the conditions of non-exportation, publicity, and supervision in the matter of the Red Cross wheat." He also expressed his personal involvement in the problem by adding that "My sympathies, and what I believe to be the practical side of my nature, are deeply engaged in the matter of relief to Spain. The situation here is really desperate. With all the official advantages that I possess, house-keeping is difficult and for the great mass of poverty-stricken folk suffering is very great." The main reason for sending the letter, however, was to insist on his recommendation for a loan and an economic agreement: "This humanitarian aspect apart, however, I cannot but believe that it is and will be worth millions of dollars to us if we can hold Spain to neutrality. And very surely if she reaches a starvation point we will see the Boches in here restoring order."[115] Just four days later he insisted again, this time by telephoning the department[116] and asking specific questions about

> what preparations have been made for the shipment of Red Cross wheat to Spain and what quantity is to be shipped; when may the announcing concerning the shipment of

Red Cross wheat be made; when may the announcement of intentions of negotiations concerning credits be made; what steps have been taken with a view to negotiations of credit; what is the probable amount of the credits being considered; has a decision been reached as to where the negotiations are to take place.

He summarized his analysis of Spain's economic situation in four points:

1. It is daily more evident that Spain is marching toward a crisis, more especially in the matter of food supplies. Basic industries are also suffering intensely from lack of raw materials while the transportation problem is acute because of depleted gasoline reserves and limited rolling stock.
2. It is not difficult to envisage a situation in which internal disorders may break on a large scale and although it is believed that the generals and the army are loyal, such events might offer the pretext for Germany to enter "to restore order."
3. Viewed from Madrid it would be not appear to be the present policy of Germany to violate this country's neutrality, for to do so it would be necessary not alone to bring its military equipment, but, as well, its gasoline and its food, no substantial body of men could live in the country.
4. Supposing the existence of, or anticipating, a far worse interior condition, Spain might easily embark on an African adventure, nourished only alone by the hope of securing food but also to fulfill the constantly manifest territorial ambitions of the present administration.

On the basis of these four points he made the following recommendations "for prompt consideration...of favorable action by our Government":

a) The declared wheat needs of Spain until the next harvest have been roughly estimated by the Government between 700.000 to a million tons.
b) It is manifest that one or two or three shipments of wheat or flour would be only palliatives of the present situation although the announcement of shipments would certainly tend to strengthen the Government's hands.
c) It is therefore evident that a prompt granting of credits by our Government and the supplying of articles made available thereunder, are essential to the maintenance of Spanish neutrality.
d) Considered in baldest terms, and leaving aside the obvious humanitarian aspects of aid to Spain, the question our Administration should ask itself is whether in view of the present world situation, the neutrality of Spain is not worth the cost of a few destroyers or less the cost of a battleship.

This country is at the parting of the ways. In our best interest it is again urged that prompt relief be extended.[117]

Washington, however, did not want to move so quickly. Therefore, a memorandum that the State Department submitted to the president and that was approved by him on 16 December 1940[118] stated that the United States of America had been informed that Great Britain had granted a loan to Spain for the purchase of Canadian and Argentine wheat and that once it had been publicly announced, the first of two or three shipments of wheat would be sent through the Red Cross. The possibility of granting loans, however, again depended on compliance with certain political and economic requirements. In particular, the following four:

> The first (...) that Spain intended to remain outside the war (...). The second (...), formal recognition by the Spanish Government of the validity of the claims of private American creditors for payment of blocking accounts owing them in Spain. The third (...) equality of opportunity and fair treatment of American citizens and firms doing business in Spain. The fourth (...), cessation of press attacks and other manifestations of hostility toward the United States in Spain and, through Spanish sources, in the Spanish-speaking countries in this hemisphere.[119]

This last point had been the object of a long previous communication from Secretary Hull to Weddell, which we shall study in greater detail below and which is fundamental for an understanding of the department's standpoint.[120]

THE SETTING UP OF THE HISPANICITY COUNCIL ON 2 NOVEMBER 1940 AND ITS EFFECTS ON U.S. POLITICS

After his appointment as foreign minister, Serrano Suñer had caused a considerable stir in the State Department with the policy he adopted toward the former Spanish colonies. Just four days before his appointment, on 12 October, Serrano had taken advantage of the celebrations of Hispanicity Day (or the Day of the Race) to make an aggressive speech against Great Britain and the United States in which he had alluded to the disappearance of the British empire and the decadence of Yankee power. He declared that the time would soon be ripe for *Hispanidad*. The following 2 November, he created a new advisory body that depended on his ministry: the Hispanicity Council.[121] As its chancellor, he appointed Manuel Halcón, who up to that time had been the director of the Academy of Fine Arts in Rome. The council's function was to centralize Spanish policy toward Spanish America and the Philippines, and to make Spain the representative of the New Europe that would arise out of the Axis victory. Thus, the (alleged) privileged ascendency of the Mother Country over its former colonies would be restored. With this policy, the regime was also attempting to gain another trump card to be used in its negotiations for colonial extensions with Germany, since Spain would be the leader of twenty Hispano-American nations.

Of course the council's activity was directed against the United States of America and its successful Pan-American policy, and its main aim was to break the "united American front." Two of the issues that Francoist propaganda was to use were the Destroyers-for-Bases Deal and the alleged advances that U.S. imperialism was making in the Western Hemisphere. The reality, however, was that Serrano's policy of Hispanicity was always severely limited because of budget problems and it essentially became an instrument of political and cultural propaganda. Contrary to popular belief in the United States and Great Britain, there was no coordination with the ad hoc policies of Nazi Germany and Fascist Italy. Neither was the joint spy service planned with Germany ever put into practice, although after Pearl Harbor, Serrano did set up a Hispano-Japanese spy service in America.[122]

What the Hispanicity Council and, in general, Franco's policy did manage to achieve was the immediate adverse reaction of the United States and the United Kingdom. In the same communication from Hull to Weddell that we have mentioned above, the ambassador was ordered to express the U.S. government's concern for what was happening and he was told in the strictest confidence that the Spanish and Germans were thought to have reached an agreement on propaganda issues for Latin America. This was contained in a State Department report of 25 November entitled "Spain as an Instrument for Axis Penetration into Hispano-American Countries" that revealed proof of the existence of Axis plans to use Spain as a channel of antidemocratic, antitotalitarian, and anti-U.S. influence, and measures had been proposed and approved for controlling and countering the activities of the Falange's Foreign Service in the Western Hemisphere and the Philippines. British directives, on the other hand, were more selective in their scope and differentiated between Francoist propaganda that propagated Nazi propaganda, which had to be combated, and merely cultural propaganda.[123]

THE REPERCUSSIONS OF THE TANGIER IMBROGLIO

All this was going on at the same time as what Denis Smyth has referred to as the Tangier Imbroglio, an explosive situation that temporarily affected the dealings between the two countries. On 3 November 1940, Spanish troops entered the city of Tangier and its International Zone, did away with the Committee of Control, the Legislative Assembly, and the Mixed Bureau of Information of the Zone, and, in so doing, sparked off a crisis in Hispano-British relations. All the bodies mentioned above were administered by the powers that had signed the convention in 1923 and the agreement in 1928: that is to say, Great Britain, France, Holland, Portugal, Italy, Sweden, and Belgium.

Britain's first reaction to the annexation was conciliatory and Sir Samuel Hoare simply presented a note of protest. In the subsequent weeks, however, complications arose and questions were asked in the House of Commons. In the middle of the controversy, news arrived of two Italian submarines that had sought shelter in the port of Tangier in their attempts to flee from the British fleet and of a crowd of Italian residents who, on 3 December, had laid siege to the British post office and the business premises of a British national.[124] All these events were given ample coverage in the British press just when the British government was interested above all else in sending supplies to Spain and had just signed the two agreements of 29 November and 2 December (see above). On 4 December, the Foreign Secretary Lord Halifax instructed Ambassador Hoare to officially request Spain to withdraw the decree of annexation and begin talks.[125]

Sir Samuel did what he had been asked, somewhat unwillingly, but the atmosphere in Great Britain was becoming more and more tense, with further questions in the Commons and articles in the press. Spain was acting with total impunity and, despite the assurances that Serrano had given Hoare, on 13 December the British officials of the International Administration were fired. To make matters worse, the two Italian submarines that had entered the port were allowed to leave without being detained. That is to say, Spain breached International Law on two further occasions.

In London, the Tangier incident made Churchill fear that Hitler was behind the Spanish annexation and was considering making a move in North Africa to counter the Italian failures in Egypt.[126] So he reacted quickly and forcefully. First, at the proposal of Halifax, he suspended economic relations with Spain. And second, on 14 December 1940, he reactivated the Brisk and Shrapnel[127] operations so that Britain could respond to what he believed to be the more than likely movement of German troops in the direction of the Iberian Peninsula, Gibraltar, and Spanish-French North Africa. However, he was mistaken. The annexation was not the preliminary stage of a German invasion: it was merely a step taken by Franco (in fact the only one to be taken throughout the war), who was attempting to lay his hands on the longed-for North African empire that Hitler was taking so long to provide for him.

In Madrid, Hoare was horrified by what his government was doing[128] and he feared that the whole strategy that he had played such a leading role in defining and implementing would come to nothing. This was particularly galling because he rightly believed[129] that what had happened in Tangier was an annexation: nothing more and nothing less. In fact, the situation deteriorated for him when on 23 December 1940 Lord Halifax was replaced by Anthony Eden, the Conservative anti-appeaser who had resigned as the foreign secretary after losing out to Chamberlain and Halifax in 1938. To make matters worse, he was one of Sir Samuel's political enemies.

The Tangier Imbroglio was to last until February 1941. Convinced by his visit to the naval attaché in Madrid, captain Hillgarth, and secret service reports on Admiral Canaris's trip to Spain that Franco was not going to enter the war for the time being, Churchill told Eden that it was no longer worth keeping the pressure on Spain and he allowed some of the vessels transporting the Canadian wheat to set sail for Spain.[130] Although Great Britain continued to protest, an agreement reached on 22 February provisionally recognized the Spanish occupation in exchange for guarantees on British political, economic, and legal interests in the city and the International Zone.[131]

THE START OF THE RED CROSS SHIPMENTS

The situation in Tangier was particularly annoying to Ambassador Weddell because it halted not only British supplies to Spain but also those of the U.S. Red Cross. In his view also, it revealed the excessive dependence of the State Department on British policy. On 20 December he impatiently asked Secretary Hull to send aid to Spain without waiting for the incident to be resolved. He complained that the delay was putting the United States "in the position of bringing pressure merely in support of British interests in Tangier which are unrelated to our fundamental aim of keeping Spain out of the war."[132] He also believed that "too close linking of our relief efforts with those of the British may also have the effect of lessening emphasis on our independent contribution to the economic rehabilitation of Spain and this may be important from the point of view of subsequent credit negotiations."[133] The secretary of state, however, paid no heed to his suggestions or his complaints[134] and stressed that the U.S. humanitarian aid was part of the general policy of collaboration with Great Britain. If Churchill had brought a halt to negotiations as a result of Spain's recent pro-Axis attitude, how could the United States justify the shipments? To Weddell's argument of excessive dependence on Britain, Hull reminded him that a few months earlier the United States had decided to provide Spain with supplies—in preparation of a subsequent trade agreement—and that Spain had responded by drawing closer to the Axis.

The secretary also mentioned another issue that was not helping to speed up the shipments: the department had included the aid to Spain in a general package for European countries that were not participating in the war, among which was Vichy France so that French children could be provided with milk.[135] This inclusion of France was raising problems with London but was essential for Washington because of the political problems involved in any sort of support for Franco. He wrote, "You have no idea of the difficulties we are facing in connection with the whole food relief problem by reason of the terrific criticism of our preparing to send relief to Spain without at the same time sending milk to children and babies, especially in unoccupied France."[136]

To get round the problem the State Department advised the president to send a message to Churchill. This he did on 31 December 1940, arguing in favor of sending milk for babies and vitamins for children in Vichy. He said:

> If Spain is given assistance and this Government is not able to send even milk for the relief of the children in unoccupied France, the distinction made between the two countries by this Government would, in my judgement, help to weaken the resistance of the Vichy Government to the pressure now being exercised upon that Government by Germany.[137]

After reading the letter, Churchill agreed to the shipments[138] and on 7 January 1941 the U.S. Red Cross announced the shipment of humanitarian aid to Spain and France.[139] Despite his annoyance at the United States' subordination to Great Britain,[140] Weddell now felt relieved. A few days before he had written the following to a relation of his in Richmond:

> As you may have learned from the newspapers, I am keeping very busy over the general question of trying to find a means to feed the civilian population and at the same time to do nothing which could help the Boche cause. Practically since September I have been engrossed with this and at least three times have been on the point of really accomplishing something and then some stupid action from the part of this Government delays everything.[141]

Deadlock over the Loan for Purchasing Raw Materials in the United States and the Franco-Mussolini Interview in Bordighera on 12 February 1941

The aid that was just beginning to be sent, however, consisted exclusively of wheat. However, there was not enough of it to cover all of Spain's requirements and the country still needed gasoline, cotton, fertilizers, and other essential products, which it hoped to purchase with the 100-million dollar loan it had requested from the United States. The fact that the Tangier Imbroglio had lasted until February 1941 had made things much worse for Britain. It was in this context that Ambassador Weddell took a further step in the demands he was making on Washington and on

29 January 1941 he asked Cordell Hull and Sumner Welles[142] to start sending much larger shipments. In his opinion, this was urgent and should take precedence over the loan negotiations. Direct offers of food should be made with the only conditions that the country should remain neutral and that the supply would be cut off if Spain were to enter the war alongside Germany or if Germany occupied Spanish territory. He believed that Spain might embark on a "mad adventure" in French North Africa in an attempt to acquire food and satisfy its territorial ambitions. To counter the arguments of all those in the United States who were highly critical of any program of relief for Spain, he explained to the department that this was not appeasement. On the contrary, it was

> A calculated policy of supporting the Spanish Government to resist German pressure in its efforts to continue as a nonbelligerent and to create a popular attitude likely to provoke at least passive resistance should the Germans invade, equally realizing that the value of say half a million tons of wheat –the minimum need of this country until the next harvest- would be less than a fourth of the cost of a battleship.[143]

It was certainly true that the situation in Spain had deteriorated and, as Franco was to say to Mussolini two weeks later, "There are still five months before the next harvest and in Spain there is only enough wheat for a few days."[144]

In Washington, however, neither the department nor the president himself saw things in this light. And events seemed to be proving them right because the Francoist leaders not only persisted in their aggressive policies against the United States and Great Britain but also continued to make worrying moves. On 12 and 13 February, for example, Franco and Serrano Suñer traveled to the Italian town of Bordighera (close to the French border and Monaco) for a meeting with Mussolini. This was one of the very few times that Franco was to go abroad in his political life and came about as the result of Hitler asking Mussolini—after Admiral Canaris had failed—to help him convince the Spanish leaders to take part in the war. What the Führer was interested in at that time was the taking of Gibraltar and in January, after Canaris had visited Franco, he made another attempt to convince the Caudillo by letter. Von Ribbentrop had also sent an urgent telegram (that was so impolitely worded that it could be described as brutal) through the ambassador in Berlin General Espinosa de los Monteros. Consequently, the German ambassador in Madrid Von Stohrer had met with Serrano Suñer several times for the same reason.[145] None of these movements, however, managed to change Spain's position. Great Britain had been informed of this pressure by General Aranda, who had confirmed that Hitler's objective was Gibraltar. Sir Samuel Hoare had immediately suggested to London that Great Britain should support the Spanish claim for extending their colonial empire on the French North African coast.[146] And Hitler asked Mussolini for support in a meeting on 19 January 1941. At that moment, the Italian leader was in an extremely weak position because his troops had been defeated by the Greeks in Albania and he was quick to agree to the request, although he did not have any great hopes of success.

The Caudillo-Duce meeting (with Serrano Suñer also present) on 12 February 1941 in Bordighera did not have the immediate effect that Hitler had been expecting. But what was discussed revealed what Franco thought about the war at that time. He explained to Mussolini that he had a real interest in taking part in the war and had in fact offered to do so in the previous September. He complained not only about how Spain was being treated by Germany but also about the "too vague promises" made at Hendaye and the fact that the Germans "inspired no confidence by subordinating any territorial compensation to the possibility of equivalent territorial expansion for he French." The Germans had also responded to the demand for territorial compensation with economic requests, which had not caused a good impression because Franco had interpreted them as an attack on the economic independence of Spain. And to justify his refusal, he referred to the appalling shortages of food throughout the country, which also affected its military strength: Spain's armies had only 300,000 men because no more could be fed. But despite all this, he made it clear to the Duce that "Spain wants to enter the war and fears entering too late."[147] Serrano Suñer pointed out that Spain wanted guarantees of territorial concessions and that in Hedaye little had been said on the subject. At this juncture, Mussolini asked Franco if he would enter the war if he had enough wheat and guarantees of colonial expansion. Franco replied that he would.[148] Mussolini also asked about the economic agreements with Great Britain and the United States, to which Franco replied that despite the economic aid they were providing he was under no political obligation to them. "Trade is one thing and honor quite another," he said.[149] His preference was clear, then, and it is quite feasible to think that if Franco had obtained what he wanted from Germany, Spain would have entered the war within a relatively short period of time.[150] In fact, in a letter that he wrote to Hitler on his return to Madrid he explained the reason for his attitude: the Hendaye Protocol was "too vague." Hitler, however, was still not prepared to give the Spanish the French territories in North Africa for the same reasons as before: he did not wish to alienate Vichy in an area that was so geostrategically important for his present and future plans. So he gave the Spanish up as a lost cause and stopped pressurizing them for a while.

Meanwhile, the Spanish leaders relentlessly went about their search for relief and at the end of January they arranged to buy 400,000 more tons of wheat from their ally the Argentine dictator general Perón.[151] And Washington continued to take little notice of the demands of the Madrid Embassy. In fact, at this point in time President Roosevelt himself was so afraid that Germany might attack Gibraltar and occupy North Africa that he suggested to Hull that they should make a show of force and send a naval squadron consisting of four or five cruisers and a dozen destroyers to Lisbon and Cadiz.[152] It is therefore fully understandable that they took no notice of Colonel William Donovan, personal friend of the president and special envoy to Spain, who was making proposals very similar to those of the Madrid Embassy.

COLONEL WILD WILLIAM DONOVAN'S VISIT TO MADRID. RELATIONS BETWEEN ALEXANDER W. WEDDELL AND SIR SAMUEL HOARE

At the end of February 1941, Colonel *Wild* Bill Donovan, First World War hero, was in Madrid and, after he had seen Weddell and met with Serrano Suñer, he gave his full support to the ambassador's point of view. His stay in the capital of Spain was the penultimate stage of a mission entrusted to him by the president to collect information and impressions about the war. It had taken him to the Balkans and the Middle East, and was to end in Lisbon.[153] A few months later, in July 1941, Roosevelt put his fact finding on an official basis and appointed him Coordinator of Information, whose task was to "collect information" and "plan covert offensive operations."[154] Subsequently, in 1942 when the United States was at war, Donovan founded the Office of Strategic Services (OSS),[155] the predecessor of the CIA.

The meeting that Donovan and Weddell had with Serrano was preceded by another meeting with Ambassador Hoare and his staff, the details of which we know because of the memorandum[156] that Weddell later sent Donovan. Sir Samuel had made a considerable effort to impress him and win his support, knowing full well the influence he had on the president. He told him that he believed that Franco and his generals (some of whom, let us remember, he was bribing) sincerely wanted to maintain Spain's status as a nonbelligerent or neutral country. However, Serrano Suñer's predominance in the cabinet was a danger, as was "the poverty of Spain, in alliance with pride" that was "a bad combination." Hoare believed that, militarily speaking, Spain and Portugal were a unit and that it was necessary to maintain what he called an "Atlantic solidarity" with them, thus preventing them from being part of the Axis. What is more, the Iberian peninsula was of great military importance for future allied landings in the south of Europe, so he also believed that Spain should be provided with economic relief, just as Great Britain was doing. It was also essential to prevent a clash in North Africa between De Gaulle's Free France forces and the Spanish. To sum up, if the relief required were not provided, Spain would be more likely to intervene in the world war and in "some mad adventure toward the south" (that is to say, toward French Morocco).

As can be seen, the similarity of the criteria—and even the words—used by the British and U.S. ambassadors was considerable and it is worthwhile taking a look at the personal relations between them. In the memorandum of conversation mentioned above Weddell included some comments about Hoare that are quite interesting. For example, he believed that the strategic ideas that Hoare had described to Donovan had been taken directly from a book that he himself had lent him.[157] With reference to the need to supply Spain expressed by the English ambassador, Weddell commented that "here he seems to accept my point of view." He was also somewhat jealous of Hoare's success with the British government, although the policy implemented was also attributable to the government itself and the military high command, because he was having very little luck with the U.S. government. None of this, however, prevented him from feeling sincere admiration for the British ambassador. To illustrate this, the previous September he had written the following to a friend:

> I believe it was Tayllerand who remarked that the fundamental error of every diplomatist lay in thinking that the entire foreign policy of his Government revolved around his own Mission; I do not go that far but I do believe that Spain is now an important point in the European picture, in which a very brilliant person, Sir Samuel Hoare, of Hoare-Laval fame, is holding the cards for the Churchill Government, and handling them with skill.[158]

Subsequently, in November, he had praised him to Sumner Welles, saying that "he is the smoothest article I have ever encountered, agreeable, polished, acute, full of ideas, an extraordinary capaccity for making contacts and not missing any moves."[159] This high opinion was not to change throughout his time at the embassy in Spain,[160] and by the end of 1941 he even thought that the British ambassador would eventually succeed Churchill.[161] Hoare, however, did not share the same opinion of his American counterpart. Although on Weddell's dismissal in the spring of 1942 he wrote "as for myself I have lost a perfect colleague, wise, cultured and sympathetic. Moreover I always felt that we had so many common interests not only in the troubled world of today but in the better world of principles and books. I shall never forget how gently you always helped me, particularly when first I came to Spain,"[162] at the end of 1940 he had described him as "completely incompetent" and prone to putting his foot in it.[163] The fact is, though, that, as we have explained above, the two ambassadors tended to coincide in many of their analyses and interpretations. They both distinguished between a proneutral Franco and a probelligerent Serrano Suñer, although Weddell was always more convinced than Hoare of Franco's (alleged) implacable desire to remain neutral[164] and his (also alleged) titanic resistance to Axis pressure to drag him into the war.[165] Be that as it may, Weddell acted autonomously from Hoare, and this autonomy has not always been faithfully reflected in the bibliography, largely because Hoare published a book on his "special mission" and Weddell did not get round to publishing his memoirs.[166]

Two days after Donovan and Weddell had their appointment with Hoare, they were received by Serrano Suñer,[167] who did not allow them to see Franco because he "was very busy." When Wild Bill questioned him on Spain's economic situation, Serrano replied with a whole battery of arguments that further convinced them of his pro-Axis stance. He even preferred not to give a direct answer to the question but to precede his response with an anti-British and anti-French diatribe that in itself was a real declaration of intent. He said that during the Civil War,

> the democracies of the world had been in opposition to Spain, and that this country had been delivered from a period of disorder and violence (under which democratic principles were nullified), by so-called totalitarian countries and that naturally as a result the gratitude of Spain flowed toward those countries. The arch enemies of Spain in this conflict (...) had been France and England whose Governments had entirely failed to recognize the basic principles involved and had encouraged in every way in their power the so-called Republican Government.

That is to say, he personally thought that Great Britain and France were more responsible than the Soviet Union, so reviled by all Francoists bar none. Without a doubt, this opinion was affected by the personal resentment he felt for the British Embassy, which he believed had denied political asylum to his two elder brothers during the war. They had subsequently been captured and shot by the Republicans just when they were doing all they could to get Serrano himself released from prison. Both ambassadors were already aware of this accusation, which, after considerable investigation, Hoare hotly denied. Serrano made an indirect reference to this situation and indignantly and bitterly denied "the failure of Ambassadors and other Chiefs of Mission during the Civil War to mitigate by their physical presence and effort the reign of blood and terror which had existed in the capital and elsewhere, recalling cases where asylum had been refused to people who shortly thereafter were assassinated." Donovan came out in defense of France and Great Britain and criticized the Nationalists lax attitude to propaganda during the Civil War. He said that "he had visited Franco's troops at the front, and was himself a Catholic" and that although there were 20 million Catholics in the USA "Franco leaders had entirely ignored the rise of propaganda as a result of which that public opinion in the United States which would have been favorable to the cause was left bewildered through lack of information –all this in sharp contrast of the activities of Republican representatives."

Serrano went straight to the point and made it clear that "we [Spain] hope for and believe in the victory of Germany in the present conflict." When he was asked why, he replied: "First of all (…) because of gratitude arising from its contribution to Spain's present independence (…) and equally in resentment of England's and France's attitude in the Spanish Civil War." And he added that he thought that "Spain's legitimate aspirations based on her 'natural rights' would be safeguarded if the hoped for event became a fact." In response to another direct question from Donovan, he denied that Germany had exerted any pressure or attempted to interfere, quite unlike what France and Great Britain had always done in Spain with their investments. He even said that "England is intervening today." When he was asked yet again whether Spain would remain neutral, he replied that Franco "would remain aloof until Spain's 'honor or interests or dignity' were in question." And the rest of his answers were along these lines. For example, when he was asked about the future of Europe after a hypothetical German victory, he said that "France and Belgium would receive special consideration and (…) there would be a general control of other countries in accordance with German ideas." As far as he was concerned, a nation such as Germany, with 80 million inhabitants was "sufficiently large to impose its will on all Europe as well as to protect greater component states from the horrors of communism coming from the East." With reference to what Spain would get out of all this, Serrano stated that "it would surely receive Gibraltar together with a further recognition of Spain's 'natural rights' in Africa." On the other hand, when asked about a hypothetical British victory, he said that a "bourgeois government" would be imposed on the rest of Europe and that "this would be an impoverished congeries of peoples too weak to resist the Red attack."

In what was surely a supreme test of his patience, Donovan explained that the United States of America wished to support Great Britain in the struggle against the Axis. He and not Serrano—who should have been the interested party—was the one to bring up the possibility that the United States could provide Spain with relief. And from that point on, it was he who seemed to be most interested in discussing a relief package and not the Spanish minister, which is a good indication of Serrano's cynicism, because at that time a sizeable part of the Spanish population was literally dying of hunger. In particular Donovan said that "he had learned from his own observation and otherwise of the general economic needs of Spain"; that Weddell had notified Washington of these necessities; and that "he was desirous of contributing in any way he could to a sympathetic consideration of these necessities." His personal proposal was that they should be discussed with the British ambassador in Madrid and perhaps in London with the British government, and that he should inform his government in person on his return to Washington. This prompted Serrano to mention "the terrific destruction in field and forest and factory, in transportation" and to point out that other countries that had engaged only in wars beyond their boundaries had secured loans for their rehabilitation while Spain of today was not alone suffering from the destruction of the past but on every frontier was feeling the repercussion of the present conflict. But he showed no enthusiasm for the offer.

The meeting had taken place in an atmosphere of tension that was not reflected in Weddell's report. Several years later Hoare mentioned that Donovan had treated Serrano "as if he were a prisoner in the dock. Using all his forensic ability he went through a long indictment that omitted nothing in the charge sheet, and left the Minister almost speechless with fury. The Minister's reactions were what might have been expected."[168] For his part, Serrano described the interview as "one of the most disagreeable scenes I have had. That man basically came to rudely condemn everything, demanding explanations..." and, what he found most difficult to believe, "threatening us."[169] In any case, the incident convinced Franco and Serrano that they were being treated with some arrogance by the United States.

It hardly need be said that although Weddell recognized the importance and the clarity of the pro-Axis statements made by the Spanish minister of foreign affairs, in the report of the interview that he sent to the State Department, he continued to argue that American policy "in dealing with this Government should be one of bald realism dictated by a careful determination of what Spanish neutrality is worth to the general cause and how it should be secured."[170] Nevertheless, neither Weddell's nor Wild Bill's reports managed to achieve anything at this point in time.

TRANSPORTING THE THOUSAND REPUBLICAN REFUGEES OF POLITICAL IMPORTANCE TO MEXICO

Since February 1941, President Roosevelt had been well aware of the issue of relief to Spain and not just because of the demands made on him by the Madrid Embassy and Colonels Donovan and Behn. On 23 January, he had received a letter from Ambassador Bowers in Chile[171] enclosing a memorandum that had been sent to him by Jay Allen. Allen had traveled to France and its North African colonies and was heavily involved in evacuating the Spanish Republicans to America via Mexico. His journey may have been connected to the international campaign—led by Swiss and U.S. journalists—denouncing the conditions in the French internment camps for the refugees.[172] In his text, Allen argued that the humanitarian aid that the North American Red Cross was beginning to send to Franco's Spain and Vichy France should be paid for on a quid pro quo basis: the same vessels that transported the supplies to France should transport some of the Spanish Republican refugees to Mexico. To be more precise, he mentioned that about a thousand of the 90,000 refugees that he calculated to be in unoccupied France and French North Africa could be shipped out in this way thus preventing the leading political figures, masons, and protestants from being extradited at the request of Franco's authorities and coming to the same sorry end as President Companys and many others. The quid pro quo that the Francoists should be asked for in private was that in exchange for supplies they should withdraw any objections they had to these refugees being shipped out. According to Allen, Vichy was only prepared to authorize transport to Mexico if Spain did not oppose it.

Although Allen's information was not altogether accurate, he described a real problem: the danger existed. On 22 August 1940, Vichy and Mexico had signed an agreement by which France accepted the offer made by the Mexican president General Lázaro Cárdenas to allow all the 100,000 or so Spanish Republicans in France who wished to do so to enter his country. Mexico would be responsible for their transport[173] as long as, in return, France were to agree "to respect the freedom and the existence of all those people who had sought asylum on French territory, restricting any extradition measures exclusively to common-law crimes and offenses, unconnected to other crimes of a political nature."[174] However, the Francoists were not opposed to the agreement[175] and Serrano Suñer, who at that time was still minister of governance, had presented Vichy with a list of 636 Republicans that the Francoist authorities wanted to be extradited. These people would find it difficult to leave the country because although the French did not want to hand over prisoners directly as the Germans had done, they were prepared to study any requests for extradition that Spain made. Allen was referring particularly to such politicians as the former prime minister and socialist leader Francisco Largo Caballero; another former Prime Minister Portela Valladares; former Ministers and Director Generals such as Nicolau D'Olwer and Ansó; former Director Generals such as Alonso Mallol or Victoria Kent, or the former mayor of Madrid Pedro Rico, among many others (e.g., Cruz Salido, Pau Casals, and Companys' widow). We know that in January and February 1941 Spain had requested the extradition of some of these figures.[176] Jay Allen also sent his proposal to the president's wife, Eleanor Roosevelt.[177]

Apparently Vichy had made a similar official proposal to Washington about using the U.S. vessels that were transporting the humanitarian aid to France. The French, however, were thinking of using vessels of their own and were negotiating with Mexico and other countries in an attempt to evacuate as many refugees as possible because they were having serious difficulties feeding them all.[178]

The president did not accept either request because the use of vessels sailing under the U.S. flag contravened the Neutrality Act. He communicated his decision to the president of the Red Cross Norman Davis, who had also taken an interest in the matter. The only possibility, said Roosevelt, was to ask Congress to pass some specific legislation authorizing such a use but he decided against making the request.[179] Under Secretary Welles wrote the letter that the president sent to Bowers in response to his proposal. In it he pointed out that the use of ships[180] "would (...) require the expenditure of large sums of money which the refugee associations in this country do not have at their disposal and in any event would involve a violation of the Neutrality Act." On the contrary, "the wisest course would seem to be for the French and Mexicans to work out the transportation problem directly without employing American vessels."

The matter went no further. Spain and Germany were afraid that some of the refugees would leave the country and join De Gaulle's troops and the pressure they exerted resulted in Vichy, one month later on 20 March 1941, prohibiting all male refugees between seventeen and forty-eight years old from leaving the country.[181] Meanwhile, Franco continued to make extradition requests, most of which were denied in compliance with the Franco-Spanish Agreement on Extradition of 1877. Nevertheless, some of the most sought-after Republicans were subsequently captured by the Germans when their troops occupied the whole of France. This was the case of Largo Caballero who was sent to a Nazi concentration camp, like thousands of other ordinary Spanish Republican refugees, most of whom were to die there.[182]

We should say that the State Department, which had learnt its lesson from the execution of Companys and the resulting international reaction, took steps to help some Republicans who had been preventively detained. Welles wrote the following:

> We have recently expressed our hope to the Spanish Government that clemency will be exercised in the treatment of political prisoners. A report recently came to our attention that the French authorities had arrested the former Prime Minister of Spain, Señor Largo Caballero, and other prominent Spanish republican refugees in France with the intention of turning them over to the Spanish Government. On two occasions during January, we requested our Embassy at Vichy to ascertain the facts regarding such reports, and the most recent report from the Embassy with respect to this matter was that it had been informed by an official of the French Foreign Office that Señor Largo Caballero and a number of other former Spanish political leaders have in fact been detained or kept under surveillance in their homes by the French authorities. The officer of the Foreign Office stated, however, that there was no intention on the part of the French Government to permit the extradition of these men to Spain or to turn over Spanish refugees in unoccupied France to the authorities in Spain. We have now followed up our previous inquiries with a telegram to the Embassy at Vichy authorizing it to bring to the attention of the French Foreign Office the concern which is felt by many people in the United States for the safety of these Spanish political refugees in France, and to express the hope that the French Government will adhere to the policy of not permitting the extradition of these refugees to Spain.[183]

As we have said above, they were not extradited. They were destined to have a different fate.

From all the above, it can be seen that by the end of February 1941 the relations between the United States of America and Franco's Spain were deadlocked. Apart from the aid provided by the Red Cross and the supplies that Spain was managing to acquire in the United States—mainly gasoline—no headway had been made. This was the result of the same criteria being adopted, although they had come to no formal agreement, by the two opposing factions within the Roosevelt administration, which meant that on the issue of the Franco regime they were both acting in the same direction. The only dissenting voice was that of Ambassador Weddell. This unity had several causes. First, Morgenthau, Ickes, and Companys distrusted the Francoists because they believed them to be allies of the Axis powers and followers of their policies (even though they had not yet taken the step of entering the war). Second, the State Department, and Cordell Hull in particular, suspected the Franco regime of respecting neither private property nor free trade, and disapproved of its alarming proximity to the Axis. And finally, a large part of the press and U.S. public opinion was exerting considerable pressure not to have any dealings with the regime in Spain. Of course, this suspicion was constantly being rekindled by Franco's and Serrano's trips to see Hitler and Mussolini, their policy of repression both at home and abroad, their declarations of friendship with Germany and Italy, Serrano's Latin American policy of an aggressive and pro-Fascist *Hispanidad*, and their hostility and that of the Spanish press to democracies in general and the United States in particular.

Nevertheless, as from March 1941, it seemed that the deadlock was about to be broken, once again because of the pressure exerted by the British in Washington. It was not until March 1942, though, that the United States of America decided to implement a policy of its own and we shall deal with this period in the next section.

THE FINAL STAGE: FROM MARCH 1941 TO MARCH 1942 AND THE DISMISSAL OF ALEXANDER W. WEDDELL AS AMBASSADOR IN MADRID

In March 1941 it seemed that the impasse in the relations between the United States and Franco's Spain was about to be broken. At that time the British were extremely interested in the United States sending more supplies to Spain because they were unable to provide sufficient amounts themselves and, once the Tangier Imbroglio had been resolved, they made an official request to Washington along these lines. The Americans agreed but, while they were deciding what they could offer, there was a diplomatic incident between Ambassador Weddell and the Minister of Foreign Affairs Serrano Suñer that brought the non natas trade talks to a halt and prevented all official contact between the ambassador, General Franco, and Serrano precisely when it was most needed, if Weddell was to present a project for new economic relations.

The incident between Weddell and Serrano was not serious in itself, but serious enough to be used by Spain as an excuse for almost breaking off diplomatic relations with the United States. It came about against a background of renewed Spanish interest in entering the war because of a fresh wave of German victories in Yugoslavia, continental Greece, Crete, and Libya in April and May 1941, which suggested that hostilities would soon end in a resounding victory for the Axis powers. Italy, in particular, was quick to perceive this interest and actively encouraged Spain to enter the war in June 1941.

Serrano Suñer exploited the incident in his personal relations with the Axis and his attempts to increase his own power. As his Falangist supporters had been demanding since the beginning of 1941, his aim was to become president of the government and to leave Franco as head of state, and he wanted to have Italy and Germany's backing. This move by the Falange culminated a year of conflict with the army for hegemony within the regime and led to the most important political crisis that Franco had to deal with in the post–Civil War period. A vein and resentful Serrano Suñer tried to use the incident to force the Roosevelt administration to remove Weddell from his post. And although he was to remain in office until 1941, the ambassador was seriously affected. His position was to worsen after another brush with Serrano toward the end of the year, and he was dismissed shortly afterward.

The incident was the main cause of the new tension between the two countries, which had paradoxically arisen just when the United States felt well disposed toward Spain. Franco, however, was once again entertaining hopes of entering the war and satisfying his territorial aspirations. The Spanish press was constantly on the attack, fresh impetus had been given to the policy of Hispanicity,[184] and the United States was constantly being snubbed (e.g., the Spanish government did not send a representative to the reception held in the Madrid Embassy on 4 July). At this time also, Franco agreed to Serrano's suggestion that the *División Azul* should be sent to Russia to fight against the Soviets alongside the Wehrmacht. And on top of everything Franco gave an aggressively anti-U.S. speech to the National Council of the Party with the whole Diplomatic Corps in attendance on 17 July.

The U.S. government responded to Spain's attitude by following Weddell's advice, suspending the shipment of the Red Cross aid and reconsidering their offer of economic support. The fact that the United States did not break off relations with the regime there and then was because the State Department was reluctant to take the initiative and put relations with Latin America at risk. The measure that caused the Franco regime most harm was the reduction in the oil supply in the summer of 1941, one of the restrictive measures adopted by the administration against Japan, Germany, and now Spain, as one of Germany's alleged suppliers. It had been proposed by Harold Ickes, the anti-Fascist secretary of the interior and oil administrator, and of course had Morgenthau's backing and Roosevelt's approval. Thus, just as had happened the previous summer in the Telefónica affair, the Serrano-Weddell dispute was finally resolved by resorting to oil restrictions. In the summer of 1941 the oil supply was restricted; then, in November, just when relations were beginning to improve it was cut off altogether in an attempt to call the Franco regime to order.

To find a solution to the incident with Weddell, in October 1941 Serrano felt obliged to initiate a process that was to involve the Spanish ambassador in Washington Francisco de Cárdenas, the British and the apostolic nuncio in Spain monsignor Cicognani. Once a solution had been found, the Americans offered a trade agreement that was different from the one they had offered six months before because they had decided not to enter into agreements with Franco's Spain merely to collaborate with British policy or to ensure that Franco had sufficient supplies to prevent him from joining forces with the Axis. Neither did they wish to please the British by making "preclusive purchases" of strategic Spanish products so that the Germans would have to go without. They now began to base their decisions on economic reasons because they were aware that the British were dealing with Spain not only for reasons of policy and strategy but also for reasons of business and profit. They also used the agreement to reinforce the progress that they were resolutely making toward rearmament. Thus, any sales they made to Spain would have to be returned in the form of Spanish products that had been unavailable to them up to that time (olive oil, for instance) and other products of a more strategic nature, such as cork, zinc, lead, or wolfram. The United States, then, finally designed and implemented a specific Spanish policy, which was based not only on political reasons (they wanted Spain to remain neutral) and their support of Great Britain, but also on their own economic and strategic interests. The policy was not what Weddell had been campaigning for. It did not subordinate economic interests to political and strategic ones, and it was tougher and more demanding than the British policy when it came to getting something in return. It put particular stress on making a profit and satisfying the strategic needs of the United States, which was in the process of rearming. Despite their differences about how to deal with Spain, the two sectors of the Roosevelt administration coincided on both these points, and particularly on the second one. This new policy was also much easier to justify to the press and public opinion than Weddell's policy or mere subordination to the British. Even so it was constantly criticized in the following years. In March 1942, the United States reached an agreement with Spain. At the same time Weddell was dismissed from his post. Let us take a closer look.

THE BRITISH PROPOSAL OF A JOINT ANGLO-AMERICAN PLAN IN MARCH 1941

In March 1941 it seemed that the deadlock between Spain and the United States would be broken thanks to new pressure brought to bear by the British ambassador in Washington. On 20 March Lord Halifax, who had substituted Lord Lothian, appeared before Sumner Welles, the acting secretary of state at the time, with a message from his government describing a joint Anglo-American plan of economic aid for Spain. And he asked the U.S. government to agree to implement their part. It was clearly the work of Sir Samuel Hoare, Her Majesty's Embassy in Madrid and Weddell himself, with whom Hoare had discussed the plan.

The plan was not restricted to the type and volume of supplies that Spain would be sent: it also specified exactly which members of Franco's government they should be involved in the negotiations and which ones should not. Particular mention was made of Serrano Suñer, who was regarded as being the enemy to be isolated. The man chosen to be in charge of receiving the supplies was the Minister of Industry and Commerce Demetrio Carceller. Of course, the plan was puerile and was never put into practice. As Willard L. Beaulac wrote forty years later, if it had been "the effect might well have been not to isolate Serrano but to destroy Carceller."[185] The message that Halifax gave to Welles was that the British government believed that "in the present state of Spanish affairs it is essential to strengthen their friends and isolate the Minister for Foreign Affairs in every possible way and as soon as possible and (…) that everything practicable should be done to create an economic bloc in the Western Mediterranean independent of the German continental system."[186] The message also stated that Spain was about to be granted a loan of £2.5 million pounds sterling and that a further £2.5 million would be made available so that Spain could make purchases in the sterling area or use the money in other areas for three months. The £2.5 million loan had been requested by Carceller at the end of December 1940 and although Serrano had put off signing it for several months he finally did so, very reluctantly, on 7 April 1941.[187] According to the message, the Spanish required £3.3 million to cover their most urgent needs for raw materials and another £1.25 million to buy oil. And they needed the United States to provide these raw materials, send specialists to Spain to counter the German economic influence, and grant the regime a loan.

The proposal was to implement the plan in the following way: (1) A public declaration would be made that the U.S. government was ready to join His Majesty's Government in making food and raw materials available for Spain (it was hoped that Portugal would also make a similar declaration); (2) A loan would be offered to the minister of industry and commerce (not to Serrano) to finance purchases in the United States; (3) Spain would be immediately provided with 100,000 tons of wheat from U.S. ports; (4) Spain would be provided with up to 200,000 tons of sulfate of ammonia; and (5) U.S. experts and purchasers should be allowed to visit Spain. The message also recommended that Spain should consider the possibility of trading with French North Africa and made it clear that none of the products received should be reexported.[188]

The British proposal came at a good time, just nine days after the Lend-and-Lease agreement had been signed. Welles was receptive and prepared for it to be implemented.[189] However, two weeks later, on 6 April 1941, the war entered a new phase when the Germans launched an offensive in Yugoslavia and Greece in support of the Italians. The offensive was quick and effective: Yugoslavia and Greece surrendered on 17 and 23 April, respectively. Crete was soon to follow and General Rommel and his Afrika Korps defeated the British in Libya. In fact, at the end of May everything seemed to suggest that Alexandria was about to fall and, therefore, that the Suez Canal would soon be in Axis hands. This would satisfy Spain's requirement for entering the war and meant that Gibraltar, the other gateway to the Mediterranean, could soon be taken.

Although the Suez Canal had not yet fallen (and in fact was not to do so because the Germans were unable to advance any further in northeast Africa), Franco and Serrano Suñer, encouraged by Mussolini and Ciano, were once again seriously considering entering the war,. What they were unaware of, however, was that the aim of the German offensive was not to take control of the central Mediterranean: it was an essential but subordinate part of Hitler's attack on the USSR scheduled for 22 June, which was of much greater importance for Germany. What is of immediate concern for us, however, is that just when the United States was responding to British pressure and seemed to be prepared to enter into a trade agreement with Spain, Franco redoubled his military efforts. And throughout the summer he was openly hostile to Great Britain and the United States.

THE SERRANO SUÑER-WEDDELL INCIDENT OF 19 APRIL 1941

While Washington was making plans for Spain, in a parallel but unconnected process in Madrid, Weddell was preparing to follow Secretary Hull's instructions and make it clear to the Spanish government that the United States of America was not prepared to wait meekly on the sidelines in the face of the totalitarian threat to the world. The instructions that Hull had given were of a general nature, based on a speech given by the president on 15 March[190] and directed at all ambassadors, consular representatives, and even U.S. citizens abroad. This is why Weddell went to see Serrano Suñer on 19 April 1941 and what happened at the beginning of their meeting was to lead to a diplomatic incident in which Spain's new expectations of entering the war were to play a role.

Although what Weddell had to say to Serrano was important, it was little more than a statement of general policy. The ambassador, however, decided to make it a much more solemn occasion and raise a variety of other issues. A letter that he wrote to a friend the day before the interview showed that he was taking it seriously: "Tomorrow I am having a heart to heart talk with the Foreign Minister (…) I shall tell him a few truths as regard our attitude and purposes. I wish you were here to help me polish the plangent phrases (…) I plan to utter to him (…) in Spanish."[191] Despite his careful planning, however, the meeting was a disaster. Weddell explained to the department that at the beginning of the interview he gave two letters to Serrano, who had just come from a meeting with Franco and seemed depressed and irritable. They were addressed to North American citizens residing in Spain and had been sent by the State Department.[192] Both the envelopes bore the stamp of the German censors. As he was handing them over, he smiled and said that he did not understand why Spain had renounced its sovereignty.[193] Serrano showed no surprise and, after listening to Weddell's explanation, took one of the envelopes and promised to investigate the matter. This version contrasts with the explanation Weddell gave to the new general consul W.L. Beaulac on 25 June, according to which he had not passed Serrano the letters but "tossed them" to him.[194] Whether he tossed them or not—and it seems that he did—the incident was the result of a confidential order received from Cordell Hull on 1 March[195] instructing Weddell to investigate the fact that some mail sent from the United States to Spain had been received with clear signs of having been tampered with by the German censors. Apparently the first to warn of the problem had been the U.S. press distribution services.[196] Weddell had specifically been told to find out whether Germany had offices for censoring mail in Spain so it occurred to him to take two alleged pieces of evidence to Serrano when he should merely have followed the more general order. Neither did his admonitory tone help matters.

Before continuing, however, it should be said that the version Weddell gave to the department of the incident is different from the version that Serrano gave in his first volume of memoirs *Entre Hendaya y Gibraltar* (*Between Hendaye and Gibraltar*), which is full of mistakes, as is the whole of this and other volumes of his memoirs.[197] Not only does he situate the event after Pearl Harbor, but also speaks of one letter not two,[198] and generally exaggerates the facts. Even so it reveals that Weddell's part in the incident was not as inoffensive as he had communicated to his superiors in Washington. Serrano says the following:

> Before he had even sat down, he arrogantly tossed an envelope onto my desk saying: "This is what remains of Spanish sovereignty." I had to control myself so as not to respond to his violent manner with even greater violence. I did not want to cause an unpleasant scene. Once I had recovered I told him that I would ignore his insulting words and that I preferred to believe that he was not fully aware of how serious they were, undoubtedly because of his lack of mastery of Spanish. He finally calmed down and—still without taking a seat—he explained that the letter in question had been sent from New York to an American citizen residing in Madrid and that it had been postmarked by the German censors in Bordeaux. It was quite clear to me: the letter had undoubtedly come from a sack taken from a ship that had been sunk or looted in the Atlantic by German submarines. It had then been taken to France and, because

nothing of great interest had been found, it was sent on to Spain. The Germans had done them a favor by sending it! As best I could, I tried to make Mr. Weddell understand that Spain was not to blame for the United States allowing its mail to be hijacked in the middle of the Atlantic. I also made a laconic offer to investigate the matter, and asked him to leave the famous envelope with me. It was at this point that something totally unexpected occurred. The ambassador grabbed the envelope, tore it in two and kept one half as a receipt.[199]

The interview then continued its course and Alexander W. Weddell stated his country's antitotalitarian standpoint. Serrano listened in silence. Weddell went on to complain about the Spanish press and how it treated the United States in particular and the democratic countries in general. He suggested that Germany had some sort of hold over the media and mentioned something that Serrano's predecessor at the ministry, Colonel Beigbeder, had said: that the Spanish press (which as we know, Serrano himself had controlled as minister of governance and even now controlled from the Ministry of Foreign Affairs) represented neither the opinion of the government nor the opinion of the people. Some of the editorials, he said, seemed as if they had originally been written in German and the press office of the German Embassy, headed by Lazar, often sent anti-U.S. articles to be published in Spanish newspapers. It was the second allusion to the loss of Spanish sovereignty in just a few minutes, spoken in the presence of one of the leading governors of the New Spain.

Serrano replied that the Spanish were quite capable of writing articles that were offensive to the North Americans by themselves. This was certainly true. Unbeknownst to Weddell, Serrano himself often wrote editorials for the newspaper "Arriba," the main organ of the single party. When Weddell asked him about the rumors that Spain would be signing the Tripartite Pact and that he would soon be traveling to the frontier to interview Von Ribbentrop, Serrano denied it and said that Spain's position on the war had not changed since the interview with Colonel Donovan and Weddell himself. The ambassador finished with a cryptic comment: "Some day peace will come to the world and (...) it will be interesting to see in what direction countries represented at the peace table or interested in its results will turn to secure the necessary help for their general rehabilitation." This could have been interpreted as a warning and the minister gave no response. Although Serrano apparently engaged in no verbal violence, he had found the interview extremely offensive because of the allusions to Spain's loss of sovereignty. Serrano was conceited and extremely resentful so this was to be very damaging for the relations between the two countries, just the opposite of what Weddell had been aiming for.

The following day Serrano told the German ambassador Von Stohrer that he should have thrown Weddell out of his office or, even better, slapped him, but he had not done so because he was the representative of a foreign power.[200] We should point out that two weeks before, Serrano had sent Weddell a note protesting about some "extremely insulting" caricatures of General Franco that had been published in two U.S. newspapers.[201] Likewise, Weddell had sent Serrano a private letter complaining of some comments in the press that he suspected referred to the philanthropic and humanitarian activities of Mrs. Weddell, although in this case he seemed to have been perfectly satisfied by the minister's denial.[202] Weddell was particularly sensitive to this issue, since both he and his wife had just been accused in the United States by the journalist Drew Pearson of having "totalitarian sympathies" and of being "appeasers"[203] because as part of the charity work she had been doing, Mrs. Weddell had been making donations to the Falangist charity organization, Auxilio Social. Serrano showed that he was extremely angry about Weddell's attitude by sending a telegram to Von Stohrer in Berlin in which he said that Weddell seemed to have acted either in accordance with "very strict instructions" or he had completely lost his self-control.[204]

In this state of great umbrage and in close contact with the German and Italian ambassadors, Serrano Suñer decided that he would no longer receive the U.S. ambassador. For his part, Weddell asked Hull for permission to request an interview with Franco, because he did not trust Serrano to inform him of the United States' antitotalitarian stand. However, because he was convinced that what he had to say could only lead to practical results if at the same time he offered economic aid, he also wanted to make specific economic proposals in connection with the collaboration that the British had asked Washington for and to which the department seemed to be receptive. In particular he asked Hull for permission to tell Franco the following:

> Save in the event of the adoption of an unfriendly attitude by Spain to the British and Allied cause, the United States Government is prepared to give sympathetic consideration to Spain's import needs for materials now subject to American embargo such as scrap iron, et cetera (...) We are also prepared to collaborate with the appropriate Spanish authorities in drawing up a program for the supply of goods for which Spain may have adequate exchange and which are now subject to licenses or other delaying controls, so as to accelerate the handling of applications covering Spain's most urgent requirements.[205]

That is to say, he was opening up a possible new way: the exchange of goods or bartering[206] between the two countries. This was the way, he believed, that Spain could promptly receive the products it needed. It did not have the disadvantages of the loan, which the department was so reluctant to authorize because of the differing views within the administration on how to deal with Spain and the possibility that it could be used against the administration for political reasons.

Hull gave his permission and told Weddell that he would shortly be sent a telegram with instructions for the economic negotiations. He should tell Franco that as soon as he received them the negotiations could begin. As the British had suggested, Hull also ordered Weddell to tell Franco that the Minister of Industry and Commerce Carceller and the Minister of the Treasury Larraz should be involved in these negotiations, in the hope that "the Caudillo will be prepared to support with them a program of American-Spanish cooperation."[207] Four days later, Weddell was authorized to initiate ministerial talks on the extension and liberalization of trade between the two countries, and to tell Franco that the U.S. government was prepared to provide Spain with surplus supplies (in particular, wheat, corn, and cotton). The immediate offer was to exchange peanut oil for 25,000 tons of olive oil and 200,000 tons of wheat. This exchange required no loans and was feasible because the British had lifted the ban on olive oil substitutes by which they had attempted to halt exports of Spanish oil to the Axis. It was also extremely interesting to U.S. importers who had been trying to acquire Spanish olive oil for some considerable time and it was envisaged that the amount involved could be increased in the future. As far as other products such as scrap iron, ammonium sulfate, and machine tools were concerned, however, the department believed that export restrictions could be lifted and the products sold but not in any great quantity given the British needs and the demand generated by the United States itself.[208]

The deal was designed not merely to exchange goods and initiate trade talks. There were also political conditions. Weddell's job was to guarantee that Franco would respect the conditions formulated by the United States the previous December, when it had seemed that talks were about to begin. That is to say,

- Spain would not enter the war or give support to the Axis.
- Spain would officially recognize the rights of U.S. citizens whose accounts in Spain had been blocked.
- Spain would not discriminate against U.S. citizens or businesses, in accordance with the most favored nation principle.
- The Spanish press would cease its attacks on the United States and Spanish sources would no longer transmit anti-American feeling to Latin American countries.[209]

One further condition was now added: the following official communiqué by which the Roosevelt administration was to inform the North American public of the beginning of talks should also be published in Spain

> The Spanish Government is very desirous of purchasing American surplus commodities for her economic rebuilding and has asked for time in which to make payments. This would probably include some Spanish commodities which we would desire. The Government of the United States is naturally interested in the mutually desirable improvement and development of commercial relations between the United States and Spain, and in the peaceful economic reconstruction of Spain. This Government feels that these objectives can only be achieved if Spain remains outside of the European conflict. Accordingly, the Government of the United States, in a spirit of cooperation with Spanish efforts for the furtherance of such peaceful economic reconstruction, has indicated that the appropriate governmental agencies are prepared to explore the possibility of an early initiation of discussions with representatives of the Spanish Government with a view to the extension of conditional, limited credits for the purchases of such surplus commodities as wheat, corn and cotton.[210]

Weddell did not object to the text, one of the aims of which was to justify the action taken by the administration in the face of public opinion. But he did object to the four conditions and he suggested that, since no loan was going to be granted for the time being, Spain should only be asked to comply with the first.[211] He believed that requiring Spain to comply with all four would make it much more difficult to reach an agreement. Personally he was elated. The British intercession had been crucial and the policy he had been fighting for was about to be implemented. However, after officially requesting an audience with the Spanish head of state on 25 April 1941 to inform him that the United States of America was prepared to enter into an economic agreement, Weddell then waited for weeks without being summoned. At first he suspected nothing because at the time Franco had his hands full with an important political problem that is now known as the May Crisis of 1941.

At this point, Serrano may not have planned to take any action against the ambassador other than not receive him for a certain period; and he may even have decided not to involve Franco for the time being. In fact, on 1 May Serrano had sent Weddell a note about one of the letters bearing the stamp of the German censors to inform him that he was investigating the matter but that "it appears from what can now be seen that the report will be completely vindicated from the Spanish point of view." He ironically added "which will constitute a real satisfaction for me and I trust for Your Excellency as well."[212] According to Weddell, the note was written "in terms of such friendliness and cordiality as to provoke comment" in the embassy.[213] What is more, on 11 May the head of protocol of the Ministry of Foreign Affairs, baron de las Torres,[214] was asked by Serrano to visit the ambassador[215] and tell him that the Generalissimo was extremely busy with the ongoing political crisis and could not receive him for the moment. The baron told him that he personally thought that he would be granted an audience some time that same week. Weddell expressed his surprise and displeasure at the delay and said that he was obliged to inform Washington. At the same time, he kept the State Department informed of the economic requests that the Spanish, and Carceller in particular, were making. Rather than wheat and cotton, which were being supplied by Argentina,[216] the most requested products were scrap iron, ammonium sulfate, machinery, electrodes, and, above all, the lubricating oils so essential for engines, all of which had export restrictions placed on them in the United States,[217] and which Weddell was in the process of trying to have removed.

BRITISH ALARM IN APRIL 1941, OPERATION PUMA AND THE REGIME'S MAY CRISIS IN 1941

At this time, a political-military bombshell that affected Spain was about to go off in London. As early as 22 April, against a background of German victories in Yugoslavia and Greece, Ambassador Hoare told Churchill that he had received secret information that the Military Governor of Cadiz (the Spanish province surrounding Gibraltar) believed that plans for attacking the Rock were in place. German troops were expected to arrive in Spain "in the near future."[218] In his message, Sir Samuel advocated that Britain should continue to supply Spain but should also consider occupying the Canary Islands, the best air and sea base after Gibraltar, if a German occupation were to take place. Churchill agreed at once and ordered plans to be drawn up. On 24 April, then, an expeditionary force known as Operation Puma was created with the main objective of taking the most strategically important of the islands, Gran Canaria. The operation, however, was not limited to the Canary Islands. As we know, for almost a year plans had been in place to occupy the Portuguese Azores and Cape Verde in the Atlantic. With this in mind, Churchill asked Roosevelt to extend the radius of action of the U.S. naval patrols to include this area. Roosevelt was reluctant to do so unless Portugal made an express request along these lines.[219]

Just when Puma was ready to be put into action, new events in Spain and Hoare's subsequent reports led to Churchill putting it on standby. On 2 May 1941, the British ambassador informed him of an imminent change in the Spanish government by which Serrano Suñer would lose some of his power. Indeed, on 5 November Colonel Valentín Galarza Morante, former under secretary to the presidency of the government, was appointed new minister of governance. Galarza was a military man and very close to Franco because he had worked with him on the political and administrative matters of the presidency. He was notoriously anti-Serrano and, according to Hoare, pro-Ally, which meant that he was one of the military staff who were being bribed—without them being aware of it—by Great Britain using Juan March's banking smoke screen. He had taken active part in resolving some of the disputes in which Weddell had been involved during his first year as ambassador in Spain.

The first consequence of the appointment was that Serrano lost the de facto power he had had over the Ministry of Governance since he had moved to Foreign Affairs because the Under Secretary Lorente Sanz was one of his right-hand men. The power that he lost was gained by the military. This was particularly significant because tension was increasing between Serrano and his Falangists, who were playing a major role in postwar Spain, and the army, which believed itself to be responsible for the victory in the Civil War. Galarza's appointment, then, was seen as a double offense: not only did the Falangist lose control of governance, they also felt that it was a hostile move against the party. Nevertheless, for the United States and Great Britain, who before the war had clearly differentiated between the attitudes of Serrano and those of Franco, the appointment meant that German troops were less likely to enter the country.

Galarza's appointment was also the immediate cause of the May Crisis of 1941. Throughout May there were more ministerial changes, which paradoxically benefited the Falange, and Serrano's political power went into decline. This did not necessarily mean that a German invasion was any less likely or that Spain would eventually decide to enter the war—as Hoare and Churchill believed—but simply that Franco decided to dispense with his brother-in-law as the link between the national headquarters of the Falange and the party's leaders. As has been said above, this marked the beginning of Serrano's political decline just when the personal relations between the two brothers-in-law were deteriorating. It turned out that Franco's wife, Carmen, had informed him that Serrano was having an extra-marital affair with the Marquise of Llanzol, which had begun shortly after he had been appointed foreign minister[220] and which was to be one of the reasons for the early termination of his career.

In fact, the events leading to the May Crisis[221] had been initiated several months before by the Falangists and it was in response to these events that Franco decided to appoint Galarza and strengthen the military sector of the government. At the end of January 1941 a representation of *legitimista* Falangists (that is to say, the most Fascist sector of the party, which had been militant even before the Unification, and was supported by the relatives and former colleagues of José Antonio Primo de Rivera), disappointed by Spain's not participating in the world war and by the semblance of a Fascist state that the regime cultivated when in fact the single party held only part of the power, presented an ultimatum to Serrano. As their interlocutor with Franco, they said he should put an end to this situation by becoming the head of government and remodeling the ministerial structure so that the main portfolios—including a new Ministry of National Syndicalist Economy, the Ministry of Governance and the Ministry of Education—would be in the hands of Falangists. The party, then, would hold the reins of political power and share government with the army. They would sweep the cabinet clean of such conservative elements as Catholics, Monarchists, Alfonsists, and Carlists who, in their opinion, opposed the National-Syndicalist policies of the single party and prevented Spain from becoming a Fascist-Falangist regime in which the party would have as much power as in Germany and Italy. They probably also tried to set the army's most pro-Falangist faction against its most hostile faction, the monarchist generals such as Kindelán, Aranda, Vigón, and Orgaz, among others, and Colonel Beigbeder, who was by then pro-Ally. In this way, they intended to falangize the whole state, making it so wholly Fascist that the Falange would not share political leadership but have total control of the country. In this new scheme of things, Serrano Suñer would be the leader and president of the government while Franco would be the Head of State, Generalissimo, and National Head of the Falange.

On hearing the proposal, Serrano must have realized immediately that it put him in a difficult situation. He had not been a Falangist before the war but he had created the regime's single party; he was the chairman of its political board and, after Franco, its leader, but he knew that his brother-in-law was hardly likely to hand over the presidency of the government or be happy to accept the position of head of state. Neither would he easily agree to giving total political hegemony to the Falangists, thus doing away with the need to find an equilibrium between the internal trends in the coalition or the Francoist block that he had been cultivating since the beginning of the regime. Even so, he decided to take the bull by the horns because he had no real alternative if he wished to maintain his position of dominance over the *legitimistas*. He was probably also tired of his position as the regime's effective but unofficial "number two." In the final analysis he was merely another minister, he insisted that the press refer to him as "Minister-President" (because he was the president of the Political Board of the Party but he liked people to think that he was president of the government). He wanted to get on in the political world and he believed he was a better politician than Franco. Also, like the Falangists, he believed that Spain should take part in the world war. And if Spain were to enter the conflict, he felt that it would be easy for him to acquire greater power and sideline not only his political enemies—among whom were the *juanista* monarchists, the Carlists, and many Catholics—but also many members of the military high command. By the end of 1940, this latter group, and particularly those who were being bribed, were against entering the war. They believed that Spain's military strength had been considerably depleted and that the country's probable defeat would put paid to everything that had been gained as a result of the Civil War. They also feared the party's increasing power. Some of them were being *helped* to hold these beliefs by the bribe they were receiving. Because they had been told that this bribe was the patriotic contribution of a group of national banks and companies that were against entering the world war, they must have felt even more patriotic. In Serrano's favor was his close relationship with the Italian and German ambassadors (which was even closer now that he was responsible for foreign affairs), and his excellent personal relationship with Mussolini's son-in-law Count Ciano and the Duce himself. And although Spain had not managed to enter the war in 1940, the victories in the Balkans seemed to be opening up another opportunity, which both he and Franco were prepared to grasp, as we shall see below.

The offensive by the Falangists lasted for several weeks and Serrano eventually agreed to become their leader. If he had refused to do so he would have lost his popular support, the only thing that enabled him to remain in power (apart from the fact that he was related to Franco). The *legitimistas* used all sorts of strategies to further their cause—political meetings, articles in the press, and dismissals—and the state of unrest intensified at the beginning of May 1941, probably because rumors were circulating that Galarza was about to be appointed minister of governance. Two great Falangist symbols resigned: Pilar and Miguel Primo de Rivera, the brother and sister of the Falange's founder José Antonio, who were National Delegate of the Female Section of the Party and Civil Governor and Provincial Chief in Madrid. Other important Falangists and colleagues of Serrano such as Dionisio Ridruejo (national chief of propaganda), Antonio Tovar (under secretary of the press for the Ministry of Governance), and several provincial party leaders also resigned. On 2 May Serrano gave a passionate speech in which he spoke with contempt of those who wanted the regime to be "an eclectic centipede" (that is to say, a mixture of tendencies). The speech, which also included a violent diatribe against the democracies, was given considerable coverage in the Falangist press.

In response to this internal strife, Franco decided to appoint Galarza, thus reaffirming his authority and clearly revealing that he did not intend to give the Falangists the hegemony they sought. This decision indirectly limited Serrano Suñer's power. He also appointed two leading Alphonsine and anti-Falangist generals—Kindelán and Orgaz—to take command of the most important military districts: the Protectorate of Morocco and the Military Region of Catalonia. Thus, he was looking to the army for support to resist the Falangist pressure. The Falangists made it clear that they were not pleased: the general Vice Secretary Pedro Gamero de Castillo refused to collaborate with Galarza in the appointment of provincial party chiefs, for which agreement between the party and the Ministry of Governance was mandatory; an article against Galarza was published in the official Falange journal *Arriba* (although he was not mentioned by name); and young university Falangists in Madrid spoke of organizing demonstrations against him. Galarza counterattacked by publishing an article that poured scorn on Falangist pretensions to determine Spain's foreign policy. On 12 May 1941 Serrano Suñer used this to present his resignation to Franco. He was taking a considerable risk.

Franco appeared not to have the stomach for a fight and he immediately asked him to reconsider because his resignation "serves the purpose of our enemies, and in these confusing times may damage Spain." He asked him to "meditate on the injustice and the wrong of your decision."[222] Serrano did just this, surely feeling relieved and hopeful. However, he was astounded when he found out that Franco had offered three *legitimista* Falange leaders ministerial posts and that all three had accepted. On 19 May 1941, the appointments were officially made: José Luis de Arrese Magra was appointed general secretary of the party, a post that had not been occupied since 1939 and took yet more power away from Serrano; Miguel Primo de Rivera was appointed minister of agriculture; and José Antonio Girón de Velasco was appointed minister of work. Another Falangist, Joaquín Benjumea Burín, the minister of agriculture moved to the Treasury Department because José Larraz,[223] who had interviewed Weddell in 1940 with Beigbeder and Alarcón de la Lastra, had resigned as the result of a campaign that Serrano had orchestrated against him.

Franco, then, had bypassed his brother-in-law in the party by dealing directly with the *legitimista* Falangists. From this point on, he was to take responsibility for all Falange matters himself, through the new general secretary of the party, José Luis Arrese, thus showing that he no longer needed Serrano. The Falange had increased its power in the government. It not only occupied more ministerial posts but also had greater power since it had taken over responsibility for the press and propaganda from the Ministry of Governance. By giving the party power in some areas, Franco had defused the Falangist maneuver to take control of the government and acquire political hegemony.

Although the *legitimistas* seemed to have come out on top, it was soon very clear that Arrese and the other ministers were completely subservient to Franco and increasingly against Serrano. The situation that arose out of the Falange's demands was very different from the situation in Rumania where, in January 1941, the Iron Guard Fascist party had risen against Marshall Antonescu in an attempt to seize power and had been crushed. In Spain, the Falange had been given *more* power but not *all* the power. More importantly, the party had started to lose its autonomy and Serrano had lost power and influence, although he was still minister of foreign affairs and president of the political board of the Falange. He had lost out to Franco in a direct head to head and little more than a year later he was to be dismissed. The man who was to play a leading role in his dismissal was a naval officer who had taken over from Galarza as under secretary of the presidency of the government. His name was Luis Carrero Blanco, the chief of operations of the general staff of the navy and author of the report used by Franco and Serrano before Franco's trip to Hitler's Alpine refuge in November 1940. From this moment on, he was the regime's number two although he was much more discrete than Serrano. He was totally faithful to Franco and incorruptible. And of much greater immediate concern he was also anti-Falange and anti-Serrano.[224]

The Worsening of the "Envelope Incident" between Serrano Suñer and Weddell between May and June 1941

Let us leave the May Crisis for the moment and return to the relations between Spain and the United States. It had seemed that the incident concerning the envelopes had done little more than anger Serrano and make him reluctant to receive Weddell but this was to change after 15 May when Mrs. Weddell received a postcard posted in Madrid itself. It was rubber-stamped by the German military censors. Weddell sent it to Serrano with a note expressing his surprise and reiterating his doubts about whether "the German government, through its military [administrative units], was maintaining a censorship of official and private correspondence within the boundaries of Spain."[225] After reading the letter and confirming this new accusation of loss of Spanish sovereignty, Serrano flew into a rage. This time he would not investigate the matter or give fresh explanations, although this is precisely what the situation demanded because it seemed to be clear that the Germans were somehow interfering with the mail being sent to the U.S. Embassy and U.S. nationals in Spain (and obligingly using a rubber stamp to prove that they were tampering with it). Instead he informed Franco, who was still upset over the interview with Weddell in November 1940, and they decided that Weddell would no longer be received.[226] The balance of the world war was increasingly tipping in Germany's favor and Spain was once again considering becoming involved. The two brothers-in-law were affected by this general atmosphere and regarded Weddell and the United States as the future enemy.

However, Weddell also showed a surprising duality on the issue of the envelopes. On 20 May, for example, he responded to the department's request of the previous 1 March to make inquiries into the matter of a U.S. publication that had arrived in Spain with a German censor's stamp on the envelope. He suggested that Spain was not involved in anything untoward:

> Within the past few weeks the Embassy has had further opportunity to investigate this matter in an informal way through a trustworthy source having a personal contact with officials in the censorship section of the post office here. In this quarter the information obtained, after the wrapper was examined, is to the effect that there is no German censorship office in Spain, and the opinion was expressed that the publication might have been missent to Biarritz [France] by error. In connection with the suggestion that publications were missent, it should be mentioned that an instance of the misrouting of letters for Spain was revealed in the receipt yesterday by a member of my staff of an air mailed letter addressed to him at the Embassy, mailed in the United States on April 28 but which also bore a Marseille stamp dated May 12, evidently affixed before the latter was received by any Spanish post office, since the Spanish stamps bore the date May 19, 1941.[227]

Was Weddell so personally involved in his dispute with Serrano Suñer that he was adding fuel to the flames in Madrid but informing the department that he did not believe that the German censors were working in the country? We do not know and probably never will. Be that as it may, his new note to Serrano on 15 May gave rise to a serious diplomatic incident. In fact, the ambassador was unaware of the regime's attitude toward him and on 25 May he attributed the delay in being granted an appointment to the "characteristic sluggishness" of the Ministry of Foreign Affairs.[228] Just the day before[229] he had been extremely surprised to receive an aide-mémoire from Hoare containing the text of a telegram he had received from the ambassador in Washington, Halifax, who had initiated talks with the department on 20 March. It said that the State Department wanted Weddell to send some suggestions. Therefore, Hoare was being sent a list of possible suggestions that Weddell might like to make so that he could attach his signature and Hoare could send them back. We now know that this list had been written by the expert in Iberian peninsula economic affairs and official of the Ministry of Economic Warfare David Eccles,[230] who was in Washington at the time advising Halifax. The list contained a variety of suggestions. For example: the United States should increase its purchases of such Spanish products as olive oil, wine, cork, and zinc; in exchange they should receive "generous instead of destructive treatment of Spain in the matter of export licenses;[231] the initiation of negotiations perhaps necessitating credits, the latter depending on amounts available through increased purchases to cover imports of cotton, scrap iron, agricultural machinery and fertilizers here, emphasis to be laid on actual purchases rather than on the fixing of a quota"; the Red Cross would continue to send aid; Portuguese colonial products would be financed for consumption in Spain; and U.S. propaganda would be increased to support that of Great Britain.[232]

As he immediately explained to the secretary of state, Weddell was surprised and upset by the way in which he had been informed by the British Ambassador when "several of the matters touched on have been already the subject of correspondence with the Department." He also complained that "the British here have been able on the basis on their representatives' reports to indicate and to their advantage in informal ways to the Spanish authorities our views and ideas rather than have these made known by this Embassy at the appropriate time."[233] But he did not merely make his displeasure heard: he also responded to Eccles' proposal point by point, reaffirming his own ideas and criticizing those of the Englishman. On the subject of purchasing Spanish olive oil, wine, cork, and zinc, he said: "This suggestion parallels recommendations I have previously made but I believe a broader range of products should be considered. The Embassy will submit further recommendations in this connection."[234] And regarding the possibility of a more generous award of export licenses he said, "This likewise follows the line of recommendations already submitted." However, it was on the issue of extending loans that he most disagreed:

> I still believe that the extension of credits to Spain may have a strong influence in strengthening its resistance to German diplomatic pressure and that we should be prepared to enter negotiations for such a credit. However, for reasons of strategy I feel that we should maneuver to have the request from them come from the Spanish authorities at which time we should suggest that they reexamine their requirements especially in the light of increased purchases by the United States.

That is to say, rather than making Spain an offer, the possible extension of credit should be used as a negotiating tactic. Neither was Weddell convinced by the three-sided deal with Portugal, although he did not rule it out definitively, or the issue of the Red Cross aid. Even though he felt that aid should be provided he made it clear that he disagreed with the British because the aid package had little propaganda value. He announced that he would be sending a telegram on the matter of propaganda the next day and, because he was sure that he would very soon be having an audience with Franco, he asked Hull for permission to tell him that the United States was prepared to start talks on buying Spanish products and flexibilizing the granting of export licenses, which would affect such essential items as oil, ammonium sulfate, and many others. We do not know what Hull replied to Weddell, who innocently continued to prepare for his meeting with Franco.

But what was the strategy that he and his staff were thinking of following in the subsequent negotiations with the Spanish? Essentially they were going to use the powerful weapon of the export licenses.[235] The Madrid Embassy firmly believed that if these licenses were to be used flexibly, the Francoists would concede on some points. They needed to be convinced that they depended as much on the American continent as on the British empire. This was fundamental because at this time in which the German exploitation of the occupied countries may have put Hitler in a position to provide Spain with economic aid in exchange for greater collaboration or even entry into the war. Weddell's opinion was that the Spanish government was politically close to the Axis and believed in its final victory. Since it was a totalitarian regime, it was more necessary to convince the government than the Spanish population in general. He also believed that the talks for the Hispano-American economic agreement should be held in Madrid.

The days passed, however, and he was not summoned by the Spanish head of state. Weddell knew that Franco was fully aware that he wanted to see him and interpreted the lack of response as increasing indifference toward the United States. He assumed that this indifference was due to the recent German victories in Crete[236] and Libya and Serrano Suñer's position in the government, which he mistakenly believed to be stronger than ever. He predicted that the Suez Canal would soon be captured and that German troops would enter Spain shortly afterward, which meant that the whole Atlantic coast from Narvik to Dakar would be in German hands. He believed that the Spanish could not and would not prevent the Germans from entering their country. But even so, Weddell still maintained that Franco wanted to remain neutral and that he did not wish to sign the Tripartite Pact.[237]

Like Weddell, Hoare also was pessimistic about the future of Spain. Sir Samuel still maintained that Franco and Serrano Suñer had very different views on Spain's participation in the war. He believed that in the following six weeks Serrano would do everything possible for Spain to become part of the Axis, blocking any influence that might convince Franco otherwise.[238] This was why the interview with Weddell could not go ahead. Hoare was right, but he was wrong in thinking that Franco's views were different from Serrano's. Although the two brothers-in-law were gradually drawing apart because of family and political troubles, they were still united in their foreign policy and particularly so on the issue of whether Spain should or should not enter the war. At that time Serrano was exultant about the Axis victories and he told the Italian ambassador that "in due course Franco and he would probably make the Axis a new offer for Spain to take part in the conflict."[239] For his part, the German ambassador informed his superiors that Serrano urgently wanted Spain to enter the war and that now that the food situation had improved "so had the possibilities of embarking on war." The big question, however, was what Franco would be offered in return.[240]

Meanwhile, Weddell was still being made to pay the price of the envelope incident by Franco and Serrano Suñer. Finally, on 27 May 1941, Weddell received the response to his request for an appointment. At last he could see it in black and white: he would not be allowed to see Franco. Should he have anything in particular to say to him, he could tell the minister, who would then pass the information on to Franco.[241] This response was a bombshell in the Madrid Embassy. An accredited ambassador's universally recognized right to be received by the head of state was being refused. Weddell and his staff, however, regarded the refusal as the confirmation of the dichotomy between the two foremost Spanish leaders, believing that Serrano was preventing Franco from making any improvements in relations between Spain and the United States. After consulting with his superiors in Washington and receiving instructions from Hull, Weddell[242] replied to Serrano Suñer with an extremely terse note that insisted on the right "of an Ambassador—a right immemorially recognized in the relations of states to be received by the Chief of State to whom he is accredited whenever such an interview is sought." He added that the U.S. government was reluctant "to believe that the Chief of State, were he cognizant of my request, would willingly sanction any undue delay in arranging an interview." But he did not stop at pointing out Franco's (alleged) ignorance: he also threatened that "if I am to conclude that the position taken in your note under reference is to be accepted as indicating a change in the views and procedures of the Spanish Government on this subject it will naturally become necessary for my Government to reconsider its policy in the light of this extraordinary development." And he went on to explain that "my request for this interview, made at the specific direction of my Government, was for the purpose of making known to the Chief of the Spanish State the policy and intentions of my Government in the present world conflict of which your own Government despite its attitude of non-belligerency should be informed." In fact, it had been the Spanish government itself that

> in recent months (...) has in formal and informal ways indicated a desire to obtain economic assistance from the United States: and that equally frequent requests have been made by representatives of your Government looking to a relaxation of existing export controls in order to make available products which the Spanish Government appear to have been particularly interested in acquiring in the United States.

Had he not been prevented from seeing the head of state, he said, his intention would have been "to discuss with him again the possibility of initiating discussions with a view to broadening and liberalizing the basis of mutual trade between Spain and the United States." And he predicted that "the outcome of such discussions could have been favorable and beneficial both to Spain and the United States." He finished the note by demanding that Serrano inform Franco of this situation and that he express his own and his government's "astonishment" that his desire to speak to Franco had been frustrated and that he had not been provided with any reasonable justification.

On 13 June 1941 Serrano sent Weddell an extremely harsh reply.[243] He denied that he had refused him an interview with the head of state and accused him of trying to avoid the Ministry of Foreign Affairs, of having "made a scene" in their interview of 19 April and of having shown "his habitual lack of moderation" and of using "crude" language in his note, which he regarded as being "offensive to the dignity of the Spanish State and its institutions." He therefore believed it to be his duty to prevent those who expressed themselves in such unacceptable terms from doing so in the presence of Franco. But he also made it clear that he was not referring to the government of the United States as such, "whose suggestions and desires" Franco and himself would consider "with all correctness"[244] but to Weddell's behavior, which was the cause of the deplorable situation of the relations between the countries.[245]

Weddell responded to Serrano Suñer's attempt—which he had very probably agreed on with Franco—to separate and isolate him from his government in the next few days by writing several notes to Serrano in which he made it clear that "each step I have taken during the past 2 months to obtain an interview with the Chief of the Spanish State for the purpose of discussing the matters of outstanding importance and interest to our two countries of which Your Excellency is aware, has been taken with the full knowledge and approval of my Government."[246] Serrano made no further replies, however. In his communications with the State Department, Weddell insisted that the whole situation had been a maneuver by Serrano to weaken his standing with Washington by denying him access to the head of state and thus forcing his dismissal. We should make it clear, though, that Franco was involved, and Weddell was ignoring the fact that he had played a role in this new incident by forwarding the postcard that his wife had received.

In the middle of this situation and unable to communicate with either of the two main leaders of the regime, Weddell had to get information about "his case" from Ambassador Hoare who, in turn, got what he knew from the Minister of Industry and Commerce Carceller. The Spanish minister was very probably going to some trouble to provide him with a watered-down version of the situation in an attempt not to make the provision of U.S. supplies even more difficult. According to Carceller, Franco knew of Weddell's attempts to see him but he did not wish to grant him an interview for two reasons. In the first place, it was a personal quarrel between Weddell and Serrano and he did not want to interfere. And in the second place, he had recently been pressured by Mussolini to sign the Tripartite Pact and so far he had resisted. He therefore felt that receiving Weddell could have been interpreted by the Axis as a sign that he was drawing closer to the the United States[247] and the democracies. Weddell was convinced that this information was reliable because it tied in perfectly with his own theory about Franco and Serrano having different projects. As far as he was concerned, if Franco did not wish to intervene it was because he had had his mind poisoned by Serrano. In his own words, "[This] is completely in line with tactics employed by Suñer in trying to give the impression of personal differences between us (...) and strengthens my conviction that he is scheming to bring about the withdrawal of the American Ambassador."[248]

THE NEW SPANISH TEMPTATION TO ENTER THE WORLD WAR IN JUNE 1941

Italy could not have asked Franco to sign the Tripartite Pact, as Carceller had said, because he had already secretly signed it. What Ciano had really asked Serrano, in a letter dated 3 June, was for Spain to make the signature public. His exact words were the following:

> I am aware of the reasons preventing your country from taking this brave step, which is such a part of Spanish tradition and your revolutionary temperament. I am aware, and you know the great respect that Italy has always had for your freedom of decision. But it now seems to me that, even if you do not wish to enter the conflict, Spain should demonstrate that the Falangist flag is on the side of the Fascist and Nazi revolutions. In a matter of days Croatia will become part of the Tripartite. The New State that is being shaped in accordance with the model of the totalitarian states and which is encountering the internal difficulties of all beginnings is in no doubt that it should align with the Axis. Why does Spain not do the same? You may say that you have

secret agreements, which I understand. But you must understand that what matters nowadays is the responsibility that men and countries assume, and it is only by assuming this responsibility that we can claim our place in the world of tomorrow.[249]

In his own hand, after the sentence asking Franco to announce that Spain had signed the Tripartite Pact, Mussolini had added the words "at least."[250] The Italians, then, were more interested now in Spain's entering the war than the Germans. In fact, Hitler had abandoned Operation Felix and the attack on Gibraltar in favor of Operation Barbarossa and the attack on the USSR. This did not mean that he had definitively decided against intervening in Spain: he merely had a new priority. The current state of the war seemed to favor Spanish participation. The campaign in the Balkans had ended more than a month before and the Germans had managed to solve the military confusion that Italy had created; the German-Italian forces were drawing ever nearer to Egypt and the Suez Canal; and, as in June 1940, the war once again seemed about to end in an Axis victory. Il Duce was exultant. If Spain were to enter the conflict at that moment, the Mediterranean theater of war would be changed because Gibraltar would be taken and Spanish Morocco would be part of the Axis. All this would contribute to Great Britain's final defeat and the end of the war.[251] It was in Spain's interests to be involved now, or at least to make public that they had signed the Tripartite Pact.

However, what the Italians (and, of course, the Spanish) did not know, because Von Ribbentrop had not told them in Brennero on the Austrian-Italian border on 2 June, was that Germany was about to launch an attack on the USSR and was no longer interested in Europe's southern flank, which was of such concern for Italy. Hitler was about to shift the focus of the conflict toward the east in an attempt to deprive the British of their one possible continental ally—Russia, their continental sword.[252] Only after he had defeated Russia would Hitler return to the southern European flank and the struggle with Great Britain. It was here that Spain could play a role. The important thing now, though, was that Spain was of no immediate interest to Hitler.

Franco and Serrano were receptive to Mussolini and Ciano's message but they immediately wanted to know—in writing—what they would be given in return. On the very day on which he had received the letter, Serrano had a long conversation with Franco about the possibility of announcing that they had signed the pact, in compliance with the Hendaye Protocol. In his reply to Ciano, he requested an "extremely private letter" in which the Axis agreed to grant Spain its territorial claims. He also asked to be invited personally to Italy, to discuss Spain's possible entry into the war. Serrano imagined that after Spain had publicly announced that it had signed the Tripartite Pact, the British would occupy the Canary Islands and make it much more difficult to acquire navicerts, which would accelerate Spain's entry into the war.[253] Everything seems to suggest that in June 1941 the two brothers-in-law envisaged a real possibility of entering the war. Serrano was undoubtedly the most enthusiastic because he was using his relationship with the Italian leaders to increase his power and overcome the internal trouble he was having after the May Crisis.

Weddell had believed Carceller when he told him that Franco was reluctant to join the Axis and he wrote to the department to explain that Spain's rapid diplomatic recognition of the puppet Croatia was merely a sop to the Duce. His suspicions that Franco and Serrano were drawing apart were confirmed when Hoare told him that Franco wanted to get rid of Serrano but that Germany and Italy were preventing him from doing so. Of course, it is perfectly feasible that Franco was fed up with his brother-in-law after the May Crisis and the family troubles he had caused. But he still needed him, and there is little to justify the Anglo-American interpretation that Franco was in favor of remaining neutral and Serrano against. What is certainly true is that Serrano was attaching increasingly more importance to foreign affairs because of his declining domestic power, and that Franco was becoming more and more distant even though he still believed that it was still possible for Spain to enter the war in exchange for territorial compensation, supplies, and more favorable circumstances. This, however, was not to be: the attack on the USSR meant that the war changed its focus and put paid to any hopes of Spain playing a role.[254] Even so, the Spanish leaders were very excited because they were convinced that the new campaign would soon end in German victory.[255] Nothing at this point in time led Franco and Serrano to suspect what was really going to happen: despite a short period of hope in 1942, the Russian campaign would put paid to Hitler's interest in Spanish participation in the war. Neither did they suspect that the Eastern Front would be the main cause of Germany's defeat. In fact, like most of the world's leaders, they believed quite the opposite.

The Sending of the División Azul to Russia and Its effects on Relations with the United States and Great Britain

The news of the attack on the USSR on 22 June 1941 led to an explosion of euphoria among the Francoists and particularly among the members of the Falange. Serrano Suñer was elated. He predicted that the quick victory of the Axis would open up new possibilities for his own political career and for the party, and he continued to weigh up the possibility of entering the war. As he said to the Italian ambassador in Madrid, also on 22 June, the German attack put an end to the German-Soviet Pact of 1939, "the last spiritual obstacle to Spain's future participation in the conflict."[256] The anti-Communist struggle had been the "moral base"[257] of the Spanish Civil War, so the Spanish were enthusiastic about fighting against Russia. On the same day, he saw the German ambassador Von Stohrer and promised to send "a few units of Falange volunteers"[258] to take part in the struggle, although Spain did not respond to his pressure to declare war on the USSR. The Council of Ministers met on 23 and 24 June in the Pardo Palace, Franco's official residence, to study the situation,[259] but caution prevailed and the ministers decided to wait and see. This decision not to declare war was crucial to Spain's future because it would have meant entry into the Second World War.

Meanwhile, the Falangists made sure that the mood in the street was at fever pitch. Demonstrations were held in various provincial capitals.[260] The one in Madrid—probably organized with the help of the German Embassy because reporters from German agencies were there to film it—marched through the center of the city demanding that war be declared on Russia.[261] The Falangists assembled in front of the party headquarters in Calle de Alcalá and Serrano spoke to them from the balcony,[262] uttering the famous phrase "Russia is guilty!" and adding, "Guilty of the murder of so many comrades and so many soldiers who fell in the Civil War caused by the aggression of Russian Communism." He finished off his speech with a crushing judgment: "Russia must be exterminated for the sake of history and the future of Europe." The demonstration did not and here. Groups of students from the Sindicato Español Universitario, the only official union, moved on to the British Embassy and stoned it. In response, Hoare and all his staff went to protest to Serrano Suñer in his private residence, from which they were ejected after Hoare told him that "this only happens in countries of savages."[263] The relations between Spain and Great Britain became even more tense when on the same day there was a military incident between the two countries: antiaircraft guns in Algeciras opened fire on a British plane that had penetrated Spanish air space, and there was an exchange of artillery fire between Gibraltar and Spain.[264]

In the following days, volunteers were recruited so that Spain could send a division to the Russian front. Inevitably, however, the tensions between the army and the Falange led to confrontation over who should be in command. Franco decided that the military unit would be recruited by the Ministry of the Army, which would also provide the officers, while the Falange would recruit troops from among its rank and file. This new unit was referred to by Falange propaganda as the División Azul (the Blue Division) because of the color of the Falange shirt, although its official title was the División Española de Voluntarios (Spanish Volunteer Division). It consisted of 18,000 men and left for Germany in July. In the middle of August, after it had joined the Wehrmacht and been trained, the newly named 250th Infantry Division of the German army was sent to the Russian front.

Not surprisingly, however, amid the enthusiasm and mobilization of the end of June, the relations between Spain and Great Britain were becoming more strained. The press vented its anger on the British, accusing them of causing the famine in Spain by imposing the naval blockade. At this time Britain had just made an alliance with the USSR and reacted to the press campaign and the recruitment of the División Azul by banning fuel exports to Spain.[265] In turn, the Germans responded by offering Spain Rumanian oil.[266]

Amid the turmoil, Sir Samuel Hoare did what he could to reduce the tension. After speaking to some leading Spanish generals, he concluded that the German attack on Russia made Spain's entry into the war less, not more, likely.[267] He was understanding about the volunteers move to the Russian front and asked London not to suspend the gasoline supplies.[268] What is more, on 28 June 1941 he spoke to both Franco and Serrano in an attempt to break the deadlock over the issue of Weddell's interview. They both made it quite clear to him that the deterioration of the situation was not a bilateral political issue: it was a personal issue caused by Weddell's character. Franco also said at this point that the North American ambassador had said "monstruous things" during a previous interview in November 1940.[269]

In this situation, at the beginning of July the apostolic nuncio Cicognani, who was also the accredited dean of the Diplomatic Corps, tried to mediate between Weddell and Serrano by proposing that the two notes exchanged in June be withdrawn. He was not successful. The State Department would only agree to Weddell's note being withdrawn if Serrano Suñer's was also withdrawn or if Weddell was granted an immediate interview with Franco.²⁷⁰ So there was no way of increasing the economic relations between the two countries, which continued to be based on the purchase of oil and the shipment of humanitarian relief by the U.S. Red Cross. Public proof of the sorry state of the relations between the Spanish government and the US Madrid Embassy was given by Weddell's reception to celebrate American Independence Day on 4 July. Although the whole of the Spanish government had been invited, only the head of protocol of the Ministry of Foreign Affairs actually went and he only stayed for a few minutes.²⁷¹ Weddell interpreted this as further proof of Serrano's influence on the cabinet, particularly after his success with the División Azul. That Serrano was orchestrating a campaign against him was also shown by the fact that the Madrid newspapers had been ordered not to quote him, that no news was given about the embassy's social events and that he had been refused an interview to introduce the new counselor Willard L. Beaulac. Weddell also believed that Carceller was not to be trusted now because although he had confronted Serrano in the past he was no longer prepared to do so: he had not even dared to speak to him on behalf of a U.S. citizen who had been working for a company of which Carceller was the chairman and who had recently been arrested by the police. And on top of everything the new minister of governance colonel Galarza, "an ardent Franco man" and staunch enemy of Serrano Suñer, had asked Weddell not to visit him to congratulate him on his appointment because he was under such close surveillance by Serrano that it would have been embarrassing.²⁷²

The Spanish minister of foreign affairs had taken advantage of the new situation to relaunch the policy of Hispanicity. Since the previous April, his right-hand man, Felipe Ximénez de Sandoval—head of the cabinet and national delegate of the Falange's Foreign Service—had been creating Falange Missionaries and Propaganda Schools entrusted with spreading the ideas of the party in Spanish America and the Philippines. The real driving force behind the diplomatic offensive of the Hispanicity Council, however, was the new alliance between Great Britain and the USSR. It aimed to exploit the antagonism between Catholicism and Communism, thwart the policy of the United States and split up the "American block."²⁷³ This offensive was to end in resounding failure.

WEDDELL'S REQUEST TO HALT THE HUMANITARIAN RELIEF TO SPAIN

At this point, the relations between Spain and the United States had deteriorated to such an extent that Alexander W. Weddell decided that the State Department should make a forceful response to the Spanish government, using the weapons they had closest at hand. In the first place, he suggested—and the Department agreed—that the Red Cross's shipments of humanitarian relief should be stopped. On 14 July he asked Under Secretary Welles to reconsider the whole of the United States' strategy toward Spain.²⁷⁴ There was no sense at all in continuing to insist on an interview with Franco, who was well aware of U.S. policy in the world war; neither was there any sense in beginning economic talks with Spain, a country that after all that had happened, and particularly after the División Azul had been sent to Russia, was not even in a position to guarantee its neutrality, precisely the condition that the Roosevelt administration required to be able to justify future economic concessions.[275]

On a more personal note, he had been under considerable pressure as a result of the envelope incident. In his own words, he was torn between "the Scylla of wishing to hold high the dignity of my office and the Charybdis of not doing what Suñer and his German friends would like for me to do. So I shall continue to hold the fort until I get a signal from Washington."[276] The month before he had written to a friend that he was starting to take notes for a future book entitled *Failure of a Mission*, but that he was not prepared to yield.[277] From the department, Sumner Welles encouraged him to continue his resistance, although he made it quite clear that the United States did not wish to give Spain any more reasons for joining the Axis—"she should not be pushed," he wrote—by forcing diplomatic relations to be broken off. This, he said, could be extremely harmful to U.S. interests, particularly in South America.[278]

Since Weddell was persona non grata, the new counselor to the Madrid Embassy, Willard L. Beaulac took it on himself to approach the Spanish authorities and find a solution. He had been appointed in April and had arrived in Madrid at the end of June to replace Flack.[279] He had come from the embassy in Havana.[280] Under Secretary Welles had instructed him to reassess the relations between the two countries and propose a policy on Spain.[281] This suggests not only that the department wanted to reconsider the policies implemented up to that point, which had culminated in the current deadlock, but also that they were somewhat dissatisfied with Weddell's work. Even so, from the outset the new counselor worked hand in hand first with Weddell and then with his successor Carlton J.H. Hayes, and he soon became one of the key men at the Madrid Embassy. However, a new incident took place that disturbed the relations between Spain and both the United States and Great Britain. This time Serrano Suñer could not be blamed because the leading role was played by the Spanish head of state, Franco himself.

Franco's Speech on 17 July 1941

On the afternoon of 17 July 1941 Franco gave a speech to the party's National Council in Madrid on the occasion of the fifth anniversary of the *Alzamiento Nacional* (National Uprising). Because of the importance of the event, the whole of the accredited Diplomatic Corps in Madrid, including Weddell and Hoare, was in the Plenary Hall of the National Council's headquarters. Franco spoke with great violence and made several allusions to the "democratic plutocracies." He expressed his conviction that Germany had already won the war and that any intervention by the United States would only serve to prolong it unnecessarily.[282] His allusions to the United States were extremely harsh and he even made reference to the recent economic relations between the two countries:

> The Council should know how others have attempted to hinder the provisionment of our fatherland. In the moments of greatest crisis of the past year when bread was short in our territory and the inevitable delays of the long journey from South America caused a shortage of grain, it was attempted to bring from North America

100,000 tons already purchased and ready for embarkation but the efforts of our representatives were shattered by the dispositions of that nation which prohibited this and the grain remained upon the wharves of the friendly country. And when there seemed to be offered to Spain a prospect of an economic collaboration in its reconstruction, behind the generous appearance of the credit operation always appeared an attempt at political mediatization incompatible with our sovereignty and with our dignity as a free people.

The first allusion (or rather accusation) was false, since the Spanish requests for a loan to buy wheat and other products in August 1940 had not been granted, so they had not purchased the 100,000 tons mentioned or any other quantity. On the other hand, the Red Cross had been shipping supplies since February although, as we have just seen, a few days before Weddell had asked for these shipments to be halted (something that Franco was unaware of). The accusation that the loan was subject to certain political conditions was not false. That is to say, Franco's allusions to the United States expressed an anger that had gradually been accumulating as a result of his dealings with the Roosevelt administration since 1939. And this anger focused on the person of Alexander W. Weddell. He also responded to what Cordell Hull had been trying to communicate to him through the American ambassador in the non nata interview and that, from what he said, he clearly knew all about.[283] His words also reproached Weddell for having dared to question Spain's sovereignty. The American ambassador must have been aware of all this while Franco was speaking—and it was to him that the speech was primarily addressed—although he gave no sign that he was, as we shall see.

But Franco did not stop there. He questioned the British blockade ("the inhuman blockade of a continent") and the support provided by the United States through the Lend-and-Lease Act. And without mentioning the United States by name, he tried to persuade them against taking part in the war with the following words:

> I would speak to you with this crudity because the time has come to take steps against these snares, pretexts, and maneuvers and for everyone to realize that nations must save themselves by their own effort and their own work and sacrifice. It is illusory to believe that the plutocracies will make use of their gold for generous or noble enterprises. Gold ends by debasing nations as well as individuals. This exchange of fifty old destroyers for various remnants of an empire is eloquent in this regard.
>
> No human force exists which is capable of diverting this destiny. But we should none the less not dismiss from our minds the possibility that the madness which directs the policy of other countries may attempt to thrust new miseries upon Europe. Against this we must prepare ourselves, offering to the world the serene example of a united people disposed to defend its independence and its right.
>
> No one is more authorized than ourselves to say that Europe has no ambitions in America. A contest between the two continents is an impossible thing. It would mean only a long war at sea without results; fabulous business for a few and unsuspected miseries for many; prodigious losses of ships and goods; a war of submarines and high speed vessels striking blows at the hitherto peaceful commerce of the world.
>
> Coasts confronting one another, strong and unapproachable by the enemy; a sea divided into zones of influence, European and American, from which the vessels of world commerce are barred... The American Continent cannot dream of intervention

in Europe without exposing itself to catastrophe nor can it say without prejudice to the truth that the American coasts are in danger from the attacks of European powers.

Thus neither the liberty at seas (...) nor international law outraged by the inhuman blockade of a continent nor the defense of invaded peoples who are dragged into hunger and misery are now more than a grandiose farce in which nobody believes.

In this situation, to say that the course of the war can be changed by the entry into action of a third country is criminal madness, is to kindle a world war without horizon which may last years and which would definitely ruin the nations whose eclipse of life is based on their legitimate commerce with the countries of Europe.

These are facts which nobody can dispute. The blockade of Europe is contributing to the building up of an autarchy prejudicial to South America. The continuance of the war will complete the work.[284]

The reference to the recent relief by the United States of the British troops occupying Iceland was clear. And there may also have been a veiled reference to the rumors that were rife in the United States about the possible occupation of the Spanish islands in the Atlantic by North American troops assisted by Republican exiles.[285] Before finishing, Franco said that Great Britain had lost the war:

The war was badly planned and the Allies have lost it. So all the peoples of continental Europe including even France have recognized; the solution of their differences confided to the fate of arms and the outcome has been adverse. They expect nothing from their own efforts, the very governments themselves declare this clearly and definitely. What is proposed is a new war between the continents which by prolonging their agony will give them an appearance of life and in the face of this we who love America feel the anxiety of the moment and pray that the evil of which we have a foreboding may not reach them.[286]

Historiography has hotly debated what General Franco intended by giving such an anti Anglo-American speech, but these debates have often not taken place in the context of the relations between the United States and Spain. First, it was another, sincere example of his belief in an Axis victory and of his disdain for the democratic countries. He was reacting to Spain's economic dependence and the foreign policy demands that offended his extreme sense of authoritarian nationalism by hurling abuse at the British, who he called one of Spain's "age-long enemies" who used "intrigues and treachery" because they "never forgave [Spain] for having been great," and particularly at the North Americans. However, his speech was also designed to give a clear message to people at home and the Axis countries: he wanted to show that he, not Serrano Suñer, directed Spain's international policy. For his part, Serrano was both surprised and upset that his brother-in-law had not consulted him about the content of the speech, and they exchanged heated words afterward.[287] Speaking to the German Ambassador Von Stohrer some days later, a resentful Serrano reproached Franco for having "opened the English and American eyes to the true Spanish position. Until now the English government in particular had believed that only he, the minister of foreign affairs, was in favor of going to war while the 'wise and cautious' Franco unconditionally wanted to preserve neutrality."[288]

Although the speech had negative consequences for Spain, it is not so clear that it had revealed Franco's true standpoint, as Serrano suspected. What Franco had just said indirectly in public was that it was he, and not Serrano, who was in charge in Spain. It was the second setback that he had received in just a short time, the first being Franco's solution to the May Crisis. The difference between these two incidents was that the former meant that Serrano lost some of his ability to influence domestic policy,[289] while the latter suggested that Franco no longer needed him by his side in foreign affairs. The personal relations between the two, then, had begun to deteriorate toward the end of 1940; the political relations had gone into decline in May 1940;[290] and now the downward spiral took another turn. Serrano's decision to become the leader of Falange discontent had backfired and now Franco was taking his first steps in foreign policy without him.

Taking into account the negative consequences of the speech, these first steps were not altogether successful, even though there was no substantial change in the policy that the two brothers-in-law had been implementing for the previous two years. Spain was still interested in taking part in the war if the conditions were right and the sought-after territory was a possible reward. The difference lay in the fact that Franco was now at the head of foreign affairs and at his side he had an *anti-Serranista* who had his own ideas: Carrero Blanco.[291]

THE BRITISH RESPONSE

Neither Weddell nor Hoare knew exactly who had written the speech nor what Franco intended by giving it. Considering his belief in the dichotomy in Spanish politics, Weddell logically held that it was all Serrano's work;[292] the more astute and better informed Hoare, on the other hand, wondered whether it had not been prompted by Franco's desire to ingratiate himself with Hitler, whether it had been a mere verbal concession to the Axis, or whether it had been designed to show the Spanish population that he and not Serrano really held the power.[293] Paradoxically, and to Sir Samuel's horror because he sensed that his Spanish policy was now under threat, it was Great Britain that reacted most forcefully to the speech.[294] On 24 July 1941, in response to a question in the House of Commons, the Foreign Secretary and anti-Francoist Anthony Eden said the following:

> His Majesty's Government have now noted that General Franco, in his speech to the Falange National Council on July 17th, displayed complete misunderstanding not only of the general war condition, but also of British economic policy towards Spain. If economic arrangements are to succeed, there must be goodwill on both sides, and General Franco's speech shows little evidence of such goodwill. His statement makes it appear that he does not require further economic assistance from this country. If that is so, His Majesty's Government will be unable to proceed with their plans, and their future policy will depend on the actions and attitudes of the Spanish Government.[295]

Eden's words were part of a more general response that also involved new preparations for an offensive. Three days before this statement to the British parliament, the Defense Committee had decided to update the plans made the previous April for occupying the Spanish island of Gran Canaria (Operation Puma): the expeditionary force was strengthened and the operation's name was changed to Operation Pilgrim.

The military occupation was planned for August. The committee also asked the Chiefs of the General Staff to study the possibility of simultaneously launching an attack from Gibraltar on the Spanish artillery positions that threatened the Rock. Secretary Eden was asked to moderate his replies to any questions in the Commons about Franco's speech so that these intentions would remain concealed. The British government approved Eden's suggestion to stop insisting that the United States should provide Spain with economic relief "against their wishes."[296] And on 29 July, the head of the Ministry of Economic Warfare, Hugh Dalton, announced that Great Britain would maintain the "utmost vigilance to ensure that nothing reaches Spain that might increase General Franco's capacity to go to war against us.[297]

It seems, however, that the exchanges between the two countries were not greatly reduced.[298] This was because the Defense Committee wanted imports to be received from Spain until very shortly before Pilgrim was launched[299] and believed timing to be of the essence. Also, on 16 August, the British Embassy in Madrid managed to partly convince Churchill to accept Sir Samuel Hoare's and Naval Attaché Hillgarth's argument that the planned military operations needed to be halted: Franco's speech, they said, was largely of domestic importance for Spain and his attempt to curry favor with Germany should be interpreted bearing in mind that he was considering dismissing Serrano in the near future. What is more, the military attaché in Madrid, Brigadier Torr, traveled to London and convinced the chiefs of the General Staff that Franco would not enter the war unless Egypt fell into the hands of the Axis or the Canary Islands were attacked. This was not the time, he said, to carry out an offensive against Spain, nor to take any other action: it was the time to wait. They would be obliged to change this tactic if Franco were to agree to the German occupation of the country. The British would then be justified in invading the Canary Islands and this invasion would also be well received by the Spanish armed forces and the Spanish people.[300] Hoare and Torr had based their opinion on information gleaned from the group of generals who were unbeknowingly being bribed. It is also highly likely that Churchill's change of heart was influenced by the fact that Spain had created a Military Junta consisting of three *Alfonsino* monarchists (General Aranda, Kindelán, and Orgaz) and Colonel Beigbeder. They were all in favor of a neutral Spain and in close contact with other generals such as Saliquet, Ponte, and Solchaga, and monarchist and/or Catholic politicians who had been punished or ostracized by Franco (e.g., the minister of National Education between 1938 and 1939 Pedro Sáinz Rodríguez and the former leader of the popular Catholic-agrarian party during the Republic, José María Gil-Robles). All these members of the military were among those being bribed. The aim of the Junta was "to coordinate efforts against the probelligerent policy of Serrano Suñer and against Franco himself should he continue to support this policy as he had done in his speech on 17 July,"[301] and to resist any German pressure to enter the war. The members of the Junta made Torr aware of their concern that Great Britain and the United States would take military action against Spanish possessions, which would prompt Germany to invade Spain.[302]

The Junta, however, did not represent all the generals, the army. or the whole of the armed forces. Generals such as Agustín Muñoz Grandes, at the head of the División Azul, and Juan Yagüe were pro-German and pro-Falange, as were most subordinate officers. Other generals such as the Minister of Air Juan Vigón were *Alfonsino* monarchists but extremely faithful to Franco and also pro-German.[303] The chain of command, then, did not share one opinion. Franco was perfectly aware of these divisions and used them to his advantage. He also used the party and Serrano himself as a focus for the anger of the monarchists even though he needed the party as the mass base for his personal power and Serrano to curb any aspirations to restore the monarchy, which would effectively have put an end to his glorious period as head of state.

THE UNITED STATES AND THE NEW REDUCTION IN THE SHIPMENT OF OIL TO SPAIN IN SUMMER 1941

The official reaction of the United States to Franco's speech was merely to deny that Spain had ever purchased 100,000 tons of wheat so it could not have been retained.[304] It was decided not to make a formal complaint about this falsehood or to announce the real value of the supplies sent by the U.S. Red Cross to Spain, the total of which was similar to that mentioned by Franco.[305] Neither did the United States occupy the Azores, which they were supposed to have done in parallel to the British occupation of the Canary Islands, as Churchill and Roosevelt had agreed at Placentia Bay. And although the quota system established in the Anglo-Spanish Oil Agreement of September had already reduced the oil exports to Spain and other countries in comparison to 1940[306] the United States decided to decrease them even further. This decrease in the summer of 1941 was substantial, but the worst was still to come. The oil supply to Spain was decreased not only because Great Britain wanted it to be provided[307] but also because it was the natural consequence of previous decisions. For example, on 20 June 1941[308] at the proposal of the Secretary of the Interior and Oil Commissioner Harold Ickes, the United States had modified the law governing the exportation of oil products.[309] Ickes had been given invaluable help by Dean Acheson,[310] the lawyer who had made a decisive contribution to finding a legal solution to the Destroyers-for-Bases deal and who had just been appointed assistant secretary of state for economic affairs. It was he who had got the department to agree to the measure, and the fact that the proposal was jointly made by the State Department helped to convince the president and get his approval. The new law meant that all exports of oil and its derivates required an export license, thus extending the system that had been in existence for aviation fuel since July 1940. Ickes had made the proposal in an attempt to prevent oil and other U.S. products from ending up in Japan and Germany. In particular, he believed that Germany was obtaining US supplies that had been exported to Spain. These exports were being made when considerable restrictions had been put on domestic consumption so that national defense needs could be satisfied, and the government was coming in for some strong criticism from the press and public opinion.

The new system came into force on 1 August.[311] And on the same day it was established that all oil exports—with the exception of those bound for the British empire and the rest of the American continent—would be restricted to the "usual prewar quantities."[312] The final reason for decreasing the supply was that on 3 August Ickes convinced Under Secretary Welles that, because of the shortage of United States tankers, they should not be used to export oil to peninsular Spain or the Canary Islands.[313] This was an added difficulty for the Spanish, who had a small fleet of tankers. The department's economic adviser, Herbert Feis, subsequently explained that, independently of Ickes' aim, the department wanted "to cause the Spanish Government to behave more decently" but "not to force a collapse."[314] So, after Franco's speech of 17 July, the policy implemented delayed deliveries or refused licenses but did not cut off the supply or impose an embargo. In all of this Dean Acheson played a key role.[315] Another measure that was to affect trade with Spain in general was adopted after a proposal made by Hull and Morgenthau led to the drafting of a "Proclaimed list of Certain Blocked Nationals." This list initially contained some 800 people or firms suspected of working for the benefit of the Axis,[316] some of which were Spanish.

The result of all this activity was that considerably less oil was sent to Spain during the summer of 1941 (to be more precise, the third term: July, August, and September), because the United States was Spain's main supplier, although some was also sent by Venezuela,[317] Colombia, and the Dutch West Indies. In these months, Spain received less than half of the gasoline stipulated by the quota agreed on with the British, slightly more than half the amount of diesel fuel, approximately two-thirds of the fuel oil and not quite all the lubricants, as can be seen in table 1.[318]

As we can see from the table, the situation was to get no better in the next term and did not improve until well into 1942. We shall discuss this below.

Counselor Beaulac's Reports on the Spanish Situation

Meanwhile, Counselor Willard L. Beaulac met with the staff of the British Embassy and then, on 31 July, with the member of Franco's government who the British were in closest contact with: namely, the Minister of Industry and Commerce Demetrio Carceller.[319] To his surprise, the minister was prepared to come to terms with the United States and told him several important—and self-interested—secrets about the internal situation of Franco's government. He also spoke out against Serrano Suñer. Beaulac told him that before he had arrived in Spain and as a result of the conversations he had had with the State Department, he had been convinced that the two countries could come to some sort of formal or informal economic agreement, but that Franco's speech and the Spanish government's unfriendly attitude toward Weddell had put paid to these hopes. He spoke of how important public opinion was in his country and of the fact that, after the speech, the prevailing opinion was that Spain was being "unfriendly" toward the United States and collaborating more and more with the Axis. He added that the Roosevelt administration, backed by public opinion, was not prepared to help those countries that hindered attempts to prevent the Axis from controlling the Atlantic Ocean. This was fundamental to the outcome of the war.

Carceller replied so frankly that Beaulac must have been surprised. He said that the United States should be more pragmatic and take notice not of the words spoken by the Spanish leaders but of their actions; the reality of the economic aid that Spain was providing the Axis was insignificant and Spain's potential for supplying Germany and Italy was limited by the country's delicate economic situation. What is more, all supplies were being controlled by Great Britain and the navicert system

Table 1 CAMPSA imports 1941

Term	Agreed quota (tons)	Amounts received (tons)	Difference (tons)
Gasoline			
1	60,000	60,154	
2	75,000	60,677	
3	75,500	38,805	
TOTAL	211,000	159,636	
4 (Scheduled shipments)	47,409	39,652	
TOTAL	258,409	199,288	
			59,121
Oil			
1	13,500	3,108	
2	23,750	3,378	
3	33,750	1,995	
TOTAL	11,000	8,481	
4 (Scheduled shipments)	1,995	1,996	
TOTAL	12,995	10,477	
			2,518
Diesel fuel			
1	43,000	36,030	
2	40,000	36,096	
3	40,000	22,999	
TOTAL	123,000	95,125	
4 (Scheduled shipments)	20,100	8,713	
TOTAL	143,100	103,838	
			39,262
Fuel oil			
1	75,000	52,215	
2	67,500	39,007	
3	57,500	45,070	
TOTAL	200,000	136,262	
4 (Shipments scheduled)	34,100	25,886	
TOTAL	234,100	162,178	
			71,922
Lubricants			
1	7,500	6,136	
2	12,000	9,894	
3	13,200	11,285	
TOTAL	32,700	27,315	
4 (Shipments scheduled)	10,480	6,689	
TOTAL	43,180	34,004	
			9,176
Total Difference			181,999

Source: CAMPSA statistics (1941) R: 2246 E: 75 Archive of the Ministry of Foreign Affairs

(which was not exactly true because trade was also being carried out by land and was therefore not subject to these restrictions). Carceller argued that it should not be forgotten that the German army was on the other side of the Pyrenees, and that Spain did not have the sufficient military strength to repel an invasion. He even told him that if Spain had adopted a less friendly attitude toward the Axis as the British and Americans had asked, the invasion may well have taken place, which would have been harmful to the interests of the democracies. Essentially, then, he said what he thought Beaulac wanted to hear, but said nothing of the "wait-and-see" attitude that the Spanish government had adopted toward their participation in the world war. Of course, what he said also served the minister's purpose of increasing the American supplies that Spain so urgently needed, in just the same way that the demands he made to the British had resulted in the agreement of 7 April 1941. In fact, he went so far in his attempts to convince Beaulac that he told him

> Given the limited amount of practical aid which Spain was extending to the Axis and the desirability from the point of view of the military situation of the democracies of keeping the Germans out of Spain, the present policy of the Spanish Government, which is to give Germany the impression of cooperation while denying any effective cooperation, should have the wholehearted support of the democracies.[320]

A more intelligent policy, he explained, would be to cooperate with Spain and set up a system for smuggling goods to Germany that had been provided by the democracies. The Germans, then, would trust Spain absolutely and not invade. After all, he said, what importance did it have if Spain were to send 500 tons of coffee from a consignment of 1,000 if, by so doing, the Germans remained convinced that the Spanish cooperation was sincere? What is more, he was finding it extremely easy to deceive the German Embassy. He explained that he had just signed an agreement to send the Germans 12,000 tons of olive oil in monthly batches of 1,000 tons. But over the course of a year anything could happen given the fact that they were in the middle of a world war! And the División Azul was merely a cheap way of cooperating in a limited fashion with the Germans and keeping them quiet.

At this point Beaulac, who was far from convinced, interjected and said that in the light of the minister's explanations he did not understand Franco's refusal to grant Weddell an audience. Carceller, who had had to give Hoare an answer to the same question on a previous occasion, said that he regretted this situation and blamed Serrano Suñer for the conflict. He also said that he personally was working to solve the problem and was optimistic. Carceller had much to be grateful to Serrano for. It was thanks to him that he had been promoted to minister in October 1940 but, even so, he was extremely critical of him. Serrano, he said, hated the United States of America and Ambassador Weddell, whom he considered to be the typical American businessman, quite unlike Lord Hoare, the typical Englishman, whom he admired. He described him as an "an evil man goaded by limitless ambition who was trying to use the Axis governments as a help to creating greater power for himself in Spain."[321] According to Carceller, Serrano believed that if Franco delayed the interview long enough, the U.S. government would eventually replace the ambassador. He went on to explain that the cabinet was united in its opposition to Serrano—which is not difficult to believe for he was a very arrogant man—and that Franco's speech had not been an attempt to take from him "the Axis banner" and attract Germany and Italy. Serrano too was fully aware of the step that Franco had taken. Carceller showered Franco with praise: he had deeply rooted democratic instincts, he said quite shamelessly, and was not a dictator but the president of the Council of Ministers. Carceller defined himself as a liberal and a friend of the United States, who wished for nothing but good and developing relations between the two countries. He also regarded himself as a friend of Sir Samuel Hoare, who did not agree with what Eden had said in the British parliament. Carceller's greatest concern, however, was the possible North American occupation of the Atlantic islands or North Africa that, should it take place, would prompt Germany to invade the Iberian peninsula. In other words, he was afraid not of the United States but of Great Britain.

Carceller said all of the above at a time that Franco and his speech were undoubtedly quite a burden for him and a source of some considerable anguish. Because the economic effects of the speech were just beginning to show and could acquire catastrophic proportions if the British were to occupy the Canary Islands, Carceller, as minister of industry and commerce, was attempting to limit the damage by influencing Beaulac and, through him, the Roosevelt administration. And he was at least partly successful since Beaulac gave some credence to what he said.

Carceller, of course, was playing a double game and one month later during economic talks in Leipzig and Berlin he spoke of the deterioration in the relations with the United States and Great Britain as the merit of the Spanish leaders. He even made them the same proposal to set up a smuggling operation.[322] At the same time as he was making economic demands and saying "it (...) [is] now up to us [Germany] to mark out the guidelines for Spain's attitude and Spain will follow them, even if it leads to war," he also asked for their consent to flexibilize Spain's antidemocracy position by arguing that "if Germany felt it was important to keep Spain in a somewhat viable and fighting condition over the next 2 to 3 months, an attempt would have to be made to restore the flow of imports from overseas."[323] He was effectively asking for Germany's permission to obtain essential supplies from the Anglo-Saxon countries while expressing his disdain for the democracies and keeping Spanish options open to join the Axis war effort. He also expressed complete indifference to Serrano Suñer and made no attempt to hide this attitude from the Germans, something that would have been unthinkable when he took up office around the time of the Hendaye meeting. Since then, however, Franco had made it clear that he was now independent of his brother-in-law, and Carceller decided to leapfrog Serrano and move closer to the head of state. Beaulac was convinced and impressed by the conversation he had with Carceller, and it had a profound influence on the action he was to take.[324]

Despite this favorable impression, though, the head of the Madrid Embassy, Alexander W. Weddell, still advised Sumner Welles not to make any economic concessions to Spain until Franco and Serrano changed their attitude toward him.[325] He did not intend the Spanish to become prodemocratic, he argued, but he did believe that they should not be so offensive to an official representative of the United States. At the same time, bearing in mind Beaulac's interview with Carceller, he was reasonably optimistic that the situation would improve, because he believed that the "moderate elements" within Franco's cabinet were working in his favor. He also had information about a conversation between Carceller and Franco on 2 August[326] according to which the latter had said that if the ambassador were to make another request for an appointment he would give him one. Considering the worsening of the gasoline situation, this was perfectly plausible. On this point, however, Welles was quite clear: Weddell was not to make any such request, but he was pleased that the Franco government was under such pressure. The only policy possible at this time, he said, was to wait for Franco to change his mind.[327]

Meanwhile, information continued to flow between the British and American Embassies in Madrid. On 11 August, Beaulac and the commercial attaché Ralph Ackerman met with Irving, the British commercial counselor; Unwin, the commercial secretary; and a representative of the Ministry of Economic Warfare.[328] At this meeting and also at a previous one,[329] the British explained that they were urging the Spanish to come to an economic agreement with the United States so that supplies such as petroleum products could be ensured. In particular, they said that

> In the past two months it has been repeatedly pointed out to CAMPSA, members of Syndicates and the Ministry of Industry and Commerce that the main problem of the Spanish Government (...) [is] no longer that of obtaining adequate quotas from the British Government but of obtaining supplies and that as a corollary to this the U.S. is now an increasingly important factor. [However], the Spanish government has not been able to improve its political situation with the United States, so the State Department refuses to grant export licenses for which we are prepared to give navicerts

Although the British had tried to persuade the United States to grant export licenses for the products that they would give navicerts, they had not been successful (as is clear from the new measures adopted by Ickes) and the situation had deteriorated.

Following these interviews, Beaulac sent a series of reports to Washington at the end of August 1941, the most important of which was a plan for coordinating and improving the economic relations between the United States and Spain, which he had written with Ackerman.[330] Weddell's accompanying letter clearly showed that he was alarmed by the consequences that the oil restrictions were having on Spain.[331] He said:

> Unless it is determined to place Spain in the category of an enemy country and to give up trading with her, which of course is not recommended, it is logical that our trade relations be placed on as good a basis as is possible within the limitations of Spain's desire and ability to trade with us and of our determination that our trade with Spain shall not result in aid to Germany.

Weddell pointed out that the combination of the system of export licenses and the navicerts ensured that goods could not be sent on to the Axis, and that if the issue of supplies was essential to relations with Spain, this was not the time to be threatening to cut them off. Secretary Hull responded emphatically:

> Despite a free access to this market in the past and a constant disposition of this Government to cooperate with Spain in the solution of its economic problems, the Franco Government has shown no desire to reciprocate and indeed has furnished no

evidence of any wish to extend or improve relations with the United States. On the contrary, its whole policy has been to exclude in so far as possible American enterprise and investment and to restrict its purchases in this country to an irreductible minimum of necessities not available in any other market or only available at great cost.[332]

More in line with the secretary's point of view than Weddell's letter was the Beaulac-Ackerman technical report, which argued that the economic relations between the two countries were unsatisfactory because the United States was providing Spain with essential products that were difficult to find in other places (e.g., gasoline and other oil products) but in return could not obtain such strategically important products as cork, zinc, or olive oil. What is more, Spain was putting "insurmountable" difficulties in the way of importing products that the United States had traditionally exported such as films, printed material (not a single American magazine or newspaper was being sold in Spain at this time) or radios, all of which were of considerable political importance. Likewise, the Spanish complained that the restrictions that the United States had placed on exports meant that they could not acquire all the products they desired or the right amounts. The overall situation, then, was the result of the juxtaposition of Spain's non–laissez-faire policy and the United States not restricting sales with the purpose of achieving a quid pro quo exchange. And at this point in time the United States of America was losing out.

In this situation, Beaulac and Ackerman suggested that there was only one way to overcome the Spanish obstacles: make intelligent use of export restrictions. To do so, however, the administration had to be able to coordinate all aspects of economic relations with Spain through the State Department. They argued that "there is not in the State Department in Washington any entity authorized or qualified to deal with the many sides of the Spanish picture and to coordinate the various elements entering into our relations with this country." Neither was there "adequate coordination between the Department and the Embassy in Madrid to enable the Embassy to discuss economic matters with Spanish authorities intelligently and successfully." To support their arguments they gave the following example:

> Our Government recently expressed interest in obtaining a certain amount of zinc from Spain. The Spanish Government immediately countered with an offer to furnish the zinc in exchange for a certain amount of ammonium sulphate. We are furnishing large amounts of petroleum products, and could furnish more; in exchange for this we have neither asked for nor received corresponding trade advantages.

This state of affairs was the result not only of the department's reluctance to put economic relations with Spain "on a trading basis" but also of the Madrid Embassy's unsuccessful attempts to convince the Spanish authorities that a more permissive export policy would be beneficial for both countries. The failure was evident: the United States had been too permissive with Spain and had been unable to satisfy their own needs.

The internal coordination of the Roosevelt administration, then, was not working as it should. From the very moment that the United States had restricted exports, Spain had responded to U.S. orders of Spanish products with a corresponding order for products on the restricted list. Because there was no coordination among the departmental sections involved in trade with Spain or with the Madrid Embassy, Weddell and his staff were "prevented from driving home the fact of the concessions we are making or to insist that Spain recognize our desires." The solution lay in

> the setting up in the Department of a body whose function it would be to coordinate the work of the various United States Government departments, agencies and divisions having to do with Spain. Some of these departments, agencies, etc., are, for example, the Treasury Department in connection with the possible use of Spanish credit by Axis powers and in connection with the furnishing of information concerning the amount of Spanish balances in the United States at a given time; the Division of Controls of the State Department, and the office of the Administrator of Export Control in connection with export licenses; the Department of Agriculture in connection with Spain's need for fertilizers, etc., and the Metal Reserves Corporation and Defense Finance Corporation in connection with the acquisition in Spain of zinc, cork and other strategic materials.

The person or office in charge would have to be informed daily "of all aspects of our economic relations with Spain and would be in a position to coordinate them" and would keep the "Madrid Embassy informed and give the Embassy the opportunity to make recommendations before export licenses for Spain were issued or other facilities were given to Spain." In this way, the embassy "would be in a position to go to the Spanish Government and obtain from the Spanish Government those commodities and facilities which we desire in exchange for the commodities we are in a position to furnish Spain." What is more, "it might permit the Embassy to check the tendency of considered discrimination against American goods which is seriously affecting our commerce in certain articles." One of the examples given was the National Syndicate of Entertainment's imposition of prohibitive taxes on tickets to see American films although films from other countries were tolerated. According to Beaulac and Ackerman, if the proposed coordination managed "to reintroduce into Spain American printed matter, moving pictures, and radios, the system would have justified itself." Another factor to consider was that the United States:

> could increase our purchases of Spanish products, which in turn would enable Spain to import more products from the United States, including products which we ourselves are interested in furnishing. This would tend to raise, to some extent at least, the lamentably low standard of living of the Spanish people today, and by placing American products in Spanish hands the United States would receive at least part of the credit for this.

This proposal of internal coordination would also give the U.S. Embassy greater influence in Spain.

Beaulac and Ackerman believed that once this system had been put into practice, the relation with the Ministry of Industry and Commerce should take priority over everything else. This would mean that they could avoid Serrano Suñer, which was one of the recurring aims of both the British and the American Embassies in Madrid, and deal directly with Carceller, who had so impressed Beaulac. They said that "if the system worked out as anticipated the ministry of Industry and Commerce would be a powerful ally within the government on any matter of importance to Spanish-American relations." What is more, trade with Spain in such products as coffee and sugar could include Latin America and set up a triangular system.[333] The proposal was absolutely reasonable as a way of optimizing economic and political relations with Franco's Spain. A month and a half later, in October 1941, new sections were set up within the U.S. administration to control foreign trade by means of export licenses. In March 1942, a specific section was set up for the Iberian peninsula (see below). Meanwhile, however, the coordination between the State Department and the Madrid Embassy was still besieged by problems.

Another of the reports sent by Beaulac to Washington—this one written by him alone—analyzed the general Spanish political situation prevailing on 27 August 1941.[334] It focused on the attitudes of both Franco and Serrano, since Beaulac, like Weddell and Hoare, had blindly accepted that the political attitudes of the two men were different. The report described Serrano as the most hated man in Spain (which was true), and stated that he owed his position of power both to his family ties with Franco (which was obvious) and to the support he received from Germany. This last observation was not so clear because support for Serrano within the Axis came more from Italy than from Germany, who since November 1940 even considered him to be an obstacle to their plans. The report mentioned the two explanations that were circulating in Spain about Serrano's involvement with the speech of 17 July: On the one hand that "he was responsible for General Franco's anti-democratic speech (...) which indicated his growing authority with the Government," or, on the other, that "Franco made his July speech in order to wrest the Axis banner from Suñer's hands, and that Suñer was greatly displeased by the speech." The report also spoke of the rumor that the Germans "are becoming disquieted over Serrano Suñer's lack of popularity in Spain and are looking for a more popular leader," which seems to have been completely untrue. In Beaulac's opinion, the first and foremost obstacle to better relations between the United States and Spain was "General Franco's continued refusal to receive the American Ambassador, and (...) the open offensive toward the United States of Serrano Suñer." It was generally held that "Serrano Suñer is personally responsible [for this situation] and that he is acting in a manner which he believes will be pleasing to the Germans who are his present sponsors in Spain," which was doubly mistaken not only because the Germans were not his sponsors but also because both brothers-in-law agreed on the policy that they were applying toward the United States. As far as the economic relations between Spain and Britain were concerned, Beaulac described the situation as being "on stand by" since the speech and said that the British cabinet was "endeavoring to arrive at a decision as to whether it will continue its present policy of limited economic assistance or whether it will abandon, or at least modify, its policy." Of course "Ambassador Hoare would appear to be opposed to any change believing that time is working in his favor."[335]

The Resolution of the Serrano-Weddell Incident between September and October 1941

At long last, in September 1941 and after months of problems with the supply of gasoline, Franco adopted a new approach. In the middle of the month Serrano Suñer was once again forced to take action to improve relations with the United States because of the desperate economic situation. On this occasion the shipments of gasoline were becoming increasingly infrequent but not only because of intentional restrictive measures. There were also other reasons: for example, the Spanish often changed their minds about the exact product they wanted to buy when the tankers were already on their way, which led to confusion and delays, and the State Department regularly received reports of oil being transferred from Spanish to German tankers.[336] The effect of the reduced supplies had been terrible and Weddell was extremely concerned that Spain might be forced into the arms of the Axis.[337]

To break the deadlock between the two countries, Serrano called Ambassador Cárdenas back from Washington so that he could act as mediator with the Madrid Embassy. Once in the capital, Cárdenas threw himself heart and soul into resolving the Serrano-Weddell dispute largely because, as a veteran Spanish diplomat of the old school, he feared that Serrano's unpredictability could affect his professional future. Before leaving Washington, he went to say farewell to Secretary Hull, who took advantage of the visit to give vent to all the anger that had been building up as a result of the disputes between the two countries, Spain's refusal to accept free trade and give priority to the United States, the spurning of his offer to negotiate a trade agreement (about which Weddell could not even inform Franco), and above all the way in which Serrano and Franco were treating the U.S. ambassador in Madrid. He said[338]

> In all of the relations of this Government with the most backward and ignorant governments in the world, this Government has not experienced such a lack of ordinary courtesy of consideration, which customarily prevails between friendly nations, as it has at the hands of the Spanish Government. Its course has been one of aggravated discourtesy and contempt in the very face of our offers to be of aid.

And he went on:

> We could not think of embarrassing, not to say humiliating, ourselves by further approaches of this nature, bearing in mind the coarse and extremely offensive methods and conduct of Suñer in particular and in some instance of General Franco.

He added that the more he thought about "the conduct of the Spanish Government toward this Government," the more inconceivable it seemed to him, and he warned Cárdenas, who by that point must have been quite upset by the harsh criticism, that he had

> little hope [that he] could make the slightest impression on Franco and Suñer for the reason that if they are capable of adopting such an unworthy and contemptible attitude toward this Government with no cause whatever, when they should in fact have been thankful, he seriously doubted whether the Ambassador can appeal to any sense of reason or courteous conduct.

Having weathered the storm as best he could, Cárdenas responded lamely that there must have been some sort of misunderstanding between Weddell and Serrano and that he would do whatever he could to find a solution.

For his part, during a visit to Germany at the beginning of September, the Minister of Industry and Commerce Carceller had already warned the Germans that they might have to accept an agreement between Spain and the United States that would put an end to the problem of the oil supply. At the same time as he was reaffirming Spain's friendship with the Axis (and even his willingness to go to war), he pointed out that Spain may have to moderate its antidemocracy attitudes in order to be able to receive vitally needed imports. And once he had returned to Madrid, he asked for permission to do just this, saying that

> It would also be highly effective (...) if the American Ambassador in Madrid would finally be granted his wish for a personal audience with the Caudillo, something which had been denied him for months. (...) If Franco would see the Ambassador for only 15 minutes, it could be assumed that the American Government would, for instance, issue export clearance for six Spanish tankers which are lying in American ports ready to sail, loaded with paid-for gasoline (...) [And] that all Franco would have to tell the Ambassador was that the Spanish Government intended to continue in its present policy. Each party could then interpret this in its own way, the Americans as a continuation of Spanish neutrality, the Spaniards as a continued policy of unlimited support to Germany. (...) Naturally the Spanish press would be bound to continue supporting the German side as before, only there would have to be a halt for the time being to sharp attacks, insults and vituperation against Germany's enemies.[339]

As soon as he was back in Spain, Cárdenas set to work to solve the conflict: he had two interviews with his minister, Serrano, and one with both Serrano and Franco. The apostolic nuncio Cicognani also acted as mediator[340] and, through him, the Pope sent telegrams to Franco.[341] Cárdenas saw Weddell several times, and on the first of these occasions he explained how hostile Serrano Suñer felt toward him and how he had "iterated and reiterated the 'offensive conduct'" of the ambassador during the interview on 19 April when he had accused Spain of "having lost her sovereignty."[342] Weddell responded by saying that the Spanish minister's anger was clearly an "afterthought" because after the interview, on 1 May, Serrano had written to him quite politely and not in the least offended. He did not, however, mention the second incident involving his wife's postcard. Cárdenas said that Weddell's note of 9 June had led to Serrano's note of 13 June. Weddell replied that his note had been dictated to him by the State Department. Cárdenas then appealed to the ambassador's spirit of sacrifice and mentioned all the things that he had had to "swallow" throughout his career, which prompted Weddell to say that "On various occasions I had 'swallowed' gross rudeness on the part of the Foreign Minister... while the outstanding fact in all my relations with him was he had thus far successfully thwarted my desire, acting under instructions of my Government, to see the Chief of State." Cárdenas persisted in asking Weddell to make some sort of conciliatory gesture toward Serrano and, in particular, to tell him that he had had no intention of offending him with the envelopes and his allusions to German censorship. Weddell, who was getting more and more upset, refused to do so. Cárdenas then suggested that they could withdraw their notes and although initially Weddell refused point blank, he then said that under no circumstances would he withdraw his note first. He insisted that, behind everything, was the question of the interview with Franco, which was still pending. At this point in the conversation, Cárdenas painted a dramatic (and real) picture of supplies that had been cut off, a population that was starving and a country that was being forced into the arms of the Axis, with all the negative consequences that this involved for the British cause. Weddell also believed in the scenario he described and was prepared to do all he could to avoid it. But he was not prepared to bow before Serrano Suñer. He said that in Serrano's twelve months as foreign minister he had never made any mention of wishing to cooperate in trade with the United States. The Ministry of Industry and Commerce, on the other hand, was a different matter and had repeatedly sought out the embassy to discuss possibilities of cooperation. Eventually, because of his "sincere friendship for Spain" he wished "to contribute to some satisfactory arrangement" so he made it clear that he would be prepared to enter into some sort of agreement. He also asked about the rumors rife in Madrid that changes in some ministries, including Serrano's, were imminent. Cárdenas told him that he sincerely doubted that these changes would take place.

These rumors, however, were in fact quite accurate and eventually proved to be one of the reasons for Serrano's dismissal as minister of foreign affairs and president of the political board of the Falange one year later. His extra-matrimonial affair with the society lady Sónsoles de Icaza y de León, the Marquise of Llanzol, was now public knowledge and it was even to lead to the birth of a daughter just three days before he was dismissed in 1942.[343] Weddell had been informed of this situation during the summer by Beigbeder,[344] who was no stranger to extra-matrimonial affairs himself and was extremely hostile to Serrano. His own relationship with Mrs. Fox had been used as the reason—or excuse—for his dismissal. Although Serrano's lover was neither English nor a spy, the situation was untenable in the ultra-Catholic environment of the Franco regime and extremely hurtful to Franco's wife Carmen Polo. The Marquise in question was an acquaintance of the Weddells and had often been invited to the embassy because, as we know, they were very fond of mixing with nobles ("Grandes de España") and members of high society.[345] Her husband, the marquis of Llanzol, was lieutenant colonel Francisco de Paula Díez de Rivera y Casares, who was considerably older than his attractive wife and who had caught typhus during the Civil War. Serrano Suñer had used his influence to get him the post of adviser to the Bank of Spain, a job for which he had had absolutely no training and which was extremely well paid.[346] Despite his family lineage, he may have needed this job because he was "penniless" (according to Weddell) or simply because he was unable to keep up with the spending of his young wife, who was always dressed in the height of fashion. Beigbeder also informed Weddell that Serrano's wife—Ramona or "Cita" Polo—had gone to the Pardo Palace to complain to her sister and that Franco himself was extremely annoyed. In this context, Beigbeder advised Weddell to be patient and wait until October, suggesting that by then Serrano would have been dismissed. Although Weddell considered Beigbeder to be a "peripatetic gas bag, talking *all* the time and therefore, as a general rule, badly informed" he believed the secret he had revealed and adopted a "time will tell" attitude to his prediction about Serrano's dismissal.[347] He was right to do so because Serrano was to stay in power for much longer than Beigbeder had anticipated.

Cárdenas, on the other hand, was determined to make the most of his time and on the day after his first interview with Weddell, he visited him again. Their conversation was largely a repetition of what they had said the previous day, but this time Cárdenas suggested that they should exchange their points of view in writing. Weddell refused to yield and complained once again about not being granted an audience with Franco. However, he wrote to the department to say that things were now being taken seriously and that the Spanish government was extremely concerned about the consequences that Serrano's attitude toward his person and the Madrid Embassy was having in the U.S. administration.[348] Washington also believed that the Spanish had decided to make a move so Secretary Hull ordered him to be more flexible with Cárdenas and suggested how he should proceed on the issue of the notes. He said:

> The Department is convinced that Cárdenas is honestly trying to clear up this unsatisfactory situation in the hope of improving general relations. His presence in Madrid may offer a satisfactory opportunity of withdrawing these notes, of which the Department feels we should not hesitate to take advantage. If, therefore, Cardenas should offer to return to you your note, the Department is of the opinion that you should reciprocate.[349]

Cárdenas continued to work against the clock. He had new interviews with Franco and Serrano Suñer, and immediately afterward with Weddell, but only to inform him that he would be received by Serrano on 30 September 1941 and subsequently by Franco.[350] He told him that Spain was now in desperate need of gasoline and that the highest political circles believed that the United States was pressurizing Spain by taking a long time to authorize export licenses (which was absolutely true). He also told him that he was looking into the problem of the attacks in the Spanish press on the United States and President Roosevelt. According to the Ministry of Foreign Affairs, he said, these attacks were in response to attacks on Spain made in the North-American press. Cárdenas had suggested that at least "Arriba," the Falange's main newspaper, should desist from offending the United States. With this he showed that, like Weddell, he was unaware that some of these editorials were written by Serrano Suñer himself.

Cárdenas, then, had devised a general strategy that included giving advice to the U.S. ambassador on how to deal with the *Cuñadísimo*. He asked Weddell not to mention the withdrawal of the notes to Serrano and he said that they should not forget that they were experienced diplomats dealing with "young and inexperienced men, men unversed in international relations." In the end, it seems that Cárdenas' advice and recommendations were not required because the interview between Serrano and Weddell took place in a relaxed atmosphere.[351] Even so, Weddell showed the extent of his ignorance of the Francoist mentality by complaining that he had found out about his alleged insult to Spanish sovereignty from Cárdenas just a few days before and that it had all been a misunderstanding. They argued for a while but eventually agreed to forget the incident. Not once did they mention the withdrawal of the notes. They had met to discuss the issue of supplies and Weddell decided to get straight to the point. There was no longer any need to offer to improve trade relations; he simply had to demand a quid pro quo relationship. Therefore, he began by saying that the United States wanted to buy various products from Spain, including cork, zinc, mercury, and olive oil. Serrano Suñer then stated Spain's needs. He said that the need for gasoline was extremely urgent, but that the other products could be discussed calmly at a later date. The economic situation of the country was so serious, he said, that gasoline was no longer just a product but a political issue, and that the delays were causing bad feeling against the United States in the government and the general population (quite a cynical statement considering that Serrano had done much to create this bad feeling with his speeches and editorials). He also said that if Spain's status as a nonbelligerent country meant something to Britain, then Spain should not be "strangled" by the shortage of gasoline. He could not understand, he continued, why the quantities of gasoline already agreed on with Great Britain and the United States were not already being supplied.

Weddell rightly replied that the United States had come to no official agreement with Spain and that between these two countries there was no trade agreement or quota system similar to the arrangement between Great Britain and Spain. Serrano's statement showed that he was unaware of this or that he was unable to distinguish between official agreements and purchases from suppliers. It also showed his lack of interest in the administrative side of foreign affairs, something that has already been pointed out by historiography.[352] Three weeks later Beaulac also spoke of the inconceivable inefficiency and lack of coordination of the Franco administration, particularly as far as the coordination between the ministries was concerned.[353] Weddell denied that there was a policy of reprisals against Spain and explained that the present situation had come about because the United States now had a new system of export licenses and that there was a shortage of gasoline, particularly on the East Coast. He also pointed out that this was the first time that Spain's minister of foreign affairs had informed the U.S. ambassador that his country was in need of gasoline, and that he had become aware of the situation only through informal and indirect means. This reference to the fact that Weddell had several interlocutors and the lack of implication of the Ministry of Foreign Affairs almost made Serrano lose his temper. To make it clear that he was closer to Franco than anyone else, he replied that the talks with the Ministry of Industry and Commerce had been "indiscreet" and were no guarantee of anything (thus playing down Carceller's role), and he made no mention of his own responsibility in the lack of contact. He then insisted on the issue of the gasoline and announced that he would draw up a memorandum that would itemize all the delays in the deliveries to date. He also said that he would arrange for Weddell to see Franco in the next few days.

He kept his word. After a wait of six days, on 1 October 1941 the ambassador was granted an audience with Franco in the presence of Serrano. During the meeting, Weddell read a memorandum[354] that he had prepared. It had been written by the embassy and modified by the State Department, and it was the expression of a fundamental change. Now, unlike the previous spring, the United States had decided not merely to act in accordance with the wishes of the British Embassy in Washington: immersed in their own program for manufacturing armaments (designed to support the United Kingdom but also as a function of their own military interests) and concerned with their own defensive needs, they wished to acquire strategic materials from Spain. And they were only prepared to acquire them on the basis of quid pro quo exchanges. The text, which made no attempt to tone down its criticism of Serrano Suñer, said the following:

> In connection with informal representations made to this Embassy indicating a desire on the part of the Spanish Government to improve trade relations with the United States, I wish to inform Your Excellency that my Government has been and is still prepared to use its efforts to increase American purchases of Spanish products and thus give Spain additional purchasing power in the United States. In turn it is prepared to sell to Spain freely those products of which it has an exportable surplus.

The ambassador went on to justify the difficulties of shipping oil and other products by saying that "if certain products cannot be supplied or can be supplied only in limited amounts it is because of shortages of such products in the United States due to our enormous defense effort." And he issued the following warning:

> Shortages of materials are becoming more acute daily and the longer we delay in placing Spanish-American economic relations on an equitable basis the more difficult it will become for the United States to make available many of the products which Spain desires. (...) In my recent conversation with the Foreign Minister, he referred to gasoline. I wish to point out that the United States has over a long period of time sold to Spain all the gasoline which Spain was able to transport with its existing tanker capacity and whatever delays have occurred in issuing export permits have become administrative delays due to the fact that exportation of gasoline is restricted in the United States for reasons of military defense. Moreover, my Government has continued to supply Spain with petroleum products and other urgently needed products [here the Department had struck from the initial draft copy the sentence "in the face of a public attitude of increasing hostility on the part of Spain"] despite the fact that Spain has excluded from its markets also American products except those which it could obtain only in the United States or which were obtainable elsewhere only at inordinately high prices. These products have been supplied to Spain in the face also of obstacles which the Spanish Government has placed in the way of the export to the United States of products of which Spain has had an exportable surplus.

He concluded by reaffirming the United States' will to send exports to Spain and even increase the current quantities as long as Spain was prepared "to place this trade on a reciprocal, friendly basis."[355]

When Weddell had finished reading, Franco had his say. He spoke at length of the difficulties that Spain was having in finding wheat, cotton, and gasoline, all of which had been easy to find in the world market before the outbreak of war. He cited the difficulties that the country was having to find the means to pay for supplies but was interrupted by Weddell who told him that Spain had not permitted the United States to buy zinc, a surplus product. If he had allowed the sale to go through, he would have obtained some of the funds that he had just said were so difficult to come by. Franco did not know what to say to this. Encouraged by his success, Weddell told him that the United States could sell Spain not only the products that he had mentioned but also typewriters, calculators, and radio sets, which were not among the Spanish orders but which the United States wished to sell. He pointedly added that during the previous year the embassy had not received a list of products that Spain wanted to purchase from the United States, although he had found out about the need for gasoline from the orders placed by CAMPSA, all of which had been informal. Franco did manage to respond to this point. Spain, he said, communicated with the North American government through two channels: the U.S. Embassy in Madrid and the Spanish Embassy in Washington. In this case, they had been using the latter. Weddell was hurt by this response and he complained that despite being prepared to help he was being marginalized. He also said that he had not been aware of what the Spanish Embassy in Washington did, which did not reflect well on the State Department and its coordination with the Madrid Embassy. This confirmed the U.S. administration's lack of internal coordination mentioned by Beaulac and Ackerman in their report two months before.

Nevertheless, Weddell was not prepared to bite his tongue in the presence of Franco despite the presence of Serrano Suñer and the delicacy of what he was about to say. He brought up Serrano's comment from the previous interview that Spain should not be "strangled" by the United States. Franco was about to respond when Serrano made a scornful gesture and said that the comment was not intended to be a threat, only a reflection: that the shortage of gasoline was paralyzing the nation and causing hostility toward the United States, and that Weddell's government should be aware of this. Weddell repeated his argument that the delays were the result of administrative adjustments caused by the fact that the export of gasoline was now restricted for defense purposes. However, he did not dwell on this issue: in Franco's presence he had managed to accuse Serrano and he innocently thought that this would weaken him. He changed tack and tried the old maneuver of attempting to exclude Serrano from any future economic negotiations. After asking whether Spain wished to improve its relations with the United States and Franco had replied in the affirmative, Weddell said that, if that was the case, he hoped the necessary instructions would be given to the appropriate ministry. He suggested that this should be the Ministry of Industry and Commerce. Franco was quick to cut him off and said that the ministry entrusted with this responsibility would be the Ministry of Foreign Affairs. So the plan to sideline Serrano and bring Carceller to the fore did not work. Getting round the most famous brother-in-law in Spain was no easy matter. The most important result of the meeting, though, was that everything seemed to suggest that trade talks were about to begin.

Spanish Haste and the Demands for Greater Coordination between the Madrid Embassy and the State Department

Franco's government decided that it would immediately take commercial advantage of the fact that a solution had been found to the conflict with Alexander W. Weddell. We have already spoken of how Carceller had sounded out the Germans about this possibility, and Cárdenas was instructed to go to the State Department and request the immediate initiation of trade talks. This he did on 9 October 1941 and he found a favorable atmosphere. Under Secretary Welles thanked him for the steps he had taken in Madrid and informed him that he "had heartily approved" of the suggestion made by the head of the department's Western Europe Division, Ray Atherton, to begin talks with the Spanish commercial attaché in Washington.

Cárdenas described Spain's current economic situation as disastrous, and said that if the United States did not send supplies forthwith, then Spain may have no other option but to come to an economic agreement with Germany, even though he personally was violently against such an eventuality. Surprisingly, however, given the nature of the remarks he had previously made to his friend Welles, he showered praise on Serrano Suñer who, contrary to general opinion in the United States, had played a fundamental role in preventing Germany from occupying Spain and in improving cooperation with the Axis.[356] He also criticized Ambassador Weddell, whom he blamed for the recently resolved dispute. In particular, he said that "the Embassy had failed to understand Spanish temperament and that notwithstanding the best intentions, the Embassy had been responsible for the creation of friction which might easily have been avoided."[357]

Meanwhile, in the days immediately following the interview between Weddell and Franco, the Madrid Embassy prepared various reports and recommendations about how to improve coordination with the department, and on 9 October 1941 Weddell sent a "Plan for the Coordination and Improvement of Our Relations with Spain."[358] Two weeks later he sent a memorandum on Spain's commercial relations written by the commercial attaché Ackerman.[359] When he found out that the Board of Economic Operations had been set up on 8 October 1941 to manage the department's remaining responsibilities after most of the functions concerning licenses and other economic matters had been transferred to the recently created Economic Defense Board,[360] Willard L. Beaulac drafted a lengthy report entitled "Recommendations for a Policy for Spain"[361] on behalf of the ambassador, who was out of Madrid at that time. In the introduction, which was written for Hull, and in a personal letter that was sent with an extra copy to Welles, Beaulac insisted on the urgent need for coordination. The report pointed out the main shortcomings of current policy. For example,

> The Embassy has already pointed out to the Department [that] one weakness in the Embassy's position in Spain is the lack of information concerning activities in the Department with reference to Spain. The Embassy occasionally learns second hand from someone in the Spanish Government, or in the petroleum industry for example, of conversations between officials of the Spanish Embassy in Washington and officers of the Department. The Embassy is by no means sure, however, that everything which is said to the Spanish Embassy is communicated accurately to the Spanish Government, and it is believed that the Department, in sending instructions to this Embassy, may sometimes assume that the Spanish Government has information concerning our attitude which in fact it does not have. It would be very helpful if this Embassy could be kept informed either by telegram or by air mail concerning these conversations and concerning decisions of the Department which may be communicated to the Spanish Embassy.[362]

In the letter to Welles[363] that was sent with the report, however, Beaulac was even more candid. He reminded him that

> Some time ago I asked that the Embassy be supplied with copies of memoranda and so forth indicating what was happening in the Department with reference to Spain. When I arrived here, I was very much struck with the complete absence of any information in the Embassy about what the Department was doing in relation to Spain.

After his years spent at the embassy in Cuba, this had been a big surprise to him since the department was particularly careful to coordinate Cuban affairs. He pointed out that "whenever an officer of the Department discusses Cuban affairs with an official of the Cuban Embassy (...) the Embassy is immediately furnished with a report of the conversation and is able to keep track of what is going on in Washington as well as in Habana." He also reminded the under secretary that before he had left for Madrid he had been told that he would be kept informed. In short, and as far as the North American policy toward Spain was concerned, "... it is still literally true that our right hand does not know what our left hand is doing."

Even though he was well aware of the criticism leveled at trade with Spain by some sectors of the U.S. administration, press, and public opinion, in the recommendations section he argued that trade relations should be continued and increased because if they were not Spain would remain in the economic orbit of the Axis, and the United States would have to do without such strategic materials as cork, zinc, and pyrite. Therefore, trade should not only be maintained but also increased, and the United States would benefit as a result. In fact, the Spanish minister of industry and commerce had already offered to double the number of vessels loaded with pyrite bound for the United States. Nevertheless, for Beaulac, the economic issue was not everything. Political and military matters were more important. And from these perspectives it was of utmost importance to keep Spain out of the war, because of the country's fundamental strategic position. If Spain were to become an adversary and/or Germany were to occupy Spanish Morocco the fate of Gibraltar and French Morocco could have been sealed. We should point out here that for some time both Great Britain and the United States had been cultivating relations with French Morocco governed by General Weygand. In February 1941 the United States had even signed a lend-and-lease agreement, the so-called Murphy-Weygand Agreement. As far as the British policy toward Spain was concerned, Beaulac pointed out that "the only possible criticism which may be directed at British policy (...) is that it has been applied in the face of a gratuitously offensive attitude towards Great Britain on the part of the Spanish Government and press" and immediately added that this could not occur in the case of the United States since "the Embassy has made it clear to the authorities that our economic relations with Spain can be improved only if the Spanish Government and Government-controlled press adopt an improved attitude toward us."[364]

One week after sending the text, Beaulac wrote to Assistant Secretaries Dean Acheson and Adolf A. Berle Jr.[365] insisting that coordination be improved and that the Madrid Embassy be consulted before each export license was granted. He even asked for the embassy to be part of the organization entrusted with managing economic relations with Spain and expressed his absolute opposition to the only channel of communication between Spain and the United States being the one already established between the Spanish Embassy in Washington and the department. He argued his case by reiterating the chaotic lack of coordination of Franco's government and particularly the bad reputation of the Ministry of Foreign Affairs. He said,

> It is difficult to conceive of the inefficiency with which this totalitarian government operates. There is practically no coordination among the various Government

departments. Each head of a department or separate office is a petty tyrant, interested only in his own immediate objectives. The Ministry for Foreign Affairs has no prestige, and other Government departments characteristically pay little or no attention to what it says. If the Department deals only with the Spanish Embassy in Washington, therefore, the probability is that its representations, if they are accurately communicated to the Ministry of Foreign Affairs here, will rot in some dark corner and that it is all there will be to it. In order that the Spanish *Government* [the underlinings are from the original] as distinguished from the Ministry of Foreign Affairs or some under official in the Ministry can be currently informed of our attitude it is necessary that the *Embassy here* go to infinite pains to make this attitude known to a varying number of persons not only within the Ministry of Foreign Affairs but in other departments and agencies. The British have been working at this for a long time and they have found it necessary themselves to bring about coordination among the various Spanish Departments and agencies in every individual case discussed. No organization exists within the Spanish Government which is itself able to bring about that coordination.

But this was not all. At times Franco's government "balks and does not want to take the steps we suggest" but more frequently it did not do so through "sheer lethargy and inefficiency" and it was only "by continuous hammering" that the embassy could break the inertia. In this process, whether or not the export licenses were granted was fundamental. The most important thing for the Madrid Embassy was that its policy of indefinitely maintaining Spain's status as a nonbelligerent country should win through.

In spite of the need for coordination, information, and intervention, the problem was not to be solved for some considerable time. After the Economic Defense Board mentioned above had been set up outside the department and the Board of Economic Operations within it, the bureaucracy got much more complicated. What is more, differences arose in the internal policy on how to deal with Spain.

Proposal for a Trade Agreement with the Franco Regime and Restrictions on Shipping Oil Products Beginning in November 1941: The "PM" Campaign, the Weygand Question, and Serrano Suñer's New Trip to Germany

When a path toward an economic agreement seemed to have been cleared in Madrid, new difficulties arose in Washington. On the same day as his interview with Franco, Weddell had received a telegram from the State Department ordering him to investigate the truth of information about alleged transfers of gasoline from Spanish tankers to Axis vessels in the Atlantic.[366] To make things worse, this information came from officers and seamen on Spanish tankers (particularly the first officer of the steamer "Monte Iciar"), it had reached the ears of the Commissioner of Customs, and had been forwarded by the Treasury Department to the State Department.[367] Weddell took immediate action and two days later[368] he replied that the British had reacted to similar information by sending an expert from their Ministry of Economic Warfare to investigate. In order to compare the amounts that arrived at their destination with the amounts that had been shipped, he studied figures supplied by CAMPSA and the tanks of unloaded oil products in both peninsular Spain and the Canary Islands. He concluded that although there may well have been the occasional transfer of small quantities of oil to Axis vessels on the high sea, this transfer was certainly not on a large scale or systematic. Neither was oil being sent to Germany or Italy from Spanish ports. Weddell accepted these conclusions and at the same time questioned whether these officers and seamen had really witnessed any transfers. The incident, however, had been reported to the government by Secretary Ickes[369] and Sumner Welles had to write to the president along the same lines as Weddell had. He based the content of his text on a report by the FBI of 9 September and concluded that the accusations seemed to be "purely circumstantial and inconclusive."[370]

Following these skirmishes, on 10 October 1941 the State Department presented President Roosevelt with a proposal for trade relations with Spain. Because of the controversy surrounding the Spanish question in the country and the administration, and as a result of recent debates, the State Department had decided to add another element, subordinate to the fundamental political-strategic considerations, and which Weddell had already discussed in his interview with Franco: the United States should receive goods in return for shipping oil and other products to Spain.[371] The memorandum coincided with the points of view of the Madrid Embassy in that it suggested that future relations with Spain should not merely be based on political and military objectives. In this respect it stated:

> It is desirable to develop United States trade with Spain on a broader basis than has existed in recent months, with the principal object of discouraging Spain from entering into closer relations with the Axis Powers. Recent conversations indicate that the Spanish Government is genuinely desirous of expanding trade relations between Spain and the United States.[372]

It argued that up to that time the United States had had no strictly commercial policy toward Spain: relations had been on a day-to-day basis and individual export licenses had been considered and granted (or suspended) depending on particular circumstances. At times the controls on U.S. exports were stricter than the British navicerts and at others they were very lax.[373] The United States had to find a way, then, of putting a stop not only to this but also to the considerable difficulties they were having in buying the products they required from Spain, largely because of the Franco government, the high prices, and German competition. From now on, whether or not licenses were granted would depend on Spain's authorizing the sale of products that the United States wanted to buy. Two products were of particular importance: cork and olive oil.[374] Preclusive purchasing was discounted because, as we shall see below, it raised considerable internal problems. The memorandum stated that products "of strategic importance to the United States" would be purchased "at current American prices or at prices not greatly in excess." In exchange, the United States offered "to supply Spain with products (in addition to petroleum and petroleum products) which we can undertake to supply subject to the limitations imposed by our defense requirements." Petroleum products would be sent under a system of monthly quotas.

The memorandum recommended that coordination be improved with Great Britain on everything connected to trade with Spain. This meant, among other things, that the U.S. official who attended the meetings of the Permits Committee in London would have more power; that requests would have to be made to the British for information about Hispano-German trade and the stocks in Spanish hands; and that the British would have to consult with the United States before granting any navicert quotas to Spain. But it also meant that the United States had to be prepared to provide the British with similar information. It also recommended that all shipments of products to Spain be suspended until "satisfactory arrangements for the improvement of the two-way exchange of goods between the United States and Spain"[375] had been made. The amounts of petroleum products that were being sent would not be reduced but their continuation would be made to depend on Spain's improving its part of the exchange.

On 31 October, Under Secretary Welles asked the president to approve the memorandum, alluding to the issue of the supplies in the following words:

> The statement recommends that petroleum exports, subject to the limitations mentioned above, be continued for the present but that the Spanish Government be at once informed that such exports cannot be long maintained unless certain Spanish products, such as cork, zinc and olive oil, which we urgently need and which we wish to keep out of German hands, are shipped to us in return. The statement further recommends that other United States exports be withheld from Spain until the Spanish Government gives tangible evidence of its willingness to provide us with these essential materials, but that when that evidence is forthcoming we shall authorize the export to Spain in moderate quantities of other commodities, in addition to petroleum, which are not vitally needed in our own defense program.[376]

Once the president gave his approval, the department would be able to begin to negotiate with Spain and the document would be sent to the official liasing with the Economic Defense Board so that it could be immediately applied to exports to Spain.[377] The president gave the document his approval.[378]

Immediately, however, new problems arose in the United States and within the administration in relation to the regime in Spain. In October, several Spanish tankers had arrived in the United States unexpectedly and been loaded in accordance with the rule of "usual prewar quantities."[379] This triggered a press campaign against all shipments of petroleum to Spain.[380] It was initiated by "PM" and based on statistics from the Department of the that which suggested that Spain was being sent large quantities of products that were banned from being exported such as aviation gasoline and lubricating oil.[381] When he found out, the Secretary of the Interior and Petroleum Commissioner Harold Ickes was outraged because he was convinced that it was all ending up in German hands. He directly blamed the "damn State Department at work again continuing its appeasement policy."[382] The press campaign was stepped up and finally the Department of the Treasury made a statement that the statistics quoted were mistaken and that the products had not been sent. Even so, feelings were still running high against the State Department, which was the constant target of all those who thought that many of its officials were incorrigible appeasers of the Spanish Fascists.[383]

The truth was that aviation gasoline had not been sent[384] but the accusation had a certain basis in fact because the rating of some of the gasoline that had been authorized in September was somewhat higher than usual. In response to internal criticism, and before the matter could be reported in the press, Welles had told the president about it:

> According to the Department's records, licenses were issued during the month of September, 1941, for the export to Spain of 5,508,000 gallons of gasoline, valued at $309,000. No other quantities of gasoline were licensed for export to Spain during the quarter ended September 30 and none have been licensed since that time. The gasoline supplied under these licenses was of a grade only slightly superior to the grade of gasoline falling within the definitions established under export schedule no. 15 applicable for the supply of gasoline to Japan. A slightly superior grade was authorized from the reasons that
> (a) gasoline suiting the definitions was apparently not available for export in this country and could only be made available after an appreciable delay,
> (b) Spanish tankers were waiting in Port Arthur, Texas, ready to load, and
> (c) in view of the fact that Ambassador Cardenas was on the point of departure for Madrid, it was desired that we should be in a position to say that pending applications had been taken care of.[385]

This was not enough to put an end to the controversy, however, and the situation was further complicated when two members of the House of Representatives, using information published in "PM" presented the Coffee-Gillette Resolution in an attempt to force an investigation into "the leakage of American war materials to the Axis."[386] By so doing, John M. Coffee, Democrat representative for Washington, was warning the House that Franco was keeping Spain "technically at peace until he can squeeze the last drop of tribute from Great Britain and the United States, and when he has effectuated that objective he will invite the Fascists to use his territory as a base of operations. Mark that prediction."[387]

The pressure exerted on the State Department from the administration, the press, and public opinion was considerable. The press mercilessly attacked those who they qualified as appeasers: that is to say, Hull, Welles, Dunn, Weddell, and Hoare. The press was pro-Loyalist and constantly made reference to the Spanish Civil War, the aid provided by Fascists and Nazis to Franco, and the atrocities committed by the *nacionales* during the war.[388] The articles denounced that "the Department [of State] is trying once again the policy that has already failed with Italy, with Japan and Vichy France. It will fail with Spain. Instead of giving Franco oil to stay neutral, how about withholding oil until he decides actively to help the democratic cause?"[389] And also "if Spain's bullfights were run in the style of our State Department, the toreador would approach the bull with a basket of flowers and curtsey."[390]

Finally, on 29 November, the State Department sent Ambassador Cárdenas the proposal for the trade agreement.[391] It had been influenced by the prevailing atmosphere, was tougher than what had been proposed in the previous Statement of Policy approved by Roosevelt, and contained a complex system of controls designed to prevent anything sent to Spain from being diverted to the Axis. After receiving the proposal and spending an anxious few days because he feared that it would not be accepted in Madrid, the ambassador asked for some modifications to the system of controls. These modifications were made a month later and the proposal was forwarded to Madrid,[392] where, as expected, Serrano objected to the system of controls because he considered them to be excessive interference. Weddell was also informed that the proposal had been sent by the department,[393] which meant that the requests for improved coordination had not fallen on deaf ears.[394] The British Embassy in Washington considered the proposal to be "definitely brusque in places."[395]

When Cárdenas was given the proposal, he was asked to provide some preliminary reports and to accept the system of controls.[396] Meanwhile, surely influenced by the "PM" campaign, the department had refused to give export licenses for diesel fuel to the two oil tankers, the "Campillo" and the "Campuzano,"[397] docked at Port Arthur. The reason given was that Spain still had sufficient reserves,[398] and Cárdenas' efforts to convince the department that these reserves were simply the result of the restrictions that had been applied for several months were to no avail.[399] What is more, on 21 of the same month General Weygand had been called back to Paris and replaced as the supreme commander of North Africa, which was a real blow for the United States and the Murphy-Weygand Agreement of February 1941. The United States reacted by suspending shipments of supplies and subjecting the Vichy government to considerable diplomatic pressure not to change policy and allow German troops to be stationed in French North Africa or the Germans to use the ports there. As far as Spain was concerned, Weddell and Hoare feared that the new situation would have a negative effect on the trade talks,[400] but in fact the United States grew more suspicious and continued to retain the tankers mentioned above. As Ambassador Cárdenas wrote to Serrano Suñer, the United States was particularly afraid that "the replacement of General Weygand might prompt a German invasion of Spain so that that they can get to the Strait and thus to North Africa."[401]

Feelings about Spain were still running high in the United States and the situation was not being improved by the anti-U.S. press campaign that had been launched in Spain in response to the supply difficulties.[402] As Cárdenas said to Serrano,

> Because of the sincerity that is your due, and my great desire to serve the interests of Spain and the government, I must add that if we really cannot find the petroleum products that we need in any other market, while the current talks are taking place and I have not completed my task here, I believe that our press should refrain from making comments about the United States since anything that is published there is immediately reproduced here but adapted and magnified to our detriment, thus hindering the task of those friends who are prepared to help us.[403]

The reference was probably to Sumner Welles and Dunn, among others. The prevailing climate was not improved by Serrano Suñer's trip to Berlin and the speech that he gave there on 25 November 1941. The aim of the trip was to renew the Anti-Comintern Pact between Spain, Germany, Italy, Japan, Hungary, and Manchuria, and to which Finland, Denmark, Bulgaria, Rumania, Slovakia, Croatia, and the Japanese puppet government in China now also wished to add their signatures. This pact seemed to be the prelude to a Federation of Europe under the Fascist banner that would replace the domination of the Anglo-Saxon countries.[404]

Before the proposal reached Madrid, however, Serrano Suñer and Weddell clashed yet again. In his speech in Berlin, Serrano had violently attacked the democracies and condemned Great Britain and the United States for siding with the USSR in the struggle against "the regeneration of Europe undertaken by Hitler." When Weddell made an official complaint on 2 December, Serrano told him that he had every right to give the speeches he liked and that he had been influenced by the fact that Welles had cancelled the export licenses to Spain.[405] This led to another argument in the course of which Weddell told him that Franco had benefited from the Embargo Act during the Civil War. To his surprise, Serrano agreed with him. Their argument, however, focused more on Germany and the future of the war, and Serrano once again expressed his conviction that the Nazis would be victorious and accused the United States of the precarious situation between both their countries. Weddell replied that his country's policy toward Spain was based on several factors, but most of them were political.

7 December 1941: Pearl Harbor and Its Effects on U.S. Policy toward Spain. The Trade Agreement Negotiations

It was in this context that the Japanese attack on Pearl Harbor took place on 7 December 1941. On the following day, the United States of America declared war on Imperial Japan. And on 11 December Germany and Italy declared war on the United States and the conflict extended to a genuine world scale. Although Spain officially confirmed its nonbelligerence, the Spanish press showered praise on the Japanese and their early victories. In the United States, the navy stopped all shipments of oil from American ports,[406] while the government in general and Hull in particular feared an immediate German advance on North Africa through Spain. Above all, they were afraid that the Germans would find gasoline waiting for them there that had just been shipped from the United States.[407] Therefore, after refusing to grant licenses to the "Campillo" and the "Campuzano" in Port Arthur, the United States refused to grant three more to Spanish oil tankers anchored just outside. The navy also feared that they were using their radios to inform German submarines of the movements in the port.[408] Venezuela, Mexico, and Holland (because of their island colonies of Aruba and Curaçao) were asked to consult the United States before selling oil to Spain, and Great Britain was asked to refuse to grant navicerts[409] to vessels bound for Spain. All this activity led to increasing shortages of oil in Spain, where not a single liter of diesel fuel, kerosene, or lubricants arrived in December 1941 and January 1942.[410] The situation was so bad that trucks that ran on diesel were banned from being used and fishing boats were allowed to put to sea only twice a week.[411] These measures in turn made the food shortages worse. Also during this period, the British captured two German submarines, one of which was shown to have taken supplies on board in Vigo. Hoare was furious and threatened to reduce the supply of oil products if Spain did not stop assisting the Germans.[412] For once the Spanish government took the threat very seriously and did as instructed. On top of all this, Serrano Suñer wound down the Hispanicity policy implemented by Ximénz de Sandoval the previous April and May and he even agreed with several Hispano-American countries to dissolve Falangist organizations. The prevailing prodemocratic and pro-U.S. feeling, and the difficulty Spain was having in getting supplies made it necessary now more than ever before to abandon a policy that had proved to be ineffective and even counterproductive. The Hispanicity that remained focused strictly on cultural and religious matters.[413]

Nevertheless, once the first few weeks had passed and nothing new had occurred in the Iberian peninsula as far as the war was concerned, the oil companies, Great Britain, and Weddell began to make themselves heard again arguing in favor of greater flexibility. The head of the department's Western Europe Division Ray Atherton responded to demands from the British ambassador in Washington Lord Halifax on 29 December by saying that this was a matter that should be dealt with at the highest level. He suggested that Churchill should speak to Roosevelt personally. This he did on 5 January 1942[414] and the result was that Welles granted licenses to three Spanish tankers in Venezuela[415]—the "Campoamor," the "Campeche," and the "Gobeo."[416]

For its part, the Madrid Embassy was concerned about the delays in communications between Madrid and Washington, where the preliminary talks were being held on the agreement, and it did everything in its power to speed things up.[417] Aware that the United States' entry into the war had complicated Atlantic communications quite considerably, Weddell insisted that the talks be held in Madrid or that Spain should send a delegation to negotiate in Washington.[418] The department agreed to the first of these two options: Weddell would make the official proposal in Madrid[419] and the talks would also be held there. At long last he had been given a prominent role to play, even though the proposal that he was asked to make was probably too hard line for his taste. This was not Weddell's only success, however. More progress was made with the coordination between Washington and the Madrid Embassy, so a problem that had recurred throughout the second half of the ambassador's term of office was close to being solved.

A specific policy for exchanging goods with Spain, then, was about to be put into practice. Commercially speaking, the United States was to be much less benevolent toward Spain than Great Britain. And Alexander W. Weddell noticed that Spain's leaders now had a different opinion of him. As he wrote at the time "I am a little more of a favourite in exclusive Spanish ministerial circles," which he correctly attributed "to the increasing pressure of economic events in this country."[420]

Just as this change was taking place, however, Weddell was on the point of causing another dispute with Serrano Suñer, this time about the bombing of the city of Manila by the Japanese and how it was reported in the Spanish press (the publication of a communiqué from Serrano Suñer's Ministry of Foreign Affairs). The ambassador sent Suñer a harshly worded note saying that he was extremely upset that his department "has apparently permitted itself to be used as a mouthpiece of the Japanese Government" by falsely reporting the events of the bombing of the city of Manila and the subsequent destruction of Catholic schools, convents, and churches. With these actions, the Japanese had infringed the Hague Convention of 1907.[421] Washington was quick to perceive the danger and Atherton advised Welles that Weddell should be gently cautioned. "I fully agree with the point of view of Mr. Weddell and every remark he has made in his recent communications on this subject to the Spanish Foreign Minister are more than justified," said Atherton but went on to recommend that he change his tone if he did not want relations with Serrano to break down yet again.[422] Hull sent a telegram agreeing with everything that he had said but questioning "the [doubtful] expediency of further notes" because of the United States' interest in keeping relations with Spain on "an even a basis as possible."[423] The incident went no further probably because Serrano Suñer decided to ignore Weddell's note: the oil deal was too important to risk another crisis with the United States. Weddell, however, did not come out of this mild incident very well, as we shall see below.

Despite this new incident, Weddell was instructed by Secretary Hull on 8 January 1942 to present the proposal to the Spanish government.[424] The system of controls to which Cárdenas had objected had been changed and it had been made to look as if the proposal had arisen out of a desire to prevent delays in oil deliveries.[425] It stated that "the proposals submitted herewith have been prepared to accommodate trade to the complexities of the present situation and to ensure that products made available shall not aid the enemies of the United States" and it established the concept of quid pro quo by saying "the proposals contemplate a movement to Spain of products, including petroleum products, conditional upon Spain making available to this country (or possibly to this country and Great Britain through a joint arrangement) in significant quantities the products of Spain mentioned below."[426] The list of goods that the United States wished to purchase was a long one and included wolfram, cork, tin, olive oil, olives, lead, zinc concentrates, mercury, aconite root, colchium seed, psyllium seed, gentian root, ergot, camomile leaves, horehound leaves, uva-ursi leaves, and white squill. The United States also wanted Spain to reinitiate imports of products such as films, printed material, and publications. However, the main aim of the proposal was to explain the system of controls designed to monitor the final destination of the products—essentially petroleum and its derivates—that were to be shipped from the United States. These products would be sent in sufficient, *but only sufficient*, quantities[427] for Spain's transport needs or other essentials. The controls required monthly reports from the two Spanish oil companies CAMPSA and CEPSA on stocks, inventories, regional consumption figures, the movement of oil tankers, and the use of petroleum products in all areas of activity per region. They also required U.S. agents attached to the Madrid Embassy to be allowed access to Spanish oil facilities. When Cárdenas objected, they justified this measure by saying that it was necessary "to minimize delays by reason of inadequate information."

Goods other than petroleum products were also subject to the sine qua non condition that they could not be exported subsequently to Germany, Italy, Japan, or any of the occupied countries. The possibility was mentioned of selling some (unspecified) foodstuffs or small amounts of fertilizer with no need of any system of control. The reason given for imposing strict controls on products such as tractors, rubber, electricity, machinery, and metals was none other than to help the war effort. And in order to purchase anything at all, Spain would have to get authorization from the Office of Production Management and the Board of Economic Warfare, and under no circumstances reexport any of the goods purchased to the Axis.[428]

Four days later, Weddell was sent some additional instructions for his personal information and to guide him in his talks with the Spanish.[429] The tone of the instructions shows the pressure that the department was under, particularly now that the United States was at war with the Axis. They also contained a fundamental contradiction with the policy designed in Washington the previous October, although this contradiction seems only to have been temporary. The instructions began by explaining the reasons that had prompted the United States to enter into a trade agreement with Spain and stating that trade talks had only been started at the insistence of the British, who needed Spain's economy to be minimally buoyant if they were to be able to purchase the goods they required. This could only be ensured if the United States were to satisfy Spain's need for petroleum products. The instructions went on to say that the U.S. policy "does not regard the effect of the proposals, if any, upon the general policy of the Spanish Government as a major factor, and will therefore base its decisions regarding the movement of supplies to Spain on whether it can obtain from Spain a tangible and valuable quid pro quo."[430] This statement was in direct contradiction with the policy that had been determined the previous November. It reflected the point of view of Secretary Hull, who was less understanding toward Spain than Under Secretary Welles, but it must also have been the result of an internal agreement between the sectors of the Roosevelt administration to justify what was being done to a U.S. public opinion that was largely against trading with Spain. Whatever the case may be, the change was only temporary, as we shall see below.

While they were waiting for the trade agreement to be signed, Weddell was ordered to ask the Spanish government to sell a quantity of wolfram to the Metals Reserve Company for the same value as the petroleum that had been authorized to be loaded onto the three tankers in Venezuela.[431] He was also informed that the amounts of petroleum products that would be sent to Spain in accordance with the terms of the agreement would be much lower than Great Britain wished, not only because of the United States' own needs but also because the department was concerned that the Spanish army had accumulated a reserve of 15,000 tons of gasoline in the Protectorate of Morocco. The department's aim was to reduce this reserve because it was convinced that with current stocks and the petroleum on board the three tankers, Spain had sufficient provisions until the middle or the end of February—as long as the supplies were used carefully. Therefore, Weddell was immediately informed that one new license would be granted to a tanker that had just arrived in Venezuela[432] at the end of January, and two more would be granted in the first half of February. But only on the condition that Spain agreed to shipping the wolfram.

Weddell presented the proposal to the under secretary of the Ministry of Foreign Affairs on 14 January 1942, despite Hoare's objections that it was "harsh and schoolmastery in tone."[433] Carceller was afraid that Serrano Suñer would not agree to it,[434] but the reality of Spain's economic situation was such that talks began nine days later. The need to resolve the problem of the petroleum supply and the modifications made to the language of the original text were enough for Serrano to back down. At the same time as the proposal was being presented, the commercial attaché Ralph H. Ackerman left for Tangiers to discuss the issue of the gasoline stocks with the representatives of the American and British oil companies that were operating in Spanish Morocco.[435] While Franco and the members of his government were studying the proposal, Weddell explained to the State Department that Spain would find it difficult to provide the quid pro quo order of wolfram because it did not have any of its own. He proposed that they should order instead 6,000 tons of zinc and 10,000 tons of pyrite, as well as a boatload of 250 tons of cork that was about to set sail for the United States. In exchange, Spain would order fertilizers, copper sulfate, and light tractors. With reference to a question he had been asked about methods of trading with Spain, he proposed that the best method of acquiring the strategic material that was most important to the United States was to work jointly with Great Britain through the United Kingdom Commercial Corporation. Another issue was the requirement that all products be transported in Spanish vessels and he informed that Spain was trying to get assurances that these vessels would not be sunk by Germany. It seemed that Germany had responded somewhat ambiguously to Spain's first approach and the Spanish government was quite uneasy.[436] The result of all this preparatory work was that the State Department eventually decided to create a corporation that was similar to the UKCC, the United States Commercial Corporation (USCC).

Before this was to happen, however, and while Spain was still assessing the proposal made by the United States, trade between the United States and Spain was largely at a standstill. The United States had been at war for more than a month and a half and very few vessels had been authorized to sail for Spain. Weddell, therefore, wrote once again to the department,[437] complaining of the lack of trade and directly blaming the U.S. administration for the situation. In his opinion, the Spanish were cooperating: they had provided all the information that had been asked for, they had offered thirty vessels for the purpose of trade with the United States and their two oil companies had accepted the presence of controlling agents. The United States, on the other hand, had increased controls on the exportation of petroleum and other products that Spain was in the utmost need of, and had not provided any information about the products that they were prepared to sell. Weddell also complained that he had sent Washington the information about petroleum he had been asked for but that as yet he had received no response. In the same communication he sent the results of Ackerman's investigations with the representatives of the oil companies and the consul general in Tangier J. Rives Childs. His conclusions were that Spain did not have anything like 15,000 tons of stocks and that the actual reserve was probably about one-third of that figure. Even so, the question of how to prevent stocks of gasoline from accumulating in the protectorate was still pending.

What most concerned Weddell at this time, however, was that trade between the two countries was at a standstill: the State Department was waiting for the Spanish government to make a move through its embassy in Washington, while the Spanish government was waiting to be informed of exactly what the United States wished to buy. As Ackerman wrote in a letter to Washington,

> The United States refused to grant export permits for any quantities of petroleum products after November 11 and until the end of January (...) Since about the middle of 1941 the United States refused all applications for export permits covering lubricants. On our insistence the British refused to grant navicerts to cargoes of crude oil and petroleum from Aruba, from Venezuela and Colombia during part of December and January. This complete cessation of supplies arose from our desire to have the Spanish Government give certain guarantees concerning ultimate destination and use of such products. However, two months intervened from the time that our Government conceived the idea of the type of control we wish to exercise until the time that the Embassy in Madrid was specifically informed concerning the full extent

of such desired control so that it was able to discuss the matter with the matter with the Spanish authorities; meanwhile no export permits were granted and naturally the condition of stocks in Spain became so dangerously low as to place the Spanish Government in almost a desperate situation.[438]

It is also worthwhile taking a look here at the commercial attaché's assessment of the circumstances involved in the effective blockade that the United States was inflicting on Spain:

> Our policy with regard to petroleum, and I might say many other products, has been to impose slow starvation. While we have been discussing ways and means for control we have denied the patient nourishment.
> A somewhat similar condition pertains regarding the supply of other materials. We have denied export permits to Spain on many articles which have been fabricated for almost a year and many of which are lying in warehouses, either in factories or in ports doing no good to our own economy and certainly of not benefit to Spain. Many of these commodities were paid for many months ago. I refer specifically to certain compressor drilling equipment and other mining machinery manufactured by the Ingersoll Rand Company which have been held in port at New York for many months; drum making machinery and repair parts for the refinery of CEPSA, drum making machinery for a concern at Barcelona, to mention only a few specific instances. This equipment was specifically made for Spain, cannot be used in the United States unless extensive changes are made, and cannot be exported elsewhere.
> We have also recently blocked certain Spanish accounts. The Spanish Government tells us there are $3,000,000 paid to the credit of the Spanish Foreign Exchange Institute by the Swiss Government to compensate for shipping services for Switzerland which have been blocked since early in December and with no indication having been given to Spain as to why or whether it will eventually be unblocked. As this payment is part of a contract involving $10,000,000, it is immediately observed that this is extremely harmful to the economy of a nation whose dollar resources are extremely limited. (...)
> We in the Embassy are not ignorant of the effect on our entire economic structure of our war effort nor or the effect of these on the ability to supply materials for export. We have also so often stressed this point to the Spanish officials that we feel they clearly understand that they must be prepared to make available to us the things we need even at a sacrifice to Spain, in return for any sacrifices we make to help the Spanish economy.[439]

In an attempt to get round the deadlock Weddell proposed that an interim plan be implemented until some form of decision had been taken on the trade agreement. His plan consisted of selling Spain 40,000 tons of petroleum, 5,000 tons of ammonium sulfate, 2,000 tons of copper, and some machinery already manufactured specially for Spain and that was in storage in U.S. ports during the months of February and March 1942. In return, he expected to obtain 1,500 tons of cork, 10,000 tons of zinc, 2,000 tons of olives, and 5,000 flasks of mercury.

Spain was extremely desirous of entering into an agreement given the country's predicament, and this was made plain on 23 January 1942 when Beaulac and Ackerman were called to a meeting of the Economic Committee set up specifically by the Spanish government to negotiate the agreement with the United States.[440] The interlocutor was Serrano Suñer's Ministry of Foreign Affairs, represented by the under secretary, and not the Ministry of Industry and Commerce, which is the interlocutor the Madrid

Embassy would have liked. At the meeting, the under secretary informed them that the Spanish government accepted the North American proposal. Ambassador Cárdenas had also been instructed to communicate this acceptance in Washington.[441] The telegram that Serrano sent instructing him to do so reveals the difficult situation of diesel fuel supplies that had led the minister to back down. It said,

> Please inform the State Department that, having analyzed Memorandum presented by American Embassy which contains and expands on proposal delivered to you, the Government authorizes you to give tentative conformity until we can study questions of detail and search for formulas that satisfy our mutual aspirations. Of course, and as requested, we confirm once again that products imported shall be exclusively for internal consumption. Stress need for immediate departure of "Campillo" and "Campuzano" to resolve situation of extreme urgency. Without their immediate departure normal conversations impossible since the pressure to receive these supplies is too great as to be compatible with friendly deliberation. Current supplies of diesel fuel approximately cover the minimum consumption for one month of essential operations with maximum restrictions including halting almost all industries and motorized agricultural work and reducing to forty per cent all fishing activities. At a moment of such vital need, damage to national supply may be irreparable. Since aforementioned vessels require twenty-five days to make journey, only if they leave immediately can they arrive before current supplies are exhausted. Talks with the Embassy (United States Embassy in Madrid) have begun. We seem to share criteria and real possibility of finding practical formulas for application.[442]

At the meeting, the Spaniards agreed that everything to do with the trade of petroleum products should be supervised and said that they were prepared to sell the United States all the products they asked for. As far as the strategic products of wolfram, mercury, and zinc were concerned, the under secretary explained that Germany had not given Spain guarantees that their ships would be safe in the Atlantic and, therefore, proposed to send them first to Great Britain using the convoy system and then on to the United States. He also stressed the need to use encrypted code to refer to these materials in their communications, so that the Germans could not keep track of them. And on behalf of the Committee he reiterated the need to allow the two tankers to set sail from Port Arthur. In exchange, and in application of the quid pro quo system that Spain seemed to have accepted, he offered to make immediate shipments of cork, zinc, and mercury.

Weddell recommended that Washington should allow the two tankers to set sail. When the department found out that a Spanish vessel loaded with cork had departed, it said that authorization would be given to load the "Campillo" and the "Zorroza"—which was in the Dutch island of Aruba—with diesel fuel but that this authorization would not take immediate effect. It was also made clear that there would be no more new authorizations until the Spanish government provided more information on the quantities of products of equivalent use that it would be sending to the United States, or until they agreed to allow U.S. officials to travel on board the tankers.[443] Cárdenas argued that it was impossible for the products sent by Spain to be of the same importance as the products received, complained about the decision not to grant any new authorizations, and insisted that permission be given for the "Campuzano" to be loaded so that it could set sail immediately.[444] The hard line adopted by the department surprised the Spanish ambassador, the Franco government, and Weddell. The latter wrote to the department saying that unless Spain was provided with a minimum quantity of petroleum products while the talks lasted, the country would not be capable of producing or transporting the strategic materials that they hoped to send to the United Kingdom and the United States. And he reiterated that Washington had still not stated exactly what quantities of strategic materials it hoped to receive from Spain, or whether or not it was prepared to enter into competition over prices in the international market.[445] Also still pending was the problem of the possible attack by German submarines on Spanish vessels, because Spain was still unaware of which products Germany considered to be contraband and therefore open to attack or interception. It requires no great effort of the imagination, however, to guess that this list of products would include wolfram, zinc, mercury, cork, and all those other products that the Germans hoped to obtain from Spain. This unawareness was the reason why the Franco regime did not want to run the risk of using Spanish vessels and why they were proposing that the goods should be sent in British vessels or in convoy.[446]

In fact, the Germans knew the full text of the North American proposal for the trade agreement, as Carceller explained to Beaulac two days later,[447] and Ambassador Von Stohrer had said that they would not allow it to be implemented. The Spanish Ministry of Industry and Commerce, however, hoped to be able to convince them to reduce the list of products classified as contraband to a maximum of eight by arguing that if the Germans were really friends of Spain they should understand Spain's need to acquire certain products from the Allies and to sell them Spanish products in return. Even so, it was not until the following 21 April that Spain and Germany signed a secret document by which the Germans agreed not to take action against Spanish freighters that they believed not to be carrying contraband goods on the condition that they would continue to be supplied with wolfram and other products. Two boats loaded with olives and wine were the first to set sail for the United States on 1 July 1942.[448]

While waiting for the United States' response, at the beginning of February 1942,[449] the Spanish negotiating committee made a new proposal by which they hoped to comply with the department's requirements: they offered to send 6,000 tons of zinc, between 800 and 1,000 tons of cork, and an unspecified amount of wolfram and mercury (but of the same value as the zinc and the cork). They also accepted the presence of U.S. inspectors on board Spanish vessels, although they did ask them to be as discreet as possible[450] (in other words, their work should be done in secret) so that Germany would not find out about them and take reprisals. In exchange, and with Weddell's support, they urged the department to grant export licenses to the two tankers in Port Arthur.

The department's response, however, must have been extremely exasperating for both Weddell and the Spanish: the ships would not set sail until Spain had given assurances that material of equal usefulness would be sent to the United States.[451] The department also asked for visas to be granted to the North American inspectors who were to travel on the ships. Spain granted the request at once but asked for the controllers to monitor the loading and unloading but not to travel, thus avoiding the considerable risk involved and safeguarding Spain's responsibilities in the event of any untoward circumstance.[452]

In this extremely difficult situation in Spain, and just after CEPSA's oil refinery in Tenerife had been forced to close down because of the shortage of crude,[453] Alexander W. Weddell traveled to the United States.

Franco's Speech on 14 February 1942 and Its Repercussions on the Talks

Willard L. Beaulac remained in Weddell's place as *chargé d'affaires*. And it was he who had to cope with the consequences of Franco's speech of 14 February 1942, two days after the Spanish head of state had had an interview with the head of the government of Portugal, Dr. Oliveira Salazar de Sevilla, in what could have been interpreted as an indirect attempt to draw closer to the Allies given the traditional Portuguese alliance with Great Britain (despite which Portugal had not entered the Second World War).

After the interview and perhaps in an attempt to justify his actions to the Axis (or as a display of his real feelings),[454] Franco gave a heated anti-Soviet and pro-German speech in which he made such threats to the Allies as the following: "If there were a moment of danger, if the path to Berlin were to be open, it would not be a division but a million Spaniards who would volunteer to go there."[455] These and other proclamations caused outrage in the United States, particularly because at the time the Japanese troops had just taken Singapore and General Rommel had the British in trouble in El Alamein. And once again fears were raised that Spain might enter the war. Washington and the State Department were particularly concerned and the Secretary of State Cordell Hull even went to the lengths of chiding Beaulac for paying too much attention to economic affairs and not enough on providing the necessary information on Spanish political affairs (such as the interview between Franco and Salazar).[456] The month before the State Department had told the Madrid Embassy that the trade agreement was strictly economic and that its possible political effects were of no interest,[457] so Beaulac immediately requested an interview with Serrano Suñer. As we shall see below, it was not to be granted until a few weeks later.

At the same time, however, Beaulac sent a spirited reply to the Secretary of State arguing that

> The Embassy has submitted in despatch form a number of basic reports on the political situation and the relation to that situation of our economic relations with Spain. It has endeavored to assist the Department in arriving at a definite policy toward Spain, the principal purpose of which would be to influence Spanish policy.[458]

And in a demonstration of plain talking, he counterattacked the secretary's ticking off saying that

> Although the Department stated in its (...) January 12 (...), that it does not regard the effect of its economic proposals upon the general policy of the Spanish Government as a major factor, the Embassy continues to attach great importance to the political and strategic results which it believes it may be possible to obtain from judicious trade with Spain.[459]

To drive home his point, he said that it was not only the embassy that attached such great importance to trade: the Axis did too.

> The fact that the Germans also are aware of the importance of this is indicated by their efforts to interfere with this trade (by spreading rumors calculated to arouse our Government's and suspicions, for example) and by their efforts to impress upon the Spanish people their own feeble accomplishments along this line. As an indication of the importance the Germans attach to this, when 57 air compressors were recently imported from Germany, the Germans arranged for them to be exhibited a whole day on Madrid's principal boulevard. Such stunts have little effect however so long as Spain continues to import principally from the democracies.

He also stressed that

> The weakness in Germany's relationship to Spain is precisely that Germany is unable to furnish Spain with the materials Spain urgently needs for its continued existence. This is interpreted in Spain as a sign of German weakness and indicates further (so long as the democracies are able to furnish goods to Spain) that however lamentable Spain's economic situation may be it can only be worsened by Spain's entry into the war on the side of the Axis. This argument will not be valid to the same extent of course if we withhold supplies of petroleum principally of gas oil so important to Spanish agriculture, fishing, communications and industry.[460]

Thus, Beaulac took advantage of the situation to repeat the arguments of the Madrid Embassy in favor of an agreement in which political and military aspects outweighed the strictly economic, and he reaffirmed the Madrid Embassy's view that there were two opposing sectors within Franco's government. He said,

> Our and Great Britain's ability in the past to furnish supplies to Spain has been interpreted as a sign of our strength. It has also encouraged the Spanish Government especially those elements in it not entirely sympathetic to the Axis to endeavor to improve Spanish-American relations and has strengthened their hands in their endeavor to counteract the efforts of the Spanish Minister of Foreign Affairs to bring about complete cooperation with the Axis.

In conclusion he pointed out that

> In recommending continuance of a modicum of trade with Spain, the Embassy is quite aware that some risks would be entailed. It believes, however, that the political and military risks from stopping trade are greater and involve Spain's possible entry into the war on the side of the Axis. Our military and naval attachés concur in this opinion.

He also believed that the Spanish situation was evolving positively: the desire to keep out of the war was growing stronger throughout the country, and in influential circles—including the cabinet—and the public in general there was an increasing feeling of friendship toward the United States of America. The relations between the embassy and the Ministry of Foreign Affairs had also recovered their former dignity, and the newspaper editorials only rarely attacked the United States, although he was quick to point out that this by no means meant that Franco's government had abandoned its policy of friendship with the Axis or that ministers and editorials had stopped showering the Axis with praise in the press.

THE AGREEMENT OF 4 MARCH 1942. THE DISMISSAL OF ALEXANDER W. WEDDELL AS AMBASSADOR IN MADRID

After these ups and downs, on 27 February 1942[461] the State Department finally considered that the assurances given by Spain were sufficient and granted the export licenses to the two tankers in Port Arthur—the "Campillo" and the "Campuzano." It also agreed to the inspectors not traveling on board.[462] But what was most important was that the decision was taken to supply Spain with petroleum products for a period of three months, which meant that a trading relationship could be physically established between the two countries.[463] They had reached the beginnings of an agreement, then, even though it had to be put to the test. The United States described it as a "patchwork agreement on a trial basis"[464] and it brought to a close a whole year of activity for Alexander W. Weddell and the Madrid Embassy. The cycle was coming to an end.

The State Department perhaps gave the go ahead not only because of a desire to regain some of the flexibility lost in the previous weeks—a flexibility that was required by the policy designed by the department and its political and strategic motivations—but also because of British pressure and the points of view that Weddell expressed in person in Washington. In fact, the day before the agreement was accepted he had been in the department and we know what he said there.[465] He had begun his journey to the United States on 7 February,[466] because of his wife's health problems, but he was never to return either to his job or to the city he had left with the conviction that he would be back within the month, after Mrs Weddell's operation.[467] They were delayed by transport problems in Madrid and did not arrive in Richmond until 25 February.[468] Weddell immediately went to the State Department[469] and then had an interview with the president. With the department he was very blunt. With reference to the communication in which Hull had poured scorn on the political effects of the agreement, he criticized the fact that relations with Spain had to be based more on economic criteria, on a strict quid pro quo, than on political and military criteria.[470] He said that

> In its most recent telegrams to the Embassy, the Department seems to take the attitude that the basis of our relations with Spain must be economic, that there must be a rough equality between goods which we may make available to Spain and goods that Spain should make available to us. Politico-military considerations appear to be relegated to a secondary position.[471]

All of this, he pointed out, "required reweighing."

As far as Weddell was concerned, there were three political options. The first was to submit Spain to a total blockade, which went against British interests. The second was to make it clear that the United States was prepared to provide economic relief without demanding any commercial quid pro quo but on the condition that Spain remained benevolently neutral toward the Allies. This option could also require Spain to stop supplying the Axis and to dismiss Serrano Suñer and the other pro-German ministers. Theoretically, the third option was the one that was being put into practice: that is to say, a policy based on strictly economic criteria and subject to the condition of quid pro quo. Only theoretically, however, because in fact the United States was implementing the first option and subjecting Spain to what amounted to a blockade. Weddell believed that the consequences of the first two options would be Spain's entry into the war on the Axis' side, in the first case, and the invasion of Spain by Germany in the second. What is more, a complete blockade of Spain would probably have the following effects:

1. The entry of Spain into the war on the side of the Axis powers.
2. To give Germany a line of ports extending practically unbroken from Narvik to Dakar.
3. Germany would gain much in manpower.
4. Germany would gain a small but effective army.
5. Germany would immediately begin receiving an even larger share of minerals and other strategic material.
6. Germany would further gain through the immediate closing of the Straits of Gibraltar.
7. Germany would gain a long coastline, offering submarine bases.
8. Germany's influence in Tangier would be economically strengthened.
9. Germany's influence in French North Africa would also be augmented.
10. A further harmful effect would be the painful repercussion in Iberian-American countries at the physical and moral wound inflicted on their mother country.

Should the United States agree to provide economic relief in exchange for benevolent neutrality, the interruption of supplies, and the dismissal of pro-Axis ministers, however, Weddell believed that the effects would be the following:

- The immediate invasion of Spain by Germany, in which case Portugal would be equally a victim.
- Terrific suffering among the civil population, although their hunger might be met by relief from us if we had access to certain ports.
- A guerrilla warfare by Spain that could be highly effective against an alien enemy, as Napoleon found out.
- Springing from anticipated German invasion, Spanish and Portuguese islands could be immediately occupied.
- These islands as well as any Spanish and Portuguese ports that could be held could form bases for operations against Germany and Italy if adequate help from us arrived in time.
- The menace to Gibraltar would be perhaps lessened.
- Depending on the efficiency and promptness of our aid we would gain a certain amount of most valuable strategic materials.
- Joint action by the United States and Great Britain in Spain arising through German invasion would doubtless provoke a favorable sentiment in Iberian-American countries.[472]

Weddell also pointed out that if the effective blockade that Spain was being subject to were to continue, Spain may well be forced to join the war. He therefore recommended that the United States reconsider its policy and make an immediate gesture of good will that would create the appropriate atmosphere for the beginning of talks. It should also be made clear which products the United States wished to obtain from Spain and which products they were prepared to provide on a monthly basis. Weddell also insisted on setting up an American Purchasing Commission or working through the UKCC, and holding the talks in Madrid, which meant providing more staff for an embassy that was already below strength in terms of personnel.[473] But above all he believed that the administration had to realize that economic issues were secondary and that military issues were much more important: in the Allies' interests Spain had to be kept out of the war.

> To repeat what I have constantly favored, I would urge that our government consider in baldest material terms just what Spain's present attitude, in its worst aspect, toward us is worth to the common cause, and to act accordingly. In my own judgement in such a weighing, economic factors fall into a secondary position; the military aspect is the cardinal one.

Without discounting the second option, then, Weddell favored the third although he criticized the insistence of the quid pro quo.

To prepare the economic part of his interviews at the department, Weddell had used a memorandum specially written by the commercial attaché Ralph H. Ackerman,[474] who first analyzed the reasons why the trade relations between the two countries had ground to a halt and then warned for the umpteenth time of the danger of forcing Spain into the arms of the Axis:

> We cannot expect to deprive Spain, as a non-belligerent, of some of those materials which we normally supply, or are supplied by countries of Latin America, which are fundamental needs, without being prepared to run the risk that this might convince the Spanish Government that it has nothing to gain from dealing with the democracies and that it may be able to better obtain at least a small part of its requirements by an open alliance with the Axis.[475]

And he insisted on the importance of political factors, saying that they could not "entirely divorce the political significance of Spain in the present world struggle from the consideration of its economic needs and to limit the problem entirely to Spain's ability to make available to us and to the British the materials which it can produce and which we need." He believed that Spain was undoubtedly a valuable source of strategic material and that although

> the British have been obtaining fairly substantial shipments of iron ore, potash and mercury, and smaller quantities of wolfram (sometimes acquired in Portugal although of Spanish origin), lead, cork, ergot of rye, woolen manufactures, in addition to certain quantities of fruits, the United States have not acquired large quantities of strategic materials because we have not made a serious effort to purchase these.

And all this was despite the fact that

> On several occasions the Spanish Government expressed a willingness to discuss with us proposals looking toward the supply by the United States of certain materials against which Spain would make available materials which we might desire in quantities within its capacity to offer, taking into consideration the fact that other nations are now actually buying such materials.

Nevertheless "these conversations were postponed as the Embassy had received no information from Washington as to its willingness to make available the commodities listed and the quantities desired or to acquire in the Spanish market the products which Spain was disposed to make available to us." Now things had changed and the department and American government officials should be prepared to enter into any negotiations on a "give and take" basis. They had an added advantage:

> The committee appointed by the [Spanish] Government to conduct these arrangements with our Embassy fortunately consists of a group most friendly disposed to us; it is very probable that by giving way on minor matters at times, we can obtain much more important concessions. With the possible exception of Blas Huete, the member from the Spanish Exchange Institute, all the other members are quite definitely pro-Ally in sentiment.

Ackerman also spoke highly of the minister of industry and commerce Demetrio Carceller and his "continued opposition (...) to Suñer, and (...) realism concerning the need to cooperate with the democracies and his reported assurances to Franco that he will be able to obtain benefits from such cooperation which will fully justify the attitude of the regime in refusing to join with the Axis."[476]

Although we have a good knowledge of the standpoint that Weddell defended in his interviews at the State Department, we know only a little of what he discussed with the president on 9 March 1942.[477] Roosevelt asked him to evaluate the consequences of a possible allied landing in Algeria or the north-west African coast. In fact, shortly after Pearl Harbor Vice President Henry Wallace urged that simultaneous attacks be launched against Hitler by invading Madeira, the International Zone in Tangiers, Spanish Morocco, Casablanca, and Dakar.[478] And a joint report by General Marshall and Admiral Stark written at the same time envisaged the possibility that after his failure to conclude the campaign in Russia, Hitler would invade Spain, Portugal, and the French colonies in North Africa.[479] Throughout the first half of 1942, the United States studied plans for making an assault on Europe via Spain, Portugal, and Norway. They even contemplated not using land forces at all and fighting a war based on air and sea superiority.[480] Roosevelt totally agreed with the use of air power and since 1939 he had been in favor of using it as a deterrent, as is shown by the plan to deploy the B17s in the Philippines throughout 1941 and the beginning of the work on the atomic bomb in October 1941.[481]

Weddell replied to the president's question two weeks later. From Richmond he sent him a specially prepared memorandum that made the following points:

1. I would earnestly recommend consideration of debarking forces on the coast of French Morocco or Río de Oro, or on both coasts simultaneously.
2. Simultaneously the Azores, the Canaries, and the Cape Verde Islands should be occupied.
3. Such activities should coincide with a real or feigned attack through France by a British Expeditionary Force.

There is now to be considered the probable effect of such action on our part:

1. In the Axis countries, in Spain and in Portugal, a howl would go up of moral indignation.
2. This in the case of the Axis countries should be ignored.
3. In the case of Spain, that country has lent and is lending sufficient aid to the Axis cause to warrant our action, while those majority elements hostile to the Franco government would welcome any move which would embarrass that administration.
4. As regards Portugal and perhaps also in the case of Spain, protest might be adequately met by solemn declaration that territories seized would be handed back following peace.

The adverse of such action would very likely be.

1. The entry into Spain and Portugal, with or without their consent of Axis forces.
2. The immediate siege of Gibraltar, the enforced departure there from of United Nations' vessels, and the loss of that port as an assembly point for convoys.
3. Germany would hold ports extending from Narvik to Dakkar, as well as additional Mediterranean ports.
4. The blocking of the straits at least during daylight hours.

Favorable results to be anticipated would be

1. The encouraging of anti-Axis elements in the peninsula.
2. To bring out elements in Northwest Africa who favor the Allied cause.
3. To provide a base from which Europe might be invaded.
4. To place hostile elements in North Africa between United Nations' forces in East and West.

In addition to this issue, however, it is very probable that they spoke of Weddell giving up his post in Madrid as when he visited Sumner Welles a few days later, on 25 March, to give him the memorandum we have just mentioned, he was given a letter from Roosevelt officially requesting his resignation. What is more, immediately after the Weddell-Roosevelt interview, Welles had started to look for his successor.[482] In his letter, which had been drafted by Welles, the president said the following:

> Owing to recent and rapid changes in our general relations with Spain, and to the very critical character of the problems which are confronting us, I have reached the conclusion that it would be helpful to the interests of this country at the present moment if I were to appoint an eminent lay Catholic as our Ambassador in Madrid. For that reason, and with very real regret, I am obliged to ask for your resignation as Ambassador to Spain.[483]

It is highly likely that the mild incident that Weddell had caused with his note to Serrano on 31 December 1941 hastened a dismissal that may have been on the cards since the previous conflicts with the same minister. But now a new period in relations between the two countries was dawning and it was unthinkable that the situation of April 1941, when relations were almost broken off, could be repeated. Sumner Welles must have been aware of all this ever since Cárdenas had complained to him about the envelope incident three months earlier. Along with this, Weddell had been diagnosed with a urological problem that needed an immediate operation and a two-month convalescence.

Despite the above, Weddell was probably very surprised when Roosevelt asked for his resignation. It seems that his dismissal was made to appear as if it had been for health reasons,[484] although in fact it had been a presidential decision in response to the new period they were about to enter into. Weddell presented his resignation on 28 March 1942 claiming that

> I am about to enter hospital to undergo an operation of some gravity which, they tell me further, even if successful, would be followed by a longish period of convalescence and observation. My return to Spain could not, therefore, under most favorable circumstances, take place for some months.[485]

He added that "my deep regret in relinquishing my post is tempered by the hope that you may later make use of my services." The president accepted it at once and told him that he would call on him again.[486] This he was never to do, however, even though it seems that Roosevelt really was prepared to take him on again after his recovery.[487] A few months after the operation, on 31 October 1942, just before his sixty-seventh birthday, Alexander W. Weddell definitively retired from the diplomatic service.[488]

Replacing Weddell was another sign of the importance that political and military factors had acquired in the relations between the United States of America and Spain in the last term of 1941, and particularly after the United States' entry into the world war. The country had now designed its own policy that did not depend directly on Great Britain's as it had in previous years. As a sign of this new will to intervene in Francoist policy and, as before, keep Spain neutral, Roosevelt decided to appoint a prominent Catholic. He chose one of the most influential and best known lay Catholics in the country, the professor of history at Columbia University Carlton Joseph Huntley Hayes (Alton, New York, 1882). His appointment, however, signified much more than this, since Hayes had supported Franco during the

Civil War by signing a declaration in October 1937 along with 175 other leading American Catholics stating that the vast majority of Spaniards supported the military uprising[489] in Spain. In this way, Roosevelt and Sumner Welles hoped to have a man in Madrid who was highly regarded by the Francoists and respected in the Catholic world so that he could use his contacts to exert an anti-Axis influence on the Spanish government.[490] Paradoxically now that Weddell had been dismissed, he would have to be tuned to the policy of the Madrid Embassy and Under Secretary Welles. All these changes were the direct result of the United States' entry into the war and particularly of the growing awareness that Spain and its North African possessions played an important role in the country's military strategy. One of the options that this strategy was considering was a landing in French North Africa.

For his part, Weddell's interviews in Washington had made him realize exactly how controversial the issue of Franco's Spain was in the administration. He expressed this new awareness in a letter to Beaulac in the following way: "Now I have a faint idea of what a red hot political potato Spain is."[491] This was undoubtedly one of the keys to the agreement that was being entered into with Spain: politically speaking it was the option that was least objectionable to the opposing sectors in the administration; that was least exploitable by the press; and which could be presented as the most demanding, the least pro-Franco and the least appeasing to the public opinion.

Even so, between the administration's acceptance of the assurances given by Spain on 27 February 1942 and the agreement becoming a reality new difficulties arose in the United States', although they were not to change Washington's decision. One of these difficulties was the sinking of oil tankers from both the United States and other allied countries by German submarines and the problems this was creating for the coastal towns of the Gulf of Mexico. Because of the concentration of refineries on the mainland and several Caribbean islands, submarine activity was particularly intense in the first two months of 1942, and numerous freighters and oil tankers were sunk. And the survivors who managed to make it to Port Arthur (Texas) pointed out that it was the well-lit Spanish tankers that were guiding the German submarines by night. In fact, Naval Intelligence was investigating the matter when[492] there was an incident in the Texan port. A new Spanish tanker—the "Campechano"—was taking on oil.[493] This had caused the families of many North American sailors to protest and, fearing sabotage, the Texas Company called off the operation and even suspended the contract with CAMPSA. The ship was finally sent to New Orleans (Louisiana), where Secretary Morgenthau and the Department of the Treasury managed to delay the loading process yet again.[494]

Another controversy was the interview that Beaulac had on 4 March with Serrano Suñer to discuss Franco's speech of 14 February.[495] Serrano responded to Beaulac's complaints of such an open expression of pro-German and anti-Soviet feeling by referring to the Hispano-Luso Treaty of Friendship and Non-Aggression of 1939 that had come about because of Spanish concern about rumors of a possible U.S. invasion of the Azores. According to Serrano, Salazar had denied these rumors. For his part, the Portuguese leader had shown his concern about a possible German invasion of Spain. Franco had told him that although Germany was worried about its "peninsular flank," as long as the Spanish continued to show their friendship this invasion would not take place. This situation would change, he added, if the democracies took any action against Spain or Portugal. In the same meeting they also spoke of the difficulties in supplying petroleum products and considered the desirability of setting identical prices for a whole range of products, wolfram in particular, which were important for all those involved in the conflict.

The atmosphere between the two men was cordial until Serrano tried to give a more detailed explanation of Franco's speech and the situation became tenser. Beaulac complained about its extreme anti-Communist tone and the effect that these sorts of public declarations had on North American public opinion. The result was merely to place yet another obstacle in the way of providing economic aid to Spain. Serrano justified his brother-in-law by using the Francoists' usual battery of arguments: that is to say, Spain was not only militarily weak but also had German troops on its Pyrenean border. He also said that as long as Spain made a public show of friendship toward Germany, they would have nothing to fear and that Spain was providing the Axis with no military support. This may have been true insofar as they were not providing German submarines with supplies but they were giving them every facility as regards information and espionage. He also claimed that his country was trading with both the Germans and the Allies, and that it was "between the Devil and the deep blue sea." However, as was his duty, he also defended the anti-Communist content of the speech in the following terms:

> Franco expressed precisely Spain's well known public attitude towards communism. Spain considered Germany a bulwark against communism. When Franco said that Spanish volunteers would go to Germany's aid in case Germany was overrun by the Russians, he was being entirely consistent with Spain's attitude towards communism; Spain quite realized it could not prevent Germany being overrun but Spaniards would be quite prepared to die in the attempt.[496]

However, he was quick to point out that "until this contingency should arise, however, Spain had no desire to become more involved than at present in the war against Russia or any other country and Spanish policy was directed against becoming involved." In response, Beaulac only reminded him of the effect that such public statements and ideas had on public opinion in the United States (and he could also have mentioned the effect they had on some sectors of the administration)

> If his theses were fully accepted, he must still realize the effect on public opinion in the United States of the public utterances of Spanish officials and if Spain had no alternative to its policy towards Germany as described, it was likewise impossible to prevent American public opinion in the United States from reacting unfavorably and suggested that he bear this in mind.[497]

As far as everything else was concerned, since the Spanish press had not ceased its biting attacks on the United States with reference to the shortage of gasoline, Beaulac was to have plenty of opportunity for making further complaints to Serrano.[498]

Despite the tension between the two men during the interview, it was not sufficient to halt the preparations that were being made by the State Department, which was being spurred on by the British[499] and which had by now been informed—and perhaps convinced—by Weddell in person. At long last, on 4 March 1942[500] Sumner Welles sent Beaulac a memorandum with the draft conditions for the trade agreement with Spain and the three-monthly plan for shipping petroleum products (which included the shipments that had already been made during February). The same text was also to be delivered to Cárdenas in Washington but it was first sent to the Madrid Embassy because the department had decided to prioritize this channel (much to the satisfaction of the staff in Madrid) and because haste was now of the essence.

Welles ordered Beaulac to informally make the Spanish authorities aware of the draft conditions, and to make it clear that "this export of petroleum from the United States at the present time is a recognition of essential Spanish need and indicative of our wish for responding to it." He was also told to stress two other aspects:

> As the Spanish authorities will understand, any movement of petroleum from the United States which by any form of accident or change in military circumstance could be of assistance to our enemies is a matter of utmost moment to us.... We hope to make headway with our program of purchase of Spanish products useful to our own defense effort and also in consideration of other Spanish needs.

The memorandum, which was based on the recognition that "both Governments are ready to proceed with the arrangements contemplated," announced that the United States would soon initiate negotiations for the purchase of Spanish products through "its Embassy in Madrid and through the special representatives that will be sent to Spain for that purpose." The plan for supplying petroleum envisaged for the February–April term included 25,000 tons of gasoline, 1,000 of kerosene, 20,000 of diesel fuel (12,400 of which had already been shipped on the "Campillo" and the "Campuzano"), 14,000 of fuel oil, and 3,000 of lubricating oil. That is to say, a total of 61,000 tons that was less than what Spain had imported in the final term of 1941 (70,644 tons), as is shown in table 2.

The total was much lower than the first three terms of 1941 (first term: 160,639 tons; second term: 149,032 tons; and third term 120,749 tons).[501] And the supply depended on the Spanish government cooperating by constantly providing information about the stocks they had available, consumption, and so on, and, above all by not reexporting any of the supplies they received to any other country (that is to say, the Axis). The memorandum also specified that the United States would

Table 2 Imports of petroleum products by Spain in the October–December term 1941 (in tons)

	Gasoline	Kerosene	Diesel fuel	Fuel oil	Lubricants	Kero + Petrol.	Total
October	14,909	1,996	0	0	356	1,996	17,261
November	17,182	0	8,713	13,598	6,329	0	45,822
December	7,561	0	0	12,228	0	0	7,561
						Total	70,644

Source: Based on Leonard Caruana and Hugh Rockoff. *An Elephant in the Garden: The Allies, Spain and Oil in World War II* (Cambridge: National Bureau of Economic Research, 2006), 44.

not send crude to be refined in Spain because the Spanish government had not satisfactorily informed about either the activity or the stocks at the only refinery in Tenerife, or the stocks in Spanish Morocco. The result of this was that none of the Spanish tankers that were in Colombian ports would be loaded with crude and the Spanish government was advised to order them to set sail for the Galveston (Texas) because "under the program being developed the necessary cargoes for Spain would be shipped from American Gulf ports." Finally, for the plan to function efficiently and the perceptive export licenses to be granted, the Spanish government was required to send to the U.S. government, in plenty of time, the schedule of their tankers.

The Founding of the Iberian Peninsula Operating Committee (IPOC) and the USCC

At the same time as he was taking the above step, Sumner Welles also took several others on an internal level to ensure that the plan could be implemented effectively. Because numerous departments and organizations were involved in some way or the other in trade with Spain—as well as the State Department there was the Department of the Navy, the Board of Economic Warfare, the Office of Strategic Services (OSS), the Reconstruction Finance Corporation, the Petroleum Administrator for War and the War Production Board—he ordered the State Department's economic adviser Herbert Feis to design the structure of an interdepartmental committee that would be responsible for managing the day-to-day business of economic relations with Spain and Portugal from Washington. This committee would also act as the link to the British government and bear the title of IPOC. In the future, it was to become the model on which similar committees responsible for trade with Turkey and North Africa would be based.

He also began to prepare the group of agents that were to control the petroleum supplies being sent to Spain. This group would be directed by Walter F. Smith, who was appointed Petroleum Attaché to the Madrid Embassy and had arrived in Madrid on the previous 1 March to start preparations.[502]

The most important aspect of the process, because of the drastic change it entailed, was the setting up of the USCC, the agency responsible for managing all purchases in the Iberian peninsula, including the "preclusive" ones (that is to say, those products that were acquired not so much for purposes of consumption but so that the enemy could not get their hands of them). To help in the preparations, the assistant chief[503] of the Division of Defense Materials,[504] Henry Labouisse, was sent to Madrid a few days after Smith.

The setting up of the USCC had not been easy and it led to the confrontation with Vice President Wallace and Jesse Jones, the Federal Loan Administrator and Chairman of the Reconstruction Finance Corporation.[505] The internal controversy dated back to the end of 1940 when the department's economic adviser Herbert Feis and the head of the Defense Materials Branch Thomas Finletter had followed Great Britain's example and recommended that the agency be set up. In fact, the United States had for some time been using the Reconstruction Finance Corporation and its subsidiaries the Defense Supply Corporation, the Metals Reserve Company, and the Rubber Reserve Company to purchase products on the international market that it believed to be necessary for the defensive needs of the country, but it had yet to adopt the British tactics of making preclusive purchases. This was the proposal that was now made. However, when the department accepted the idea, it came up against the reluctance of Jesse Jones, who believed that "our purpose should not be to buy merely to keep someone else from getting the same materials, but rather to have on hand an ample supply of what we might want."[506] This heralded a period of hard bargaining although it did not prevent some preclusive purchases from being made: for example, during the summer of 1941 the United States acquired all the Bolivian copper, tin, and wolfram, and most of Argentina's zinc and Brazilian manganese. In the following Autumn, they also managed to cut off the sale of war materials from Latin America to Japan, with the only exception of those materials being sold by Argentina. The case of Spain, however, and that of the neutral European countries in general, was more difficult since there was fierce competition among the belligerents both to control the deposits and purchase strategic products. This situation was exploited by neutral governments—and particularly Spain—to get what they wanted from them. This was the situation in November 1941 when a British request for the United States to help out with a preclusive purchase of wolfram in the Iberian peninsula reopened the controversy in both the Roosevelt administration (between the State Department and the Reconstruction Finance Corporation) and the press. At the time the Germans were paying between $300 and $370 for a unit of wolfram in Portugal when just three months before it had cost $19.5 (and $21 in the United States).[507] Spain was producing less than Portugal but that was to change very quickly. Germany was in vital need of wolfram so that metals could be hardened for the manufacture of arms. Great Britain's aim was to deprive them of it. A few days before Pearl Harbor, encouraged by the State Department and in his capacity as chairman of the Economic Defense Board Vice president, Wallace had had an interview with Jesse Jones to convince him of the need to initiate a program of preclusive purchases but he had not been able to. However, the prices at the time were so astronomical that even Secretary Hull had agreed with Jones and the issue had been shelved. Then in February 1942 Feis and Finletter gained the support of the head of the department's Western Europe Division Ray Atherton and, once again, of Vice president Wallace (who was now also head of the recently created Board of Economic Warfare). Wallace put Jones in the uncomfortable position of having to accept the USCC or lose his authority over it, so he finally came round and accepted it.[508] Shortly afterward, in April, it was put under the control of the Board of Economic Warfare.

All the preparations for the agreement with Spain coordinated by Sumner Welles were included in a new statement of policy that he presented to the president himself during a cabinet meeting. But before he had time to do so, new difficulties arose. Reports were received that Spain had hired and sent Portuguese freighters to Central and South America,[509] and also that Spain and Argentina had reached a new agreement in January for buying wheat.[510] And to make matters worse, all the heads of the Spanish General Staff and Air Force had gone to Berlin.

The fears that this news had raised soon faded, however, and Welles had his new statement of policy approved by Roosevelt in a government meeting held on

20 March 1942. This did not put a stop to internal reluctance and the day after it had been approved, the under secretary sent the memorandum containing the details of the agreement for the next three months to the president so that he could confirm his approval. It seemed that the various departments and agencies involved in trade with Spain were reluctant to implement it. Welles explained the situation to the president in the following terms:

> In so far as the execution of this program by our own Government is concerned many departments and agencies of the United States are necessarily involved. Speaking very frankly, certain subordinate officials of these departments and agencies appear to be opposed to the carrying out by this Government of any program which involves the shipment of commodities from the United States to Spain.

His aim now was to inform these organizations that the execution of the agreement during this test period was "specifically approved and authorized by you."[511]

Chance would have it that in this period at the end of March 1942 Alexander W. Weddell resigned, thus bringing to an end a period in the relations between the United States of America and Franco's Spain. His last acts as ambassador, however, raised some considerable controversy. When interviewed by the press, he spoke of Spain and its current situation in a "somewhat more sympathetic light than was usually given" and his words were widely reported in Latin America. In particular, Argentine newspapers that supported the Franco regime used them to respond to attacks on Franco. Weddell's justification of Hispanicity as essentially a cultural phenomenon that was not, as many believed it to be, at the service of the Axis actually prompted the U.S. ambassador Norman Armour to lodge a formal complaint to the State Department.[512]

Conclusion

The Roosevelt Administration did not have a specific policy on Franco's Spain throughout the two-year period in which the United States was not involved in the Second World War: that is to say, between its outbreak on 1 September 1939 and the attack on Pearl Harbor on 7 December 1941. The foundations of a Spanish policy began to be formulated only in October 1941, two months before the Japanese attack. This lack of a specific policy meant that their actions were governed by a mixture of three factors.

The first factor was the controversy over the Franco regime in the Roosevelt administration—the press and public opinion. Spain was a red hot potato, partly because of the more general problem of Fascism, which created rifts between the high-ranking officials of the government and the administration. At various times it led to the Secretaries Morgenthau, Ickes, Stimson, and Knox, and the Vice President Wallace clashing with the secretary and the under secretary of state, Hull and Welles. The president himself was often undecided about whether to take action or not, but he tended to support the policy of the State Department. This policy aimed to increase North American presence (and business) in Spain but conflicted with the extremely anti–United States attitudes of the regime's leaders. Within the State Department itself, the issue of Spain was sometimes just one more manifestation of the general tension between Cordell Hull and Sumner Welles, a personal friend of Franco's Ambassador in Washington Juan Francisco de Cárdenas. Alexander W. Weddell and the Madrid Embassy also had their differences with the department, particularly because they had been in favor of designing a specific Spanish policy since 1939. This led to regular clashes with the State Department, which was intent on following British policy and under constant pressure by the anti-Franco press and public opinion. The Spanish policy implemented by Washington between 1939 and 1941, then, was largely erratic, much to the frustration of the Madrid Embassy. For their part, the anti-Francoists in the government and the Roosevelt administration wanted a much tougher and more aggressive policy than the one advocated by the State Department, and on occasion they were successful in getting it. In fact the Franco regime continually supplied the anti-Franco press with ammunition because of the ferocious repression of the Republicans who had been defeated in the Civil War, the shooting of political leaders who had been captured by the Germans and sent back to Spain, and their constant expression of antidemocracy and anti–United States feeling. All this affected and limited the State Department's policy on the Franco regime.

The second factor that explains U.S. policy on Spain in the period under study was that, after the outbreak of the Second World War, President Roosevelt and his government wanted to do all they could to assist the democracies in their struggle against the Axis. As far as Spain was concerned, this meant agreeing to go along with the British who had a specific policy but needed the United States to be able to implement it (that is to say, to be able to provide Spain with particular supplies). Nevertheless, not all of the U.S. policy consisted of helping the British. Some private U.S. companies were doing good business with Spain and they were to continue to do so although with some interruptions. And because of the continuous conflicts between the regime and the United States the collaboration with Great Britain had its ups and downs.

The third and final factor explaining U.S. policy on Franco's Spain in the first two years of the world war is directly related to these ups and downs, which were largely caused by the aggressive attitude of the regime toward Roosevelt and the United States in general. The Spanish were proud and ultranationalist, disdained the democracies, and secretly helped the Axis. In both the second half of 1940 and the spring of 1941 they tried to reach an agreement with Germany for Spain to participate in the war alongside the Axis in exchange for imperial expansion. All this was negotiated on "mysterious" trips to Berlin, Rome, Hendaye, and Berchtesgaden. Spain even dared challenge the Pan-Americanism fostered by the United States with an aggressive policy of Fascist Hispanicity.

The State Department had been surprised by the aggressive antidemocracy stance of the Franco regime when it first manifested at the end of the Civil War. It was the department that had established the political guidelines for dealing with the two sides during the war, in accordance with the policy of nonintervention designed by the United Kingdom and France to restrict the conflict within the Spanish frontiers and prevent it from becoming the spark that would ignite a continental conflagration. President Roosevelt himself had accepted this policy, although from the beginning of 1938 the attitudes of his immediate family and colleagues in government and the Nazi and Fascist demands in Europe led him to gradually change his noninterventionist point of view. He even organized secret operations to help the Spanish Republic without once modifying the official policy that was being implemented.

What is more, as soon as the war ended, the possibilities of having an economic relation with Spain in line with the precepts of free trade that Hull had been implementing since 1934 with his Reciprocal Trade Agreements were short circuited by the ultraprotectionist, interventionist, and autarkic policy adopted by Franco, and the regime prevented certain U.S. citizens and companies from having free access to their possessions in Spain. One such case was La Telefónica, which dominated the diplomatic relations between the two countries for more than a year. Another was the issue of the release of the Lincoln Brigade prisoners.

When these disputes had been resolved, new problems arose particularly in the second half of 1940: first Spain attempted to enter the Second World War on the side of the Axis; and then Franco tried to extend Spain's empire by occupying and annexing the city of Tangiers and its International Zone.

Great Britain, however, desperately needed Spain to be neutral. Between 1939 and 1941, the Axis conquered numerous territories in Europe and one of the main

British fears was that Spain would enter the war. To prevent this from happening, Great Britain designed a sophisticated policy, the aim of which was to keep Spain supplied so that Franco would "not be forced into the arms of the Axis." This is where the United States came in, as a complementary but essential source of supplies (particularly gasoline). Other elements of the policy involved bribing Spanish generals and maintaining a state of military alert so that they could respond to any hostile movement by the regime. As a result of the British requests for collaboration, in the spring of 1941 the United States agreed to provide Franco with more petroleum products than up to that point and increase humanitarian aid, which was being sent by the Red Cross so that Roosevelt could avoid the political risk of being accused of supporting Franco. The United States was even prepared to grant an important loan that Spain had been trying to get for months. However, just when negotiations were about to begin, there was an incident between Weddell—the great advocate of the Spanish cause but who had mistakenly interpreted Franco's intentions—and the Minister of Foreign Affairs Serrano Suñer. This incident put everything back by five months.

The incident was partly the fault of both men and came about just when the Francoists were again considering entering the world war on the side of the Axis, after deciding against doing so in 1940 because Hitler had not wanted to satisfy their colonial aspirations. They used the incident to their advantage in their relations with Germany and Italy, but the country paid a high price because the loan they had been seeking was not granted and, above all, the supply of petroleum products was cut off for a short time, just as it had been in the summer of 1940. And in September–October 1941, just as had happened in August 1940 with La Telefónica and the Lincoln Brigade, economic pressure had the desired effect and the regime backed down and reestablished contacts with Weddell. The result of all this was that in October 1941 the United States designed a specific policy to govern relations with the Franco regime. It was based on a strict commercial quid pro quo, was much tougher than the policy that would have been proposed in March–April, and which the Weddell-Serrano incident had prevented and depended on Spain not forwarding any of the supplies received to the Axis. It also meant that the amount of petroleum products supplied would be lower than in the previous two years. In accordance with British policy, then, the issue of supply was used as a weapon to oblige the Francoists to behave themselves during the world war; that is to say, to remain neutral.

Pearl Harbor and the entry of the United States into the Second World War led to restrictions in the supplies to Spain, but the rudiments of the U.S. policy on the Franco regime had been established two months before the Japanese attack. As a result of this new situation, ambassador Weddell, disillusioned by his confrontations with Madrid, was dismissed. He was replaced at the beginning of 1942 by a similar diplomat who was maybe even more in favor of the regime than Weddell had been: an influential Catholic and pro-*nacional* during the Civil War, Carlton J. H. Hayes. His policy was a continuation of that of the Madrid Embassy between 1939 and 1941, but he was more determined and often had to struggle against his own administration, which was increasingly less inclined to put up with the Franco regime. He was fortunate not to have to contend with Serrano Suñer, who was dismissed in September 1942. His replacement, Jordana, was much more neutral. During his time in Madrid, Spain gradually moved away from the Axis, which throughout 1943 and 1944 was on the retreat.

To sum up, it should be pointed out that the British and U.S. policies on the Franco regime were based on a dichotomy and a mistaken assessment of the ideologies and attitudes of Franco and Serrano Suñer, his main political adviser and brother-in-law. This appreciation was shared by the Foreign Office, the British ambassador in Madrid Hoare, the State Department, and both Weddell and Hayes, who all believed that Franco was a convinced neutralist while Serrano was a passionate pro-Nazi and interventionist. Serrano, then, was the real enemy to be isolated although recent historiography has clearly shown that both brothers-in-law and a large part of the army and the single party wanted to join forces with the Axis in the Second World War in exchange for imperial compensation. And if the Axis powers had come out on top, they would have willingly participated in Hitler's New Order. Of course this does not mean that they did not have their differences but their agreement on who they should support outweighed all other considerations.

Roosevelt and Franco never met. However, the dislike and hostility they felt for each other and their respective regimes had to take second place to the dictates of a realistic policy during the two years of United States neutrality at the beginning of the Second World War. In conjunction with Great Britain, the United States tried to prevent Spain from joining forces with the Axis. Despite the fact that their policy was based on the mistaken belief that Franco was against participation, it finally seemed to be successful. Spain's policy toward the United States, on the other hand, had to accept the reality of their economic dependence on the most reviled and powerful of the democracies. This mutual disagreement, dislike, and dependence led to a fascinating relationship between the two countries. I hope I have been able to capture the readers' interest with it.

NOTES

ACKNOWLEDGMENTS

1. Particular mention should be made of the valuable studies by Ángel Viñas Los Pactos secretos de Franco con Estados Unidos. Bases, ayuda económica, recortes de soberanía (Barcelona: Grijalbo, 1981) and En las garras del águila. Los pactos con Estados Unidos, de Francisco Franco a Felipe González (Barcelona: Crítica, 2003), by Arturo Jarque Iñiguez (Queremos esas bases. El acercamiento de Estados Unidos a la España de Franco [Madrid: Universidad de Alcalá, 1998]) and by the authors coordinated by Lorenzo Delgado and Mª Dolores Elizalde in the volume España y los Estados Unidos en el siglo XX (Madrid: CSIC, 2005).

1 ROOSEVELT AND FRANCO DURING THE SPANISH CIVIL WAR (18 JULY 1936–1 APRIL 1939)

1. Richard Hofstadter. *Franklin D. Roosevelt: The Patrician as Opportunist,* ed. Richard Hofstadter. *The American Political Tradition and the Men Who Made It* (New York: Alfred A. Knopf, 1962), 338.
2. Frederick W. Marks III. *Wind over Sand. The Diplomacy of Franklin Roosevelt* (Athens and London: University of Georgia Press, 1988), 277.
3. Ibid.
4. John Morton Blum. *From the Morgenthau Diaries. Years of Crisis, 1928–1938* (Boston: Houghton Mifflin, 1959), 485.
5. Hofstadter. *Franklin D. Roosevelt: The Patrician as Opportunist*, 339.
6. David Reynolds. *From Munich to Pearl Harbor. Roosevelt's America and the Origins of the Second World War* (Chicago: Ivan R. Dee, 2001), 158–159.
7. To bring about his downfall they used a homosexual incident in which he was supposedly involved: Irwin F. Gellman. *Secret Affairs. Franklin Roosevelt, Cordell Hull, and Sumner Welles* (Baltimore and London: Johns Hopkins University Press, 1995). On the Hull-Welles power struggle and FDR's preference for the latter, see Letter from the Ambassador Juan Francisco de Cárdenas Rodríguez de Rivas to the Minister of Foreign Affairs General Conde de Jordana on 30 August 1943 AMAE R: 1434 E.
8. Reynolds. *From Munich to Pearl Harbor*, 33–34.
9. Robert Dallek. *Franklin D. Roosevelt and American Foreign Policy, 1932–1945* (New York and Oxford: Oxford University Press, 1995), 177; Reynolds. *From Munich to Pearl Harbor*, 174.
10. Or the Slavs disinclined toward Slavs and Spaniards; Marks. *Wind over Sand*, 254.

11. Frank Freidel. *Franklin Delano Roosevelt. A Rendezvous with Destiny* (Boston: Little, Brown, 1990), 270
12. Ibid. 272.
13. On my characterization of Franco's regime as fascistized, see Joan Maria Thomàs. *La Falange de Franco. Fascismo y fascistización en el Régimen Franquista, 1937–1945* (Barcelona: Plaza y Janés, 2001).
14. Richard P. Traina. *American Diplomacy and the Spanish Civil War* (Bloomington and London: Indiana University Press, 1968), 47.
15. Gerald Howson. *Armas para España. La historia no contada de la Guerra Civil española* (Barcelona: Península, 1998).
16. Ángel Viñas. *El oro de Moscú. Alfa y omega de un mito franquista* (Barcelona: Grijalbo, 1979); Pablo Martín Aceña. *El oro de Moscú y el oro de Berlín* (Madrid: Taurus, 2001).
17. Dominic Tierney. "Franklin D. Roosevelt and Covert Aid to the Loyalists in the Spanish Civil War, 1936–39," *Journal of Contemporary History*, 39 (July 2004), 299–313.
18. Blum. *From the Morgenthau Diaries. Years of Crisis*, 506.
19. Joseph P. Lash. *Eleanor and Franklin. The Story of Their Relationship Based on Eleanor Roosevelt's Private Papers* (New York: W.W. Norton, 1971), 569–570.
20. Ronald Radosh, Mary R. Habeck, and Gricory Sevostianov. *Spain Betrayed: The Soviet Union in the Spanish Civil War* (London: Yale, 2001), 428–429.
21. Freidel. *Franklin Delano Roosevelt*, 271.
22. Cordell Hull. *The Memoirs of Cordell Hull* (London: Hodder & Stoughton, 1948), 1:506.
23. Ibid. 271–272.
24. Ibid. 272.
25. Harold L. Ickes. *The Secret Diary of Harold L. Ickes. The Inside Struggle*, vol. 2 (New York: Simon & Shuster, 1954), 424, note of 12 May 1938.
26. Traina. *American Diplomacy and the Spanish Civil War*, 150–152.
27. Dallek. *Franklin D. Roosevelt and American Foreign Policy*, 177–178.
28. F. Jay Taylor. *The United States and the Spanish Civil War* (New York: Octagon Books, 1971), 81.
29. Harold Ickes to FDR, 23 November 1938, Franklin Delano Roosevelt Presidential Library (FDRPL). President's Secretary's File (PSF) Box 50; Taylor. *The United States and the Spanish Civil War*, 183, n. 87.
30. Dallek. *Franklin D. Roosevelt and American Foreign Policy*, 176.
31. Sumner Welles to FDR, 30 November 1938, FDRPL, Official File (OF).
32. Dallek. *Franklin D. Roosevelt and American Foreign Policy*, 178.
33. FDR to the Attorney General 28 November 1938 FDRPL OF.
34. Reynolds. *From Munich to Pearl Harbor*, 50–51.
35. Dallek. *Franklin D. Roosevelt and American Foreign Policy*, 79.
36. Reynolds. *From Munich to Pearl Harbor*, 49.
37. Ibid.
38. Dallek. *Franklin D. Roosevelt and American Foreign Policy*, 179–180.
39. Reynolds. *From Munich to Pearl Harbor*, 49.
40. Dallek. *Franklin D. Roosevelt and American Foreign Policy*, 180.
41. And he went on: "There were times when this annoyed me very much. In the case of the Spanish Civil War, for instance, we had to remain neutral though Franklin knew quite well he wanted the democratic government to be successful. But he also knew that he could not get Congress to go along with him. To justify his action, or lack

of action, he explained to me, when I complained, that the League of Nations had asked us to remain neutral. By trying to convince me that our course was correct, though he knew I thought we were doing the wrong thing, he was simply trying to salve his own conscience, because he himself was uncertain." Eleanor Roosevelt. *This Is I Remember* (New York: Harper & Brothers, 1949), 161–162.

42. Douglas Little. "Antibolshevism and Appeasement: Great Britain, the United States, and the Spanish Civil War," ed. David F. Schmitz and Richard D. Challener. *Appeasement in Europe. A Reassessment of U.S. Policies* (Westport: Greenwood Press, 1990), 41.
43. Cited in Enrique Moradiellos. "La política europea, 1898–1939," *Ayer* (2003), 49, 76.
44. Douglas Little. *Malevolent Neutrality. The United Status, Great Britain, and the Origins of the Spanish Civil War* (Ithaca and London: Cornell University Press, 1985), 31–33.
45. Ibid. 214–215.
46. Little. "Antibolshevism and Appeasement: Great Britain, the United States, and the Spanish Civil War," 26; Little. *Malevolent Neutrality*, 232–233.
47. Little. *Malevolent Neutrality*. 26–27.
48. Ibid. 34.
49. Little. "Antibolshevism and Appeasement: Great Britain, the United States, and the Spanish Civil War," 26; Little, *Malevolent Neutrality*, 233–234.
50. Taylor. *The United States and the Spanish Civil War*, 43.
51. Reynolds. *From Munich to Pearl Harbor*, 31–32.
52. Taylor. *The United States and the Spanish Civil War*, 58, n. 44.
53. Douglas Little. "Claude Bowers and His Mission to Spain: The Diplomacy of a Jeffersonian Democrat," ed. Kenneth Paul Jones. *U.S. Diplomats in Europe, 1919–1941* (Santa Barbara: ABC-Clio, 1983), 140.
54. Moradiellos. "La política europea, 1898–1939," 77.
55. Ricardo Miralles. "Las iniciativas diplomáticas de la Segunda República durante la Guerra Civil 1936–1939," ed. Javier Tusell, Juan Avilés, and Rosa Pardo. *La política exterior de España en el siglo XX* (Madrid: Biblioteca Nueva, 2000), 246.
56. Enrique Moradiellos. *Neutralidad Benévola. El gobierno británico y la insurrección militar española de 1936* (Oviedo: Pentalfa Ediciones, 1990), 250.
57. Ibid.
58. Taylor. *The United States and the Spanish Civil War*, 81; Dallek. *Franklin D. Roosevelt and American Foreign Policy*, 136.
59. Cited in Taylor. *The United States and the Spanish Civil War*, 86.
60. Neutrality Act of 1 May 1937 in U.S. Department of State, *Peace and War: U.S. Foreign Policy 1931–1941* (Washington: 1983), 355–365.
61. Reynolds. *From Munich to Pearl Harbor*, 32.
62. Dallek. *Franklin D. Roosevelt and American Foreign Policy*, 140.
63. "New York American" 1 February 1937 quoted in Taylor. *The United States and the Spanish Civil War*, 81.
64. Von Stohrer. German Minister of Foreign Affairs 16 July 1939 quoted in Manuel Ros Agudo. *La guerra secreta de Franco (1939–1945)* (Barcelona: Crítica, 2002), 303.
65. Hull. *The Memoirs of Cordell Hull*, 479.
66. Sumner Welles. *The Time for Decision* (New York: Harper & Brothers, 1944), 59.
67. Little. *Malevolent Neutrality*, 263.
68. Quoted in Little. "Antibolshevism and Appeasement: Great Britain, the United States, and the Spanish Civil War," 30.
69. Ibid. 31; Dallek. *Franklin D. Roosevelt and American Foreign Policy*, 143.

70. Dallek. *Franklin D. Roosevelt and American Foreign Policy*, 143.
71. Ibid. 147.
72. Ibid. 158.
73. Ibid. 117.
74. Ibid. 168.
75. Ibid. 232.
76. Ibid.
77. Little. "Antibolshevism and Appeasement: Great Britain, the United States, and the Spanish Civil War," 23, 24, 36.
78. Taylor. *The United States and the Spanish Civil War*, 185.
79. Little. "Antibolshevism and Appeasement: Great Britain, the United States, and the Spanish Civil War," 40.
80. Taylor. *The United States and the Spanish Civil War*, 187.
81. Michael R. Beschloss. *Kennedy and Roosevelt. The Uneasy Alliance* (New York: W.W. Norton, 1980), 164.
82. Ibid. 186.
83. Ickes. *The Secret Diary of Harold L. Ickes. The Inside Struggle*, vol. 2, 389–390.
84. In a letter to Claude G. Bowers on 31 August 1938 FDR had written that "perhaps a little later on—if the Czech situation does not end disastrously—I can make some kind of a move for the purpose of at least aiding in ending the Spanish War." FDRPL PSF Spain Box 50.
85. Note from Fernando de los Ríos to Cordell Hull on 26 January 1939 FDRPL PSF Spain Box 50.
86. Note from Sumner Welles to FDR on 27 January 1939 FDRPL PSF Spain Box 50.
87. Dallek. *Franklin D. Roosevelt and American Foreign Policy*, 180.
88. Little. "Antibolshevism and Appeasement: Great Britain, the United States, and the Spanish Civil War," 42 43.
89. Letter from Bowers to FDR on 16 February 1939 FDRPL PSF Spain Box 50.
90. Ibid.
91. Undated telegram from Hull to Roosevelt although FDR's reply on 23 February 1939 means that it must have been sent before this date. FDRPL PSF Spain Box 50.
92. In fact, the United Kingdom and France diplomatically recognized Franco's Spain on 27 February 1939
93. *Naval Message* on 23 February 1939 FDRPL PSF Spain Box 50.
94. Undated telegram from Hull to FDR FDRPL PSF Spain Box 50.
95. Quoted in Little. "Antibolshevism and Appeasement: Great Britain, the United States, and the Spanish Civil War," 43.
96. Bowers. *Misión de Guerra en España;* Barcelona, Grijalbo, 1977, 431.
97. Ibid. 433.
98. Letter from Bowers to FDR St. Jean de Luz 25-V-1939 FDRPL PSF Spain Box 50.
99. Taylor. *The United States and the Spanish Civil War*, 200.
100. Little. "Antibolshevism and Appeasement: Great Britain, the United States, and the Spanish Civil War," 43.
101. Tusell et al. *La política exterior de España en el siglo XX*, 294.
102. Bowers. *Misión de Guerra en España*, 432.
103. Notes of a Sumner Welles-De los Ríos conversation 27 March 1939 FDRPL PSF Spain Box 50.
104. Little. "Claude Bowers and His Mission to Spain: The Diplomacy of a Jeffersonian Democrat," 144; Little. "Antibolshevism and Appeasement: Great Britain, the United States, and the Spanish Civil War," 43.

105. Taylor. *The United States and the Spanish Civil War*, 207.
106. Enrique Moradiellos. *Franco frente a Churchill. España y Gran Bretaña en la Segunda Guerra Mundial (1939–1945)* (Barcelona: Península, 2005), 27.
107. Ibid. 28; Little. "Antibolshevism and Appeasement: Great Britain, the United States, and the Spanish Civil War," 33.
108. Ibid. 35.
109. Dallek. *Franklin D. Roosevelt and American Foreign Policy*, 182–183.

2 BETWEEN TWO WARS: FROM THE SPANISH CIVIL WAR TO THE SECOND WORLD WAR (1 APRIL–1 SEPTEMBER 1939)

1. Neither was it over in the press. In 1951, the former counselor for the Madrid Embassy, Willard L. Beaulac, spoke of the situation in 1941 in the following terms: "... except for Franco's pro-Axis speeches, which were given wide publicity, most of this Franco propaganda was not printed in the United States. What the American press presented as news concerning Spain came usually from Mexico City, Montevideo, New York, London, Moscow, and other cities more or less distant from Spain. Conservatively speaking, 90 per cent of this also was propaganda—anti-Franco propaganda, in this case (...) We knew that a very large part of it was false because we were in Spain and had opportunities to check it. Practically all this "news" was unfavorable to the Spanish government. The sins of the Franco Régime were well known. But those sins were not accurately set forth in the American press (...) On the basis of these reports the American public formed its impressions not only about Spain but, what was more important, about American policy toward Spain. A common reaction was that if the Spanish Government was so bad we should not have relations with it. The Spanish Civil War, which had officially ended in 1939, was dragged out and fought all over again in the press." *Career Ambassador* (New York: Macmillan, 1951), 158–159.
2. Letter from Jay Allen to Eleanor Roosevelt 10 July 1939 FDRPL PSF Spain Box 50.
3. Mark H. Leff. "Franklin D. Roosevelt, 1933–1945," ed. Alan Brinkley and Davis Dyer. *The Reader's Companion of American Presidency* (Bosto and New York: Houghton Mifflin, 2000), 367–385.
4. Letter from Negrín to Morgenthau on 10 July 1939 in FDRPL *The Morgenthau Diaries* Roll 54. Both Allen's and Negrín's letters refer to the meeting with Mrs. Roosevelt on the previous Saturday.
5. Reynolds. *From Munich to Pearl Harbor*, 70.
6. Mrs. Roosevelt sent Allen's letter to the president, who asked Sumner Welles to comment on it, as we shall mention below.
7. Reynolds. *From Munich to Pearl Harbor*, 58–59.
8. Ibid.
9. Ibid. 61; Dallek. *Franklin D. Roosevelt and American Foreign Policy*, 194.
10. Ibid. 195, 237–238.
11. Reynolds. *From Munich to Pearl Harbor*, 62.
12. Beschloss. *Kennedy and Roosevelt. The Uneasy Alliance*, 189.
13. Dallek. *Franklin D. Roosevelt and American Foreign Policy*, 207.
14. Ibid. 227.
15. Reynolds. *From Munich to Pearl Harbor*, 66–67, 173.
16. Hull to the Minister of Foreign Affairs Jordana on 3 April 1939: FRUS 1939, 2:772, n. 52.

17. National Archives and Record Administration (NARA): U.S. Department of State, *Relations between the United States and Spain 1936–1942*, Research Project No. 34, May, 1947, Foreign Policy Studies Branch, Division of Historical Policy Research, Office of Public Affairs.
18. Matthews to Hull on 1 May 1939 FRUS, 1939, 2:810–811.
19. Joan Clavera, Joan M. Esteban, M. Antònia Monés, Antoni Montserrat, and J. Ros Hombravella. *Capitalismo español: De la autarquía a la estabilización (1939–1959)* (Madrid: Edicusa, 1973), 1:78.
20. Ibid.: When the center-right government led by Alejandro Lerroux had replaced the main supplier, the USSR, by this company.
21. Howson. *Armas para España*, 111; Guillem Martínez Molinos. "El suministro de petróleo," in *La Guerra Civil Española*, vol. 16 (Madrid: Historia 16), 95, 97, n. 10.
22. Molinos. "El suministro de petróleo," 95.
23. Herbert Feis. *The Spanish History. Franco and the Nations at War* (New York: Alfred A. Knopf, 1948), 271.
24. Howson. *Armas para España*, 110.
25. Traina. *American Diplomacy and the Spanish Civil War*, 168.
26. Contract between the Nacional Telephone Company of Spain and the International Telephone and Telegraph Corporation 29 August 1924. Office of the Head of State. Archive of the Presidency of the Government, L01714EC009001.
27. Ángel Bahamonde Magro and Luis Enrique Otero Carvajal. "El teléfono: El nacimiento de un nuevo medio de comunicación," ed. Ángel Bahamonde Magro, Gaspar Martínez Lorente, and Luis Enrique Otero Carvajal. *Las comunicaciones en la construcción del Estado contemporáneo en España: 1700–1936* (Madrid: Ministry of Public Works, Transport and Environment, 1993).
28. Adoración Álvaro Moya. "Redes empresariales, inversión directa extranjera y monopolio: El caso de Telefónica, 1924–c1965," 7th Congress of the Spanish Association of Economic History (Santiago de Compostela, 13–16 September 2005).
29. Note from the head of Military Court No. 16 to the War Auditor of the Guadarrama Armed Forces on 7 June 1940: The accused, apart from Behn and Caldwell, were the also U.S. citizen Antonio Ahumada Valdés and the British citizen David Graham: AMAE, R: 1676 E: 6.
30. Matthews to Hull on 11 May 1939 FRUS 1939, 2:820–824.
31. Weddell to Hull on 24 August 1939 FRUS 1939, 2:815.
32. Matthews to Hull on 21 April 1939 FRUS 1939, 2:809–810.
33. Bowers to FDR on 20 April 1939 FDRPL PSF Spain Box 50.
34. Memo of a conversation between Pierrepont Moffat, Chief of the Division of European Affairs and Truelle, Counselor of the French Embassy in Washington 16 February 1939 FRUS 1939, 2:801.
35. Ibid.
36. Memo of a conversation between Moffatt and Murphy, First Secretary of the Embassy in Paris on 21 April 1939 FRUS, 2:808.
37. Setter from Weddell to Mrs. William K. Draper on 17 October 1939 announcing the move at the end of that week: A.W. Weddell Papers.
38. Virginia House was inherited by the Virginia Historical Society and is currently a house-cum-museum dedicated to the Weddells.
39. Vide guest lists and visiting cards from receptions, teas, and so on: A.W. Weddell Papers.
40. "The United States and Spain 1936–1942," 26.

41. A.W. Weddell, "Memorandum of Conversation with the President," 10 May 1939: A.W. Weddell Papers.
42. Setter from Weddell to Mrs. W.K. Draper 26 November 1940: A.W. Weddell Papers.
43. Address of Ambassador Alexander W. Weddell on being received by His Excellency, the Chief of the Spanish State: A.W. Weddell Papers.
44. List of appointments during diplomatic career in A.W. Weddell Papers.
45. In 1942 and after he had been dsimissed as ambassador in Spain we find him acting as president of the Virginia Museum of Fine Arts, as campaign manager for the Children's Home Society for 1943 and for the Red Cross, among other posts: Letter from Weddell to Arthur Garrels on 23 November 1942: A.W. Weddell Papers.
46. Alexander W. Weddell, *Introduction to Argentina* (New York: Greystone Press, 1939).
47. His category in 1928 was "Foreign Service Officer of class one" (since 1925): Curriculum Vitae A.W. Weddell: A.W. Weddell Papers.
48. Setter to Arthur Garrels on 10 January 1940: A.W. Weddell Papers.
49. Setter to Mrs. W.K. Draper on 1 February 1941: A.W. Weddell Papers.
50. Correspondence of A.W. Weddell with Dunn on 6 and 7 April 1939; Letter from *Scotten* to Weddell on 20 April 1939: A.W. Weddell Papers.
51. Letter from A.W. Weddell to Alesandro Padilla on 15 June 1942: Bert Allan Watson. *United States-Spanish Relations, 1939–1946* (Washington, DC: Ph.D. Dissertation, George Washington University, 1971), 122.
52. Also cited in Ramón Serrano Suñer. *Entre Hendaya y Gibraltar*, 2nd ed. (Barcelona: Nauta, 1973), 357: "Hablaba bastante español."
53. Marks. *Wind over Sand*, 281.
54. Charles R. Halstead. "Diligent Diplomat: Alexander W. Weddell as American Ambassador to Spain," *Virginia Magazine of History and Bibliography*, 82 (January 1974): 4. He might be able to efface some memories in "Franco Spain."
55. *Newsweek* 24 April 1939, cited in Watson. *United States-Spanish Relations*, 10.
56. Javier Tusell. *Franco, España y la Segunda Guerra Mundial. Entre el Eje y la Neutralidad* (Madrid: Temas de Hoy, 1995), 246.
57. Rosa Pardo Sanz, *Con Franco hacia el Imperio. La política exterior española en América Latina 1939–1945* (Madrid: UNED, 1995), 132; Lorenzo Delgado Gómez-Escalonilla. *Imperio de papel. Acción cultural y política exterior durante el Primer Franquismo* (Madrid: CSIC, 1992), 28; Florentino Rodao. *Franco y el imperio japonés. Imágenes y propaganda en tiempos de guerra* (Barcelona: Plaza & Janés, 202), 262.
58. Ángel Viñas, Julio Viñuela, Fernando Eguidazu, Carlos Fernández Pulgar, and Senén Florensa. *Política Comercial Exterior de España 1931–1975*, vol. 1 (Madrid: Banco de España, 1979), 303.
59. Ros Agudo. *La guerra secreta de Franco*, xiii–xiv.
60. Ibid. 98.
61. José Mª Benítez Toledo, *Una política española de petróleo* (Madrid: Bolaños y Aguilar, 1936), 125.
62. Moradiellos. *Franco frente a Churchill*, 44.
63. Viñas et al. *Política Comercial*, 1:366.
64. On 19 February 1939, cited in Moradiellos. *Franco frente a Churchill*, 33.
65. Christian Leitz. "'More Carrot Than Stick': British Economic Warfare and Spain, 1941–1944," *Twentieth Century British History*, 9 (1998), 246–273; the besat and most recent síntesis in Moradiellos. *Franco frente a Churchill*, 33–83, who we follow in the text.
66. Moradiello. *Franco frente a Churchill*, 62.
67. Ibid. 64.
68. Letter from Cárdenas to Jordana on 30 August 1943.

3 THE FIRST STAGE OF ALEXANDER W. WEDDELL'S EMBASSY (MAY 1939–AUGUST 1940)

1. Dallek. *Franklin D. Roosevelt and American Foreign Policy*, 213.
2. Ibid. 215.
3. Reynolds. *From Munich to Pearl Harbor*, 72–75.
4. Dallek. *Franklin D. Roosevelt and American Foreign Policy*, 216.
5. Reynolds. *From Munich to Pearl Harbor*, 75.
6. Ibid. 72, 78.
7. Dallek. *Franklin D. Roosevelt and American Foreign Policy*, 221.
8. Ibid. 227.
9. Reynolds. *From Munich to Pearl Harbor*, 78–79.
10. Ibid. 81–82.
11. Dallek. *Franklin D. Roosevelt and American Foreign Policy*, 224.
12. Reynolds. *From Munich to Pearl Harbor*, 79.
13. Ibid. 174.
14. Ibid. 79.
15. Norman J.W. Goda. *Tomorrow the World. Hitler, Northwest Africa, and the Path toward America* (College Station: Texas A&M, 1998), 26.
16. Julius W. Pratt. *Cordell Hull*, vol. 2 (New York: Cooper Square, 1964), 694.
17. Dallek. *Franklin D. Roosevelt and American Foreign Policy*, 235.
18. Reynolds. *From Munich to Pearl Harbor*, 87–88.
19. Ibid. 89.
20. Ibid. 89–90; Dallek. *Franklin D. Roosevelt and American Foreign Policy*, 241.
21. Ibid. 157.
22. Ibid. 241.
23. Reynolds. *From Munich to Pearl Harbor*, 70 and 82.
24. Letter from Weddell to Mrs. Bliss on 28 November 1939: A.W. Weddell Papers; It is also mentioned by Willard L. Beaulac in his two memoirs: *Career Ambassador* and *Franco. Silent Ally in World War II* (Carbondale: Southern Illinois University Press, 1986).
25. Letter from Weddell to Benito N. Anchorena on 10 July 1941: A.W. Weddell Papers.
26. Letter to Mrs. W.K. Draper on 27 July 1939: A.W. Weddell Papers.
27. Von Stohrer's office to the German Ministry of Foreign Affairs on 27 July 1941: *Documents of German Foreign Policy*, 13, 157.
28. Letter from Sumner Welles to FDR on 19 July 1939 FDRPL PSF Welles Box 50.
29. Letter to Mrs. Draper.
30. Letter from Weddell to Mrs. W.K. Draper on 27 July 1939: A.W. Weddell Papers.
31. Letter from Weddell to Dr. John Stewart Bryan on 27 December 1939: A.W. Weddell Papers.
32. According to the official *Breve resumen de la obra del Ministerio de Justicia por la pacificación espiritual de España* published in 1946, in 1940 the number of inmates was 280,000. An interdisciplinary approach to the prisons and detention centers of Franco's Spain in the immediate postwar period can be found in C. Molinero, M. Sala, and J. Sobrequés, eds. *Una inmensa prisión. Los capos de concentración y las prisiones durante la Guerra Civil y el Franquismo* (Barcelona: Crítica, 2003).
33. Letter from Weddell to Thomas Benjamin Gay on 11 March 1940: A.W. Weddell Papers.
34. Letter from Weddell to Hull on 8 December 1939: A.W. Weddell Papers.
35. Ibid.
36. Letter from Weddell to Hull on 31 July 1939: A.W. Weddell Papers.

37. Letter from Weddell to Sumner Welles on 7 November 1939: A.W. Weddell Papers.
38. By means of an agreement between the Holy See and Spain signed on 7 June 1941 that reestablished the privileges of the Concordat of 1851 until a new one was signed. This did not happen until 1953: Antonio Marquina Barrio. *La diplomacia vaticana y la España de Franco 1936–1945* (Madrid: CSIC, 1986), 287–291.
39. Letter from Weddell to Hull on 8 December 1939: A.W. Weddell Papers.
40. Letter from Weddell to Welles on 29 August 1939 FDRPL Sumner Welles Box 57.
41. Ibid.
42. *ABC* 3 November 1939.
43. Text from Weddell to Hull entitled *Extra-official Activities of Ambassador and Mrs. Weddell in Promoting a Good Understanding between the United States and Spain* 16 November 1939 NARA RG 84; Letter from Weddell to Welles on 7 January 1941: A.W. Weddell Papers.
44. The best overall study on Francoist represión, which is also compared to Republican represión, can be found in Santos Juliá, Julián Casanova, Josep Maria Solé Sabaté, Joan Villarroya, and Francisco Moreno, eds, *Víctimas de la Guerra Civil* (Madrid: Temas de Hoy, 1999).
45. He referred to them as "misguided and misinformed volunteers" in a letter to Thomas Benjamin Gay in April 1940.
46. Letter to Mrs.William K. Draper on 17 October 1939: A.W. Weddell Papers.
47. Letter to Mrs. William K. Draper on 9 January 1940: A.W. Weddell Papers.
48. There are numerous examples in the private and public letters contained in the collection A.W. Weddell Papers at the Virginia Historical Society (Richmond, VA).
49. Marks. *Wind over Sand*, 257.
50. Welles to Weddell (via Bullitt, ambassador to Paris) 29 May 1939 FRUS 1939, 2:830–831.
51. Matthews to Hull 1 May 1939 FRUS 1939, 2:810–811 and 22 May 1939 FRUS 1939, 2:812–813.
52. Weddell to Hull 22 June 1939 FRUS 1939, 2:812–813.
53. For more details about this lawsuit, see Weddell to Hull on 4 November 1939 FRUS 1939, 2:816.
54. Matthews to Hull on 21 May 1939 FRUS 1939, 2:824–826. There is an extensive dossier on Telefónica in the Head of State's collection in the Archive of the Presidency of the Government. It was begun in 1939 with a copy of the contract between the CTNE and ITT, mentioned above.
55. Welles to Weddell on 29 May 1939.
56. Joan Maria Thomàs. *Falange, Guerra Civil, Franquisme. FET y de las JONS de Barcelona en els primers anys del Règim franquista* (Barcelona: Publicacions de l'Abadia de Montserrat, 1992), 407.
57. Marina Casanova. *La diplomacia española durante la Guerra Civil* (Madrid: Ministerio de Asuntos Exteriores, 1996), 51, 226, and 245.
58. He had begun his diplomatic career in 1904 and served in Lisbon, Montevideo, Havana, Mexico, Bucharest, and Tokyo. He was also in Washington as first secretary of the embassy in 1915 and 1917; as minister counselor and counselor in 1920; and as ambassador in 1932. He was married to the sister of F.C. Nano, former counselor of the Rumanian legation in Washington: Note on Cárdenas FDRPL PSF Spain Box 50. Cárdenas was, then, a man with considerable experience in dealing with the United States. Remember his personal friendship with Sumner Welles.
59. In Paris, on 20 July 1936, he had personally taken the telegram from the President of the Cabinet of the Spanish Republic José Giral to President León Blum requesting

that arms be sent. He did so fully believing that the French would refuse to help, which, as we have mentioned above, they did but only several days later and partly due to British pressure: Casanova. *La diplomacia española durante la Guerra Civil*, 51.

60. Memorandum of conversation between Welles and Cárdenas on 10 May 1939 FDRPL PSF Welles.
61. Ibid.
62. Report from José María Milá y Camps, count of Montseny to the minister of industry and commerce on the proceedings of the Comisión for Commercial and Industrial Incorporation No. 2 of 12 May 1939, Historical Archive of the Chamber of Commerce, Industry and Navigation of Barcelona. Barcelona cited in Thomàs. *Falange, Guerra Civil, Franquisme*, 407 and 489.
63. The agencies were the Reserve Federal Bank of New York, the United States. Assay Office in New York and the U.S. Lines Company: Letter from the general counsel of the Treasury Department to the Secretary of Commerce Harry Hopkins on 20 June 1939 in FDRPL Harry Hopkins Secretary of Commerce 1938–1939 Container 119.
64. Memorandum of conversation on 10 May.
65. Report on negotiations to obtain loans to buy cotton, Cárdenas, 16 June 1939: AMAE, R: 1898 E: 2.
66. Ibid.
67. Feis' version, although he does not say that he was present at the meeting in *The Spanish Story*, 11.
68. FDRPL *The Morgenthau Diaries* Roll 51 Note on 26 May 1939.
69. Feis. *The Spanish Story*, 11.
70. Memorandum from Roosevelt to Warren Pierson on 27 May 1939 FDRPL OF 1937–1945.
71. Memorandum from the Adviser of International Economic Affairs Herbert Feis on the conversation between Welles and Cárdenas, witnessed by Feis. 12 June 1939 FRUS 1939, 2:832–834.
72. Welles to FDR 26 June 1939 FDRPL OF 422 Spain.
73. Telegram from Cárdenas to the Minister of Foreign Affairs Conde de Jordana on 12 June 1939: AMAE, R: 1898 E: 2 AMAE.
74. Memorandum from Hopkins to Jesse Jones on 9 June 1939 FDRPL Hopkins, Secretary of Commerce, 1938–1940 Box 19.
75. Memorandum sent by the Treasury Department to Hopkins on 20 June 1939 FDRPL Hopkins, secretary of commerce 1938–1940 Container 119.
76. Ibid.
77. Ibid.
78. The Spanish government states (1) that the cotton will be exclusively put to domestic use in Spain; (2) the Spanish government states that the agreed payments shall be made and that no appeals shall be lodged against these payments as the result of litigation or disputes initiated by Spain or any Spanish interest, financial or otherwise, resulting from the purchases of silver that the secretary of the treasury made from the Spanish government: Memorandum from Welles to FDR on 26 June 1939.
79. Ibid.
80. Memorandum of conversation between Welles and Cárdenas on 29 May 1939 FRUS 1939, 2: 838.
81. Welles to Weddell via the ambassador in France Bullitt on 29 May 1939 FRUS 1939, 2:830.
82. Report on negotiations to obtain loans for buying cotton, Cárdenas, 16 June 1939 AMAE, R: 1898 E: 2.

83. Memorandum from Feis on 12 June 1939. Cárdenas' version was sent by telegram to Jordana on 12 June 1939 AMAE, R: 1898 E: 2.
84. Telegrams 149 and 153 from Cárdenas to Jordana. The latter was dated 12 June 1939: AMAE, R: 1898 E: 2.
85. Report on negotiations to obtain loans for buying cotton, Cárdenas, 16 June 1939 AMAE, R: 1898 E: 2.
86. He had received a telegram from the Ministry of Foreign Affairs "describing the situation of the Catalan industry while waiting for the loans to be granted for the cotton that was being negotiated in the United Status": AMAE Memorándum s/f: R: 1898 E: 2.
87. Hull to Weddell on 1 June 1939 FRUS 1939, 2:835–836.
88. Ibid.
89. Hull to Weddell on 5 July 1939 FRUS 1939, 2:837 note 10.
90. Weddell to Hull on 19 July and 20 July 1939 FRUS 1930, 2:837–838.
91. Letter from Jay Allen to Eleanor Roosevelt on 10 July 1939; Setter from Negrín to Morgenthau on 10 July 1939.
92. Ibid.
93. Letter from Sumner Welles to FDR on 19 July 1939.
94. Text sent by Jay Allen on 28 July 1939 FDRPL PSF Spain Box 50.
95. Vide "Mr. Roosevelt, the British Tories and Franco," *The Christian Century*, July 19, 1939, 892; Frank L. Kluckhon. "Credits on Cotton Extended to Spain," *New York Times*, 8 August 1939 cited in Watson. *United States-Spanish Relations, 1939–1946*, 23.
96. Vide letter from Cárdenas to Jordana on 1 August 1939 AMAE, R: 1898 E: 2.
97. Feis. *The Spanish Story*, 10 note 1: The appeal was to be definitively rejected in January 1941.
98. Weddell to Hull on 20 July 1939 FRUS 1939, 2:838–839.
99. Hull to Weddell on 22 July 1939 FRUS 1939, 2:839–841.
100. Ibid. 841.
101. Weddell to Hull on 25 July 1939 FRUS 1939, 2:841–843.
102. Ibid.
103. Hull to Weddell on 22 July 1939, 840, n. 13.
104. Letter from Cárdenas to Pierson on 29 July 1939 AMAE, R: 1898 E: 2.
105. Letter from Cárdenas to Jordana.
106. Letter from Weddell to Welles on 29 August 1939 FDRPL Alex Weddell Box 57.
107. Memorandum s/f AMAE.
108. According to *Instruction No. 15* on 14 July 1939 contained in Weddell to Hull 17 August 1939 NARA RG 84.
109. Weddell to Hull on 17 August, 1939 NARA RG 84.
110. Weddell to Hull on 14 August 1939 FRUS 1939, 2:814; Hull to Weddell 26 June 1939 FRUS 1939, 2:813.
111. Weddell to Hull 24 August 1939 FRUS 1939, 2:815.
112. Text from the judge of Military Court No. 16 to the *Auditor de Guerra* (Judge Advocate) of the Army Corps of Guadarrama on 7 June 1940 AMAE, R: 1676 E: 6.
113. We do not know on which date the investigation began. As far as the use of the indictment for politically clearing the Ministry of Governance is concerned, see text written by the judge of Military Court No. 16.
114. Weddell to Hull 30 November 1939 FRUS 1939, 2:849.
115. Weddell to Hull 14 December 1939 FRUS 1939, 2:849–850.
116. Memorandum of conversation Moffatt-Cárdenas 18 October 1939 FRUS 1939, 2:846–847.

117. Weddell to Hull 26 September 1939 FRUS 1939, 2:843–844.
118. Weddell to Hull 2 October 1939 FRUS 1939, 2:845–846.
119. Memorandum of conversation Moffatt-Cardenas.
120. A play on words. *-ísimo* is a superlative suffix in Spanish so the title of *generalísimo* awarded to Franco means "the most powerful of all generals." Therefore, his brother-in-law (*cuñado* in Spanish) was the *cuñadísimo*, the most powerful of all brothers-in-law.
121. Weddell to Hull on 22 December 1939 FRUS 1939, 2:853.
122. Letter from Welles to Weddell on 20 November 1939: A.W. Weddell Papers.
123. Hull to Weddell on 28 December 1939 FRUS 1939, 2:856.
124. Weddell to Hull on 8 January 1940 FRUS 1940, 2:855–856.
125. Weddell to Hull on 22 December 1939 FRUS 1939, 2:853.
126. Original note for the North American ambassador in response to the one he sent on the previous 29 December: AMAE, R: 1676 E: 6. The note in English in Weddell to Hull 8 January 1940 FRUS 1940, 2:855.
127. Weddell to Welles 8 January 1940 FRUS 1940, 2:857.
128. Memorandum of conversation Welles-Cárdenas 30 January 1940: FDRPL PSF Spain.
129. Ibid.
130. Welles to Weddell on 4 December 1939: A.W. Weddell Papers.
131. Weddell mentioned the CTNE affair in a letter to a friend in the United States at this time: "The thorniest issue I am involved in at the moment is to get some American prisoners of war released and to prevent the Government from putting an end to a small organization called Telephone Company. It belongs to a herd of sheep known as I.T.&T. I remember buying some shares ten years ago at their nominal value and then I got rid of them, some time before I came here at $5.75." Letter to George W. Hinman on 11 January 1940: A.W. Weddell Papers.
132. Weddell to Hull on 16 January 1940 FRUS 1940, 2:859.
133. 19 January 1940 AMAE, R: 1676 E: 6.
134. Weddell to Hull on 17 January 1940 FRUS 1940, 2:857–858.
135. Ibid.
136. Telegram from Cárdenas to Beigbeder on 3 February 1940 AMAE, R: 1676 E: 6.
137. Telegram from Beigbeder to Serrano Suñer on 5 February 1940 AMAE, R: 1676 E: 6.
138. Letter from Weddell to Welles on 1 March 1940: A.W. Weddell Papers.
139. As Weddell wrote to his relative Elizabeth Wright Weddell on 5 April 1940, "I am trying to straighten out my principal remaining difficulty with the Spanish Government, which concerns the Telephone Company. You may have learned that I was able to obtain the liberation of the last of the American prisoners of war, one of whom, Mr. Dahl, appears to be just now enjoying the hospitality of the City of New York, a reception committee of the Police Department having met him on arrival": A.W. Weddell Papers. Information about these events is not given in Peter N. Carroll's work, *La odisea de la Brigada Lincoln* (Sevilla: Espuela de Oro, 2005) although reference is made to the arrival in March of Reuben Barr, "the last member of the Lincoln Brigade to arrive home" (291).
140. Letter from Cárdenas to Beigbeder on 29 February 1940 AMAE, R: 1676 E: 6.
141. Ibid.
142. Memorandum on 26 February 1940 AMAE, R: 1676 E: 6.
143. He was the only one on the cited list of future high-ranking officials. The men who fell foul of the political clearance process were Caldwell, Ralph, Sacksteder, Hall, Stark, McKim, Ahumada, and Graham: Letter from Weddell to Beigbeder on March 13, 1940 AMAE, R: 1676 E: 6.
144. Weddell-Hull on 14 March 1940 FRUS 1940, 2:860–861.

145. Memorandum of conversation Moffatt-Page 30 April 1940 FRUS 1940, 2:880–881.
146. Text from the judge of Military Court No. 16 to the *Auditor de Guerra* of the Army Corps of Guadarrama on 7 June 1940: AMAE.
147. Letter from Weddell to Beigbeder on 13 March 1940. AMAE, R 1676 E: 6; Ander, secretary of governance to the minister of foreign affairs, on 15 March 1940.
148. Weddell to Hull on 28 March 1940 FRUS 1940, 2:863: "it would appear abundantly clear from the entirely unsatisfactory results obtained after a nearly one year of constant pressure that any assurances received from the Foreign Minister alone may not only be valueless but at times definitely misleading since the forces in the Government opposed to the company appear to be in a sufficiently strong position to nullify any promises given by him."
149. Ibid. 862.
150. Ibid. 864.
151. Hull to Weddell on 2 April 1940 FRUS 1940, 2:865.
152. Letter from Weddell to Beigbeder on 3 April 1940 AMAE, R: 1676 E: 6.
153. Weddell to Hull on 9 April 1940 FRUS 1940, 2:866–869.
154. Hull-Weddell on 11 April 1940 FRUS 1940, 2:869–870.
155. Weddell-Hull on 11 April 1940 FRUS 1940, 2:870–871.
156. Letter from Weddell to Welles on 1 April 1940: A.W. Weddell Papers.
157. Hull-Weddell on 13 April 1940 FRUS 1940, 2:872–873.
158. Memorando of conversation Welles-Cárdenas on 16 April 1940 FRUS 1940, 2:873–874.
159. Moradiellos. *Franco frente a Churchill*, 100–101, 107.
160. Viñas et al. *Politica Comercial*, 1:321.
161. Ibid. 427.
162. Ibid. 366.
163. Moradiellos. *Franco frente a Churchill*, 105–106.
164. Weddell to Hull on 25 April 1940 FRUS 1940, 2:877.
165. Weddell-Hull on 5 May 1940 FRUS 1940, 2:882–884.
166. Weddell to Hull on 29 April 1940 FRUS 1940, 2:879.
167. Memorandum of conversation Moffatt-Page on 30 April 1940 FRUS 1940, 2:880.
168. "I saw the under secretary of state (…) He told me that the issue of the people who have to be replaced is no problem at all." Telegram from Cárdenas to Beigbeder on 19 April 1940 AMAE, R: 1676 E: 6.
169. The news about the presentation of the appeals is given in Weddell-Hull on 5 May 1940 FRUS 1940, 2:882–883; The text is given in a setter from Weddell to Beigbeder on 4 May 1940 AMAE, R: 1676 E: 6.
170. Text from the judge of Military Court No. 16 to the *Auditor de Guerra* of the Army Corps of Guadarrama on 7 June 1940. We do not know the result of the lawsuit, although it is reasonable to assume it was dismissed, given the lack of any reference to it in U.S. documentation on relations with Spain in the following years.
171. Weddell to Hull on 5 May 1940 FRUS 1940, 2:882–883.
172. Bucknell-Hull on 7 May 1940: A.W. Weddell Papers
173. The post of counselor at the Madrid Embassy was extremely unstable, and Weddell eventually complained about this to Under Secretary Welles in May 1941. By then the appointment of Willard L. Beaulac to the post had just been announced. Matthews spent thirty-one days with Weddell; Scotten nine months; and Bucknell not even seven. Before Beaulac there was one other appointment: Flack, who spent less than five months in the post: Letter from Weddell to Welles on 12 May 1941: A.W. Weddell Papers.

174. Bucknell to Hull on 18 May 1940 FRUS 1940, 2:886–887.
175. Bucknell to Hull on 15 May 1940 FRUS 1940, 2:885–886.
176. Memorandum of conversation Welles-Cárdenas on 15 May 1940 FDRPL PSF Spain.
177. Welles to Weddell on 28 May 1940 FDRPL PSF Spain; Also in Hull to Weddell on 28 May 1940 FRUS 1940, 2:803–804.
178. Welles did not forget such other pending issues as the return of the loans granted by North American organizations to the Loyalists during the Civil War. These loans amounted to a total of 40 million dollars and Franco's government had decided to freeze them. He made it clear that a solution had to be found. Since the Civil War had ended, Franco's government had been arguing that both the United States and Great Britain had been warned that the funds deposited by the Spanish Republic in their countries should be frozen. This had not been done, so the official stance was to accept a possible recognition of the debt but not to be in any hurry to pay it back.
179. Moradiellos. *Franco frente a Churchill*, 136–137.
180. Weddell-FDR 28 August 1940: A.W. Weddell Papers
181. Ramón Serrano Suñer. *Entre Hendaya y Gibraltar (Noticia y reflexión, frente a una leyenda, sobre nuestra política en dos guerras)*, 1st ed. (Madrid: Ediciones y Publicaciones Españolas, 1947), which the author also had translated into French and published in Switzerland in the same year (*Entre les Pyrénées et Gibralta: Notes et réflections sur la politiques espagnole depuis 1936*. Geneva: Les Éditions du Chevail Ailé, 1947); Ramón Serrano Suñer. *Entre el silencio y la propaganda, la Historia como fue* (Barcelona: Planeta, 1977). For a criticism of Serrano's version, see Joan Maria Thomàs. "Serrano Suñer, el personaje real y el personaje inventado," ed. Adriano Gómez Molina and Joan Maria Thomàs. *Ramón Serrano Suñer* (Barcelona: Ediciones B, 2003), 193–319.
182. Javier Tusell and Genoveva García Queipo de Llano. *Franco y Mussolini. La política española durante la Segunda Guerra Mundial* (Barcelona: Planeta, 1985), 84–85.
183. Cited in ibid. 85.
184. Goda. *Tomorrow the World*, 58.
185. Fundación Nacional Francisco Franco. *Documentos Inéditos para la Historia del Generalísimo Franco*, vol. 11–1 (Madrid: Azor, 1992), 135.
186. Ibid. 136.
187. Ibid.
188. Michel Catala. *Les relations franco-espagnoles pendant la Deuxième Guerre Mondiale. Rapprochement nécessaire, réconciliaton imposible 1939–1944* (Paris: L'Harmattan, 1997), 125.
189. Catala., "Papiers Noguès," 125.
190. Norman J.W. Goda. "Una hipótesis: La entrada de España en la Segunda Guerra Mundial," ed. Joan Maria Thomàs. *La Historia de España que no pudo ser* (Barcelona: Ediciones B, 2007).
191. Catala. *Les relations franco-espagnoles*, 125.
192. Ibid. 126.
193. Matthieu Séguéla. *Franco-Pétain. Los secretos de una alianza* (Barcelona: Prensa Ibérica, 1994), 85.
194. In response to a telegram from Lequerica: Fundación Nacional. *Documentos Inéditos*, 243.
195. Beigbeder to Asensio 26 July 1940. Ibid. 273–275.
196. Ibid.

197. Cited in Moradiellos. *Franco frente a Churchill*, 117.
198. Ibid.
199. Ros Agudo. *La guerra secreta de Franco*, 104; Charles B. Burdick. "*Moro*: The Resupply of German Submarines in Spain, 1939–1942," *Central European History*, 3.3 (1970), 256–284.
200. Ros Agudo. *La guerra secreta de Franco*, 99–100.
201. Moradiellos. *Franco frente a Churchill*, 117–118.
202. For a systematic study of all the issues mentioned, see Ros Agudo. *La guerra secreta de Franco*.
203. Pardo. *Con Franco hacia el Imperio*, 132.
204. Ibid. 165.
205. Ros Agudo. *La guerra secreta de Franco*, 303.
206. Weddell-Hull 22 June 1940 FRUS 1940, 2:887–888.
207. It should be pointed out that the memorandum of conversation Serrano-Weddell FRUS 1940, 2:887–889 is slightly different from the memorandum sent by Weddell himself to the department, which was classified until very recently. Nevertheless, none of the differences justifies its being classified. I have used both versions here.
208. FBI dossier "Axis Aspirations through South America" on 24 April 1942 FDRPL Hopkins Papers FBI Reports Container 144.
209. Pardo. *Con Franco hacia el Imperio*, 174.
210. Letter from Weddell to Mrs. W.K. Draper on 17 October 1939: A.W. Weddell Papers.
211. Letter from Weddell to Welles on 3 July 1940: A.W. Weddell Papers.
212. Moradiellos. *Franco frente a Churchill*, 136.
213. Sir Samuel Hoare. *Ambassador on Special Mission* (London: Collins, 1946).
214. James C. Robertson. "The Hoare-Laval Plan," *Journal of Contemporary History*, 10.3 (1975).
215. David Eccles. *By Safe Hand. Letters of Sybil & David Eccles 1939–1942* (London: Bodley Head, 1983), 101, n. 1.
216. Moradiellos. *Franco frente a Churchill*, 136.
217. Ibid.
218. He was promoted to the rank of Captain of the Royal Navy in 1940: Josep Massot i Muntaner. *El cònsol Alan Hillgarth i les Illes Balears (1936–1939)* (Barcelona: Publicacions de l'Abadia de Montserrat, 1995), 13.
219. Moradiellos. *Franco frente a Churchill*, 140.
220. In the 1950s Eccles was appointed minister of trade: Viñas et al. *Política Comercial*, 1:302, n. 62.
221. And he adds: "He was a man of parts. His staff soon came to admire his knowledge of the world, his social gifts, and his talent for administration, but they never got over the bouts of physical and moral cowardice. A bat circled the ceiling of his study. He flung himself under the sofa calling out for me to kill it with his tennis racquet. On other occasion when rumours reached him that German troops were about to cross the Pyrenees he invented an offer of a place in the War Cabinet which it was his duty at once to go home and consider. We knew that this story was pure fantasy but we saw how much he needed the pretence of going back into government as a tranquilliser for his nerves": Eccles. *By Safe Hand*, 100–101.
222. A.W. Weddell, official memorandum from the American Embassy in Madrid 30-VII-1940 NARA RG 84.

223. William L. Langer and S. Everett Gleason. *The Undeclared War 1940–1941* (New York: Harper & Brothers, 1953), 737.
224. Division of European Affairs, memorandum for the under secretary, 14 June 1940 cited in State Department. *Relations between the United States and Spain 1942–1945*, Research Project No. 69, May, June 1948, Division of Historical Policy Research, Office of Public Affairs, 23: NARA; Feis. *The Spanish Story*, 37.
225. Memorandum from the British Embassy on 17 June 1940 cited in *Relations between the United States and Spain 1942–1945*, 9.
226. Ibid.
227. Feis. *The Spanish Story*, 274.
228. Ibid. 38.
229. Moradiellos. *Franco frente a Churchill*, 154, n. 94.
230. Feis. *The Spanish Story*, 39.
231. "Gestión en Nueva York en relación con los abastecimientos petrolíferos" 28 June 1940 AMAE, R: 2246 E: 75.
232. "El problema de petróleo de España en la actualidad" 22 July 1940 AMAE, R: 2246 E: 75.
233. Feis. *The Spanish Story*, 41.
234. Ibid. 274–275.
235. *National Petroleum News* July 3, 1940 AMAE, R: 2246 E: 75.
236. John Morton Blum. *From the Morgenthau Diaries. Years of Urgency 1938–1941 (Boston: Houghton Mifflin, 1965) 323; Proclamation 2412 June 27, 1940: Sec. 191. Regulation of anchorage and movement of vessels during national emergency.*
237. Memorandum from Morgenthau to President Roosevelt on 2 July 1940: FDRPL *The Morgenthau Diaries*, Roll 279.
238. Blum. *From the Morgenthau Diaries. Years of Urgency*, 325.
239. Ibid. 324.
240. Ibid.
241. Ibid.
242. Feis. *The Spanish Story*, 42–43.
243. Note from the government's subdelegate in CAMPSA to the under secretary of the Ministry of Foreign Affairs, 19 June 1940 AMAE, R: 2246 E: 75.
244. Telegram from Cárdenas to Beigbeder on 20 June 1940 AMAE, R: 2246 E: 75.
245. Telegram from Cárdenas to Beigbeder on 24 June 1940 AMAE, R:2246 E: 75.
246. CAMPSA to the plenipotentiary minister of Rumaniain Madrid on 27 June 1940 AMAE, R: 2246 E: 75.
247. CAMPSA. "How turning to the Rumanian market would affect our stock of gasolina and the extraordinary expenditure involved"; 27 June 1940 AMAE, R: 2246 E: 75.
248. "Gasoline Supply" 30 July 1940 AMAE, R: 2246 E: 75.
249. Ibid.
250. Ángel Viñas. "Factores comerciales y de aprovisionamiento en la neutralidad española en la Segunda Guerra Mundial," Ángel Viñas, *Guerra, Dinero, Dictadura. Ayuda fascista y autarquía en la España de Franco* (Barcelona: Crítica, 1984), 251.
251. "Gestión en Nueva York en relación con los abastecimientos petrolíferos" 28 June 1940 AMAE, R: 2246 E: 75.
252. Telegram from Cárdenas to Beigbeder on 16 July 1940: Fundación Nacional. *Documentos Inéditos*, 262. Leonard Caruana and Hugo Rockoff believe that Britain made its request to interrupt the supply of oil to Spain on 16 July 1940, and cite a document in support of this view (NARA Microfilm Publications), cited in Leonard Caruana and Hugh Rockoff. *An Elephant in the Garden: The Allies, Spain*

and Oil in World War II (Cambridge: National Bureau of Economic Research, May 2006), 12.
253. Telegram from Cárdenas to Beigbeder on 22 July 1940 and from Beigbeder to Cárdenas on 23 July 1940 in Fundación Nacional. *Documentos Inéditos*, 262–264.
254. Telegram from Cárdenas to Beigbeder on 22 July 1940 in Fundación Nacional. *Documentos Inéditos*, 262; Telegram from Beigbeder to Cárdenas on 24 July 1940: ibid. 264.
255. "Notas para Franco sobre telegramas de la Embajada estadounidense en Madrid captados por los españoles": ibid. 268.
256. Ibid.
257. Telegram from Beigbeder to Cardenas on 23 July 1940: ibid. 263.
258. "Notas para Franco sobre telegramas de la Embajada estadounidense en Madrid captados por los españoles," 266.
259. Dallek. *Franklin D. Roosevelt and American Foreign Policy*, 239.
260. Blum. *From the Morgenthau Diaries. Years of Urgency*, 348.
261. Ibid. 165.
262. Ibid. 319.
263. Dallek. *Franklin D. Roosevelt and American Foreign Policy*, 239.
264. Blum. *From the Morgenthau Diaries. Years of Urgency*, 351.
265. Ibid. 352.
266. It stated: The president may, whenever he deems "necessary in the interest of national defense," prohibit or curtail the exportation of military equipment, munitions, tools, materials, and so on. Export Control Act, 2 July 1940.
267. Memorandum of telephone conversation Ickes-Morgenthau on 23 July 1940 FDRPL "*The Morgenthau Diaries,*" n. 285 Roll 78.
268. "07/26 Fri. President invokes the Export Control Act and prohibits exportation, without license, of aviation gasoline and certain classes of iron and steel scrap." A few weeks before he had instituted another series of prohibitions directed against Japan: "07/05 Fri. President invokes the Export Control Act against Japan by prohibiting exportation, without license, of strategic minerals and chemicals, aircraft engines, parts, and equipment." We believe that, in spite of the reference to the need for export licenses, the reality was that of a virtual embargo.
269. "On 25 July 1940, and on the basis of the Treasury memoranda, Roosevelt ordered that scrap iron, oil and oil derivates be included on the list of basic materials that could not leave the country": Blum. *From the Morgenthau Diaries. Years of Urgency*, 352.
270. Feis. *The Spanish Story*, 45.
271. Blum. *From the Morgenthau Diaries. Years of Urgency*, 352.
272. "Henry [Morgenthau] sent a memorandum to the president that showed that the oil and gasoline that they had sent to Spain had ended up fuelling German submarines in Spanish docks. When he found out, Welles replied that oil was also being sent to Germany through Spain from Mexico, Colombia and Venuela, and that we should not lose our share of this market"; Harold L. Ickes. *The Secret Diary of Harold L. Ickes*, vol. 3, *The Lowering Clouds, 1939–1941* (New York: Simon & Schuster, 1954), 273.
273. Ibid. 273–274; Feis. *The Spanish Story*, 45.
274. Ibid. 270.
275. After his resignation, it was significant that he occupied the post of chief buyer for CAMPSA in the United States: ibid. 271.
276. Caruana and Rockoff. *An Elephant in the Garden*, 44; By the same authors, see also "A Wolfram in Sheep's Clothing. Economic Warfare in Spain, 1940–1944," *Journal of Economic History*, 63 (2003), 65–99.
277. Moradiellos. *Franco frente a Churchill*, 154.

278. W.N. Medlicott. *The Economic* Blockade, vol. 1 (London: His Majesty's Stationery Office-Longmans, Green, 1952), 509.
279. Viñas. "Factores comerciales y de aprovisionamientos," 251.
280. Ibid. 154.
281. Ibid. 151.
282. Eccles. *By Safe Hand*, 112–113, 124–125; Moradiellos. *Franco frente a Churchill*, 159.
283. Telegram from Beigbeder to Cárdenas on 25 July 1940: Fundación Nacional. *Documentos Inéditos*, 265.
284. Telegram from Beigbeder to Cárdenas on the same date as the one cited in the above note in Ibid. 265; "Apunte sobre la situación actual de los problemas de abastecimiento en el exterior" 12 August 1940 AMAE, R: 2243 E: 33.
285. Ibid.
286. Moradiellos. *Franco frente a Churchill*, 165.
287. Letter from Beigbeder to Hoare on 27 August 1940 AMAE, R: 2246 E: 75.
288. Feis. *The Spanish Story.*, 275.
289. B.R. Mitchell, *European Historical Statistics 1750–1970* (London: Macmillan, 1981) cited in Jordi Catalán. *La economía española y la Segunda Guerra Mundial* (Barcelona: Ariel, 1995), 253.
290. Consumption in 1935 had been 797,548 tons while in 1940 it was 750,953: Hayes-Hull. *Proposed Program of Petroleum Supplies* 26 May 1942 NARA RG 84.
291. Denis Smyth. "Les Chevaliers de Saint George": La Grande Bretagne et la corruption dés généraux espagnols (1940–1942)," *Guerres Mondiales*, 162 (1991), 29–54; Denis Smyth. *Diplomacy and Strategy of Survival. British Policy and Franco's Spain 1940–1941* (Cambridge: Cambridge University Press, 1986), 35.
292. Massot i Muntaner. *El cònsol Alan Hillgarth*, 270.
293. Moradiellos. *Franco frente a Churchill*, 146–147.
294. Ibid.
295. Ibid. 150.
296. Ibid. 142–145.
297. Telegram from Beigbeder to Cárdenas on 9 August 1940. Fundación Nacional. *Documentos Inéditos*, 284–285.
298. Ibid.
299. He also wrote about the CTNE problem: "Last night Behn came to see me and now I am going to speak to Serrano, who will tell you about this alligator's childish maneuver. He acts independently of and differently from his ambassador. The latter requested that the board should meet (and went off quite happily) while Behn behaved like the pettifogging lawyer who sticks to the rule book and said that we had to wait for thirty days. Tomorrow they are going to see Serrano": ibid. 285.
300. Weddell-Hull on 19 August 1940 FRUS 1940, 2:896–897.
301. Ibid. 897.
302. Hull to Weddell on 30 August 1940 FRUS 1940, 2:897.
303. "Extracto del Memorándum de la Embajada en Washington al Ministerio de Hacienda de 28 de Agosto último" 10 October 1940 AMAE, R: 1676 E: 6.
304. Note sent by the Ministry of Foreign Affairs s/f (1945): AMAE, R: 1676 E: 6.

4 THE SECOND STAGE OF ALEXANDER W. WEDDELL'S EMBASSY (AUGUST 1940–MARCH 1942)

1. Goda. *Tomorrow the World*, 61–72.
2. Weddell-FDR 28 August 1940: A.W. Weddell Papers.

3. A reference to the probation that was being granted to some prisoners in an attempt to ease overcrowding.
4. Weddell-Hull on 7 September 1940 FRUS 1940, 2:805.
5. Viñas et al. *Política Comercial*, 1:366.
6. Weddell-Hull on 7 September 1940 FRUS 1940, 2:805.
7. Hull-Weddell on 19 September 1940 FRUS 1940, 2:808–809
8. Gellman. *Secret Affairs*, 232–234.
9. Ibid.
10. Goda. *Tomorrow the World*, 72–89
11. Ibid. 71–91.
12. Tusell and García Queipo de Llano. *Franco y Mussolini*, 107.
13. Weddell-Hull on 30 September 1940 FRUS 1940, 2:810.
14. Tusell and García Queipo de Llano. *Franco y Mussolini*, 108–109.
15. Ibid.
16. Weddell-Hull on 30 September.
17. Weddell-Hull on 4 October 1940 FRUS 1940, 2:812.
18. Ibid. 2:812–813.
19. Ibid.
20. Ibid.
21. Moradiellos. *Franco frente a Churchill*, 171.
22. Memorandum of conversation, Hull 7 October 1940 FRUS 1940, 2:813.
23. Moradiellos. *Franco frente a Churchill*, 171–172.
24. Weddell-Hull on 8 October 1940 FRUS 1940, 2:814–815.
25. Hull-Weddell on 12 October 1940 FRUS 1940, 2:815–816.
26. Ibid.
27. Weddell-Hull on 16 October 1940 FRUS 1940, 2:818–819.
28. Francisco Gómez-Jordana Souza. *Milicia y diplomacia. Los Diarios del Conde de Jordana 1936–1944* (Burgos: Dossoles, 2002), 104.
29. The police report on Beigbeder's dismissal; Fundación Nacional. *Documentos Inéditos*, 381–382. The chief of the Police Force went on to say that "this version is accepted as true in military circles and will also be accepted in the more popular circles when the news reaches them since it offends not only patriotic dignity, because of the German imposition, but also the economic sensitivity of the workers, because of the bread rationing. And, of course, it also presents the United States—which in this case means England—as desirous of favouring Spain. Of the numerous versions that are circulating, the one that is reflected in the present report on the last crisis is, in my opinion, the one that is most dangerous."
30. Tusell and García Queipo de Llano. *Franco y Mussolini*, 108.
31. Charles R. Halstead. "Un 'africain' méconnu: Le colonel Juan Beigbeder," *Revue d'Histoire de la Deuxieme Guerre Mondiale*," 21 (1971), 31–60.
32. Gabriel Tortella and Francesc Cabana. "Demetrio Carceller Segura (1894–1968)," ed. Francesc Cabana. *Cien empresarios catalanes* (Madrid: LID, 2006), 473–480; Thomàs. *Falange, Guerra Civil, Franquisme*, 62; Serrano Suñer, *Entre Hendaya y Gibraltar*, 38.
33. Weddell-Hull on 17 October 1940 FRUS 1940, 2:820–822.
34. Eccles. *By Safe Hand*, 158–159.
35. Moradiellos. *Franco frente a Churchill*, 174–175.
36. Ibid.
37. According to David Eccles, physical courage was not one of his character traits: "His career comes first, although he is a patriot and a strong monarchist, and would be

a statesman if he could forget himself. This is no bigger defect than a belief in God prompted solely from a desire to save one's own soul—in Sam it slightly corrupts purity of action and judgement, and, added to a lack of physical courage, produces bouts of hesitation and compromise that mark the limits of a 'highly gifted nature.'" *By Safe Hand*, 158.
38. Hoare. *Ambassador on Special Mission*, 75–76.
39. Weddell-Hull on 17 October 1940 FRUS 1940, 2:820–822.
40. Moradiellos. *Franco frente a Churchil*, 189–190.
41. Hull-Weddell on 18 October 1940 FRUS 1940, 2:822–823.
42. Hull-Weddell on 19 October 1940 FRUS 1940, 2:823.
43. Letter from Welles to Roosevelt on 28 October 1940; Letter from Ickes to Roosevelt on 23 October 1949 FDR PSF Spain.
44. Letter from Ickes to Roosevelt on 23 October 1940 FDRPL OF 307-A
45. Goda. *Tomorrow the World*, 94–112; Tusell and García Queipo de Llano. *Franco y Mussolini*, 112; Thomàs. "Serrano Suñer, el personaje," 289.
46. Ibid. 292–293; Goda. *Tomorrow the World*, 106.
47. Serrano Suñer. *Entre el silencio y la propaganda*, 299.
48. Josep Benet. *El President Companys, afusellat* (Barcelona: Empúries, 2005), 185.
49. Ibid. 182.
50. Letter from Hull to Roosevelt on 30 October 1940; Letter from Roosevelt to Hull on 31 October 1940; Letter from Bowers to Roosevelt on 26 October 1940 FDRPL OF 422.
51. Information contained in a letter from Hull to Roosevelt on 30 October 1940.
52. Ibid.
53. Memorandum of conversation between Welles and Cárdenas on 31 October 1940 FDRPL OF 422.
54. Luis Alcofar Nassaes. "Las visitas de Ciano y Himmler," in *Cataluña durante el Franquismo* (Barcelona: La Vanguardia, 1985), 15; Wayne H. Bowen. "Spaniards into Germans: Himmler, the Falange, and the Visigothic Ideal," ed. Joan Maria Thomàs. *La Historia de España que no pudo ser*; Wayne H. Bowen. *Spaniards and Nazi Germany. Collaboration in the New Order* (Columbia and London: University of Missouri Press, 2000), 10; Wayne H. Bowen. *Spain during World War II* (Columbia and London: University of Missouri Press, 2006), 35–36.
55. Letter from Weddell to Welleson 23 November 1940: A.W. Weddell Papers
56. Ros Agudo. *La guerra secreta de Franco*, 304.
57. Memorandum of conversation between Welles and Cárdenas on 31 October.
58. Ibid.
59. Weddell-Hull on 31 October 1940 FRUS 1940, 2:824–826.
60. Hull-Weddell on 5 November 1940 FRUS 1940, 2:826–827.
61. Weddell-Hull on 31 October 1940.
62. Hull-Weddell on 5 November 1940.
63. Weddell-Hull on 6 November 1940 FRUS 1940, 2:828–829
64. Tusell-García Queipo de Llano. *Franco y Mussolini*, 115–116.
65. Ibid.
66. Ibid.
67. Weddell-Hull on 6 November.
68. Hull-Weddell on 8 November 1940 FRUS 1940, 2:829–831
69. Ibid.
70. Memorandum of conversation between Welles and Butler on 11 November 1940 FRUS 1940, 2:833; Aide-Mémoire British Embassy-State Department on 9 November 1940 FRUS 1940, 2:831–832.

71. Ibid.
72. Moradiellos. *Franco frente a Churchill*, 196.
73. Ibid.
74. Ibid. 191–193.
75. Leitz. "'More Carrot Than Stick,' British Economic Warfare and Spain, 1941–1944."
76. Gellman. *Secret Affairs*, 232–234.
77. Ibid. 232–233.
78. Ibid. 234.
79. Accusations about his alleged homosexuality were used to have Welles dismissed: in particular, an incident involving the under secretary on a train in September 1940. Gellman. *Secret Affairs.*, 235.
80. Ibid.
81. Weddell-Hull on 17 November 1940 FRUS 1940, 2:835.
82. Letter from Weddell to Welles on 18 November 1940: A.W. Weddell Papers.
83. Letter Weddell to Mrs. W.K. Draper on 26 November; in a previous letter to Mrs. Draper—on 4 October 1940—he had written in the same vein, saying that "I shudder to think that this country may be pushed into the struggle by the Boche, because it will simply be suicide. Fortunately, I believe that Franco wishes to keep his country aloof, but Stalin's allies are on the northern border in enormous numbers and Franco's task is a difficult one." A.W. Weddell Papers.
84. Letter from Weddell to John Stewart Bryan on 18 November 1940: A.W. Weddell Papers.
85. Ibid.
86. Letter from Weddell to Hull on 18 November 1940: A.W. Weddell Papers.
87. Letter from Weddell to Mrs. W.K. Draper on 26 November 1940: A.W. Weddell Papers.
88. This was the case, for example, of Berlin: Exchange of letters between Leland B. Morris (Chargé d'Affaires, American Embassy, Berlin) and W. Weddell on 29 April and 7 May 1941: A.W. Weddell Papers.
89. He was to arrive in France on 5 January 1941, after passing through Madrid as Weddell's guest at the embassy: Fleet Admiral William D. Leahy, *I Was There. The Personal Story of the Chief of Staff to Presidents Roosevelt and Truman Based on His Notes and Diaries Made at the Ttime* (London: Victor Gollanz, 1950), 15 and 20; also, letter from Weddell to Welles on 7 January 1941: A.W. Weddell Papers.
90. Smyth. *Diplomacy and Strategy*, 120.
91. Memorandum of conversation between Welles and Butler on 19 November 1940 FRUS 1940, 2:836.
92. Tusell and García Queipo de Llano. *Franco y Mussolini*, 166.
93. Javier Tusell. *Carrero. La eminencia gris del Régimen de Franco* (Madrid: Temas de Hoy, 1993), 40–43.
94. Goda. *Tomorrow the World*, 125.
95. Tusell and García Queipo de Llano. *Franco y Mussolini*, 117.
96. Weddell-Hull on 19 November 1940 FRUS 1940, 2:837–838.
97. Ibid.
98. Ibid.
99. Welles-Weddell on 20 November 1940 FRUS 1940, 2:838.
100. Ibid.
101. Johnson (*Chargé d'Affaires* in London) Hull on 20 November 1940 FRUS 1940, 2:839; On the pressure exerted by Ambassador Lothian on *Hull v. Cordell Hull. The Memoirs of Cordell Hull*, 876.

102. Letter from Churchill to Roosevelt on 23 November 1940: Francis L. Loewenhein-Harold and D. Langley-Manfred Jonas. *Roosevelt and Churchill. Their Secret Wartime Correspondence* (New York: Saturday Review Press/E.P. Dutton, 1975), 121; Tusell. *Franco, España y la Segunda Guerra Mundial*, 183.
103. Smyth. *Diplomacy and Strategy*, 122–123.
104. Ibid.
105. Moradiellos. *Franco frente a Churchill*, 198.
106. Smyth. *Diplomacy and Strategy*, 131.
107. Moradiellos. *Franco frente a Churchill*, 215–216.
108. Weddell-Hull on 29 November 1940 FRUS 1940, 2:839–841.
109. This was the first time that the 250 German divisions had been mentioned, and they were subsequently to be used by the Francoists to justify the alleged pressure that Spain had been put under by Germany and Italy to enter the war.
110. Weddell-Hull on 29 November 1940.
111. Hoare to the British Foreign Office, 28 June 1941, Templewood Papers, Section 8: 3 In Charles R. Halstead. "The Dispute between Ramón Serrano Suñer and Alexander Weddell," *Rivista di Studi Politici Internazionali*, 3 (1974), 459.
112. Weddell-Hull on 2 December 1940 FRUS 1940, 2:841–843.
113. Weddell to Hull on 3 December 1940 FRUS 1940, 2:843.
114. Ibid. 2:844.
115. Letter from Weddell to Welles on 3 December 1940: A.W. Weddell Papers.
116. We do not know who his interlocutor in Washington was, although it was probably Hull or Sumner Welles. *Memorandum for Telephone Conversation American Embassy*, Madrid 7 December 1940: A.W. Weddell Papers.
117. Ibid.: Supplementary Points: A.W. Weddell Papers.
118. Hull. *The Memoirs of Cordell Hull*, 879–880.
119. Ibid. 880.
120. Hull-Weddell on 10 December 1940 FRUS 1940, 2:845–846.
121. Delgado Gómez-Escalonilla. *Imperio de papel*, 267.
122. Rodao. *Franco y el imperio japonés*, 262.
123. Pardo. *Con Franco hacia el Imperio*, 212.
124. Smyth. *Diplomacy and Strategy*, 135.
125. Ibid. 137.
126. Ibid. 148–149.
127. Ibid. 141.
128. Ibid. 155.
129. Eccles. *By Safe Hand*, 192.
130. Smyth. *Diplomacy and Strategy*, 169.
131. Ibid. 171–172.
132. Weddell-Hull on 20 December 1940 FRUS 1940, 2:851
133. Ibid.
134. Hull-Weddell on 27 December 1940 FRUS 1940, 2:852.
135. Ibid.
136. Ibid.
137. Hull. *The Memoirs of Cordell Hull*, 881.
138. Ibid. 882.
139. Hull-Weddell on 8 January 1941 FRUS 1940, 2:855.
140. The previous day, 6 January, to mark the celebration of the Epiphany he had attended a reception at the Royal Palace where he saw Franco. He wrote the following about the meeting: "Very frankly, in view of our rather suspended negotiations

with these people in the matter of foodstuffs, and keeping in mind that we are now waiting on Britain before taking action, I rather avoided a chat with the Chief of State who in my brief greeting was, however, most cordial. This was not, altogether, the case with his Foreign Minister, and thereby hangs a tale!"; Letter from Weddell to Welles on 7 January 1941: A.W. Weddell Papers.

141. Letter to Miss Elizabeth Wright Weddell, 3 January 1941: A.W. Weddell Papers.
142. Langer and Gleason. *The Undeclared War*, 364.
143. Weddell-Hull on 29 January 1941 FRUS 1941, 2:880–881.
144. Cited in Moradiellos. *Franco frente a Churchill*, 207.
145. Tusell. *Franco, España y la Segunda Guerra Mundial*, 188.
146. Tusell and García Queipo de Llano. *Franco y Mussolini*, 118.
147. Ibid. 120–121.
148. Ibid. 119–122.
149. Ibid. 121.
150. Ibid. 122.
151. Smyth. *Diplomacy and Strategy*, 174; *La Vanguardia* 8 February 1941.
152. Langer and Gleason. *The Undeclared War*, 364.
153. Corey Ford. *Donovan of OSS* (Boston: Little, Brown, 1970), 98; Loewenheim. *Roosevelt and Churchill*, 133.
154. Dallek. *Franklin D. Roosevelt and American Foreign Policy*, 290.
155. And in 1947 he was to play a role in the foundation of the CIA.
156. Weddell. "Memorandum for Colonel Donovan" on 26 February 1941 NARA RG 84.
157. "The ambassador [Hoare] has recently borrowed my Napier's Peninsula War." The book he was referring to was by Sir William F.P. Napier. *History of the War in the Peninsula and in the South of France 1807–1814* (London: 1828–1840).
158. Letter from Weddell to Miss Claire Boothe on 4 September 1940: A.W. Weddell Papers.
159. Letter from Weddell to Hull on 23 November 1940: A.W. Weddell Papers.
160. In January 1941 he wrote the following to a relative in Richmond: I see my British colleague almost daily; he is Sir Samuel Hoare who has been at the head of the Foreign Office, the Admiralty, the Air Ministry, and has occupied other administrative posts in England. He is very able and very charming. He has a wife who is "heavy county" and who perhaps unconsciously nourishes a certain pity for anyone who is not born English or into exactly the right caste: Letter from Weddell to Miss Elizabeth W. Weddell on 3 January 1941: A.W. Weddell Papers.
161. He mentioned this in a letter to William and Winifred Gordon: "I continue to see a good deal of your Ambassador here; he drops in almost daily for a discussion of affairs of mutual interest. If anything should happen to Churchill I think he is the man to take his place; great culture, great wisdom, great experience"; Letter dated 5 December 1941: A.W. Weddell Papers.
162. Letter from Sir Samuel Hoare to Weddell on 6 April 1942: A.W. Weddell Papers.
163. Letters from Hoare to Halifax on 8 November 1940 and to Cadogan on 11 November 1940 cited in Marks. *Wind over Sand*, 4.
164. Vide, for example, what he wrote to T. Norman Jones Jr. in March 1941: "I do believe (…) that, despite contrary elements, Franco himself is trying to keep the country neutral; but with German troops on the frontier, German money being spent here like water, and the grip they have on the entire country, it is a terrific task"; Letter from Weddell on 24 March 1941: A.W. Weddell Papers.
165. According to Eccles, Hoare was convinced by his staff: *By Safe Hand*, 102–103.
166. The only specialized treatment of the whole of Weddell's time in Madrid is by Charles R. Halstead. "Diligent Diplomat. Alexander W. Weddell as American

Ambassador to Spain, 1939–1942," *The Virginia Magazine of History and Biography*, 82 (January 1974), 3–38.
167. Weddell-Hull on 1 March 1941 FRUS 1941, 2:881–885.
168. Hoare. *Ambassador on Special Mission*, 110.
169. Heleño Saña. *El Franquismo sin mitos. Conversaciones con Serrano Suñer* (Barcelona: Grijalbo, 1982), 243.
170. Ibid.
171. I have been unable to locate the letter from Bowers to Roosevelt on 23 January 1941, to which there are several references in FDRPL OF Claude Bowers 1941–1945. On the other hand, I did find Jay Allen's memorandum of 10 January of the same year, sent from Orne. It is in FDRPL OF Claude Bowers 1941–1945.
172. Denis Peschanski. *La France des Champs (1938–1941)*, Université Paris-1, 2001.
173. Catala. *Les relations franco-espagnoles*, 189.
174. Séguéla. *Franco-Pétain*, 265.
175. Catala. *Les relations franco-espagnoles*, 190.
176. Séguéla. *Franco-Pétain*, 321–324.
177. Presidential Memorandum for Mrs. Roosevelt on 24 January 1941 FDRPL OF 422-A.
178. Letter from Welles to Bowers on 14 February 1941 FDRPL OF Claude Bowers 1941–1945.
179. Presidential Memorandum.
180. Ibid.
181. Séguéla. *Franco-Pétain,* 288.
182. Benito Bermejo and Sandra Checa. *Libro Memorial. Españoles deportados en los campos nazis (1940–1945)* (Madrid: Ministerio de Cultura, 2006).
183. Ibid.
184. Pardo. *Con Franco hacia el Imperio*, 228.
185. Beaulac. *Franco. Silent Ally*, 115.
186. Memorandum of conversation between Welles and Halifax on 20 March 1941 FRUS 1941, 2:886–887.
187. Moradiellos. *Franco frente a Churchill*, 216.
188. Ibid.
189. During this period, but quite unconnected to Welles' activity, C.W. Lewis. Jr of the Division of Near Eastern Affairs also made a proactive proposal in support of Spain. He proposed an "aggressively benevolent policy on the part of the United States toward Spain" that would respond to Spain's invasion of the International Zone in Tangiers and the military situation in North Africa. More specifically, his proposal was for the United States to recognize that Spain had taken over the International Zone and to use its contacts with the Vichy government to make territorial concessions to Spain in Morocco. He pointed out that even the French were aware that they were occupying some territories that should be Spanish possessions under the terms of the 1912 treaty. What is more, the United States should provide Spain with food supplies but ensure that these supplies did not end up in the hands of the Axis. Lewis predicted that Great Britain would be opposed to such a policy. With the Germans in North Africa, the United States, Great Britain, and France should implement a benevolent policy with Spain to reinforce Franco's (alleged) desires to remain out of the war. With the Germans in North Africa, Serrano Suñer would once again try to get involved, he added. According to Lewis, Weddell should take a leading role in this policy. His exact words were: "Ambassador Weddell (who speaks Spanish well, a consideration of more importance in dealing with Spanish

speaking peoples than is generally realized) has the respect and esteem of General Franco. The Spaniards respond to sympathy and generosity. If the Spanish problems receive sympathetic and generous consideration from us, and I believe that Mr. Weddell would be an excellent agent in that connection, I am convinced that Suñer and his pro-Axis group can be thwarted in any desires they may have to enter the war on the side of Germany or to render assistance to the Axis powers."

190. Hull-Weddell on 10 April 1941 FRUS 1941, 2:887–888.
191. Letter from Weddell to Mural W. Williams on 18 April 1941: A.W. Weddell Papers.
192. Beaulac says that the State Department "had forwarded to the embassy in a routine way": Beaulac. *Franco. Silent Ally*, 109.
193. Weddell-Hull on 19 April 1941 FRUS 1941, 2:888–890.
194. Beaulac. *Franco. Silent Ally*, 109.
195. Weddell-Hull on 20 May 1941 NARA RG 84.
196. Halstead, "The Dispute between Ramón Serrano Suñer and Alexander Weddell," 450, n. 38.
197. Thomàs. "Serrano Suñer. El personaje real y el personaje inventado," 198.
198. One of them was addressed to the International General Electric in Bilbao and was investigated by the Ministry of Foreign Affairs: Vide Weddell-Hull on 15 June 1941 FRUS 1941, 2:906–907.
199. Serrano Suñer. *Entre Hendaya y Gibraltar*, 359.
200. Smyth. *Diplomacy and Strategy*, 181.
201. Note from Serrano to Weddell on 31 March 1941: Enclosure no. 1 to despatch no. 888, April 5, 1941 from American Embassy, Madrid, on the subject of "Complaint by Spanish Government concerning Caricatures Appearing in the Press of the United States" NARA RG 84.
202. Letter from Serrano Suñer to Weddell on 2 April 1941 answering one from Weddell on 27 March and Weddell's response on 4 April 1941: A.W. Weddell Papers.
203. Letter from Weddell to T. Norman Jones on 24 March 1941: A.W. Weddell Papers.
204. Stohrer to German Foreign Ministry: Doc Núm. 375, April 20, 1941, DGFP, XII, 590–591 cited in Halstead. "The Dispute Between," 453.
205. Welles-Hull on 21 April 1941 FRUS 1941, 2:891.
206. Smyth. *Diplomacy and Strategy*, 182.
207. Hull-Weddell on 26 April 1941 FRUS 1941, 2:893.
208. Hull-Weddell on 30 April 1941 FRUS 1941, 2:893–895.
209. Ibid.
210. Hull-Weddell on 19 December 1940 FRUS 1940, 2:850.
211. Weddell-Hull on 3 May 1941 FRUS 1941, 2:895–896.
212. Note sent to the department on 1 May 1941 (Weddell-Hull on 15 June 1941) regarding the letter addressed to the International General Electric Company of Bilbao "to which Your Excellency referred in our conversation of April 19": FRUS 1941, 2:906–907.
213. Weddell-Hull on 23 September 1941 FRUS 1941, 2:918.
214. His name was Luis Álvarez de Estrada.
215. Weddell-Hull on 11 May 1941 FRUS 1941, 2:897.
216. Weddell-Hull on 3 May 1941 FRUS 1941, 2:896.
217. Weddell-Hull on 3 May 1941 FRUS 1941, 2:896; Weddell-Hull on 17 May 1941 FRUS 1941, 2:898.
218. Cited in Smyth. *Diplomacy and Strategy*, 222–223.
219. Ibid. 224–225.

220. On the *Affair v. Ana Romero, Historia de Carmen. Memorias de Carmen Díez de Rivera* (Barcelona: Planeta, 2002).
221. Thomàs. *La Falange de Franco*, 264–276.
222. By letter on 13 May 1941: Serrano Suñer. *Entre el silencio y la propaganda*, 200.
223. For further information on Larraz, see the recent biography by Nicolás Sesma Landrín. *En busca del bien común. Biografía política de José Larraz López (1904–1973)* (Zaragoza: Ibercaja-Biblioteca Aragonesa de Cultura, 2006).
224. Tusell. *Carrero*, 47.
225. The matter was mentioned in a subsequent letter from Weddell to Hull on 17 June 1941 in *Unpublished Documents of United States Foreign Policy* cited in Halstead. "The Dispute Between," 454, n. 68.
226. This is the version that Serrano himself gave to Halstead in 1972: ibid. 455.
227. Weddell-Hull on 20 May 1941 RG 84 NARA.
228. Weddell-Hull on 25 May 1941 FRUS 1941, 2:899–900.
229. Aide mémoire by the British Embassy on 24 May, 1941 RG 84 NARA.
230. Ibid.
231. Ibid. and Weddell-Hull on 25 May 1941 FRUS 1941, 2:899–900. The note in FRUS uses another expression: "The liberal granting of export licenses."
232. Ibid.
233. Ibid.
234. Ibid.
235. Weddell-Hull on 26 May 1941 FRUS 1941, 2:901–902.
236. The fighting in Crete lasted from 20 to 31 May 1941.
237. Weddell-Hull on 29 May 1941 FRUS 1941, 2:902–903.
238. Weddell-Hull on 31 May 1941 FRUS 1941, 2:903–904.
239. Tusell and García Queipo de Llano, *Franco y Mussolini*, 138.
240. Ibid.
241. Weddell-Hull on 9 June 1941 FRUS 1941, 2:905–906. We have been unable to find in any of the archives consulted Serrano's response on 27 May 1941.
242. Ibid.
243. Serrano's note—which was not published in FRUS—has been reconstructed on the basis of Halstead, "The Dispute Between," 458 and Weddell's telegram to Hull on 15 June 1941 cited in Smyth. *Diplomacy and Strategy*, 182–183.
244. Ibid.
245. Halstead. "The Dispute Between," 458.
246. Text from Hull to Weddell on 18 June 1941 authorizing a response along these lines to Serrano Suñer's note of 13 June: FRUS 1941, 2:908.
247. Weddell-Hull on 17 June 1941 FRUS 1941, 2:907–908.
248. Ibid.
249. Tusell and García Queipo de Llano. *Franco y Mussolini*, 139.
250. Ibid.
251. The Duce's standpoint is analyzed thus in Tusell and García Queipo de Llano. *Franco y Mussolini*, 138.
252. Heinz Magenheimer. *Hitler's War. Germany's Key Strategic Decisions 1940–1945* (London: Cassell, 1998), 58.
253. Ibid. 139–140.
254. Tusell. *Franco, España y la Segunda Guerra Mundial*, 225.
255. Ibid. 264.
256. Tusell and García Queipo de Llano. *Franco y Mussolini*, 140.
257. Ibid. 141.

258. Tusell. *Franco, España y la Segunda Guerra Mundial*, 263; Klaus-Jörg Ruhl. *Franco, Falange y III Reich. España en la Segunda Guerra Mundial* (Madrid: Akal, 1986), 22.
259. Xavier Moreno Juliá. *La División Azul. Sangre española en Rusia, 1941–1945* (Barcelona: Crítica, 2004), 69; Luis Suárez Fernández. *Francisco Franco y su tiempo*, vol. 3 (Madrid: Fundación Nacional Francisco Franco, 1984), 274 relieves that it was on 22 and 23.
260. Moreno. *La División Azul*, 77.
261. Suárez. *Francisco Franco y su tiempo*, 274.
262. Thomàs. *La Falange de Franco*, 284.
263. Serrano Suñer. *Entre Hendaya y Gibraltar*, 373; According to Hoare, he curtly presented his protest and left: Hoare. *Ambassador on Special Mission*, 116.
264. Moreno. *La División Azul*, 78.
265. Ibid. 81; Suárez. *Francisco Franco y su tiempo*, 275–276; Moreno. *La División Azul*, 81.
266. Report by the German naval ataché in in Legajo 1, fol. 41 Archivo Francisco Franco, cited in Suárez. *Francisco Franco y su tiempo*, 276.
267. Tusell. *Franco y Mussolini*, 141.
268. Moreno. *La División Azul*, 89.
269. Halstead. "The Dispute Between," 459.
270. Halifax-Foreign Office on 5 July 1941 cited in ibid. 460.
271. Weddell-Welles on 14 July 1941 FDRPL Sumner Welles Box 75.
272. Ibid.
273. Pardo. *Con Franco hacia el Imperio*, 228, 240; Ros Agudo. *La guerra secreta de Franco*, 305.
274. Ibid. Among Weddell's documents we found a draft of this letter (addressed, however, to Cordell Hull and not Sumner Welles) headed by the inscription "Never Sent." It includes such recommendations as "Scrutinize with extreme care every application for licenses to cover exports to this country, taking care to avoid anything that could suggest that we are now embargoing such shipments." The same text, written in July 1941, also gives further proof of how far from the mark Weddell was in his appreciation of the figure of Serrano Suñer, of whom he said the following: "The real ruler of Spain today is the Foreign Minister. His grip on the country, if seemingly weakened some weeks ago, is now thought to be stronger than ever, while his ascendency over his brother-in-law has been heightened": A.W. Weddell Papers.
275. Weddell-Welles on 14 July 1941.
276. Ibid.
277. "We are well, busy, and discouraged. I am already beginning to take notes for a work to be entitled, à la Henderson, 'Failure of a Mission.' However, if my head is bloody, it is still unbowed." Letter from Weddell to William Brown Baker on 19 June 1941: A.W. Weddell Papers.
278. Letter from Welles to Weddell on 25 July 1941 (FDRPL Sumner Welles Papers 75) in response to Weddell's letter of 14 July. The draft of Welles's letter was written by James Clement Dunn.
279. Letter from Weddell to Welles on 12 May 1941: A.W. Weddell Papers.
280. Beaulac. *Career Ambassador*, 152.
281. Beaulac-Welles on 9 July 1941 FDRPL Sumner Welles Papers Box 67 Office Correspondence A-B.
282. Weddell-Hull 18 July 1941 FRUS 1941, 2:908–910.
283. Halstead. "The Dispute Between," 460.

284. Ibid.
285. On these rumors versus various communications between Cárdenas and Hull (7 May 1941) and Weddell and Hull (10 June 1941; 1 August 1941) published in UDUSFP and cited by Halstead. "The Dispute Between," 461, n. 114.
286. Ibid.
287. Saña. *El Franquismo sin mitos*, 252; Serrano Suñer. *Entre el silencio y la propaganda*, 349.
288. Von Stohrer's office on 27 July 1941 in DGFP, 13, 157, cited in Moradiellos. *Franco frente a Churchill*, 237.
289. On the speech, see Tusell and García Queipo de Llano. *Franco y Mussolini*, 142–143; Suárez. *Francisco Franco y su tiempo*, 278; Hoare. *Ambassador on Special Mission*, 113–114.
290. Tusell. *Franco, España y la Segunda Guerra Mundial*, 267.
291. Tusell. *Carrero*, 47.
292. Weddell-Hull on 20 August 1941 FDRPL Sumner Welles Box 75 Alex Weddell.
293. Hoare. *Ambassador on Special Mission*, 114.
294. On these fears, see Eccles. *By Safe Hand*, 301.
295. Cited in Hoare. *Ambassador on Special Mission*, 113.
296. Smyth. *Diplomacy and Strategy*, 231–232.
297. Moradiellos. *Franco frente a Churchill*, 238–239. This author believes that "the food and petroleum supplies bound for Spain were discontinued and Great Britain asked the United Status for asístanse in this policy of virtual trade embargo."
298. Smyth. *Diplomacy and Strategy*, 232.
299. Ibid. 234.
300. Ibid. 236; Moradiellos. *Franco frente a Churchill*, 247; Smyth. *Diplomacy and Strategy*, 236.
301. Moradiellos. *Franco frente a Churchill*, 243.
302. Ibid. 244.
303. Ibid. 245.
304. Weddell-Welles on 20 August 1941.
305. Weddell-Hull on 19 July 1941 FRUS 1941, 2:910–911.
306. Weddell-Hull on 16 September 1941 FRUS 1941, 2:915.
307. Moradiellos. *Franco frente a Churchill*, 238.
308. Medlicott. *The Economic Blockade*, 547; Watson. *United States-Spanish Relations*, 83; *The New Republic* 28 July 1941, 105.
309. Ickes. *The Secret Diary of Harold Ickes, The Lowering Clouds*, 3:547.
310. Dean Acheson. *Present at the Creation. My Years in the State Department* (New York: W.W. Norton, 1969), 21.
311. Medlicott. *The Economic Blockade*, 287; Watson. *United States-Spanish Relations*, 82.
312. Feis. *The Spanish Story*, 138.
313. Ibid. 139.
314. Ibid. 139.
315. Ibid. 138.
316. Blum. *From the Morgenthau Diaries*, 337.
317. Where CEPSA, as we know, had deposits.
318. CAMPSA statistics (1941) AMAE, R: 2246 E: 75. The information in this table coincides exactly with the monthly figures provided by Caruana and Rockoff in *An Elephant in the Garden*, 44. Feis cites unpublished data from the Department of Trade to show that 185,000 and 156,000 barrels of gasoline and diesel fuel were received, respectively: Feis. *The Spanish Story*, 139 n. 1.

319. Weddell-Hull on 6 August 1941 NARA RG 84; There is a slightly different version in "Memorandum by Mr. Perry George of the Division of European Affairs Addressed to the Acting Chief (Atherton) and the Assistant Chief (Culbertson) of the Division of European Affairs, and to the Under Secretary of State (Welles)" on 14 August 1941 FRUS 1941, 2:911–913.
320. Weddell-Hull on 6 August 1941.
321. Ibid. The version published in FRUS is slightly different.
322. Memorandum by the Director of the (German) Economic Policy Department, Berli, September 3, 1941, Documents on German Foreign Policy, 1918–1945, 444–446.
323. Ibid. 445.
324. This can be seen in his interpretation of Franco's intentions in his book *Franco. Silent Ally in World War II*.
325. Weddell-Welles on 6 August 1941 NARA RG 84.
326. Ibid.
327. Welles-Wedell on 21 August 1941 NARA RG 84.
328. Weddell-Hull on 23 August 1941 NARA RG 84.
329. Ibid.
330. Weddell-Hull on 25 August 1941 NARA RG 84.
331. Ibid.
332. Hull-Weddell on 18 September 1941 FRUS 1941, 2:917.
333. "The system likewise would offer an opportunity for furthering our policy of economic aid to Latin America by developing a triangular trade between Spain, the United States and certain other American republics in such tropical products as coffee and sugar": ibid.
334. Enclosure no. 1 to despatch no. 1132 27 August 1941 Transmitting memorandum by Counselor Beaulac regarding the situation in Spain. NARA RG 84.
335. Ibid.
336. Feis. *The Spanish Story*, 141–142.
337. Memorandum by Counselor Beaulac regarding the situation in Spain (Confidential) on 27 August 1941 NARA RG 84; Weddell-Hull on 16 September 1941 FRUS 1941, 2:915.
338. Conversation between Hull and Cárdenas on 13 September 1941 FRUS 1941, 2:913.
339. Memorandum by the Director of the (German) Economic Policy Department, 446.
340. Weddell-Hull on 28 September 1941 FRUS 1941, 2:923.
341. Weddell-Hull on 7 October 1941 NARA RG 84.
342. Weddell-Hull on 23 September 1941 FRUS 1941, 2:917.
343. Carmen Díez de Rivera Icaza was born on 29 August 1942: Romero, *Historia de Carmen*, 51. Serrano Suñer was dismissed on 2 September 1942. The girl was given the surname of her legal father, although she should really have been called Carmen Serrano Icaza or Carmen Serrano-Suñer Icaza, because over the years all of Serrano's legitimate children took both of their father's surnames. Also like their father, they incorrectly added an accent (Súñer), surely in an attempt to make the spelling and pronunciation less Catalan.
344. Letter from Weddell to Welles on 17 September 1941 FDRPL Sumner Welles Box 75 Alex Weddell
345. Several files containing invitations and visiting cards in A.W. Weddell Papers.
346. List of members of the Council of the Bank of Spain: A.W. Weddell Papers.
347. Weddell to Welles on 17 September 1941.

348. Weddell-Hull on 24 September 1941 FRUS 1941, 2:921.
349. Hull-Weddell on 27 September 1941 FRUS 1941, 2:923.
350. Weddell-Hull on 28 September 1941 FRUS 1941, 2:923.
351. Weddell-Hull on 30 September 1941 FRUS 1941, 2:924–926.
352. Tusell-García Queipo de Llano. *Franco y Mussolini*, 171.
353. Text from Beaulac to Berle, Assistant Secretary of State on 21 October 1941 NARA RG 84.
354. Weddell-Hull on 1 October 1941 FRUS 1941, 2:927.
355. Ibid.
356. Economic assistance needed by Spain, memorandum of conversation between Under Secretary Welles and Ambassador Cárdenas on 9 October 1941 FDRPL PSF Sumner Welles.
357. Difficulties encountered by American Embassy in Madrid, ibid.
358. Which we have been unable to locate: cited on page 8 of W.L. Beaulac, *Recommendations concerning American Policy in Spain* on 14 October 1941 NARA RG 84.
359. Ackerman. *Spanish Foreign Trade Relations*, with reference to a memorandum sent to the State Department on 22 October 1941 NARA RG 84.
360. On 15 September 1941: "Economic Activities of the State Department during World War II, General Records of the Department of State. Records on the War History Branch. Drafts of Chapters for an Overall History of the Department of State during World War II," NARA RG 59 Entry 714 Box No. 4.
361. Beaulac. *Recommendations concerning American Policy in Spain*.
362. Ibid.
363. Beaulac-Welles on 15 October 1941 NARA RG 84.
364. Beaulac. *Recommendations concerning American Policy in Spain*.
365. Beaulac-Berle on 21 October 1941 NARA RG 84; Beaulac-Acheson on 21 October 1941 NARA RG 84.
366. Hull-Weddell on 6 October 1941 FRUS 1941, 2:929–930.
367. On 2 October 1941: Memorandum from Welles to FDR on 9 October 1941 FDRPL OF 422.
368. Weddell-Hull on 8 October 1941 FRUS 1941, 2:930.
369. The White House dossier includes the memorandum of 9 October 1941 and a letter from Sumner Welles to the president on 31 October 1941. It is entitled *Question of Oil Raised* by Ickes et al. FDRPL PSF OF.
370. Memorandum from Welles to Roosevelt on 9 October 1941.
371. Feis. *The Spanish Story*, 148–149.
372. *Economic Relations with Spain. Summary and Recommendations* NARA RG 84 Dean Acheson.
373. Ibid.
374. Zinc was mentioned in the accompanying text written by Sumner Welles to Roosevelt on 31 October 1941 FDRPL PSF OF.
375. "4. As regards petroleum and products, it is recommended (...) (d) that no steps be taken to reduce the aggregate amount of petroleum and petroleum products authorized for export to Spain (e) that the continuance of exports on the foregoing basis be made dependent upon the satisfactory improvement of the two-way exchange of goods between Spain and the United States 5. That, in general, outstanding applications for exports to Spain (other than of petroleum and petroleum products) be held in abeyance pending the conclusion of satisfactory arrangements for the improvement of the two way exchange of goods between the United States and Spain, and that this suspension be likewise applied to the allocation of priority ratings, subject to individual exceptions in special cases: Economic Relations with Spain."

376. Text from Welles to Roosevelt on 31 October 1941.
377. Ibid.
378. He wrote "OK, FDR" on the text of 31 October 1941.
379. Feis. *The Spanish Story*, 148.
380. Ibid.
381. I.F. Stone. "Franco Gets More Oil Than He Needs.... Beyond Question, Hitler Is Using," *PM* 14 November 1941, press cutting attached to a letter from Cárdenas to Serrano Suñer on 5 December 1941 AMAE, R: 2246 E: 75.
382. Ickes. *The Secret Diary of Harold L. Ickes*, 3:640. Note on 15 November 1941.
383. At this time, Weddell was also required to provide information on Spanish companies and individuals who should be added to the "Proclaimed List of Certain Blocked Nationals" and to another (secret) black list. Weddell-Hull on 12 November 1941 *Proclaimed and Confidential Lists of Blocked Firms and Individuals in Spain* NARA RG 84.
384. Caruana and Rockoff. *An Elephant in the Garden*, 44: Between August 1940 and October 1943 no aviation fuel was sent to Spain. And with the exception of May 1942, between August 1940 and June 1943, neither was any paleoil.
385. Memorandum from Welles to Roosevelt on 9 October 1941.
386. "The Leakage of American War Materials to the Axis," *PM* 21 November 1941.
387. U.S. Congressional Record, 77th Cong., 1st Sess., 1941, Volume 87, Part 13, A3640–A3644 cited in Watson. *United States-Spanish Relations*, 83–84.
388. *The New Republic* on 28 August 1941 cited in Watson. *United States-Spanish Relations*, 82.
389. *The New Republic* on 15 September 1941 cited in Watson. *United States-Spanish Relations*, 82.
390. *The New Republic* on 16 August 1941 cited in Watson. *United States-Spanish Relations*, 82.
391. Hull-Weddell on 8 January 1942 FRUS 1942, 3:248.
392. Telegram from Serrano Suñer to Cárdenas on 24 January 1942 AMAE, R: 2246 E: 75.
393. Feis. *The Spanish Story*, 150.
394. Ibid.
395. Medlicott. *The Economic Blockade*, 293.
396. Hull-Weddell on 13 December 1941 FRUS 1941, 2:935.
397. Weddell-Hull on 24 January 1942 FRUS 1942, 3:263–265; Letter from Cárdenas to Serrano Suñer on 4 December 1941.
398. Hull-Weddell on 13 December 1941 FRUS 1941, 2:935.
399. Letter from Cárdenas to Serrano Suñer on 4 December 1941.
400. *Relations between the United States and Spain 1936–1942*, 141.
401. Letter from Cárdenas to Serrano Suñer on 4 December 1941.
402. Ibid.
403. Ibid.
404. *New York Times* on 25 November 1941 cited in *Relations between the United States and Spain 1936–1942*, 142.
405. Weddell-Hull on 2 December 1941 FRUS 1941, 2:932–934.
406. Watson. *United States-Spanish Relations*, 109.
407. Feis. *The Spanish Story*, 151–152.
408. Ibid. 152.
409. Ibid.
410. Caruana and Rockoff. *An Elephant in the Garden*, 44. During November and December 1941, and January 1942, respectively, the following amounts were imported: 17,182, 7,561, and 18,000 tons: ibid.

411. *Relations between the United States and Spain 1942–1945*, 11.
412. Ros Agudo. *La guerra secreta de Franco*, 103–105.
413. Pardo. *Con Franco hacia el Imperio*, 243, 247, 259.
414. Warren F. Kimball. *Churchill and Roosevelt. The Complete Correspondence*, vol. 1 (Princeton: Princeton University Press, 1984), 303.
415. Feis. *The Spanish Story*, 152.
416. Max Thornburg, special assistant to the under secretary, *Oil Supplies to Spain* 1 January 1942, 5: NARA RG 84 Acheson.
417. Weddell-Hull on 9 January 1942 FRUS 1942, 3:253.
418. Ibid.
419. Medlicott. *The Economic Blockade*, 293.
420. On 24 November 1941 he said in a letter to his friend Richard B. Baker: "This past year has not been an agreeable one. Just now I am a little more of a favorite in exclusive Spanish ministerial circles. This has nothing to do with me, as the phrase is, nor to any resurgence of otherwise fading charm, but only to the increasing pressure of economic events in this country": Letter from Weddell to Richard B. Baker on 24 November 1941: A.W. Weddell Papers.
421. Note 1339 on 31 December 1941 cited in *Relations between the United States and Spain 1936–1942*, 31.
422. Letter from Atherton to Welles on 6 January 1942 FDRPL Sumner Welles Box 85.
423. *Relations between the United States and Spain 1936–1942*, 31–32.
424. Hull-Weddell on 8 January 1942 FRUS 1942, 3:248–252.
425. Feis. *The Spanish Story*, 151; Hull-Weddell on 8 January 1942 FRUS 1942, 3:250: "In order to minimize delays by reason of inadequate information, it is suggested that the Governments of the United States, Great Britain, and Spain establish in consultation a method of subjecting movements of petroleum products to regulation. For this purpose this Government would appoint agents who, in consultation with the British and the Spanish, will carry out the necessary work."
426. Hull-Weddell on 8 January 1942 FRUS 1942, 3:248.
427. "It is proposed to permit the supply of petroleum products to be continued in quantities sufficient but only sufficient to meet Spain's requirements for transportation and other essentials": ibid.
428. Ibid.
429. Hull-Weddell on 12 January 1942 FRUS 1942, 3:254–257.
430. Ibid. 254.
431. Specifically, "2 months' production, at a price roughly equivalent to the 'extra blockade' price prevailing here, or alternatively, half that quantity of wolfram plus a specified quantity of cork to be agreed upon": ibid. 257.
432. We know that this tanker was the "Campanario": Thornburg. *Oil Supplies to Spain*, 5.
433. *Harsh and Schoolmastery in Tone*: Medlicott. *The Economic Blockade*, 294.
434. Ibid.
435. Weddell-Hull on 15 January 1942 FRUS 1942, 3:257; Weddell-Hull 22 January 1942 FRUS 1942, 3:261.
436. Ibid.
437. Weddell-Hull on 22 January 1942 FRUS, 1942, 3:260.
438. Ackerman. *Memorandum for the Ambassador* on 7 February 1942: A.W. Weddell Papers.
439. Ibid.
440. Weddell-Hull on 24 January 1942 FRUS 1942, 3:263–265.

441. Ibid.
442. Telegram from Serrano Suñer to Cárdenas on 24 January 1941.
443. Hull-Weddell on 31 January 1942 FRUS 1942, 266–267.
444. Memorandum from the Spanish Embassy to the State Department on 5 February 1942 FRUS 1942, 3:272–273 in response to the memorandum from the State Department to the Spanish Embassy on 2 February 1942 FRUS 1942, 3:267–268.
445. Weddell-Hull on 4 February 1942 136 FRUS 1942, 3:270–271.
446. Ibid. 268–270.
447. Memorandum of conversation from Carceller to Beaulac on 6 February 1942: A.W. Weddell Papers.
448. *Relations between the United States and Spain* 1942–1945, 21–26.
449. Weddell-Hull on 4 February 1942 No. 134.
450. Ibid.
451. Hull-Weddell on 5 February 1942 FRUS 1942, 3:271.
452. Memorandum from the Spanish Embassy to the State Department on 16 February 1942 FRUS 1942, 3:274–275.
453. Feis. *The Spanish Story*, 155.
454. Suárez. *Francisco Franco y su tiempo*, 320.
455. *Palabras del Caudillo* (Madrid: Editora Nacional, 1943), 204 cited in ibid. 321.
456. Hull-Beaulac on 18 February 1942 FRUS 1942, 3:275.
457. Beaulac-Hull on 20 February 1942 FRUS 1942, 3:275–278.
458. Ibid. 276.
459. Ibid.
460. Ibid.
461. Memorandum from the State Department to the Spanish Embassy on 27 February 1942 FRUS 1942, 3:278–279.
462. Ibid. 279.
463. Ibid.
464. Watson. *United States-Spanish Relations*, 94.
465. Memorandum of 26 February 1942: A.W. Weddell Papers.
466. Letter from Weddell to Hull on 25 February 1942: A.W. Weddell Papers.
467. Telegram from Weddell to Hull and Welles on 2 February 1942 requesting permission to travel to the United States for an urgent operation on his wife and asking to "be telegraphically instructed to report for consultation thus avoiding revealing cause": A.W. Weddell Papers; Telegram from Hull a Weddell on 4 February 1942 calling him for consultation: A.W. Weddell Papers.
468. Letter from Weddell to Hull on 25 February 1942.
469. Letter from Weddell to Arthur Garrels on 3 March 1942: A.W. Weddell Papers.
470. Memorandum of 26 February 1942.
471. Ibid.
472. Ibid.
473. Ibid.: "An already unstaffed mission," he wrote.
474. Ackerman. Memorandum for the Ambassador on 7 February 1942.
475. Ibid.
476. Ibid.
477. Memorandum for the president (Handed to Sumner Welles, under secretary of state) of 25 March 1942: A.W. Weddell Papers.
478. Memorandum from Henry A. Wallace to Hopkins, Washington, 12 December 1941 FDRPL Hopkins—special assistant to the president 1941–1945. Papers Box 28 (Decisions on Grand Strategy).

479. Cited in Watson. *United States-Spanish Relations*, 130.
480. Dwight D. Eisenhower. *Crusade in Europe* (New York: Doubleday, 1948), 59.
481. Reynolds. *From Munich to Pearl Harbor*, 185.
482. Letter from Sumner Welles to FDR explaining his contacts with Archbishop Spellman of New York on 12 March 1942 FDRPL OF 4848 Carlton J.H. Hayes.
483. Letter from Roosevelt to Weddell on 25 March 1942 and Welles to Roosevelt on 24 March 1942 in FDRPL Sumner Welles Box 85. In the first Roosevelt said, "I appreciate deeply the loyal, consistent, and exceedingly effective way in which you have represented the interests of this Government during the six years of your Embassy in Buenos Aires and during the three years of your mission in Spain. You have been untiring in your work for this country during all of that period and you have maintained at the highest level the best traditions of our diplomatic service. I wish to express to you my very sincere gratitude for the great service you have rendered the Government and the people of the United States during a unique and difficult period. For the time being I know you and Mrs. Weddell will wish to take a rest and one to which you are both so fully entitled, but I wish you to know, however, that I will call upon you again for further service in the not distant future."
484. "Weddell's retirement was announced and attributed to ill health," Watson. *United States-Spanish Relations*, 122. When he wrote to Beaulac in Madrid on 24 March 1942—that is to say, the day before receiving Roosevelt's letter—he had not mentioned that he was about to be dismissed: A.W. Weddell Papers.
485. Letter from Weddell to Roosevelt on 28 March 1942: A.W. Weddell Papers.
486. Letter from Roosevelt to Weddell on 1 April 1942: A.W. Weddell Papers.
487. "As a matter of fact the President has told me through Welles that he has something in mind for me so my present job is to get well although the actual "cutting scrape" only begins tomorrow": Letter from Weddell to Arthur Garrels on 2 April 1942: A.W. Weddell Papers.
488. In fact, the president had allowed him to remain on active service after turning sixty-five, the age of retirement. His age and his state of health were probably crucial in his decision to retire. Letter from Weddell to Arthur Garrels on 23 November 1942: A.W. Weddell Papers. The Weddells died in a train crashin 1948 in Missouri, when they were traveling from Virginia to Arizona on 1 January 1948: Watson. *United States-Spanish Relations*, 122.
489. *The Nation*, 11 April 1942 cited in Watson. *United States-Spanish Relations*, 124.
490. *Relations between the United States and Spain 1942–1945*, 32.
491. Letter from Weddell to Beaulac on 24 March 1942: A.W. Weddell Papers.
492. Welles-Beaulac on 19 March 1942 FRUS 1942, 3:283–284.
493. Feis. *The Spanish Story*, 158–159.
494. Ibid.
495. Beaulac-Hull on 4 March 1942 FRUS 1942, 3:281–282.
496. Ibid.
497. Ibid.
498. Telegrams from Beaulac to Hull on 18, 20, and 24 March 1942 cited in *Relations between the United States and Spain 1942–1945*, 15
499. "The execution of this program is being most intensively urged by the British Government. The British Government has informed us that it regards the execution of this program as being of vital importance to its own production effort and to its own political interests": Welles-Roosevelt on 21 March 1942 FRUS 1942, 3:285.
500. Welles-Beaulac on 4 March 1942 FRUS 1942, 3:279–281.

501. Taken from Caruana and Rockoff. *An Elephant in the Garden*, 44.
502. *Relations between the United States and Spain 1942–1945*, 15.
503. Medlicott. *The Economic Blockade*, 297.
504. The Acting Secretary to the Chargé in Spain (Beaulac) on 19 March 1942 FRUS 1942, 283–284. *Relations between the United States and Spain 1942–1945*, 17. Feis. *The Spanish Story*, 160–164.
505. Ibid. 164–171; Watson. *United States-Spanish Relations*, 93.
506. Cited in Feis. *The Spanish Story*, 165.
507. Ibid. 168.
508. Ibid. 169.
509. Ibid.
510. Viñas et al. *Política Comercial*, 1:368–369.
511. Welles-Roosevelt on 21 March 1942 FRUS 1942, 3:284–285.
512. Ibid. 32.

Sources and Bibliography

Archive Sources

Archive of the Ministry of Foreign Affairs (Madrid)
Archive of the Presidency of the Government. Head of State's Collection (Madrid)
Franklin D. Roosevelt Presidential Library (Hyde Park, New York)
General Archive of the Administration (Alcalá de Henares)
National Archives and Record Administration (NARA-II, College Park, Maryland)
Virginia Historical Society (Richmond, Virginia)

Libraries

Memorial Library. University of Wisconsin (Madison, Wisconsin)
University of Otago Central Library (Dunedin, New Zealand)
Wisconsin Historical Society (Madison, Wisconsin)

Published Documents

United States, *Foreign Relations of the United States. Diplomatic Papers.* 1936, 1937, 1938, 1939, 1940, 1941, 1942.

Bibliography

Unpublished Doctoral Theses

Alexander, Jack Dwyer, *A Case Study in Non-belligerency: The Changing Nature of Spanish Foreign Policy and Its Influence on Allied Military Operations in Europe during World War II*, Ph.D. Dissertation University of Notre Dame, 1970.
Bristol, William B., *Hispanidad in South America 1936–1945*, Ph.D. Dissertation University of Pennsylvania, 1947.
Darrow, Robert Morton, *Catholic Political Power: A Study of the Activities of the American Catholic Church on Behalf of Franco during the Spanish Civil War 1936–1939*, Ph.D. Dissertation Columbia University, 1953.
Halstead, Charles Raymond, *Spain, the Powers and the Second World War*, Ph.D. Dissertation University of Virginia, 1962.

Sister St. Callista Begnal, *The United States and Spain, 1936–1946: A Study in Press Opinion and Public Reaction*, Ph.D. Dissertation Fordham University 1959.

Valaik, John David, *American Catholics and the Spanish Civil War, 1931–1939*, Ph.D. Dissertation, University of Rochester, 1964.

Watson, Bert Allan, *United States-Spanish Relations, 1939–1946*, Ph.D. Dissertation, George Washington University, 1971.

Books

Acheson, Dean, *Present at the Creation. My Years in the State Department* (New York: W.W. Norton, 1969).

Alcofar Nassaes, Luis, "Las visitas de Ciano y Himmler," in *Cataluña durante el Franquismo* (Barcelona: Ediciones La Vanguardia, 1985).

Avilés Farré, Juan, *Pasión y farsa. Franceses y británicos ante la Guerra Civil Española* (Madrid: Eudema, 1994).

Bahamonde Magro, Ángel, Gaspar Martínez Lorente, and Luis Enrique Otero Carvajal, *Las comunicaciones en la construcción del Estado contemporáneo en España: 1700–1936* (Madrid, Ministerio de Obras Públicas, Transportes y Medio Ambiente, 1993).

Bahamonde Magro, Ángel and Luis Enrique Otero Carvajal, "El teléfono: El nacimiento de un nuevo medio de comunicación," in Bahamonde Magro, Ángel, Gaspar Martínez Lorente, and Luis Enrique Otero Carvajal, *Las comunicaciones en la construcción del Estado contemporáneo en España: 1700–1936* (Madrid: Ministerio de Obras Públicas, Transportes y Medio Ambiente, 1993).

Balfour, Sebastian and Paul Preston, eds., *España y las grandes potencias en el siglo XX* (Barcelona: Crítica, 1999).

Beard, Charles A., *President Roosevelt and the Coming of the War 1941. A Study in Appearances and Realities* (New Haven: Yale University Press, 1948).

Beaulac, Willard L., *Career Ambassador* (New York: Macmillan, 1951).

———, *Franco. Silent Ally in World War II* (Carbondale: Southern Illinois University Press, 1986).

Benet, Josep, *El President Companys, afusellat* (Barcelona: Empúries, 2005).

Benítez Toledo, José Mª, *Una política española de petróleo* (Madrid: Bolaños y Aguilar, 1936).

Bermejo, Benito and Sandra Checa, *Libro Memorial. Españoles deportados en los campos nazis (1940–1945)* (Madrid: Ministerio de Cultura, 2006).

Beschloss, Michael R., *Kennedy and Roosevelt. The Uneasy Alliance* (New York: W.W. Norton, 1980).

Blum, John Morton, *From the Morgenthau Diaries. Years of Crisis, 1928–1938* (Boston: Houghton Mifflin, 1959).

———, *From the Morgenthau Diaries. Years of Urgency 1938–1941* (Boston: Houghton Mifflin, 1965).

Bowen, Wayne H., *Spain during World War II* (Columbia and London: University of Missouri Press, 2006).

———, *Spaniards and Nazi Germany. Collaboration in the New Order* (Columbia and London: University of Missouri Press, 2000).

———, "Spaniards into Germans: Himmler, the Falange, and the Visighothic Ideal," in Joan Maria Thomàs, ed., *La Historia de España que no pudo ser* (Barcelona: Ediciones B, 2007).

Bowers, Claude G., *Misión de Guerra en España* (Barcelona: Grijalbo, 1977).

Brinkley, Alan and Davis Dyer, eds., *The Reader's Companion of American Presidency* (Boston: Houghton Mifflin, 2000).
Burdick, Charles B., *Germany's Military Strategy and Spain in World War II* (Syracuse: Syracuse University Press, 1968).
Burns, Richard Dean, *Guide to American Foreign Relations since 1700* (Santa Barbara: ABC-CLIO, 1983).
Cabana, Francesc, ed., *Cien empresarios catalanes* (Madrid: LID, 2006).
Carroll, Peter N., *La odisea de la Brigada Lincoln* (Sevilla: Espuela de Oro, 2005).
Caruana, Leonard and Hugh Rockoff, *An Elephant in the Garden: The Allies, Spain and Oil in World War II* (Cambridge: National Bureau of Economic Research, 2006).
Casanova, Marina, *La diplomacia española durante la Guerra Civil* (Madrid: Ministerio de Asuntos Exteriores, 1996).
Catala, Michel, *Les relations franco-espagnoles pendant la Deuxième Guerre Mondiale. Rapprochement nécessaire, réconciliaton imposible 1939–1944* (Paris: L'Harmattan, 1997).
Catalán, Jordi, *La economía española y la Segunda Guerra Mundial* (Barcelona: Ariel, 1995).
Clavera, Joan, Joan M. Esteban, M. Antònia Monés, Antoni Montserrat, and Jacint Ros Hombravella, *Capitalismo español: De la autarquía a la estabilización (1939–1959)*, 2 vols. (Madrid: Edicusa, 1973).
Coloquio Internacional "Españoles en Francia 1936–1946." Salamanca 2,3 y 4 de Mayo de 1991 (Salamanca: Universidad de Salamanca, 1991).
Cortada, James W., *Relaciones España-USA 1941–45* (Barcelona: Dopesa, 1973).
———, ed., *Spain in the Twentieth-Century World. Essays on Spanish Diplomacy 1898–1878* (Westport: Greenwood press, 1980).
———, *United States-Spanish Relations, Wolfram and World War II* (Barcelona: Manuel Pareja, 1971).
Dallek, Robert, ed., *The American Diplomacy and World War II* (New York: Holt, Rinehart and Winston, 1970).
———, *Franklin D. Roosevelt and American Foreign Policy, 1932–1945* (New York and Oxford: Oxford University Press, 1995).
Davis, Kenneth S., *FDR. Into the Storm 1937–1941. A History* (New York: Random House, 1993).
DeConde, Alexander, Richard Dean Burns, and Fredrik Logewall, eds., *Encyclopedia of American Foreign Policy* (New York: Charles Scribner's Sons, 2002).
Delgado Gómez-Escalonilla, Lorenzo, *Imperio de papel. Acción cultural y política exterior durante el Primer Franquismo* (Madrid: CSIC, 1992).
Delgado Gómez-Escalonilla, Lorenzo and Mª Dolores Elizalde, eds., *España y Estados Unidos en el siglo XX* (Madrid: CSIC, 2005).
———, *España y los Estados Unidos en el siglo XX* (Madrid: CSIC, 2005).
Dreyfus-Armand, Geneviève, *El exilio de los republicanos españoles en Francia. De la guerra civil a la muerte de Franco* (Barcelona: Crítica, 2000).
Eccles, David, *By Safe Hand. Letters of Sybil & David Eccles 1939–1942* (London: Bodley Head, 1983).
Edwards, Jill, *The British Government and the Spanish Civil War, 1936–1939* (London and Basingstoke: Macmillan, 1979).
Espadas Burgos, Manuel, *Franquismo y política exterior* (Madrid: Rialp, 1987).
Essenwein, George and Adrian Schubert, eds., *Spain at War. The Spanish Civil War in Context 1931–1939* (Harlow: Pearson Education, 1995).
Estes, Kenneth W. and Daniel Kowalsky, *History in Dispute*, vol. 18, *The Spanish Civil War* (Farmington Hills: Thomson-Gale, 2005).

Falcoff, Mark and Fredrick B. Pike, eds., *The Spanish Civil War 1936–1939. American Hemispheric Perspectives* (Lincoln and London: University of Nebraska Press, 1982).
Feis, Herbert, *The Spanish Story. Franco and the Nations at War* (New York: Alfred A. Knopf, 1948).
Findling, John E., *Dictionary of American Diplomatic History* (Westport: Greenwood press, 1980).
Flynn, George Q., *American Catholics and the Roosevelt Presidency 1932–1936* (Lexington: University of Kentucky Press, 1968).
Ford, Corey, *Donovan of OSS* (Boston: Little, Brown, 1970).
Freidel, Frank, *Franklin Delano Roosevelt. A Rendezvous with Destiny* (Boston: Little, Brown, 1990).
Fundación Nacional Francisco Franco, *Documentos Inéditos para la Historia del Generalísimo Franco*, vols. 11-1 and 11-2 (Madrid: Azor, 1992).
García Pérez, Rafael, *Franquismo y Tercer Reich. Las relaciones económicas hispano-alemanas durante la Segunda Guerra Mundial* (Madrid: Centro de Estudios Constitucionales, 1994).
Gellman, Irwin F., *Secret Affairs. Franklin Roosevelt, Cordell Hull, and Sumner Welles* (Baltimore and London: Johns Hopkins University Press, 1995).
Goda, Norman J.W., *Tomorrow the World. Hitler, Northwest Africa, and the Path toward America* (College Station: Texas A&M, 1998).
———, "Una hipótesis: La entrada de España en la Segunda Guerra Mundial," in Joan Maria Thomàs, ed., *La Historia de España que no pudo ser, Barcelona* (Barcelona: Ediciones B, 2007).
Gómez-Jordana Prats, Rafael, *Francisco Gómez-Jordana Souza. Milicia y diplomacia. Los Diarios del Conde de Jordana 1936–1944* (Burgos: Dossoles, 2002).
Gómez Molina, Adriano and Joan Maria Thomàs, *Ramón Serrano Suñer* (Barcelona: Ediciones B, 2003).
Graebner, Norman A., ed., *An Uncertain Tradition. American Secretaries of State in the Twentieth Century* (New York: McGraw-Hill, 1961).
Guttmann, Allen, *American Neutrality and the Spanish Civil War* (Boston: D.C.Heath, 1963).
———, *The Wound in the Heart. America and the Spanish Civil War* (New York: Free Press of Glencoe, 1962).
Hayes, Carlton J.H., *Wartime Mission in Spain, 1942–1945* (New York: Da Capo Press 1976).
Heinrichs, Waldo, *Threshold of War. Franklin D. Roosevelt and American Entry into World War II* (New York: Oxford University Press, 1988).
Hoare, Sir Samuel, *Ambassador on Special Mission* (Londres: Collins, 1946).
Hofstadter, Richard, *The American Political Tradition and the Men Who Made It* (New York: Alfred A. Knopf, 1962).
———, "Franklin D. Roosevelt: The Patrician as Opportunist," in Richard Hofstadter, *The American Political Tradition and the Men Who Made It* (New York: Alfred A. Knopf, 1962), 311–347.
Howson, Gerald, *Armas para España, La historia no contada de la Guerra Civil Española* (Barcelona: Península, 1998).
Hull, Cordell, *The Memoirs of Cordell Hull*, 2 vols. (London: Hodder & Stoughton, 1948).
Ickes, Harold L., *The Secret Diary of Harold L. Ickes*, vol. 2, *The Inside Struggle* (New York: Simon & Shuster, 1954).
———, *The Secret Diary of Harold L. Ickes*, vol. 3, *The Lowering Clouds, 1939–1941* (New York: Simon & Schuster, 1954).
Jarque Iñiguez, Arturo, *Queremos esas bases. El acercamiento de Estados Unidos a la España de Franco* (Madrid: Universidad de Alcalá, 1998).

Jenkins, Roy, *Churchill* (Barcelona: Península, 2001).
Jones, Kenneth Paul, *U.S. Diplomats in Europe, 1919–1941* (Santa Barbara: ABC-Clio, 1983).
Juliá, Santos, eds., Julián Casanova, Josep Maria Solé i Sabaté, Joan Villarroya, and Francisco Moreno, *Víctimas de la Guerra Civil* (Madrid: Temas de Hoy, 1999).
Keenan, George F., *American Diplomacy 1900–1950* (Chicago: University of Chicago Press, 1951).
Kimball, Warren F., *Churchill and Roosevelt. The Complete Correspondence* (Princeton: Princeton University Press, 1984).
Langer, William L., *Our Vichy Gamble* (New York: Alfred A. Knopf, 1947).
Langer, William L. and Gleason, S. Everett, *The Challenge of Isolation. The World Crisis of 1937–1940 and American Foreign Policy*, 2 vols. (Gloucester: Peter Smith, 1970).
———, *The Undeclared War 1940–1941* (New York: Harper & Brothers, 1953).
Lash, Joseph P., *Eleanor and Franklin. The Story of Their Relationship Based on Eleanor Roosevelt's Private Papers* (New York: W.W. Norton, 1971).
Leahy, William D., *I Was There* (London: Victor Gollancz, 1950).
Leff, Mark H., "Franklin D. Roosevelt, 1933–1945," in Alan Brinkley and Dyer Davis, eds., *The Reader's Companion of American Presidency* (Boston: Houghton Mifflin, 2000), 367–385.
Leitz, Christian, *Economic Relations between Nazi Germany and Franco's Spain 1936–1945* (Oxford: Clarendon Press, 1996).
———, *Nazi Germany and Neutral Europe during the Second World War* (Manchester: Manchester University Press, 2000).
Leitz, Christian and David J. Dunthorn, eds., *Spain in an International Context, 1936–1959* (New York and London: Berghahn, 1999).
Little, Douglas, "Antibolshevism and Appeasement: Great Britain, the United States, and the Spanish Civil War," in David F. Schmitz and Richard D. Challener, eds., *Appeasement in Europe. A Reassessment of U.S. Policies* (Westport: Greenwood Press, 1990), 21–45.
———, "Claude Bowers and His Mission to Spain: The Diplomacy of a Jeffersonian Democrat," in Kenneth Paul Jones, ed., *U.S. Diplomats in Europe, 1919–1941* (Santa Barbara: ABC-Clio, 1983), 129–146.
———, *Malevolent Neutrality. The United States, Great Britain, and the Origins of the Spanish Civil War* (Ithaca and London: Cornell University Press, 1985).
Loewenheim, Francis L., *The Historian and the Diplomat. The Role of History and Historians in American Foreign Policy* (New York: Harper & Row, 1967).
Loewenhein, Francis L., Harold D. Langley, and Manfred Jonas, *Roosevelt and Churchill. Their Secret Wartime Correspondence* (New York: Saturday Review Press/E.P. Dutton, 1975).
Magenheimer, Heinz, *Hitler's War. Germany's Key Strategic Decisions 1940–1945* (London: Cassell, 2002).
Marks III, Frederick W., *Wind over Sand. The Diplomacy of Franklin Roosevelt* (Athens and London: University of Georgia Press, 1988).
Marquina Barrio, Antonio, *La diplomacia vaticana y la España de Franco (1936–1945)* (Madrid: CSIC, 1986).
———, *España en la política de seguridad occidental 1939–1986* (Madrid: Ediciones Ejército, 1986).
Martín Aceña, Pablo, *El oro de Moscú y el oro de Berlín* (Madrid: Taurus, 2001).
Martínez Molinos, Guillem, "El suministro de petróleo," in *La Guerra Civil Española* (Madrid: Historia 16, 1986), 84–97.
Martínez Ruiz, Elena, *El sector exterior durante la autarquía. Una reconstrucción de las balanzas de pagos en España (1940–1958)* (Madrid: Banco de España, 2003).

Massot i Muntaner, Josep, *El cònsol Alan Hillgarth i les Illes Balears (1936–1939)* (Barcelona: Publicacions de l'Abadia de Montserrat, 1995).

McGregor Burns, James, *Roosevelt: The Lion and the Fox* (New York: Harcourt, Brace, 1956).

Medlicott, W.N., *The Economic Blockade*, vol. 1 (London: His Majesty's Stationery Office-Longmans, Green, 1952).

Miralles, Ricardo, "Las iniciativas diplomáticas de la Segunda República durante la Guerra Civil 1936–1939," in Javier Tusell, Juan Avilés, and Rosa Pardo, eds., *La política exterior de España en el siglo XX* (Madrid: Biblioteca Nueva, 2000), 245–262.

Molinero, C., M. Sala, and J. Sobrequés, eds., *Una inmensa prisión. Los capos de concentración y las prisiones durante la Guerra Civil y el Franquismo* (Barcelona: Crítica, 2003).

Moradiellos, Enrique, *Franco frente a Churchill. España y Gran Bretaña en la Segunda Guerra Mundial (1939–1945)* (Barcelona: Península, 2005).

———, *Neutralidad Benévola. El gobierno británico y la insurrección militar española de 1936* (Oviedo: Pentalfa Ediciones, 1990).

Morales Lezcano, Víctor, *Historia de la No Beligerancia española durante la Segunda Guerra Mundial* (Las Palmas: Mancomunidad de Cabildos de Las Palmas, 1980).

Moreno Juliá, Xavier, *La División Azul. Sangre española en Rusia, 1941–1945* (Barcelona: Crítica, 2004).

Pardo Sanz, Rosa, *Con Franco hacia el Imperio. La política exterior española en América Latina 1939–1945* (Madrid: UNED, 1995).

Parish, Peter J., *Reader's Guide to American History* (London: Fitzroy Dearborn, 1997).

Payne, Stanley G. and Delia Contreras, *España y la Segunda Guerra Mundial* (Madrid: Editorial Complutense, 1996).

Payne, Stanley G. and Javier Tusell, eds., *La Guerra Civil. Una nueva visión del conflicto que dividió España* (Madrid: Temas de Hoy, 1996).

Pereira, Juan Carlos, ed., *La política exterior de España (1800–2003). Historia, condicionantes y escenarios* (Barcelona: Ariel, 2003).

Pratt, Julius W., *Cordell Hull*, 2 vols. (New York: Cooper Square, 1964).

Preston, Paul, *Franco, Caudillo de España* (Barcelona: Grijalbo, 1994).

Puzzo, Dante A., *Spain and the Great Powers, 1936–1941* (New York: Columbia University Press, 1962).

Radosh, Ronald, Mary R. Habeck, and Gricory Sevostianov, eds., *Spain Betrayed: The Soviet Union in the Spanish Civil War* (London: Yale, 2001).

Rafaneau-Boj, Marie-Claude, *Los campos de concentración de los refugiados españoles en Francia (1939–1945)* (Barcelona: Omega, 1995).

Rein, Raanan, ed., *Spain and the Mediterranean since 1898* (London-Portland: Frank Cass, 1999).

Reynolds, David, *From Munich to Pearl Harbor. Roosevelt's America and the Origins of the Second World War* (Chicago: Ivan R. Dee, 2001).

Rodao, Florentino, *Franco y el imperio japonés. Imágenes y propaganda en tiempos de guerra* (Barcelona: Plaza & Janés, 2002).

Romero, Carmen, *Historia de Carmen. Memorias de Carmen Díez de Rivera* (Barcelona: Planeta, 2002).

Roosevelt, Eleanor, *This Is I remember* (New York: Harper & Brothers, 1949).

Ros Agudo, Manuel, *La guerra secreta de Franco 1939–1945* (Barcelona: Crítica, 2002).

Roulet, Louis-Edouard (Actes publiés par), *Les États Neutres Européens et la Seconde Guerre Mondiale. Colloque International* (Neuchatel: Le Passé Présent, 1985).

Ruhl, Klaus-Jörg, *Franco, Falange y III Reich. España en la Segunda Guerra Mundial* (Madrid: Akal, 1986).

Rusbridger, James and Eric Nave, *Betrayal at Pearl Harbor: How Churchill Lured Roosevelt into World War II* (New Jersey: Touchstone Books, 1992).
Saña, Heleno, *El Franquismo sin mitos. Conversaciones con Serrano Suñer* (Barcelona: Grijalbo, 1982).
Schmitz, David F. and Richard D. Challener, *Appeasement in Europe. A Reassessment of U.S. Policies* (Westport: Greenwood Press, 1990).
Schulzinger, Robert D., *The Making of the Diplomatic Mind. The Training, Outlook, and Style of United States Foreign Service Officers 1908–1931* (Middletown: Wesleyan University Press, 1975).
Serrano Suñer, Ramón, *Entre el silencio y la propaganda, la Historia como fue* (Barcelona: Planeta, 1977).
———, *Entre Hendaya y Gibraltar* (Barcelona: Nauta, 1973).
———, *Entre Hendaya y Gibraltar (Noticia y reflexión, frente a una leyenda, sobre nuestra política en dos guerras)* (Madrid: Ediciones y Publicaciones Españolas, 1947).
———, *Entre les Pyrénées et Gibraltar, Notes et réflections sur la politiques espagnole depuis 1936* (Génève, Les Éditions du Chevail Ailé, 1947).
Sesma Landrín, Nicolás, *En busca del bien común. Biografía política de José Larraz López (1904–1973)* (Zaragoza: Biblioteca Aragonesa de Cultura, 2006).
Sherwood, Robert E., *Roosevelt and Hopkins. An Intimate History* (New York: Harper & Brothers, 1948.
Small, Melvin and Otto Feinstein, *Appeasing Fascism* (Lanham: University Press of America, 1991).
Smith, Gaddis, *American Diplomacy during the Second World War 1941–1945* (New York: McGraw-Hill, 1985).
Smyth, Denis, *Diplomacy and Strategy of Survival. British Policy and Franco's Spain 1940–1941* (Cambridge: Cambridge University Press, 1986).
Suárez Fernández, Luis, *Francisco Franco y su tiempo*, vol. 3 (Madrid: Fundación Nacional Francisco Franco, 1984).
Taylor, F. Jay, *The United States and the Spanish Civil War* (New York: Octagon Books, 1971).
Thomàs, Joan Maria, *La Falange de Franco. Fascismo y fascistización en el Régimen Franquista, 1937–1945* (Barcelona: Plaza y Janés, 2001).
———, *Falange, Guerra Civil, Franquisme. FET y de las JONS de Barcelona en els primers anys del Règim franquista* (Barcelona: Publicacions de l'Abadia de Montserrat, 1992).
———, *La Historia de España que no pudo ser* (Barcelona: Ediciones B., 2007).
———, *Lo que fue la Falange* (Barcelona: Plaza & Janés, 1999).
———, "Serrano Suñer, el personaje real y el personaje inventado," in Gómez Molina, Adriano-Thomàs, and Joan Maria, *Ramón Serrano Suñer* (Barcelona: Ediciones B, 2003), 193–319.
Tortella, Gabriel and Francesc Cabana, "Demetrio Carceller Segura (1894–1968)," in Francesc Cabana, ed., *Cien empresarios catalanes* (Madrid: LID, 2006), 473–480.
Toynbee, Arnold and Veronica M. Toynbee, *The War and the Neutrals* (London: Oxford University Press, 1956).
Traina, Richard P., *American Diplomacy and the Spanish Civil War* (Bloomington and London: Indiana University Press, 1968).
Tusell, Javier, *Carrero. La eminencia gris del Régimen* (Madrid: Temas de Hoy, 1993).
———, *Franco, España y la Segunda Guerra Mundial. Entre el Eje y la Neutralidad* (Madrid: Temas de Hoy, 1995).
Tusell, Javier, Juan Avilés, and Rosa Pardo, eds., *La política exterior de España en el siglo XX* (Madrid: Biblioteca Nueva, 2000).

Tusell, Xavier and Genoveva García Queipo de Llano, *Franco y Mussolini. La política española durante la Segunda Guerra Mundial* (Barcelona: Planeta, 1985).
Viñas, Ángel, *El oro de Moscú. Alfa y omega de un mito franquista* (Barcelona: Grijalbo, 1979).
———, *En las garras del águila. Los pactos con Estados Unidos, de Francisco Franco a Felipe González* (Barcelona: Crítica, 2003).
———, "Factores comerciales y de aprovisionamiento en la neutralidad española en la Segunda Guerra Mundial," in Ángel Viñas, *Guerra, Dinero, Dictadura. Ayuda fascista y autarquía en la España de Franco* (Barcelona: Crítica, 1984), 238–264.
———, *Guerra, Dinero, Dictadura. Ayuda fascista y autarquía en la España de Franco* (Barcelona: Crítica, 1984).
———, *Los Pactos secretos de Franco con Estados Unidos. Bases, ayuda económica, recortes de soberanía* (Barcelona: Grijalbo, 1981).
Viñas, Ángel, Julio Viñuela, Fernando Eguidazu, Carlos Fernández Pulgar, and Senén Florensa, *Política Comercial Exterior de España (1931–1975)*, 2 vols. (Madrid: Banco de España, 1979).
Visme, René de, *Culture and Policy: The United Status and the Hispanic World* (Knoxville: University of Tennessee Press, 1949).
Weil, Martin, *A Pretty Good Club. The Founding Fathers of the U.S. Foreign Service* (New York: W.W. Norton, 1978).
Welles, Sumner, *The Time for Decision* (New York: Harper & Brothers, 1944).
Wylie, Neville, *European Neutrals and Non-belligerents during the Second World War* (Cambridge: Cambridge University Press, 2002).

Articles

Álvaro Moya, Adoración, "Redes empresariales, inversión directa extranjera y monopolio: El caso de Telefónica, 1924–c1965." Comunicación presentada en el VII Congreso de la Asociación Española de Historia Económica (Santiago de Compostela, 13–16 September 2005).
Burdick, Charles B., "Moro: The Resupply of German Submarines in Spain, 1939–1942," *Central European History*, 3.3 (1970), 256–284.
Caruana, Leonard and Hugh Rockoff, *An Elephant in the Garden: The Allies, Spain and Oil in World War II* (Cambridge: National Bureau of Economic Research, May 2006).
———, "A Wolfram in Sheep's Clothing. Economic Warfare in Spain, 1940–1944," *Journal of Economic History*, 63 (2003), 65–99.
Cortada, James W., "Spain and the Second World War," *Journal of Contemporary History*, 15.14 (1970), 65–75.
Goda, Norman J.W., "The Riddle of the Rock: A Reassessment of German Motives for the Capture of Gibraltar in the Second World War," *Journal of Contemporary History*, 28.2 (April 1993), 297–314.
Halstead, Charles R., "Diligent Diplomat: Alexander W. Weddell as American Ambassador to Spain," *Virginia Magazine of History and Bibliography*, 82 (1974), 3–38.
———, "The Dispute between Ramón Serrano Suñer and Alexander Weddell," *Rivista di Studi Politici Internazionali*, 3 (1974), 445–471.
———, "A Somewhat Machiavellian Face: Colonel Juan Beigbeder," *The Historian*, 37 (1974), 46–66.
———, "Un 'africain' méconnu: Le colonel Juan Beigbeder," *Revue d'Histoire de la Deuxieme Guerre Mondiale*, 21 (1971), 31–60.
Halstead, Charles R. and Carolyn J. Halstead, "Aborted Imperialism: Spain's Occupation of Tangier 1940–1945," *Iberian Studies*, 7 (1978), 53–71.

Leitz, Christian, "'More Carrot Than Stick': British Economic Warfare and Spain, 1941–1944," *Twentieth Century British History*, 9, 2 (1998), 246–273.

Lindley, Ernest K. and Edward Weintal, "How We Dealt with Spain. American Diplomacy in Madrid, 1940–1944," *Harper's Magazine* (December 1944), 23–33.

Marquina Barrio, Antonio, "La etapa de Ramón Serrano Suñer en el ministerio de Asuntos Exteriores," *Espacio, Tiempo y Forma* Serie V Historia Contemporánea, 2 (1989), 145–167.

Moradiellos, Enrique, "La política europea, 1898–1939," *Ayer*, 49 (2003), 55–80.

Padelford, N. "International Law and the Spanish Civil War," *American Journal of International Law,* 31 (1937), 226–243.

Preston, Paul, "Franco and Hitler: The Myth of Hendaye 1940," *Contemporary European History*, 1 (1992), 1–16.

Robertson, James C., "The Hoare-Laval Plan," *Journal of Contemporary History*, 10 (1975), 433–464.

Smyth, Denis, "'Les Chevaliers de Saint George': La Grande Bretagne et la corruption dés généraux espagnols (1940–1942)," *Guerres Mondiales*, 162 (1991), 29–54.

Thomàs, Joan Maria, *Getting to know Ramón Serrano Suñer: Reality and Invention, 1937–42*, *International Journal of Iberian Studies*, 18, 3 (2005), 165–179.

Tierney, Dominic, "Franklin D. Roosevelt and Covert Aid to the Loyalists in the Spanish Civil War, 1936–39," *Journal of Contemporary History*, 39, 3 (2004), 299–313.

Index

Abraham Lincoln Brigade   31, 33, 52, 58, 60, 69, 75, 216, 217
Abyssinia   6, 14, 17
Acheson, Dean   169, 170, 186
Ackerman, Ralph H.   70, 110, 174, 175, 176, 195, 196, 197, 204, 205
Afrika Korps   145
Agadir   109
Alarcón de la Lastra, colonel   53, 73, 110, 112, 113, 114, 125
Albania   121
Alfonsinos   54
Alfonso XIII   31, 55, 106
Algeciras   162
Algeria   50, 205
Alicante prison   25
Allen, Jay   25, 26, 66, 67, 115, 124, 139, 140
Almanach de Gotha   106
American Civil War   57
Anarchists   22
Anglo-Spanish Oil Agreement   169
Anglo-Spanish Financial Agreement   126
Anschluss   17, 23
Ansó, Mariano   140
Anti Fascist Policy   15
Anti-Comintern Pact   5, 13, 27, 38
Anti-Communism   15, 16, 23
Antonescu, Marshall   154
Aranda, general Antonio   124, 134, 152, 168
Argentina   37, 51, 104, 150
Armour, Norman   213
Arrese Magra, José Luis de   153, 154
Arriba   181
Asensio, general   86, 88
Asociación Cultural Hispanoamericana   89
Athens   36

Atherton, Ray   184, 193, 212
Atlantic Refining Co   30
Atomic bomb   205
Attlee, Clement   115
Auditoría de Guerra de Ocupación   32
Australia   106
Austria   6
Autarchy   30, 40
Auxilio Social   50, 57, 90
Azaña, Manuel   32, 117
Azores   150, 169, 206

B17   205
Baldwin, Stanley   12
Balearic Islands   30, 86
Balkans   160
Bank of Spain   64, 68
Barcelona   19, 118
Bárcenas, Domingo de las   29, 60, 68, 72, 73
Basque Country   34
Bates, John   viii
Battle of the Ebro   7, 19
Battle of Guadalajara   16
Baume, La   118
Beaulac, Willard L.   144, 146, 163, 164, 170, 172, 173, 174, 175, 176, 177, 182, 185, 186, 197, 199, 200, 201, 208, 209
Behn, colonel Sosthenes   31, 32, 33, 60, 61, 64, 65, 68, 69, 70, 71, 72, 73, 74, 77, 79, 82, 90, 101, 139
Beigbeder, colonel Juan   39, 50, 53, 73, 74, 75, 76, 78, 79, 82, 85, 86, 87, 89, 96, 99, 101, 105, 109, 110, 111, 112, 113, 114, 118, 125, 152, 168, 180
Beirut   36
Belgium   48
Berchtesgaden   125, 216
Berle, Adolf   7, 186

Berlin   48, 88, 116, 119, 173
Biarritz   155
Bingham, Robert W.   16
Blackthorn   122
Blue Division   143, 161, 162, 163, 172, *see also* División Azul
Blum, Léon   12, 14
Board of Economic Warfare   194, 211, 212
Bohemia   23
Bolshevism   12
Borbón Battenberg, Juan de   106
Bordighera   134
Bowen, Wayne H.   viii
Bowers, Claude G.   5, 16, 18, 20, 21, 22, 33, 35, 37, 38, 50, 55, 139
Bradsher, Greg   viii
Brennero   160
Brussels Conference   17
Bucknell   82, 110
Bulgaria   191
Bullitt   21, 22
Bureau of Narcotics   97
Burgos   61
Burín, Joaquín   154
Burma Road   51
Butler   122, 124

Cádiz   89, 150
Calcutta   36
Caldwell, Fred   32, 71, 75, 77, 83, 101, 102
Campechano   208
Campeche   193
Campillo   191, 192, 198, 202
Campoamor   193
CAMPSA   30, 94, 99, 113, 114, 174, 184, 187, 194, 208
Campuzano   191, 192, 202
Canada   22
Canaris, admiral Wilhelm   125, 134
Canary Islands   32, 35, 94, 105, 109, 113, 122, 150, 160, 168, 169, 173, 188, 206
Cape Verde   150, 206
Carceller Segura, Demetrio   54, 113, 114, 120, 125, 126, 144, 148, 150, 159, 163, 170, 172, 173, 174, 176, 179, 184, 195, 199, 205
Cárdenas, general Lázaro   9, 26, 140
Cárdenas Rodríguez de Rivas, Juan Francisco de   42, 62, 63, 64, 65, 68, 69, 70, 72, 75, 76, 83, 95, 101, 118, 143, 178, 179, 181, 184, 185, 190, 191, 194, 198, 210, 215
Carlists   54
Carrero Blanco, Luis   125, 154, 167
Casablanca   205
Casado, Pilar   viii
Casals, Pau   140
Castillo, Ramón del   51
Catalonia   10, 54, 61
Catania   36
CEPSA   30, 94, 113, 114, 194, 197, 200
Challenger   122
Chamberlain, Neville   7, 18, 23, 41, 48, 91, 97, 132
Chappell, Christopher C.   viii
Chateu d'Acoz   85
Chiang-Kai-Shek   17, 27, 28
Chicago   35
Chiefs of Staff   126
Childs, J. Rives   196
Chile   22, 50, 90
China   5, 16, 17, 26, 27, 51, 52, 96
China Sea   17
Churchill, Winston   23, 48, 49, 84, 92, 111, 112, 115, 120, 126, 132, 133, 136, 137, 150, 151, 168, 169, 193
CIA   135
Ciano, count Galeazzo   109, 113, 145, 152, 159
Cicognani   143, 162, 179
Clark, Robert   viii
Coffee, Representative John M.   190
College of William and Mary   37
Collier's Magazine   52
Colombia   40, 97, 170, 196
Columbia University   107
Comisaría de Carburantes Líquidos   95
Commission for Industry and Commerce of the Junta Técnica del Estado   114
Comité Americano del Auxilio Social   57
Committee of Non-Intervention   6
Companys, President Lluís   117, 140, 141
Consejo de la hispanidad   118
Consejo Superior de Misiones   89
Conservative Party   91
Copenhagen   36
Copyright Office of the Library of Congress   36
Cortada, James W.   vii, viii

Craigie, Robert 27
Craigie-Arita Agreement 27
Crete 142, 145
Crisis of May 1941 73, 150, 151, 160, 161, 167
Croatia 159, 161, 191
Cruz Salido 140
CTNE 31, 32, 47, 52, 60, 61, 65, 75, 76, 77, 84, 102, see also La Telefónica
Cuba 39
Cuerpo de Mutilados del Ejército 54, 58
Cummings, Homer S. 9
Curaçao 192
Czechoslovakia 8, 19, 23

Dahl 76
Dakar 109, 116, 157, 205
Daladier, Edouard 7
Dalton, Hugh 99, 168
Davis, Norman 108, 140
De Gaulle, general 116, 125, 140
Decree of unification 39
Defense Committee 168
Defense Material Branch 211
Defense Supply Corporation 211
Democrat Party 59
Denmark 36, 47, 48, 93, 191
Dennis 77
Department of Agriculture 176
Department of War 50
Destroyers-for-Bases Deal 130, 169
Dictatorship of general Miguel Primo deRivera 89
Díez de Rivera, Francisco 180
Directorio 31
División Azul 143, 161, 162, 163, 172, see also Blue Division
D'Olwer, Lluís Nicolau 140
Donovan, colonel William *Wild* 135, 136, 137, 138, 139
Dougherty, cardinal 18
Dunn, James Clement 18, 22, 37, 108, 122, 190
Duque de Alba 118
Dutch West Indies 170

East Indies 51
Eccles, David 92, 99, 115, 155
Economic Defense Board 185
Eden, Anthony 23, 92, 132, 167

Edison 50
Egypt 40, 132, 160
El Alamein 200
El Pardo, Palace of 34
Elis-Rees, Hugh entre 92
Embargo Act 192
Espinosa de los Monteros, general 116, 134
Espionage Act 94
Ethiopia 91
Export-Import Bank 26, 62, 63, 108
Exxon 30

Falange Española Tradicionalista y de las J.O.N.S. (FET y de las JONS) 39, 53, 56, 67, 111, 113, 114, 162
Falange's Foreign Services 131
FBI 91, 188
Federal Loan Administration 211
Feis, Herbert vii, 63, 98
Finland 191
Finletter, Thomas 211, 212
First World War 49
Ford 31
Fox, Rosalind 112, 180
France 11, 39, 40, 41, 47, 49, 50, 51, 53, 54, 81, 85, 86, 90
Franco, Carmen Polo de 151, 180
Franco, general Francisco 3, 6, 15, 20, 25, 33, 35, 43, 52, 53, 61, 68, 69, 72, 73, 82, 84, 90, 92, 103, 105, 109, 111, 112, 114, 115, 116, 117, 119, 124, 125, 126, 127, 128, 133, 134, 135, 137, 138, 142, 145, 147, 148, 152, 154, 155, 156, 157, 158, 159, 160, 161, 162, 164, 166, 167, 170, 173, 174, 177, 181, 183, 184, 187, 195, 200, 201, 208, 209, 215, 216, 218
French Catalonia 116
French Protectorate of Morocco 84, 85, 105, 116, 121, 126
Friends of the Abraham Lincoln Brigade 34

Galarza, colonel 72, 73, 76, 151, 153, 154, 163
Gamero del Castillo, Pedro 125, 153
General Motors 31, 48
Generalitat 117
George Washington University 36

German submarines   89
Germany   6, 23, 26, 39, 40, 41, 49
Gibraltar   39, 41, 85, 86, 88, 105, 116, 122, 125, 132, 134, 138, 145, 160, 162, 168, 186
Gil Robles, José María   168
Girón de Velasco, José Antonio   153
Gleason, S. Everett   42
Gobeo   193
Goda, Norman   viii
Goering, Hermann   30
Gomá, cardinal   35
Good Neighbor Policy   8
Goya   34
Gran Canaria   150, 167
Greece   121, 142, 145, 150
Green, Joseph   7
Grind   122
Guernica   62
Gulf of Guinea   81, 105
Gulf of Mexico   93, 208

Hachiro, Arita   27
Hague   21
Hague Convention   193
Halcón, Manuel   130
Halifax, Lord   23, 131, 132, 144, 155
Hall   42
Halstead   vii
Hammond   76, 77
Hampden-Sydney College   37
Havana Convention 1928   18, 90, 91, 164
Hawaii   49
Hayes, Carlton Joseph Huntley   43, 107, 164, 217, 218
Hendaye   88, 109, 114, 115, 116, 117, 118, 207
Hendaye Protocol   116, 135, 160
Himmler, Heinrich   117, 118
Hispanicity Day   130
Hispanidad   39, 42, 50, 84, 89, 130, 142
Hispano-luso Treaty of Friendship and Non-Aggression of 1939   208
Hitler, Adolf   4, 5, 6, 23, 28, 68, 85, 88, 92, 103, 104, 105, 109, 112, 116, 118, 132, 134, 157, 160, 167, 192, 205, 217
Hoare, Sir Samuel   84, 92, 99, 108, 115, 121, 126, 128, 131, 132, 134, 136, 137, 139, 144, 150, 151, 155, 159, 161, 162, 167, 168, 172, 190, 192, 195, 218

Holland   47, 51, 93, 192
Holy Grail   118
Hoover   18, 50
Hopkins   63, 122
House of Representatives   28
Hudson river   35
Hudson Valley   26
Hull, Cordell   4, 7, 9, 15, 18, 19, 20, 21, 22, 23, 26, 27, 29, 30, 42, 49, 55, 59, 66, 68, 69, 78, 80, 93, 95, 97, 98, 108, 109, 111, 117, 122, 131, 134, 135, 141, 146, 148, 156, 158, 165, 170, 174, 181, 190, 193, 194, 195, 200, 212, 215, 216
Hyde Park   26

Iberian Peninsula Operating Committee (IPOC)   211
Ibero-American Institute   118
Ickes, Harold   4, 5, 7, 8, 19, 27, 42, 51, 97, 98, 109, 115, 122, 141, 143, 169, 174, 188, 189
India   40
Indochina   51
Indonesia   97
Ingersoll Rand Company   197
International Telephone & Telegraph (ITT)   13, 31, 47, 52, 69, 75, 78, 101, 102
International Zone of Tangier   84, 86, 205
Iron Guard   154
Irving   174
Italian submarines   89
Italy   6, 52, 191

Japan   16, 17, 27, 98, 190, 191
Jones   63, 211, 212
Jordana, conde (count) de (of)   29, 33, 60, 69, 218

Kennedy, Joseph   18, 28
Kerensky   12
Kindelán, general Alfredo   152, 153, 168
Kirk, Alexander   37
Knox, Frank   42, 50, 51, 94, 96, 97, 98, 109, 215

La Telefónica   33, 43, 79, 101, 104, 216, 217, *see also* CTNE
Land, admiral   94
Langer, William L.   42

Lankford, Nelson D.   viii
Largo Caballero, Francisco   141
Larraz, José   72, 73, 110, 125, 154
Lausanne   36
Laval, Pierre   127
Lawyers's Committee on American Relations with Spain   8
League of Nations   14
Leahy, admiral William D.   124
Leipzig   173
Lend-and-Lease Act   145, 165
León, Quiñones de ENTRE   14–31
Lequerica, ambassador   87
Lerroux, Alejandro   32
Library of Congress   38
Libya   87, 142, 145, 157
Lima Conference   7, 8, 19, 20
Lincoln   43
Llanzol, marquis of   180
Llanzol, marquise de (Sónsoles de Icaza y de León)   151, 180
London   48
Lorente Sanz, José   151
Lothian, Lord   81, 93, 144
Loyalists   5, 11
Luxembourg   47
Luz, Saint Jean de   34

Madeira   205
Madrid   20
Mallol, Alfonso   140
Manchukuo   27
Manchuria   16
March, Juan   151
Maritime Commission   95
Marseille   155
Marshall, General   49, 205
Martínez Barrio, Diego   32
Martínez Fuset, Lorenzo   33
Matthews, H. Freeman   29, 31, 33, 61
Maud, Lady   92
Maura, Miguel   32
McCabe, Louis F.   8
Mercer, Lucy   26
Mers-el-Kébir   87
Mestre Fernández, Demetrio   32
Metal Reserves Corporation   176, 195, 211
Mexico   6, 139, 192
Mexico City   25, 36

Military Junta   168
Millán Astray, general   58
Moffat, Pierrepont   18, 22, 23, 37, 72, 73, 82
Mogador   109
Molins, Casimiro   viii
Molins Gil, Joaquín María   viii
Molins López-Rodó, Joaquim Maria   viii
Monaco   134
Montsalvat   118
Montseny, conde del   62
Montserrat   118
Moore, R. Walton   14
Moradiellos, Enrique   viii
Moral embargo   13
Moravia   23
Moreno, admiral   124
Morgan, J.P.   78
Morgenthau, Henry   4, 5, 6, 27, 42, 49, 51, 52, 63, 66, 68, 94, 95, 96, 98, 109, 141, 143, 160, 170, 208, 215
Morocco   85
Mundelein, cardinal   18
Munich Conference   4, 7, 19
Muñoz Grandes, general Agustín   168
Murphy-Weygand Agreement   186, 191
Mussolini   5, 23, 68, 103, 105, 109, 133, 134, 135, 145

Nanking   17, 27
Narvik   157
National City Bank   77
National Council   38
National Defense Act   51
National Petroleum news   96
Naval Intelligence   208
Navascués, Emilio   70
Navicerts   41, 80, 174, 188
Nazi, Germany   5, 6
Negrín, Juan   26, 66, 115
Nelly, commander   58
Neutrality Act   47, 49, 50, 140
Neutrality Act of 1 May 1937   7, 9, 14
Neutrality Act of 1935   14
Neutrality Act of 31 August 1935   13
New Antwerp Telephone and Electric Works   31
New Deal   15
New Orleans   208
New York Herald Tribune   65

New York Times   38, 96
Newsweek   38
Night of Broken Glass   10
Noguès, general   87
North Africa   116
Norway   47, 48, 93, 205
November elections of 1936   15
Nye, Senator   18

Office for Arms and Ammunition Control   7
Office of Production Management   194
Office of Strategic Services   136, 211
Operation Ballast   122
Operation Barbarossa   160
Operation Brisk   132
Operation Felix   125, 160
Operation Pilgrim   167
Operation Puma   150, 151, 167
Operation Shrapnel   132
Operation Torch   42
Orgaz, general   152, 153, 168

Pact of Steel   38
Page, Frank   82
Palma   61
Pan-Americanism   39
Panama Conference   28, 51, 89
Paris   48, 62
Payne, Stanley G.   vii, viii
Pearl Harbor   42, 43, 102, 104, 130, 205, 212, 217
Pearson, Drew   122, 124, 148
Perú   21
Pétain, maréchal   38, 49, 87, 88, 116
Peterson, sir Maurice   38, 84, 91
Petroleum Administration for War   212
Philippines   39
Phillips, William   13, 16
Phony war   38
Picasso, Pablo   62
Pierson, Warren   69, 70
Pittman, senator Key   10, 19
PM   189, 190, 191
Poland   23, 28
Ponte, general   168
Poo, Fernando   105
Port Arthur (Texas)   192, 198, 202, 203, 208
Portela Valladares, José   140

Portugal   38, 85, 145
Preclusive purchasing   188
Preston, Paul   viii
Primo de Rivera, general Miguel   31, 39, 153, 154
Primo de Rivera Sáez de Heredia, José Antonio   25, 113, 114, 151, 153
Primo de Rivera Sáez de Heredia, Pilar   153
Puerto Rico   39
Pyrenees   91

Quarantine Speech   17

Reciprocal Trade Agreements   216
Reconstruction Finance Corporation   63, 211, 212
Republican Party   50
Republican Zone   114
Reynaud, Paul   49
Ribbentrop, Joachim von   85, 87, 104, 109, 116, 124, 134, 147
Richmond   34, 133
Richmond Times   67
Ridruejo, Dionisio   153
Rieber, captain Thorkid   30, 95, 96
Rif   86
Río de Oro   206
Río Tinto   12
Ríos, ambassador Fernando de los   19, 22, 62
Rivas Cherif, Cipriano   117, 118
Rodao, Florentino   viii
Romania   95, 191
Romanones, Conde de   55
Rome   48, 88, 119
Rommel, general Erwin   200
Roosevelt, Eleanor   4, 6, 11, 18, 25, 42, 62, 66, 108, 140
Roosevelt, Franklin Delano   3, 4, 5, 7, 9, 11, 14, 15, 16, 20, 22, 23, 25, 26, 35, 42, 48, 49, 50, 51, 52, 55, 63, 70, 84, 90, 93, 97, 112, 117, 122, 126, 127, 139, 150, 169, 181, 190, 205, 206, 207, 208, 212, 215, 216, 217
Rovira i Virgili University   viii
Rubber Reserve Company   212
Ruiz Alcaín, Ignacio   viii
Russia   93, 143, 160

INDEX

Saavedra Lamas 75
Sainz Rodríguez, Pedro 168
Salamanca 61
Salazar, Oliveira 298, 200, 208
Saliquet, general 168
San Sebastián 34, 61, 116
Sandoval, Felipe Ximénez de 163, 192
San Bachiller, Mercedes 57
Sapphic 122
Scott, Byron 18
Scotten, Robert M. 37, 68, 82
Second Spanish Republic 4, 5, 8, 12, 17, 56, 57
Second World War 5, 47, 104, 215, 216, 218
Secret Service 97
Selby, Sir Walford 92
Senate 10
Senate Committee of Foreign Relations 10
Senegal 50
Serrano Suñer, Ramón 29, 33, 39, 41, 43, 50, 53, 54, 57, 59, 67, 71, 72, 73, 77, 81, 82, 88, 89, 90, 91, 101, 103, 104, 105, 106, 107, 108, 109, 110, 111, 112, 114, 115, 116, 118, 119, 120, 123, 124, 127, 128, 130, 131, 134, 135, 136, 137, 138, 139, 140, 142, 143, 144, 145, 146, 147, 148, 150, 151, 152, 153, 154, 157, 158, 159, 161, 162, 163, 166, 167, 170, 172, 177, 178, 179, 182, 184, 191, 192, 193, 195, 207, 208, 209, 217, 218
Seville 61
Shanghai 16, 27
Shea, dean Francis 8
Shell 30
Sicily 36
Sindicato Español Universitario 16
Singapore 200
Slovakia 191
Smith, Walter 211
Smyth, Denis 131
Sociedad de Telefonos Ericsson 31
Socony Vacuum Oil Company 94
Socony Vacuum-Standard Oil of New York 30
Solchaga, general 168
Soviet Union 6, 15, 23, 49
Spanish Church 56

Spanish Civil War 4, 5, 6, 11, 12, 13, 17, 25, 26, 29, 32, 38, 42, 50, 55, 56, 57, 91, 105, 138, 190
Spanish embargo 7
Spanish Embargo Act 14, 15
Spanish Protectorate of Morocco 122, 160
Stalin 15, 28
Standard Oil Company 94
Standard Oil of New Jersey 30
Stark, admiral 49, 205
State of the Union Address of 4 January 1939 10
Sterling Area 81
Stimson, Henry L. 18, 42, 50, 51, 63, 96, 97, 109, 215
Stohrer, ambassador von 161, 166, 199
Suanzes, Juan Antonio 62
Sudeten conflict 19
Sudetenland 6, 19
Suez 41
Suez Canal 125, 145, 160
Suri, Jeremy viii
Switzerland 21

Taft 18
Tangier 84, 86, 88, 132, 203, 216
Tangier Imbroglio 131, 132
Tarifa 86
Tayllerand 136
Tenerife 94, 200
Texas Oil Company 30, 93, 94, 95, 98, 208
Tiensin 27
Torr, Brigadier 92, 168
Torres, barón de las 150
Tovar, Antonio 153
Treaty of Versailles 6
Tripartite Pact 109, 110, 116, 127, 147, 159, 160
Tunisia 87
Turner, Mark 99

United Kingdom Commercial Corporation (UKCC) 196
United States Commercial Corporation (USCC) 196, 211
University of Virginia 49
Urquijo, marquis of 32
Uruguay 21

U.S. Congress   7, 9, 10, 48, 49, 95
U.S. Red Cross   59, 111, 112, 115, 119, 122, 127, 128, 132, 133, 140, 143, 156, 163, 164, 169, 217

Valencia   20
Val-Kill   26
Vansittart, Robert   23
Varela, general José   76, 124
Vargas, Getulio   51
Vatican   56
Venezuela   40, 97, 170, 192, 193, 195, 196
Vichy   105, 116, 117, 123, 133, 140
Vichy France   87, 139, 190
Victor Manuel III   86
Victory Day   23
Vigo   192
Vigón, general Juan   85, 124, 152, 169
Virginia   37

Wagner   118
Wallace, Vice President   122, 205, 211
Walsh, Frank P.   8
War Cabinet   91
Warwick   34
Warwickshire   34
Washington   32, 121
Washington, George   52
Watson, Bert Allan   vii
Weddell, ambassador Alexander W.   29, 31, 33, 34, 35, 36, 37, 38, 42, 43, 47, 52, 54, 55, 57, 59, 69, 73, 74, 77, 78, 79, 80, 90, 91, 92, 96, 101, 103, 104, 105, 106, 107, 108, 109, 110, 112, 113, 114, 115, 118, 119, 120, 123, 125, 127, 128, 131, 133, 135, 136, 137, 139, 141, 142, 144, 146, 147, 148, 149, 150, 151, 154, 155, 156, 157, 158, 159, 162, 163, 165, 167, 170, 173, 174, 175, 178, 181, 182, 183, 184, 185, 188, 192, 193, 194, 195, 196, 197, 199, 200, 202, 203, 204, 206, 208, 210, 213, 215, 218
Weddell, Mrs (Virginia Chase Steedman)   36, 57, 58, 59, 147, 154, 202
Wehrmacht   162
Welles, Sumner   4, 6, 9, 22, 42, 48, 52, 60, 62, 64, 65, 70, 73, 75, 79, 83, 91, 95, 97, 106, 108, 115, 118, 121, 122, 124, 126, 128, 134, 137, 140, 141, 163, 164, 169, 174, 185, 188, 189, 190, 193, 195, 206, 207, 208, 210, 212, 213, 215
Wendell   77
Weygand   186
Wilkie   90
Wilson, President   108
Winterhilfe   57
Wolfram   212
Woodring   47, 48, 50

Yagüe, generañ Juan   168
Yencken, Arthur   92, 99
Yugoslavia   145, 150

Zanzibar   36
Zarauz   105
Zorroza   198
Zugazagoitia, Julián   117, 118